California
Edge of American History

Second Edition

Volume I

Ronald Genini

For information address Book Writing Cube

8 The Green STE 300, Dover DE 19901

866-600-0036

https://www.bookwritingcube.com/

Published by Book Writing Cube

Printed in the United States

Dedication

This book is dedicated to Roberta, my wife and more.

Table of Contents

Foreword

Ronald Genini's *California: On the Edge of American History, Second Edition*, expands on the original 2017 edition. Like its predecessor, it is a magisterial survey of the entire history of the most populous American state and also the source of the greatest popular cultural influence of any place on earth. Ron Genini's family has been in California for more than a century, since Los Angeles was a town, and apart from San Francisco and its port, the transitory gold rush, the state was best known as a place of startling geographic variety, from the depths of Death Valley to the Sierra Nevada Mountain tops, and as a mystical last stop in the westward march of America, a paradise on earth. California's development from pre-historic times to Spanish outposts among the natives, the Mexican interlude, the Republic of California, to its integration into the United States and its phenomenal growth to become the greatest U.S. state by most measurements and the most trend-setting one, is laid out thoroughly and readably with enough, but not an excess, of detail. Astonishingly, a comprehensive and balanced history of the state has not appeared for many years, and I am advised by authorities in the field that little remotely as contemporary, thorough, accessible, and authoritative is available.

If California were an independent country, it would be in what would become the G-8 of economically powerful free market economies. The skirmishes of the Mexican War and the controversies of the first Republican presidential candidate, John C. Fremont, the gold rush, the vast migrations from the east, the rise of the motion picture industry, and all the major cross-currents of the state's increasing ethnic diversity, all are presented, thoroughly researched, but always a lively read. The period between the wars, when California was seen, in the words of philosopher Bertrand Russell, as "the ultimate segregation of the unfit" and by California gubernatorial candidate (1934), radical novelist Upton Sinclair, as a haven for swindlers and hucksters, was only a decade or so before Ron Genini was born in Oakland. Politically, it has produced probably the two most important presidents of the last sixty years, Richard Nixon and Ronald Reagan, who, along with the state's many other important and colorful political figures, are memorably described.

The author spent 34 years as a very respected high school history teacher in Fresno, professionally recognized for his talent and erudition, and also taught the history of the American West, focusing on California in the Osher Lifelong Learning Institute at California State University Fresno. He has worked on the preparation of this authoritative volume for many years and his meticulous research and professional insistence on balance are visible throughout. Like the original work, this is a valuable contribution to American historiography. It will surely take its place as an authoritative source on its uniquely important subject from the day of publication, and deserves no less.

--Conrad Black, M.P., author of *Franklin Delano Roosevelt, Champion of Freedom*; *Richard M. Nixon, A Life in Full*; and *Flight of the Eagle, the Strategic History of the United States*.

Preface to the Second Edition

The second edition of *California: On the Edge of American History*, coming seven years after its debut, is inspired by my desire to help my native state achieve its best years and avoid an abyss that threatens it by showing its people what has been achieved, allowing them to use past success to model its future.

In the 2017 edition, I described how and why I chose to emphasize popular history rather than the kind in vogue in schools when I sat in a classroom. I also emphasized Mark Sullivan's use of the press as the "diaries of history." Open a newspaper from any day in the past and you will find not just news but the opinions, feelings, amusements, and advertisements that surrounded us or our forebears. That is what I seek to capture and report. Since my extended family has been part of California since 1905, as has my own since 1910, I heard many stories (which I cherished) of their life experiences, their views of what was happening, and of the personalities who marked the time. Those stories made the past alive for me and I strove to pass it on to my students and readers. Like any history major, I was taught to interpret, but I have always preferred reporting the story and letting my readers or listeners interpret it for themselves; I have opinions but would rather let you decide on an event's significance; what was important to me might not be to you, and vice versa. The past is done, it can't be changed or undone. It shouldn't be forgotten, and it shouldn't be lied about. It is not there for us to like or dislike; it just is. It can be discussed, and events may be judged, good aspects retained as inspiration for the future and bad points reformed – but it should never be erased, or "canceled." Since elementary school, I have figuratively "worshipped" at the temple of Clio, the Muse of History. That is why I reject the ignorant statue topplers, the politically correct re-namers and re-writers (not to be confused with scholarly revisionists), as well as the Orwellians who would destroy the past to build their new Marxist future.

Since 2019, California has experienced a new governor, and with him, some profound changes to the state. His terms have seen events that, while not unprecedented, have been traumatic to our social fabric. My original intention in this updating was simply to address the Gavin Newsom impact on California. I soon realized that there were a number of items I had not covered sufficiently, or at all, items that I felt should and must be included to round out a history of California. Among the changes and additions, I have brought my treatment of the state's geography up to date (including weather phenomena and natural disasters), added connections with the Philippines in colonial times and during World War II, provided more details on the Franciscan missions and peoples' personal experiences in the Gold Rush, California's combat participation in the Civil War and World War II, Chinese and Japanese immigrant experience, as well as coverage of different European ethnic groups, urban developments and deterioration, athletic teams, art and literature, the speedy rise of food and auto manufacturing plants, Southern Californian radicals' involvement in the Mexican Revolution, the local role of the Ku Klux Klan, the Mafia, black migration from the South, the significant roles of two Fresno County men in the ending of World War II, some influence of the LGBT movement in culture, the growing, unprecedented flight from California as well as updates to the lives of people mentioned. The phenomena of broadcast radio, the proliferation of new religions, and that *sine qua non* of modern economies, the credit card, all originated in California.

As in the original edition, I use John Caughey's subject outline and emulate Thomas Costain's and Barbara Tuchman's genre of popular history within a political-economic-judicial framework. Likewise, measurements are both Imperial and Metric, and money conversion utilizes davemanuel.com for prices in 1774-2019 and Coin News's usinflationcalculator.com for prices in 1913-2024.

If you liked or found the first volume useful, I can guarantee you will feel the same about this update.

In a book review of a volume of old photographs many years ago, I wrote that "the past lives in what were once living eyes, now closed, but once very alive," so please join me on this walk-through California's past, as we contemplate what others witnessed long (and not so long) ago.

This second edition takes the reader up to April 2024. Internet endnotes were working as of April 30, 2024.

Acknowledgements

Those who helped with research assistance include Christina Moretta and Lisa Palella, San Francisco Public Library Photo Curator and assistant; Marissa Friedman, Archival/Special Collections librarian, California State Library; and Jonathan Waltmire, the History Room Supervisor of the Tulare Public Library; Carol Norbert, the Senior Project Manager of Book Writing Cube and her staff at the Amazon KDP book publishing services company (if a book looks good, it is because of them).

Those who helped by reading all or parts of the book and giving feedback include Janet Lynn Ballinger, Joe Bracamonte, Ian Buljung, Lisa Cowan, Lillian Dei, Eric Engleman, Jeannie French, Capt. Paul Goodwin, Denise Harrison, Cliff Hata, Sharee Hemsley, Lary Henkel, Geraldine Mecca Hogan, E. Curtis Johnson, Renee Heffington Johnson, Mike Kloster, Jeff Lockie, Darlene West Miller, Chelsea Milliorn, Debbie Monet-Lebeau, Diane Muñoz, Sandra Pearce, Hon. Michael T. Price, Annette Reamer, Anthony Scheideman, Diane Thomas-Garner, Melissa Ward Vega, Rev. Msgr. Robert Wenzinger, and Aimee Voss Williamson. Some of these were classmates, coworkers, or my students, while others are good friends made over the years.

Ms. French, my former student and later co-worker, was instrumental in helping me to nail down information about Herbert Bybee while Mr. Vince Nishikawa helped me to find information on Yoshito Fujimoto; both of these gentlemen played very significant roles in the conclusion of World War II (Mr. Bybee had been a student at Central Union High School). Ms. Harrison generously shared her geologic expertise with me. My son, Nicholas Genini, came across the information concerning the credit card's origin in California.

I also want to thank my friend, Conrad Black, M.P., for graciously consenting to the use of the 2017 edition foreword, with some minor changes. I want to thank Ben Bergthold, a friend, our Mac guru, for helping out and rescuing the work when the computer became temperamental.

Not to be forgotten is my wife and helpmate for over 54 years, Roberta Tucker Genini, mother of our children, and my slave-driving editor and enemy of all misplaced modifiers, dangling participles, and split infinitives. If the book looks good to you, it is due to her efforts to pound a grammatically correct work out. I provided the material. In this symbiotic effort, she provided the structure, and, thus, what she judges a marvelous work was brought forth.

About the Author

Ronald Genini

Ronald Genini is a third-generation Californian who holds a BA and an MA in history from the University of San Francisco. Genini was born in Oakland in 1946, and his extended family has lived in California since 1905. Genini taught high school history for 35 years and was named Fresno County's Outstanding Young Educator in 1978, the first of several professional and civic awards. After retirement in 2004, he taught history courses on California and the American West at the Osher Lifelong Learning Institute at California State University, Fresno.

From 1972 to 2014, over a dozen of his history articles appeared in *The Journal of the West, Revue Hellénique du Droit International*, the *California Historical Quarterly, Fresno Past & Present, Pacific Historian, International Review of Natural Family Planning, American Heritage, The Californians*, and *The Fresno Bee*. Genini has worked as a book reviewer for the California Historical Society, as well as for the former publication *The Californians*. He has written a biography (*Theda Bara: a Biography of the Silent Screen Vamp, with a Filmography*) and cowritten two others (*Romualdo Pacheco: a Californio in Two Eras* with Richard Hitchman of Cuesta College, and *Darn Right It's Butch, Memories of Our Gang* with Tom Bond). In 2017, he published the first edition of *California: On the Edge of American History*. Between 2006 and 2013, Genini helped edit two of author Conrad Black's history books, *The Invincible Quest: The Life of Richard Milhous Nixon* and *Flight of the Eagle: The Grand Strategies That Brought America from Colonial Dependence to World Leadership*.

Genini lives in Fresno with his wife, Roberta. Together, they have three married sons, four grandchildren, and one great-grandchild.

**NASA image of the Eastern Pacific from Baja to Vancouver
Island (via Wikimedia Commons)**

California Counties Map (Courtesy U.S. Bureau of the Census)

California State Map (Credit: © Map Resources)

Page Blank Intentionally

Part 1 The Origins (The Beginning-1768)

Chapter 1: The Land and People Prior to European Settlement

Geography

"If California were a separate country, it would have the world's seventh largest economy, from the Hollywood movie studios to the San Francisco fishing fleets. . ." so ran a 2003 Union Bank commercial. What made that powerhouse economy? Was it favorable geography? Was it a hostile geography that people tamed? Was it because the state is on the western end of a tilted continent that seems to slide to the sea? Is it an impressive array of economic assets - companies like Wells Fargo, Union Oil, Chevron, Pacific Bell, Apple? What grocery shopper is unfamiliar with Sunkist oranges, Del Monte canned vegetables, SunMaid raisins, Ghirardelli chocolate, Folgers' coffee or C&H Sugar? Is it in the state's education system - the University of California on ten campuses, a law school and a national laboratory, Stanford, the University of Southern California, the state college system, the Jesuit colleges? Is it in California's natural resources - the redwood forests, the San Joaquin Valley's farms and ranches, the industrial minerals in the desert, the fish, the waterpower? More importantly, is it the same high-powered economy more than two decades later?

Another question: "What is a Californian?" Is he or she the lumberjack or marijuana grower on the north coast, the Central Valley farmer, the Berkeley intellectual, the Hollywood star or the mountain resort hotel clerk? Is it the corporation CEO who seeks to build a coastal nuclear power plant or the anti-nuclear activist, the computer programming engineer, the anti-technology hermit, or the homeless person in many of the state's cities? Obviously, if they live in

California, they are all Californians. The answer to the question then is that Californians are strikingly diverse, in no way homogeneous - much as the land that produced such variety in its inhabitants.

And another question: "What is California's position in the world of diplomacy and business?" The United States maintains diplomatic relations with 178 nations. Not including the United Nations Organization, based in New York City or Washington, DC, New York City has the most consulates (116) of any American city. California hosts 83 consulates (34 of which are duplicates in the state), with Los Angeles hosting 65, while 18 that are not located in Los Angeles are in other California cities (Fresno, Palo Alto, San Bernardino, San Diego, and San Francisco). No other state or territory hosts more than California.

These are the questions that this book will attempt to answer.

**

"Such room of sea! Such room of sky! Such room to draw a soul-full breath."

-Joaquin Miller

**

"My country is abundant."

-Salvador Palma, Yuma chief, 1776

**

California's diversity reveals itself in topography, climate, population density, flora, fauna and industry. If anyone doubts the state's almost infinite variety let him take the aerial tramway near Palm Springs. This is the steepest ascent in the

3

nation, moving a person from the desert floor to above the timberline in a quarter of an hour. The rider can see many zoological and botanical zones and may notice the great variations as if in geological layers.

To the north, about 200 miles (320 km) as the crow flies, the heterogeneous topography is accented by an 84.6-mile (136.2 km) descent from the state's highest elevation Mt. Whitney, 14,505 feet (4,421 m) to its lowest. Death Valley at -282 feet (-86 m) is the lowest point in the "lower 48" and the third lowest point on the face of the Earth.

Land determines, to a great extent, climate, drainage, soils, and natural vegetation. These, then, influence population, land usage and communications. (Try using a cell phone in remote parts of the Sierra Nevada[1]) There are eight distinct regions in California, but their general patterns are generally bounded by mountain ranges, chiefly the Sierra Nevada and the Coast Ranges, and the Central Valley, which lies between them.

Four of these regions are in the Coast Ranges: the North Coast Mountains and Valleys, the San Francisco Bay Area, the Central Coast Mountains and Valleys, and the Southwestern Mountains and Valleys. The Sierra Nevada and the Central Valley make up two regions while the final two are the Southeastern Mountains and Deserts and the Northeastern Mountains and Tablelands.

The North Coast region: Majestic Trees, Fish, Marijuana, and Wine

The North Coast Mountains and Valleys include the Klamath Mountains and the Coast Ranges from the Oregon border south 250 miles (402 km) to the Sonoma and Napa Valleys. Included in this area are the counties of Del Norte, Humboldt, Trinity, Mendocino, Lake, Sonoma, and Napa.

The Klamaths include several smaller ranges, such as the Siskiyou, the Salmon, and the Trinity mountains, the most rugged of the Coastal Ranges with many peaks of 9,000 feet (2.743 km). The Trinity Alps, so named because they resemble the Swiss Alps, contain jagged peaks that rise above the timberline with rough ridges and deep glacier-cut canyons. 2.42% of the state's population lives there. Its three largest cities are Eureka (50,000 people), Arcata (over 17,000 people), and Ukiah (about 16,000 people).

In the north, the principal industry is lumber, for here are California's magnificent stands of coast redwood (*Sequoia sempervirens*) in a narrow strip 10 to 30 miles (16 to 48 km) wide and rising from the sea to 3,000 feet (914.4 m) in height. Humboldt County is the leading producer, accounting for a quarter of the state's total lumber output (which, as of 2016, accounted for 6% of US softwood lumber). Few other trees approach the redwoods in size, height, or botanical interest. In this region, four out of five acres are forested, and half of this forest area is in private commercial hands; here are stands of trees with an average age of 500 years (the more famous 2,000-year-olds are usually found in state and national parks) over 350 feet (106.7 m) high.

Over the last 1,200 years, the South Fork of the Eel River has deposited more than eleven feet (3.35 m) of new soil, and it is here on the river flats in soil of that kind that coast redwoods grow best. The Douglas fir, occurring in almost pure stands (unlike the redwoods), is found in the Klamaths and south through the Coast Ranges. Redwood lumber companies such as Pacific Lumber (the largest, based in Scotia), Sierra Pacific (among the top five in US lumber production), and Crown Zellerbach (now a part of Georgia-Pacific) once practiced clear-cutting but in later years they and their successors found that conservation was a better way, expressed by the industry as "wasting nothing but the tree's shadow." The lumber industry has been hurt in recent years by the environmental controversy that evolved from the 1990 listing of the northern spotted owl (*Strix occidentalis caurina*) as endangered. Within the US Forest Service and in the press a debate began over logging old growth forests in Oregon and Washington, environmental groups urging its reduction or abolition to preserve the trees and the owls versus the loggers who wanted to save their jobs and those who saw the need to clear out dead wood for fire prevention. The recent direction of environmentalism had shifted from forest management (clearing out dead trees and cleaning the forest floor) to hands-off. Environmentalists filed lawsuits to prevent any logging, and while most of these failed, the plaintiffs made sure to keep the matter before the public to garner sympathy. Timber sales decreased and prices went up, the public seemed interested in preservation giving impetus to more lawsuits, cheaper timber was imported from Asia to make up the decline in production. The timber industry reacted by closing mills, putting many out of work.[2]

In the forests of Humboldt and Del Norte counties' many national and state parks, one walks in shadows and semi-darkness. Even when the sun is at its zenith only a fraction of the light filters through the closely growing trees and their protective branches. Sounds are shut out by the profusion of plant life, and the wind is tempered by tall trees. The stillness of the forest is not easily forgotten.

Here also are important fisheries, Crescent City and Eureka leading California in the catch of market crab since World War II. At Fields Landing, near Eureka, most of the catch is in sole. In Fort Bragg, Albion and Point Arena salmon leads in value and weight, but crab, albacore, sole and rock fish are also important. Eureka's oyster beds in the mudflats

6

north of the Samoa Bridge are a commercial operation that, at low tide, provides 90% of the oysters produced in California.

The most lucrative crop in the north is marijuana, and because of hard times in the lumber industry, law enforcement for many years was reputedly lax in controlling it. In 2012-15, this changed when officers from the state and federal agencies, the Yurok tribal police, lumber companies, and local sheriffs' departments struck several illegal growers, with some public support. Apparently, the laissez-faire attitude of the public was eroded by the growers' increasing violence. Here is the Emerald Triangle, named for being the largest cannabis-producing area in the US (in Humboldt, Trinity, and Mendocino Counties.), Cannabis became a lifestyle in the 1960s San Francisco "Summer of Love," and soon nearly all the local population was involved, directly or indirectly, with its cultivation. With de-criminalization, effected in 2015-16 by California Proposition 215 (the Medical Marijuana Initiative) and Proposition 64 (Adult Use of Marijuana Act), the California industry exploded, reportedly due to its reputation for producing a cannabis with exceptionally good flavor and cannabinoid profiles[3] It remains (as of 2024) illegal under federal law, although 21 states (plus the District of Columbia and Guam) have decriminalized its use, and 14 have legalized its medical use.

South of the Redwood Empire are the famous wineries of the Napa and Sonoma Valleys, producing mostly dry table wines of high quality (found superior to French wines for the first time in the 1976 Judgment of Paris wine competition).[4] Here are over 1,700 wineries, and the region is famous for these as well as its cuisine, Michelin star restaurants, boutique hotels, luxury resorts, historic architecture, and culture. In western Lake County are stands of commercial walnut groves, as well as pears, olives, and apples. In 2017, many portions of the Wine Country were devastated by wildfires, which damaged precious vineyards, ruining the fruit through prolonged smoke, exposure.

Sheep find the coastline excellent for year-round grazing, but a more important domestic animal in the region is the chicken, pushing California into national leadership in egg production. Poultry ranches are characterized as "egg factories," where the product goes from the chicken to the frying pan hardly touched by human hands; Sonoma County is the leading producer, with Petaluma claiming to be the "World's Egg Basket." In this area also are found such native fauna as the black-tail deer, beaver, muskrat, ruffled grouse, mountain quail and the imported wild turkey, making the area attractive to hunters.

"Make no mistake stranger -- San Francisco is west as all hell."

- Bernard de Voto

"DAY AFTER DAY, MORE PEOPLE COME TO L.A.

SSH! DON'T YOU TELL ANYBODY THE WHOLE PLACE IS SLIPPING AWAY.

WHERE CAN WE GO WHEN THERE'S NO SAN FRANCISCO?

SSH! BETTER GET READY TO TIE UP THE BOAT IN IDAHO."

Tommy Reynolds, Stuart Magolin, Jerry Ripelle, "Day After Day"

The San Francisco Bay region: Wealthiest in the U.S.A.

Immediately south of the North Coast region is the San Francisco Bay Area, embracing the counties of Marin, San Francisco, San Mateo, Alameda, Contra Costa, Solano, and the northern part of Santa Clara, an area of 3,293 square miles (8,529 km2). Only here, at the Golden Gate, is there a real break in the Coast Ranges. Continuing south from the north coast are redwood stands, less dense than in the north. Some beef cattle are to be found in the East Bay and dairy cows add to the economy of Marin County, but most of the natural wealth is in minerals. Clay, stone, limestone, cement, salt, sand, and gravel are found in abundance in the Bay Area.

The principal industries are manufacturing, finance, computers, shipping, and tourism. 18.8% of the state population lives there. Contrary to popular belief, products are still "Made in America" as a reading of the Help Wanted sections in the local newspapers and trade papers show; the Bay Area is proof of this. Steel and auto manufacturing plants have closed but they have been replaced by other manufactured products such as computer parts, electric signals parts, circuits, plastic injection molding and other products needed by modern industries in this country and throughout the world. Wells Fargo Bank's (one of the four largest financial institutions in the nation) headquarters is in San Francisco (Bank of America was bought and moved to North Carolina in the 1990s and the Pacific Coast Stock Exchange merged into the New York Stock Exchange in 2006, although their magnificent former headquarters offices still stand proudly, occupied by new business ventures). The local economy's dependence on innovation and high-tech skills has led to a more educated population. It has also led to a high concentration of wealth, making the Bay Area the wealthiest region in the US; the East Bay city of Pleasanton has the third-highest household income in the country.[5] Tourism employs so many people that whenever the San Francisco Board of Supervisors discusses getting rid of the cable cars to modernize Powell and adjacent streets and to free themselves from negligence law suits involving car mishaps, the tourist industry howls so loudly that the politicians give in. They know that the clang, clang of the cable car translates into a plink, plink of coins in the city's coffers; thus, both sentimentalists who want to preserve the past and pragmatists who count the coins are pleased. Tourism has also suffered a 30% decline in the last few years because of growing street crime and homelessness, with accompanying drug addicts and the mentally unbalanced filling the once-fashionable streets in the downtown and around Union Square **(Chapter 20)**. Still, areas such as Pier 39, Little Italy, Chinatown, Fishermen's Wharf, Nob Hill, Castro, Presidio, and the Marina are arguably safe, as are Golden Gate Park and the Mission District during the day; Covid-19 restrictions exacerbated the decline in tourism by restricting travel, cultural exhibits, public places, and restaurants, among other things by closing these venues in an attempt to limit contagion.[6] Across the bay Oakland is the most modern port on the West Coast, utilizing up-to-date facilities, a combined government-business program that began in the late 1960s.[7]

The Central Coast region: Beauty and Tech Capital

From San Jose south to Point Conception and constituting the next region, stretch the Central Coastal Mountains and Valleys, an area of ranching, fishing, and farming. These are the counties of Santa Clara, Santa Cruz, Monterey, San Benito, San Luis Obispo, and Santa Barbara. It is home to 3.7% of the state population but is growing as people leave the metropolitan areas for cheaper housing and better neighborhoods. The Coast Ranges, which run in a northwest-southeast direction parallel to the coastline at elevations of between 2,000 and 4,000 feet (610 to 1,220 m), officially terminate at Point Conception in ranges which have an east-west trend known as the Transverse Ranges. But the traveler along U.S. 101 or State Route 1 would probably not notice the "line" between one geomorphic province and another. Here in the Central Coast are numerous valleys of all sizes nestling between the mountains, the most important being the Santa Clara, which fronts on San Francisco Bay; the Salinas, which fronts on Monterey Bay; the San Luis, the Santa Maria, and the Santa Ynez. In Monterey County the coast redwood stands halt their southern march, and the most prominent representative of native vegetation is the woodland oak, covering the foothills below 2,500 feet (762 m) elevation.

Once the habitat of the Tule elk, the pronghorn antelope and the grizzly bear, this area is now the home of the black-tail deer and the California mule deer, the wild turkey, and the wild European boar. The boar found the mountain terrain hospitable, mated with domestic pigs which had gone wild and rooted harmlessly for bulbs, mushrooms, and insects - and then, unfortunately, developed a taste for ground crops. In the boar, the fierce grizzly has been respectably replaced - for it is one of the most dangerous game animals when wounded, cornered, or encountered with its young.

Agriculture in this area centers on beef cattle, some barley fields and vineyards, fruits (especially strawberries), and vegetables - especially tomatoes, lettuce, Irish potatoes, and artichokes (of which Castroville, in Monterey County, claims to be world capital). The flower industry, based in greenhouses, and now dominated by Matsui Nursery, has become a major philanthropic benefactor to Salinas, the

11

largest city in the region with 163,542 people counted by the 2020 census. While agriculture is the economic base of Salinas, over 100 manufacturing companies call it home. Fisheries, alas, have declined as they have in the San Francisco area; squid accounts for most of Monterey's small catch, while, just to the north at Moss Landing, the catch is divided among anchovies, salmon, and albacore. The sardines, breeding in the cold, nutrient-rich offshore water of the California Current had once been the mainstay of Monterey's world-famous Cannery Row but in the half-century from 1916 to 1967 they were overfished, leading to legislative suspension of the industry.

World famous Silicon Valley is here, manufacturing most of the nation's computers and related products. Here Apple, Google, PayPal, Yahoo, and others have headquarters. All of these had their origins in the mid-1970s as young electronics hobbyists running small-time shoe-string operation out of their garages. Within 20 years they grew into multi-billion-dollar industries spreading around the world, at their best, accounting for one-third of the venture capital investment in the United States. (It's now at about 22%, a drop exacerbated by the failure of the Silicon Valley Bank in March 2023, although it remains a significant player).[8]

Tourism is a major money-maker for the region. The Santa Cruz Mountains have numerous parks and protected areas, boasting trails for hikers, horse-riding, mountain biking, rock climbing, and backpacking. The Monterey Peninsula, comprising the cities of Monterey, Carmel-by-the-Sea, and Pacific Grove, and the Pebble Beach resort community, boast artist colonies, golf courses, fine dining, theater, boutiques, and hotels. Big Sur, south of the Monterey Peninsula, has been praised as "one of the most beautiful coastlines anywhere in the world, an isolated stretch of road, mythic in reputation," and drawing from between 4.5 and 7 million visitors annually, it ranks among the top US tourist destinations.[9]

The Southwestern region: Movies, Oil, People, and the San Andreas Fault

The Southwestern Mountains and Valleys run from Santa Barbara to the Mexican border along the coast. Included are the counties of Santa Barbara, Ventura, Los Angeles, Orange, San Diego, and the sheep's tail part of Riverside and San Bernardino. Here, what appear to be the Coast Ranges merge into the Transverse, with peaks as high as 10,000 feet (3.05 km), and effectively separate northern from southern California. Below this barrier is the Los Angeles Basin, the largest lowland area fronting on the Pacific Ocean, making possible profitable agricultural endeavor and the state's greatest population concentrations. The Peninsular Ranges, extending southward into Baja California, include the Santa Ana, San Jacinto, and Santa Rosa ranges. Here are lofty peaks more than 10,000 feet (3.05 km) - San Bernardino, San Jacinto, and San Antonio.

Once the land of grizzlies, Nelson bighorn sheep and pronghorn antelope, it now boasts two species of mule deer: the California and the Southern.

As a sign of a diverse economy the primary industries are agriculture, shipping, oil, finance, tourism, and films. This is the most populated region of the state – 43.15% of Californians live there. In addition to these, its industries include software, automotive, finance, biomedical, and regional logistics.

Oil production from Newhall to Orange County and refining at Long Beach became one of the state's leading industries; however, offshore oil production accounts for an increasing share of the state's production. The Santa Monica and Venice areas are known as "Silicon Beach," due to the concentration of financial and marketing technology-centered firms located in the region. Retail outlets such as Macy's, Marshall's, Bloomingdale's, Nordstrom, Saks Fifth Avenue, Nieman Marcus, and many others, fill the business sections of many of the cities in Los Angeles, Orange, and San Diego Counties. Agriculture remains important in this region, and the traveler on Interstate 5, having passed through the concrete south from Los Angeles to Anaheim, is pleasantly surprised by the beautiful fields and orchards below Santa Ana. Beef cattle, chickens, strawberries, avocados, oranges, grapefruit, lemons, vegetables, and walnuts account for the bulk of the area's agricultural wealth - though urbanization has voraciously consumed many of the farms and ranches.

Los Angeles and San Diego are the state's top commercial fishing ports, the latter ranking fourth in the nation. Some 2,000 commercial boats based in Los Angeles harbor fish the coastal waters as far south as Peru. "Fish Harbor" on Terminal Island is the site of several canneries and processing plants, with San Pedro handling most of the fresh fish trade. San Diego formerly handled more than a hundred million pounds of fish annually, four-fifths of the catch being some variety of tuna which went to Starkist Tuna's cannery (since moved to Kentucky due to labor cost). Most of California's population is located on the coast, especially in the metropolitan areas of San Francisco (4.75 million+), Los Angeles (13.2 million+), and San Diego (3.30 million+). In Southern California there are 14 cities with more than 200,000 population and 48 cities with more than 100,000 residents. Although it has a century-old reputation for high growth rate, its population has grown more slowly than the state population average since 2000, due to increasing concentration of population in the Bay Area and Greater Sacramento region with their stronger, tech-oriented economy.

Entertainment and tourism provide much of the revenue for the area. The motion picture, television, and music industry are centered in the Los Angeles area. Hollywood, a Los Angeles district, gave its name to the movies. In Los Angeles are the headquarters of The Walt Disney Company (currently the owner of ABC), MGM, Paramount Pictures, Sony Pictures, Universal Pictures, and Warner Brothers. Southern California is also the home of a large surf and skateboard culture, with companies such as Body Glove, No Fear, Quicksilver, RVCA, Stussy, Vans, and Volcom headquartered there. It is also the home of many sports franchises and television stations such as Fox Sports Net, and is the center of many athletic competitions. Southern California's beaches, amusement parks, and snow skiing are the bases of a prosperous tourist industry.

Transportation is omnipresent in Southern California, with ten airports, three commercial ports, a commuter rail system extending from Los Angeles outward to Ventura, Riverside, San Bernardino, and San Diego. It also serves as a hub for Amtrak, freight hauling railroads, and highway interstates.

The San Andreas Fault System formed the eastern boundary of this region. It is also the boundary of the greater Pacific Tectonic Plate ringed by the Pacific Basin Seismic Belt (extending from New Zealand to Japan to Alaska to Mexico to Chile). 80% of the world's earthquakes occur along the belt as the Pacific Plate moves forward or slides by other plates. The San Andreas Fault System, a huge fissure stretching about 650 miles (1,046 km) from Point Arena southeast to Baja California, is not in fact a single break but is composed of several roughly parallel lines of activity with numerous minor faults branching off. The San Andreas has been responsible for most of the Golden State's shakers since they were first recorded two centuries ago, so it has been studied extensively. Its location has prompted several fantasists to predict that the area west of the fault will someday break off and fall into the sea, when a better description would be that San Francisco and Los Angeles continue to move toward each other, to become one in the very distant future.

California is honeycombed with faults, and no part of it is free from the threat of earthquake. Those who fear earthquakes should keep in mind that no part of the earth is safe from natural disasters, our country's midsection being subject to tornados and floods, while hurricanes whip the Atlantic seaboard and Gulf Coast, and many regions occasionally suffer from droughts and crippling snowfalls.

The Coast Range, thrust up by earthquakes and the meeting of the Pacific and North American tectonic plates, runs parallel to the coast. In some places, such as Santa Lucia (Monterey County) they rise directly from the sea with nary a beach to behold while elsewhere they rise far inland. The hills in the coastal cities, such as San Francisco's famous hills, are part of this range. The sandy beach areas of California are rather small, for if every Californian were allotted some beach property it is estimated that there would be about 0.63 square inch (1.6 cm2) for each.

The Southeastern region: Desertscapes and Imperial Valley Oasis

The Southeastern deserts, mountains and valleys occupy the eastern edge of the state from the Mexican border north to Mono Lake. This region includes the counties of Imperial, Riverside, Inyo, Mono, most of San Bernardino, and the eastern part of Kern. Here reside 12.2% of Californians, most of whom live in eleven cities with over 100,000 population in

2020, in Riverside and San Bernardino counties (Riverside, San Bernardino, Moreno Valley, Ontario, Rancho Cucamonga, Corona, Victorville, Murrieta, Temecula, Jurupa Valley, and Menifee). The lower portion is a great expanse of desert terrain, interspersed with short, rugged mountain ranges, large sandy valleys, and dried lake bottoms. This area is mostly in the Mojave Desert, with its northeastern reaches, east of the Sierra, in the Great Basin and includes Owens Valley. The Mojave, lying between the Great Basin and the Colorado, includes fascinating Death Valley. The Great Basin Desert is the only "cold desert" in the US, as most of the precipitation falls as snow, while its dryness is caused by the "rain shadow effect" of the Sierra Nevada, which allows only 20% of Pacific Ocean rain clouds to cross over.

The Salton Trough is a continuation of the great trough in which the Gulf of California (or Sea of Cortés) lies. South and adjacent to the Mojave Desert is the Sonoran Desert, consisting of approximately 7 million acres (2.8 million ha), reaching deep into the Mexican state of Sonora.

This is an area of native desert shrub, about 24.2 million acres (97,930 km2) of it. The desert soil tends to be alkaline, adding to the stress of drought on plants. Its forage potential is somewhat limited, though the Nelson bighorn sheep have always called it home. It is rich in such minerals as clay, barite, tungsten, limestone, uranium, lead, zinc, borate, potash, silver, gold, sand and gravel, cement, stone, gypsum, and iron (mainly in the Mojave).[10] The Mojave Desert is the home of the *Yucca brevifolia* (the Joshua Tree), the Colorado Desert hosts the saguaro cactus, and the Great Basin features the Pinyon pine and sagebrush.

Death Valley and Joshua Tree National Parks, along with the Mojave National Preserve (the "secret sibling to Death Valley") attract their share of tourists, where visitors can see unique landscapes, plants, and animals. Accommodations are few but there are some hotels and campsites. Touring is best outside of summer months, as the heat is unforgiving.

In contrast to the northwest Coast, which receives about 100 inches (2.54 m) of rain each year, the southeast deserts receive about three inches (7.62 cm) annually. A freak storm on the morning of August 5, 2022, flooded Death Valley as it dropped 1.5 inches (3.81 cm) in just a few hours; fifteen days later, Tropical Storm Hilary tore through the park, dropping more than a year's worth of rain - 2.2 inches (5.59 cm) – in a day, forging new gullies, displacing heavy rocks and undercutting roadways.[11] Combined with this lack of rainfall is the blistering heat of the summers. Nevertheless, the Coachella and Imperial Valleys, through irrigation from the Colorado River, have become an agricultural paradise, raising beef cattle, sheep, grapefruit, tangerines, dates, melons, vegetables, hay, and barley. The Imperial Valley's major crop is grapefruit, while barley, raised under irrigation, is the state's most important grain.[12]

The Sierra Nevada region – Grand Beauty

To the north and west of the Southeastern Deserts are the Sierra Nevada Mountains, an 80 mile (129 km) wide range stretching 400 miles (644 km) from the North Fork of the Feather River south to the Kern River. This is one of the most impressive mountain ranges in the world, containing many peaks - including Whitney - over 13,000 feet (3.96 km) elevation. The mountain counties are Plumas, Sierra, El Dorado, Amador, Alpine, Calaveras, Tuolumne, Mariposa and the eastern parts of Placer, Nevada, Madera, Fresno, Tulare, and a part of Kern.

The Sierra Nevada is the spine of California running from the deserts to the far north. At its southern end they curve west and southwest to connect, via the Transverse Ranges, with the Coast Ranges; on the north it merges with the Southern Cascade Mountains. The Sierra gently slopes on its western side but drops off abruptly to the east along a major fault scarp, a barrier to transportation in the early days of exploration and building. Some of its notable features include the General Sherman, the largest tree in the world by volume, Lake Tahoe, the largest alpine lake in North America, Mount Whitney, the tallest mountain in the "Lower 48" states, and the granite-sculptured Yosemite Valley. As so much of it was inaccessible, the Sierra was not fully explored until 1912.[13] When the Forty-niners came west, they thought that the range resembled a huge, looming elephant. Thrown up by volcanic upheaval and earthquakes they are high enough, as noted, to create a rain shadow effect that keeps at least 80% of Pacific rain clouds in California, which is why Nevada and Utah are so dry. Unlike their surroundings, the mountains receive a substantial amount of snowfall, resulting in many watersheds. On the western slope they drain into the Central Valley, through which their water is carried by the Sacramento and San Joaquin Rivers to the Pacific via San Francisco Bay. On the eastern slope, watersheds are much narrower and their water flows into the Great Basin, into the usually dry lakes and sinks of western Nevada.

A few scattered stands of redwood (*Sequoia gigantea*) surrounded by coniferous forests mark the higher Sierra while oak woodland is found in the foothills. The very high Sierra is an alpine area and is also used for summer grazing and recreation. In the Sierra are found such natives as the Sierra Nevada black bear, the California bighorn sheep, the California and black-tail deer, muskrat, beaver, Sierra grouse, golden trout, mountain quail, and such imports as the wild turkey and striped bass.

In 1975, when the federal government permitted citizens to buy, sell, and own gold without a license for the first time in 40 years, gold prices soared from a set $35 per troy ounce (31.103 g) to $198.[14] Immediately, there was a rush of hopeful amateur prospectors to the mountains all over the West with pans and other permitted non-mechanical devices. They found that any streams that drained the Sierra northwest of Mariposa to be especially productive.

Much of the range is federal lands and is either protected from development or strictly managed. There are three national parks (Yosemite, Kings Canyon and Sequoia), two national monuments (Devils Postpile and Giant Sequoia), ten national forests, and 26 wilderness areas, which together protect 15.4% of the Sierra Nevada from logging or grazing. The US Forest Service and Bureau of Land Management control 52% of the land in the range. Logging and grazing are generally allowed on this land, under federal regulations that balance land development and recreation.

Sheep are raised in the San Joaquin Valley but in May they are moved to mountain meadows to graze until November. This practice, called transhumance, is practiced in many parts of the world to provide seasonal pastures by moving flocks or herds. The flocks of the San Joaquin are moved more than 300 miles (483 km) over trails marked and set aside by the Bureau of Land Management.

Lumbering operations of the redwood and pine forests share the economy with mineral production: gold, silver, stone, sand, and gravel. Since World War II there has been a continuous increase in lumber production, with pine declining in favor of white fir and Douglas fir, but environmentalist pressures have cut into the lumber industry with resulting unemployment. Gold, the mineral suddenly found in rich veins in 1848, set the trajectory for modern California as nothing else could have done. The echo of that early abundance is still to be found in many Sierra streams, varying in size from microscopic (flour gold) to nuggets weighing several pounds or kilograms.

The Sierra Nevada is a vast area with a tiny population - only 2.73% of the state's total. As is happening in the Central Coast, many metropolitan dwellers are moving there to escape high property costs and crime. Most of the Sierra's dwellers live around Lake Tahoe. There, tourism - fueled by Nevada's gambling industry legalized in 1931, more than fifty years before California followed suit, as well as by the resorts dotting the remarkably clear, blue water - is the mainstay of the local economy, although Nevada is no stranger to the economic recession that gripped the world in 2008-13. This economic slump slowly improved until reimposed by the Covid-19 pandemic of 2020-22. Many of the Tahoe area communities benefit from cultivating a Gold Rush ambiance: places like Truckee, Grass Valley, Sonora, Placerville, Auburn, Pollock Pines, and Colfax.

The Northeastern region: Volcanoes

To the north of the Sierra Nevada, extending to Oregon, are the Northeastern Mountains and Tablelands, including the South Cascade Mountains, Modoc Plateau, and part of the Great Basin. Included are the counties of Siskiyou, Modoc, Lassen, and the eastern part of Shasta. The Cascades are a separate mountain range, although on relief maps and from the highway they may appear to be an extension of the Sierra. The Sierra are primarily granite while the Siskiyou are lava; the boundary between them is roughly the county line between Plumas and Shasta. Representative spots in the area are Yosemite for the Sierra granite and Lassen for the Siskiyou lava. Mt. Lassen (10,457 feet [3.187 km]), only

21

recently became an active volcano, and continues this status, with a great eruption in 1914-21 after a dormancy of over 1,000 years. It was still venting steam into the 1950s. With Mt. Shasta (14,162 feet [4.317 km]) it dominates the area. In the extreme northeast corner of the state, the Modoc Plateau, with an average altitude of 5,000 feet (1.52 km), gives way to the Warner Mountains, towering a mile above the plateau.

The principal money-maker here in the shadow of the Siskiyou Mountains is grazing. Less than one percent (0.07%) of the state population resides in the northeast.

To the west grow almost pure stands of Douglas fir. Sagebrush is found between 4,000 and 7,500 feet (1.22-2.29 km) in the Modoc Plateau and chaparral is scattered throughout the region. Once the grizzly, California bighorn sheep, Rocky Mountain elk, and the pronghorn antelope ranged here; now it's a habitat of the Pronghorn, the Rocky Mountain mule deer, the muskrat, goose, and sage grouse.

The grizzly, once feared in all of California except the southeast, gave all western species of bear their evil reputation. Notoriously fierce and intractable, and one of the largest of American carnivores, the grizzly cannot tolerate human presence; while most bears would avoid human contact before human food corrupted their appetite, grizzlies reputedly would go out of their way to attack a human upon detecting the scent. They are now extinct in California, the last recorded kill occurring in Tulare County in 1922. Extinct, that is except for one grizzly family in the Big Bear Alpine Zoo, Big Bear Lake, California, as symbol of strength and resistance on the California state flag, and as mascot of many sports teams.[15]

The bighorn sheep, while not extinct, declined rapidly

22

because of the introduction of domestic sheep, which overgrazed their range and communicated infectious diseases and parasites. The pronghorn antelope, principally ranging in the northeast, went from near extinction to several thousand head, as indicated by airplane surveys.

Some gold fields, copper, sand and gravel pits, iron and uranium deposits are found in this area, as well as over 11 billion board feet (3,352,800.2 km) of coniferous forest saw timber and some herds of beef cattle.

The Central Valley region -- the Nation's Agricultural Heartland

The Central Valley runs 450 miles (644 km) from Mt. Shasta to the Tehachapi Mountains and an average of 60 miles (96.56 km) from the Coast Range to the Sierra. It includes the counties of Tehama, Glenn, Butte, Colusa, Sutter, Yuba, Yolo, Sacramento, San Joaquin, Stanislaus, Merced, Kings, and the western parts of Nevada, Madera, Fresno, Tulare, and Kern. 16.6% of the state population is in the valley, mostly in Redding, Sacramento, Stockton, Fresno, and Bakersfield; three quarters of the Central Valley's population live in these five metropolitan areas, with the remainder in the Chico, Hanford-Corcoran, Madera, Merced, Modesto, Visalia-Porterville, and Yuba City metropolitan areas. Primarily flat with a few heights (as in the Sutter Buttes and Coalinga hills) it is California's agricultural heartland and a world food supplier. In 1945 the Valley's agriculture filled several Liberty ships.[16] Places once scorned by city dwellers are rapidly filling up with the homes of commuters to the metro areas. Photos of the Earth taken from the Moon since 1969 clearly show this increase in home construction.

Essentially a treeless grassland and marshy region, its largest original inhabitants were the grizzly, tule elk, and pronghorn, "flocks of herons, egret, and similar large birds, while bald and golden eagles, hawks and falcons were higher on the food chain."[17] Of those natives, only the duck and valley quail remain, having been joined by the imported chukar, pheasant and striped bass. Originally, the Central Valley had several types of vernal (seasonal) pools, especially around Merced, and several large lakes, such as the now usually dry Tulare Lake, once the largest fresh-water body west of the Mississippi River (three times the size of Lake Tahoe), Buena Vista Lake and Kern Lake. Between 1880 and 1900 farmers began to drain Tulare Lake off through an intricate system of canals, dams, and levees, eventually making it disappear. The J. G. Boswell Company, a large agricultural concern, eventually owned the entire lakebed.

As a world food and fiber supplier it boasts a long list of products. Beef and dairy herds, sheep, turkeys, chickens, ostriches, almonds, oranges, lemons, tangerines, kiwi fruit, vegetables, peaches, grapes, figs, cotton, hay, barley, and rice head the list.

As urbanization rooted out many of the orange groves of the south coast, orange acreage steadily increased in the San Joaquin, the southern half of the Central Valley; early sweet navels also grow in pockets as far north as Oroville in the Sacramento Valley, the northern half. Tangerines, kiwi fruit, and lemons are major products of Tulare County. Peaches thrive in the low humidity, ample sunshine and high temperatures of the Valley; canning varieties dominate production in the north, fresh and dried in the south. So prominent is agriculture that from the NASA earth resource satellite passing 560 miles (901 km) overhead, something trackable with iPhones, a large pattern of valley farms and orchards can be seen while Freeway 99 is barely discernable as a thin line.

Cotton had prospered since the advent of the mechanical picker, and the San Joaquin is ideal for its cultivation because of the long, hot growing season and lack of rain during the harvest period. Unfortunately, Pima cotton has all but disappeared because of the drought of 2011-17. Rice is cultivated along both sides of the Sacramento River, from Artois on the west to Butte City on the east. The area has the proper environmental conditions for rice culture, with plenty of level land, hot summers, impervious subsoil which makes drainage difficult because of a lack of pores, and an abundance of manageable water. California rice culture is probably the world's greatest example of agricultural engineering - a special rice seed specific to local conditions was developed, fields are flooded to kill weeds, seeding and fertilizing are performed by low-flying biplanes, self-propelled combines harvest the crops after the fields have been drained and the complex machinery dries it.

The drought that hit Pima cotton was not unusual in California. In the last century, there were droughts in 1922-26, which encouraged farmers to use irrigation more regularly, 1959-62, which led to the creation of the state water project, 1976-77, which inspired the discovery of the influence of El Niño on the climate, 1986-92, which was ended by El Niño events in the Pacific combined with the eruption of Mount Pinatubo in the Philippines producing heavier rainfalls, and 2007-09, which might have aggravated some of the severest wildfires in the state's history and the first in which a statewide emergency proclamation was issued.

Unfortunately, the severe, politically aggravated droughts that afflicted the state in 2011-17 and 2020-22 severely impacted California agriculture from raising food prices to impoverishing small farm-worker communities. In May 2015 the Aquarium of the (San Francisco) Bay called it "a man-made drought" in part due to a lack of rainfall and the absence of reservoirs and dams to catch what rain does fall.[18] Water authorities understand that much is unnecessarily wasted and cities such as Los Angeles have adopted laws to catch rainwater in new neighborhoods. In 2018 voters gave their support to new water reservoirs, but environmental groups generally opposed their construction because of danger to wildlife and possible damage to the land, using lawsuits and having the support of governors and other elected officials since 2010. Instead, they proposed such solutions as desalination plants, recycling wastewater for irrigation, recirculating the water that flows through rivers, installing pumps to move water from overflowing lakes to ones not expected to overflow, repairing fragile levees, and more radical solutions such as rationing water to residents, eliminating golf courses, swimming pools, and high-water use crops (such as almonds and wine vineyards).

**

Climate Diversity or Squandering of Abundance?

California's climate may be heralded in song and chamber of commerce slogans such as "Livable, Loveable Lodi," "San Clemente … The Good Life Comes in Waves," "Be World Class – Be Fresno," or "San Francisco – So Close But Worlds Away," but in reality, California has diverse climates. While most of the United States has four seasons, California has only two, cool and wet and hot and dry. Normally rain falls mainly from October to March, with a concentration between December and February. Except for occasional desert storms, rain is rare in the summer months. The dry seasons result from a continual high-pressure system which sends hot, drying winds westward to the coast, deflecting the cool, moist breezes moving south from the Gulf of Alaska. When winter approaches, this high-pressure system dissolves.

In January temperatures usually change one degree for every 330 feet (100.6 m) of elevation, for the mountain contours are the primary influences. The Sierra Nevada-Cascade barrier range protects the area to the west from the icy air masses of the continental interior, while they retain 80% of the Pacific rain clouds in that protected area. Coastal temperatures change very little - at Crescent City the mean minimum is 40o F (4.4o C) while at San Diego it increases only to 42o F (5.6o C); this in spite of the fact that Crescent City's latitude is that of Chicago while San Diego's is that of Savannah.

The July maximums often change one degree for every mile of the first 50 miles inland from the shoreline. The coast averages 60o to 72o (15O-22.2O C), while a few miles inland it's very hot, and in some areas, summers have recorded world records. When the mercury climbs above 100o (37.8o C) people become uncomfortable despite modern air conditioning, but low relative humidity makes it more tolerable than in other parts of the nation. Human adaptation to California's July and August has been greatly aided by the relative accessibility of the cooler coasts and mountains, plus ubiquitous insulation and central and vehicle air conditioning.

As just noted, California has recorded temperature extremes. On July 10, 1913, 134o (56.7o C) was recorded in Death Valley. This is the world record although some climate historians think it's four or five degrees too high; still, Death Valley recorded 129o (53.9o C) five times between July 1960 and June 2013. In the winter of 1932-33 -56o (-48.9o C) was noted at the summit of Mount Lassen. This was far from the world record set in 1983 at a research station in Antarctica: -128.6o (-89.2o C).

The state's rainfall is notoriously unreliable. Although Southern California is described as having a "Mediterranean climate" with dry summers, wet winters, and generally favorable temperatures, it is more the story of years with above- or below-normal rainfall with consecutive years of nearly waterless drought with wild fires alternating with years with flash floods and mudslides.[19] In some years, such as 1955-56 when 12 rivers from the Klamath to the Kings were affected, several times the average amount of precipitation can be recorded, resulting in extensive flooding. (This occurred again around New Year's 1997). In other years, such as 1975-77, a fraction of the annual average rainfall descends, causing disastrous droughts. The largest annual precipitation was 153.54 inches (3.9 m) at Monumental, Del Norte County, in 1908-09; the greatest monthly amount was 71.54 inches (1.817 m) at Helen Mine, Lake County, in January 1909, and the heaviest precipitation within 24 hours was 26.12 inches (65.345 cm) on January 22-23,1943 at Hoegees Camp, near Mt. Wilson, at an elevation of 2,760 feet (841.2 m). By contrast, the wettest spot in the world is on the Hawaiian island of Kauai with 460 inches (11.684 m) per year. Not so impressive in terms of inches but certainly in terms of cost was the storm which battered northern California on January 4, 1982. It blocked roads with mud slides (including the Marin approach to the Golden Gate Bridge). These mudslides instantly destroyed dozens of hillside homes, and caused auto and airplane wrecks, and cost 31 lives from the Bay Area and Santa Cruz to Yosemite National Park. The storms that hit around New Year's Day 1997 flooded towns, washed away trailer parks and caused nearly $200 million ($382,500,000 in 2023 dollars) in damage to Yosemite National Park. The El Niño phenomenon, in which waters off the west coast of South America warm, alters climates all over the world. In 1997-98 it brought record rainfall (in many places twice the

28

normal) to California and kept temperatures unseasonably cool (by 15 to 20 degrees [-9.4o to -6.7o C]) until the middle of June. On the other hand, no measurable rain fell at Bagdad, San Bernardino County, from October 3, 1912 to November 8, 1914; but this pales when compared to a dry spell in the Lake Tahoe area which began in AD 1040 and finally broke in AD 1160! Tree ring research at the University of Arizona discovered this long-ago drought.[20] A dry spell spanning 1928 to 1934 inspired the building of the big federal and state water systems.

Hurricanes which routinely strike the Mexican Pacific coast, are an anomaly in California, eventually spawning monsoon conditions over Arizona, yet they can and do occur. One struck in September 1939. Another, Hurricane Hilary, struck Baja California in August 2023 and moved up the coast to make landfall east of San Diego, sparing the city but flooding the Inland Empire and the desert to Las Vegas. La Jolla recorded wind gusts of 51 mph (82.07 km/h). Los Angeles and San Diego did receive significant rainfall, but Death Valley got more than, and Palm Springs almost as much as, falls in a year. Mount San Jacinto received an "incredible" 11.74 inches (29.82 cm) in a day, and people were stuck on roofs in Cathedral City, where roads were awash under a thick layer of mud. Turning north, it blew into the San Joaquin Valley.[21]

Snowfall has also kept pace with rainfall totals at different stations; for example, it has been measured at Mammoth Mountain in the Eastern Sierra since 1969-70. In 1982-83 there was a record snowfall at Mammoth of 668.5 inches (16.98 m). The 2022-23 season, when 17 atmospheric rivers passed over California, beat that record by measuring 702 inches (17.83 m); the water measure for that much snow was 235% of normal.[22] Unfortunately, the rain-filled reservoirs were insufficient to hold the rainfall, and much was allowed to flow out to sea; more reservoirs, routinely halted by environmental groups, could have saved it for the inevitable dry years.

There are other - and less catastrophic - statistics to describe the state. California is 100 million acres (407,700 km2). It is the third largest state (after Alaska and Texas.) The average width is 275 miles (440 km), the coastline is 2,100 miles (3,360 km) (the distance from Maine to Georgia.) Its length along Interstate 5 is 750 miles (1,207 km). Its 2020 population was nearly 40 million (38,940,231 on January 1, 2023), and, as noted above, the International Monetary Fund in 2018 ranked California's economy the fifth richest power in the world (after the United States, China, Japan, and Germany) in terms of GNP, and its economy is larger than Africa's or Australia's and is almost as large as South America's.[23] Of the 2022 Fortune 500's top 100 companies, 10 are headquartered in California (down from 30 ten years earlier, a phenomenon owing to California's increasing reputation as a comparatively unlivable state, generally unfriendly to business, small or large.) Half of the remaining Fortune 500 companies are in the computer industry.[24] Still, California is the richest state in the Union in per capita income, and it contributes 13.34% of the total US gross national product, yet it is 16th in per capita federal aid. Only 1.9 million Californians receive AFDC, a sign that poverty is not as widespread as is sometimes thought, though the San Joaquin Valley's poverty level is comparable to Appalachia, California has the highest number of welfare recipients and highest welfare payout of all the states.

**

With such a spectacular array of facts, it would be too much to expect that California would not be the subject of a pseudo-geographical collection of silly notions. One of these is that the climate is changing. This myth is usually perpetuated by old timers whose memories of the weather are rose-tinted with age. It suffices to say that the U.S. Weather Bureau denies the charge but a Fresno statistic should serve as evidence to contradict the myth: on July 8, 1905 the mercury reached 115oF (46.1oC) and on July 26, 1980 it climbed to 111o (43.9oC). A theory promoted by former Vice President Al Gore (1948- , served 1993-2001), which has become widely accepted, contends that the world's climate is heating because of an increased greenhouse effect caused by human-made carbon dioxide through use of fossil fuels, which might result in long droughts, severe storms, and rising sea levels. Interestingly, some of its proponents continue to invest in coastal property. A few years before this was promulgated, there was another theory that equally alarmed people about global cooling, a phenomenon caused by a regular replacing of the warm ocean surface by cooler water from the bottom through churning at 25–30-year intervals. A look at California's climate history will not settle this dispute because of the difference in topography in such a large area. A recent University of California study points to a history of climate stability with just a few anomalies since the 1850s and in September 2023, a group of 1,609 scientists claimed that "the so-called climate emergency is a myth."[25]

A persistent myth concerns the Golden Gate, the entrance to the deepest Pacific coast harbor between Puget Sound and the Panama Canal. It seems strange that early explorers and ordinary ship captains missed the Gate prior to 1769. Is it new, geologically speaking? There are rumors about a gigantic earthquake in the 1760s - alleged Indian legends about the gods stomping up and down the coast, resulting in the opening of the Gate. This notion was especially popular after the 1906 earthquake. There is, however, a non-legendary bit of evidence to counter this myth: the location of shell mounds on the Bay, which prove that the shoreline has been in approximately the same place for thousands of years.

One completely justified popular perception of California is that - regardless of doomsayers - the state's ability to produce is limited only by constraints on ingenuity. In a short two centuries California evolved from an acorn-based economy, through a period of hides and tallow and another of gold and wheat, to the present complex scene, where urban life, industry and farming intersect. The environment proved readily adaptable to each successive economy. If California declines it will be because its people have declined, have lost the ability to fend for themselves and to display an adventure spirit. Terrible government with increasingly oppressive regulation that drives out business, coupled with an unbridled, illegal immigration of unskilled people replacing those who contribute rather than take, will cause California to decline unless the situation is halted and reversed by the voters. Recent years have seen unprecedented numbers of mostly productive citizens relocate to states deemed more livable; for the first time, after the 2020 census, California lost a Congressional seat, one of 53, one of its electoral college votes, and eligibility for as much federal money as before. Natural disasters there have been aplenty, and California always bounced back, but against human greed, laziness, mismanagement, and stupidity there aren't any defenses.

Before the Age of Human Beings: The Land

"The more things change, the more they remain the same." This aphorism aptly describes the geologic history of California, which is, after all, part of the story of the changing four-billion-year-old Earth. Where once was sea, mountains and valleys have been created. Earthquakes and volcanoes were the forces which once raised the mountains from the sea, and they continue to add height to the Coast Range and Sierra, and to the world's great ranges such as the Rockies. Within the past few moments of time (geologically speaking) California's familiar features have been shaped by ice, wind, and water.

This is a part of the story that goes back 4.5 billion years ago to the Earth's beginning. When its surface cooled, and gravity could hold rain-producing clouds, the Pacific became Earth's first ocean some two or three billion years ago. 200 million years ago the Earth was a single vast continent. It split and these continents then began to drift apart. The Eastern and Western hemispheres became distinct 120 million years ago. This spreading continues to affect the continents, the Atlantic Ocean Sea floor expanding two inches (five cm) per year and the Pacific Ocean floor three times that.

**

"In the beginning there was no land, no light, only darkness and the vast Ocean where Earth-Maker and Great-Grandfather were afloat in their canoe."

- California Native creation myth

**

Glimpsing the Paleozoic, Mesozoic, and Cenozoic Eras

Elsewhere in California during the Precambrian Era what was happening is not clearly known. It might have been a period when most of the land was mountainous, or the mountains may have been undergoing erosion, or the record itself might have eroded. We just do not know as there is no rock record.

The next great geologic era, the Paleozoic (570-228 million years ago) left many more rocks. The best preserved are found in Death Valley and the adjacent ranges of the Mojave Desert, but others are found in the Sierra, the Klamath Mountains, the Coast, Transverse and Peninsular Ranges.

Those found in Death Valley and the Mojave show evidence of having been deposited in shallow, quiet seas, arms of the Pacific which then extended as far as Utah. Those rocks found in the Sierra Nevada and Klamath Mountains are types found at ocean shores. The Paleozoic rock layers are as often as not chemically pure limestone and marble. This was the time when California's huge limestone deposits were formed.

The more recent Mesozoic Era (230-65 million years ago) left many more clues than the two earlier ones. California as we know it, with the Sierra Nevada backbone risen from the sea, began to take shape.

Midway through the Mesozoic, the oldest rocks had been upended, twisted, broken, and so chemically altered as to become different rocks. For 130 million years, until almost 80 million years ago, these strata were pushed aside and introduced into existing rocks by magma rising from the depths of the Earth. During this period the Sierra Nevada was taken from the Pacific and added to the North American shoreline. At the same time much of California's natural wealth was added by granite intrusions: Gold-bearing veins shot through the rock of what was becoming mountains, joined by silver, copper, zinc, lead, tungsten, molybdenum, and granite itself.

While the mountains were rising, they were being eroded by wind and water. Mineral fragments that were torn away from these mountains were tossed into the sea that was the

Central Valley. Eventually these fragments consolidated into rock layers. The Sierra was still low: Mt. Whitney probably stood at only one-fourth its present height.

The great dinosaurs which stalked much of the earth left no traces in California, apparently because most of the present land was undersea. (However, in June 1997, a local firefighter found bones from a Tyrannosaurus Rex relative near Rocklin, in the Sierra, a location that 80 million years ago was the shoreline).[26] The existing land was mountainous rather than the grassy floodplains favored by the gigantic beasts. On the other hand, there are abundant fossil remains of marine life, the large variety such as the plesiosaur and mosasaur, and the microscopic variety of single-celled shelled animals (called *Foraminifera*) and single-celled plants the size of diatoms. Both these microscopic forms are living today. In December 1980 alone, researchers from the San Diego Natural History Museum recovered fossils from a dolphin, whale, albatross, cormorant, sea cow, and walrus dating back to the Pleistocene Epoch (10-1 million years ago) as far as seven miles (11.2 km) from the ocean.[27]

The Cenozoic Era, stretching from the end of the Mesozoic time until two million years ago, has been subdivided, and further subdivided, into periods and epochs, and unlike the earlier eras, the Cenozoic story is nearly complete. The most significant of these epochs was called Miocene (26-12 million years ago).

The great mountain mass of the Sierra Nevada, which had extended the length of California and beyond to the north, south and east (as the Klamath and Peninsular Ranges of today), continued its erosion down to small hills by the time of the Miocene Period. Slower-moving streams meandered westward across the mountains, heading somewhere east of today's crest, and dumping their debris into the inland areas of the Central Valley.

As the mountains eroded, their gold deposits were also eroded, and yellow fragments were carried downstream towards the sea. As the streams rounded bends, they dropped the gold to form placer pockets in the ancient streambeds. These rivers poured into seas that were along the mountain front. Their sediment has been the source of much of the gas and oil now produced in the Central Valley.

The shores of these ancient seas are marked by formations that before the Miocene were the soils of a tropical region, a red clay characteristic of areas that are humid and hot. These clay beds are important today as the resources of a thriving ceramics industry.

By the Miocene the Sacramento Valley and the northern part of the San Joaquin Valley remained a slowly shoaling arm of the Pacific, meaning that mud flats were gradually raised above sea level. By the end of the Miocene, the Central Valley had been transformed into a series of intermittent freshwater lakes.

Meanwhile in the northern Sierra volcanoes were rising, throwing tons of ash into the air that blanketed the earth and clogged the lakes and streams of the Sierra Nevada foothills. The streams sought new beds, flowing over and through the lava and down the mountains. Thanks to continental drift crashing the Pacific and North American Plates together mountains rose again, rapidly enough to give the rivers greater cutting power, yet slowly enough to allow them to maintain their new courses. Their increased strength and abrasiveness gave the rivers ability to cut into the lava cover; where it was thick the streams knifed deeply into the underlying old Paleozoic rocks. These are today's Sierra Nevada streams and, for those who can read the record of the rocks, much of the story of the mountains is written along the river's courses through steep-walled canyons.

While the mountains were still slowly rising and being eroded, the most striking part of the Sierra Nevada story was unfolding. After the mountains had nearly reached their present height, great glaciers formed and crept down the river canyons both to the west and east. The moving ice sharpened the peaks, reshaped the canyons, pushed ahead long ridges of unsorted rock and sand, hewed stone basins to hold jewel-like lakes and hanging waterfalls, and heaped up long ridges of broken rocks to form much of the spectacular scenery of Yosemite National Park and the surrounding High Sierra.[28]

Northeastern California is almost a different world from the Sierra Nevada. A region of thick volcanic sheets, dotted with cinder cones where an occasional volcano projects through, this is the southern edge of an extensive volcanic region that commences far northward in Washington, as Mt. St. Helens loudly reminded us in 1980. Some of these lava sheets are quite new. Mt. Shasta, on the western margin of the area, last erupted in the 18th century, and Lassen Peak in 1914-17, culminating in a furious burst in May 1915. The great mass of Lassen Peak began as stiff, pasty lava forced from a vent on the north slope of a larger extinct volcano known as Tehama. The lava was squeezed up to form a rough, dome-shaped mass, plugging the vent from which it came. After this plug dome was formed, Lassen Peak was calm for long periods until 1914.[29]

The Cenozoic in the Coast Ranges has left an interesting record. Great faults have torn the land apart, and still do. Slowly sinking arms of shallow seas appeared, only to disappear as they filled with mud and sand, leaving behind rocks thousands of meters thick. Oil seeps formed pools in which unlucky creatures were trapped forever - leaving their bones to give us a clear picture of those who lived in ancient California.

Much of the landscape is controlled by faults. High-angle and nearly vertical, they occupy a zone running southeast from near the northwestern corner of the state to the Los Angeles area, where the whole zone is interrupted by faults trending eastward. The southeasterly aligned zone continues southeast from this interruption through the Peninsular Range into Baja California. Its effect on the landscape has been profound - land on the west side of this fault zone, dominated by the San Andreas fault, has moved as much as 348 miles (560 km) northwestward in the last 30 million years. (In some rural areas the 1906 earthquake moved fences 20 feet [6.1 m] farther apart.).

The Cenozoic period is easily seen in the Coast Ranges, as the records of the waxing and waning of the seas, of the rise and fall of mountains, and of the carving of rock sea shelves and the building of beaches at many levels are geologic tales told in the coastal rocks. In the Palos Verdes Hills southwest of Los Angeles, for example, one can discern 13 terraces, the highest 1,181 feet (360 meters) above present sea level, dating from about two million years ago.

It was then that continental drift, ever moving northward, took what became California's scenic coastline from Mexico, and in geologic terms, temporarily deposited it in its present location. To put it in perspective, Monterey would have been where Acapulco is today. So, one might ask where did the original California coastline end up? According to geologists at the U.S. Geological Survey in Menlo Park it probably ended up in Alaska and "if things keep going for millions of years, not only will Los Angeles be adjacent to San Francisco, but it'll keep right on going."[30]

In the Great Basin, of which the Mojave Desert is a part, the close of the Ice Age (about 20,000 years ago) saw many of these basins filled with glacial saltwater which formed a chain of large lakes. As the climate warmed the lakes dried, leaving playas (dried lakes), some of which are mined for such chemicals as salt with calcium chloride. In the Mojave there are more than 50 such playas and the region's streams disappear into the sand before reaching the dry lakes. Then and now a brief desert storm erodes sand from the mountains to fill river channels and form steep-crested dunes.

Volcanoes have been active in the Mojave, where lava flows spread over a large area and cinder cones dot the landscape. The many hot springs testify that volcanic activity has not subsided, for as late as 1898, lava erupted from beneath the waters of Mono Lake.

**

"Coyote then created and placed on the hills trees, brush and grass. Then Coyote went away."

- Pomo creation myth

**

Somewhat earlier, about 10 million years ago, most of the Central Valley had become dry land, only a small part of the sea still reaching here and there across the new Coast Ranges. Then a small volcano began to rise, culminating in Ice Age volcanic explosions. Today that 9.3-mile (15 kilometer) wide volcano is the Valley's most important topographical feature, the Sutter Buttes, 49 miles (75 kilometers) northwest of Sacramento. Another set of small volcanoes, the Mono Craters ranging from Mono Lake southward, last erupted about 250 or 30 years ago and since 1980 have been threatening to erupt, as evidenced by frequent earthquakes in the vicinity.[31]

About 600,000 years ago much of the Central Valley was the huge freshwater Lake Corcoran, fed by glacial saltwater. Gradually the lake dried, but as late as our century, winter rains and heavy storms commonly transformed much of the valley into what appeared to be an inland sea. In 1907 a flood equal to 100 Sacramento Rivers hit the Delta with a fury, forcing residents to row over orchards and wharves to reach safe landing and wait for steamboat rescue. In 1955 Marysville and Yuba City had a flooded Christmas. In 1958 and 1969 melting snow water ran over the man-made levees that guard the San Joaquin River system, and usually dry Tulare Lake temporarily became the largest freshwater lake in the state, covering 130 square miles (338 square km). In 1997 the levees broke and towns like Manteca had to be evacuated while Delta towns were again washed away, and again Tulare Lake appeared. In 2023 the lake returned due to record Sierra Nevada snowfalls and valley rainfall, threatening disastrous flooding for nearby towns such as Allensworth and destruction of orchards that take several years to mature.

Anza-Borrego: Three Geologic Snapshots

So many things have happened since the beginning of the land mass that came to be California that there are very few clues left which allow us to reconstruct the most remote events. Precambrian rocks, the oldest of which are 1.8 billion years old as measured by radiometric dating, have been so extensively changed by heat, pressure and chemical reactions that it is nearly impossible to tell what they once were. They have been found only in southern California - along the San Andreas fault system, scattered through the Mojave Desert and in Death Valley.

Since so many undecipherable centuries elapsed before the

oldest known rocks were deposited, and so many years lie between the geologic clues which do exist, the clues have been compared to "snapshots" in the absence of the total picture for those hundreds of millions of years. At least three such snapshots exist.

The first snapshot shows part of southern California as it was nearly 1.7 billion years ago. A great sea filled the Death Valley area, laying down thousands of meters of sediments, interspersed with the products of subsea volcanoes. Consolidating with rock these sediments were later deformed by unrest in the Earth's crust.

The second is along the San Andreas Fault System, where very distinctive rocks, as old as 1.7 billion years, are to be seen. One of these unusual rocks is called anorthosite; an eight-colored rock containing aluminum, made almost entirely of plagioclase feldspar. It is found in the western San Gabriel Mountains between the San Gabriel and San Andreas faults. Countertops and many other construction uses are made of it today.

The third snapshot, dim like the others with the passing millennia, is similar to the second. Again, the rare anthracite is seen, this time just north of the Salton Sea, in the Orocopia Mountains. To see the development of this snapshot one must go to Anza-Borrego Desert State Park, located in the Colorado Desert. Most visitors think of Anza-Borrego they envision wildflowers, bighorn sheep, or vast arid landscapes framed by rugged mountains. Few realize that the eroded badlands of Anza-Borrego provide a contrasting view, a window into the region's vanished past. The Park was not always the arid desert we experience today. Palaeontologic studies first began in the Anza-Borrego Desert during the mid-1930's, and they continue today.

Anza-Borrego has an exceptional fossil record. Over 500 different types of organisms have been identified, ranging from microscopic plant pollen and spores to the largest of mammoth elephants. Not only are the bones and teeth of long extinct animals preserved, but in some places, also their tracks. The Salton Trough, a geologically active rift valley, which bounds the eastern edge of the park once held a northward extension of the Sea of Cortés. Sediments laid down 5 million years ago in these warm clear tropical waters now yield the preserved shells of a variety of clams, snails, crabs, and corals. These organisms have ties with the Caribbean Sea and record a time before the Isthmus of Panama had formed. The remains of fish, walrus, baleen whales and even sea cows help us to more fully picture this long extinct marine ecosystem.

About 4 million years ago, the ancestral Colorado River began cutting through the Colorado Plateau of Arizona and Utah. The sediments eroded during the formation of the Grand Canyon spilled into the Salton Trough, creating a vast delta. These brackish marine deposits are recognized in Grand Canyon today by their extensive fossil oyster shell reefs and fossilized wood. The types of trees represented now live along the Pacific coast of southern California, suggesting that any mountains west of the Trough must have been low.

As the Salton Trough was filled with sediment carried by the ancestral Colorado River, what was to become Anza-Borrego gradually changed from a predominately marine environment to a system of interrelated terrestrial habitats. By about 3 million years ago, most of the area once covered by the Sea of Cortés held a large inland lake. Here, the remains of freshwater clams, snails, and fish are not uncommon. Streams and rivers draining the new uplifted Peninsular Range Mountains, which border the western side of Anza-

Borrego today, spread an apron of alluvium and floodplain deposits eastward into the Salton Trough. It is these sediments that provide us an almost uninterrupted record of terrestrial habitats spanning a period from about 3 million to less than a half million years ago. There are other snapshots, but they are even less distinct, for the rocks may or may not be of equal age. These rocks contain what may be the oldest forms of life in California, some resembling algae while others resemble bacteria.

Forgotten Animals

In contrast to the cold world of the Ice Ages, elsewhere in California and the world there is a different geological scene that is revealed to us in the various tar pits of southern California. In the world-famous La Brea Tar Pits and Museum (the George C. Page Museum) in the heart of downtown Los Angeles, one may see a drama that began 38,000 years ago in the Ice Age and continues.

More than half a million creatures of more than 200 species expired there, and even today an unsuspecting creature may venture too far into the sticky mass and be unable to escape. The plant life, typical of a climate much like that of modern Los Angeles, tells us why the tar was so enticing. Here were shimmering pools in open, rolling, semi-arid country where water holes were few and far between.

Among the fossilized extinct specimens to be seen are the American lion (*Felis Atrox*), proportioned like the modern lion only much larger; the saber-tooth (*Smilodon californicus*), a pouncing, ambushing cat about the size of a modern lion; Harlan's ground sloth (*Paramylodon harlani*), a large creature with armor-like protection in the form of bony nodules embedded in its skin; the smaller Shasta ground sloth (*Northrotheriops shastensis*), whose diet consisted of the various desert shrubs it browsed; the giant long-horned bison (*Bison latifrons*), with its two-meter (6.5 feet) spread of horns; the short-faced bear (*Arctodus simus*), larger than the modern Kodiak bear; the very common dire wolf (*Aenocyon dirus*); the equally rare tapir (*Tapirus*); the extinct camelops (*Camelops hesternus*), similar to the modern dromedary; the long-necked, long-legged Steven's llama (*Hemiauchenia stevensi*), related to modern llamas; the western horse (*Equus occidentalis*); the long, pig-like flat-headed peccary (*Platygonus compressus*); the dwarf pronghorn (*Capromeryx minor*); the grazing imperial mammoth (*Mammuthus imperator*); and the forest-loving American mastodon (*Mammut americanum*). There are, in addition, one hundred species of birds, mostly carnivorous, such as the scavenger Merriam's giant condor (*Teratornis merriami*), attracted to the carcasses of trapped animals, the extinct California turkey (*Parapave californicus*), and rare waterfowl such as spoon bills, herons, storks, and cranes. In addition, there are coyotes (*Canis latrans*), bobcats, skunks, rabbits, many kinds of rodents, fish, frogs, toads, lizards, turtles, snakes (including the western rattler), shrews, spiders, millipedes, and insects which are the same species living today.

A museum located in Fairmead, near Chowchilla, in Madera County, features fossils encountered during excavation for a construction site in 1993. Fossils dating back 700,000 years ago were found. As of 2023 they are still being recovered.[32]

During this same time Anza-Borrego supported a rich diversity of wildlife. Herds of mammoth elephants, tapirs, zebra-like horses, several species of camels, and llamas ranged across a landscape of stream border woodlands and savannah-like grassy scrublands. And, had we been there, we may have glimpsed a foraging giant ground sloth, beaver, or even a saber-tooth or American cheetah on the hunt.

The extinction of the western horse and the extinct camel raises an interesting question. Both lived there until about 8,000 years ago. In the 1760s the Spaniards brought horses, and in the 1850s the US Army introduced dromedaries. The two latter species readily adapted to California's environment. Why, then, did their earlier forms die out?

In 1973 the California state legislature, not without long debate, adopted the saber-tooth as California's official state fossil. It joined the state mineral (gold) and the state rock (serpentine) as the third geoscientific state emblem.

As noted, most of the creatures found in the tar pits were unsuspecting animals who wandered into the sticky ooze. One creature was probably very unwilling and not unaware of her fate. A single human, in her late 20's, suffered from a sinus-bone disease and was apparently left there to die 10,000 years ago. The structure of her skull indicates that she was probably one of the Chumash people of the Channel Islands area.[33]

Chapter One END NOTES

[1] Coverage Locator, LTE Data Coverage, Generated 05/06/2016, https://vzwmap.verizonwireless.com/dotcom/coveragelocator/

[2] USDA Forest Service, Pacific Northwest Research Station: California,
https://www.fs.usda.gov/research/pnw/search?content=california; Stephanie Elam, "Drought and disease in California forests leaves behind an estimated 36 million dead trees, survey finds," CNN, February 10, 2023, https://www.cnn.com/2023/02/10/us/california-drought-millions-trees-dead/index.html; University of Montana, California Timber Harvest, http://www.bber.umt.edu/fir/HarvestCA.aspx. Forest History

Society, "The Northern Spotted Owl," https://foresthistory.org/research-explore/us-forest-service-history/policy-and-law/wildlife-management/the-northern-spotted-owl/; Jason Vondersmith, " 'Timber Wars': OPB looks back at environmentalists vs. timber industry" *Portland Tribune*, September 29, 2020, https://www.portlandtribune.com/lifestyle/features/timber-wars-opb-looks-back-at-environmentalists-vs-timber-industry/article_facb2a8f-3137-5167-9aae-3245e0be8323.html

[3] Chris Roberts, "Why No Cash Crop is More Vulnerable To California Wildfires Than Cannabis", *Forbes*, September 10, 2020, https://www.forbes.com/sites/chrisroberts/2020/09/10/why-no-cash-crop-is-more-vulnerable-to-california-wildfires-than-cannabis/?sh=5cfc97305a48 ; Cf "Marijuana could effectively trigger a primary psychotic disorder, meaning that once the substance is removed, the symptoms are still there," Juliann Garey, "Marijuana and Psychosis" Child Mind Institute, February 9, 2023, https://childmind.org/article/marijuana-and-psychosis/; "The main differences between cannabis today and cannabis in the 1960s – that is to say, hippie weed – lands mainly on THC content. In the sixties, cannabis strains rarely exceeded 5% of THC content. Today, the mildest strains have between 10-12%, many land around 15% to 20%, and the strongest ones can be as high as 25%. Basically, 'the cannabis in your average joint these days is on average 4 to 5 times stronger than the hippie weed enjoyed in the 60s.' And in some cases, it can even be more than that," Cannabis Flower Power & Its Influence in the Sixties, Cleveland School of Cannabis, July 13, 2020, https://csceducation.com/blog/cannabis-flower-power-its-influence-in-the-sixties#:~:text=The%20main%20differences%20between%20cannabis,be%20as%20high%20as%2025%25.

[4] "Historic Paris Wine Tasting of 1976 and Other Significant Competitons," http://www.alcoholproblemsandsolutions.org/Controversies/20060517115643.html

[5] Glenn Wohltmann, "Which city is richest? Depends on how the numbers are run," *Pleasanton Weekly*, May 24, 2013, https://www.pleasantonweekly.com/news/2013/05/23/which-city-is-richest-depends-on-how-the-numbers-are-run

[6] "Is San Francisco Safe to Visit?," https://freetoursbyfoot.com/is-san-francisco-safe-to-visit/; Ray Appleton on the Ray Appleton On Air, KMJ-580-AM, April 11, 2023; Kevin Truong and Maryann Jones Thompson, "Economic Recovery Elusive in SF as Workers, Tourists Stay Away," *San Francisco Standard*, February 1, 2022, https://sfstandard.com/business/economic-recovery-elusive-in-sf-as-workers-tourists-stay-away/; Todd Johnson, "S.F. tourism recovery modest in 2021, but in some areas slides backwards," *San Francisco Business Journal*, March 3, 2022, http://www.bizjournals.com/sanfrancisco/news/2022/03/03/sf-travel-forecast-2022-conference-hotels.html; Stephanie Sierra, "SF's 'dirty streets' hurting international tourism as conventions struggle to come back," ABC-7 News, September13, 2022, https://abc7news.com/sf-tourism-san-francisco-streets-international-travelers-conventions-in/12227886/

[7] Tracy Elsen, "[Robert Manduca] Here's a Pointillist-Style Map of All the Jobs in the Bay Area. 2015." VOX Media, http://sf.curbed.com/2015/7/15/9940276/heres-a-pointillist-style-map-of-all-the-jobs-in-the-bay-area.

[8] Chris Bibey, "Silicon Valley Is Losing Its Edge After Double-Digit Decline in VC Funding Dominance," Yahoo!Finance, March 7, 2023. Note critical comment by Tony on March 8, 2023, https://finance.yahoo.com/news/silicon-valley-losing-edge-double-000406529.html#:~:text=According%20to%20PitchBook's%2020 22%20US,26%25%20only%2010%20years%20ago.

[9] "Big Times in Big Sur," *Washington Times*, July 7, 2006, https://www.washingtontimes.com/news/2006/jul/7/20060707-084209-3823r/; Gregory Thomas, "Big Sur is fed up with 'selfie tourism.' Here's its new plan to transform travel in the region," *San Francisco Chronicle*, December 30, 2020, https://www.sfchronicle.com/travel/article/New-Big-Sur-plan-aims-to-control-tourists-at-15836501.php

[10] Robert Norris and Robert Webb, *Geology of California* (New York: Wiley, 1990), p. 211 passim.

[11] Best Things to do in Death Valley, California, https://capturetheatlas.com/visit-death-valley/#stay; National Park Service, Mohave National Preserve, https://www.nps.gov/moja/index.htm; Hayley Smith, "TS Hilary

damage to keep Death Valley National Park closed for months," *Fresno Bee*, September 5, 2023, p. 1.

[12] *Encyclopædia Britannica Online*, s.v. "Imperial Valley," http://www.britannica.com/EBchecked/topic/283969/Imperial-Valley

[13] Steve Roper, Sierra High Route: Traversing Timberline Country (np: The Mountaineer Press, 1997), p. 81.

[14] It has fluctuated over the years, reaching $1,780 on October 3, 2012, on July 21, 2015 selling for $1,102 and 9 April 9, 2023 selling for $2002. Source: Kitco.com

[15] Big Bear Cool Cabins, "Big Bear Alpine Zoo," https://www.bigbearcoolcabins.com/things-to-do-big-bear/big-bear-alpine-zoo# (accessed February 2, 2024).

[16] Frederick Simpich, "More Water for California's Central Valley," *National Geographic*, November 1946, pp. 645-664.

[17] *Fresno Bee*, "Valley changes 'staggering' in last 200 years," December 27, 1981, B1. Cites work of Dr. Joseph Medeiros, in 2012 professor emeritus of botany at Modesto College.

[18] Some water released from overflowing dams in the January 2017 storms would recharge the groundwater supply that had been lost during the 2011-17 drought, as required by the passage of SGMA (Sustainable Groundwater Management Act) in 2014 which set forth a statewide framework to help protect groundwater resources over the long term; SGMA was revised in 2020, "Storm Runoff in Valley May Help Replenish Groundwater," *Fresno Bee*, January 11, 2019, A1. Hannah Fry and Alejandra Reyes-Velarde, "California wastes most of its rainwater, which simply goes down the drain," *Los Angeles Times*, February 20, 2019, https://www.latimes.com/local/lanow/la-me-rainwater-lost-wet-winter-california-20190220-story.html ; Michael Zakaras, "Why Does California Let Billions of Gallons of Fresh Water Flow Straight Into The Ocean?" *Forbes*, April 15, 2015, https://www.forbes.com/sites/ashoka/2015/04/15/why-does-california-let-billions-of-gallons-of-fresh-water-flow-straight-into-the-ocean/?sh=48e086c7517c ; Hayley Smith, "With all this rain and snow, can California really still be in a drought? Look deeper," *Los Angeles Times*, February 22, 2023,

https://www.latimes.com/california/story/2023-02-22/is-california-still-in-a-drought

[19] William Blomquest, *Dividing the Waters: Governing Groundwater in Southern California.* San Francisco: G Press, 1992. http://pdf.usaid.gov/pdf_docs/pnabm801.pdf

[20] *Fresno Bee*, "Tree Rings – drought clues." January 19, 1981, p. A1.

[21] Rong-Gong Lin II and Grace Toohey, "Hilary's pattern of damage had some surprises for California," *Fresno Bee*, August 23, 2023, p. A1.

[22] Jason Samenow and Ian Livingston, "California's snowpack soars to record high after 17 atmospheric rivers," *Washington Post*, March 30, 2023, (accessed April 27, 2023), https://www.washingtonpost.com/weather/2023/03/30/california-snowpack-record-sierra/

[23] In 2022 Governor Gavin Newsom claimed that the state's economy was the world's fourth largest overtaking Germany's; however, it remained in fifth place in 2024 while others predict it will slip to sixth place, behind Germany and India. Andrew Sheeler, "Could California Drop Down to Sixth Largest Economy?" *Sacramento Bee*, April 3, 2024, https://www.sacbee.com/news/politics-government/capitol-alert/article287305070.html

[24] The Center Square: California, https://www.thecentersquare.com/california/53-companies-headquartered-in-california-made-fortune-500-list/article_8b3a9c42-a600-11ea-a4db-93d48d36b34e.html

[25] Amanda MacMillan, "Global Warming 101" National Resources Defense Council, March 11, 2016, https://www.nrdc.org/stories/global-warming-101; Cf Peter Ferrara, "To the Horror of Global Warming Alarmists, Global Cooling Is Here" *Forbes*, May 26, 2013, Opinion http://www.forbes.com/sites/peterferrara/2013/05/26/to-the-horror-of-global-warming-alarmists-global-cooling-is-here/#6f93b4d69bb0 ; Frances Malamud-Roam, "Holocene Megadroughts and Megafloods in California's Central Valley," "A 3000-Year History of Climate and Environmental Change in

California," http://cepsym.org/Sympro2009/Malamud-Roam.pdf Federal Newswire Report, "Over 1,600 Scientists Claim That the Climate Emergency is a Myth," Federal Newswire, September 18, 2023, https://thefederalnewswire.com/stories/649656011-over-1-600-scientists-claim-that-the-climate-emergency-is-a-myth Katy Grimes, "'NO Climate Crisis' Says Coalition of 1,600 Actual Scientists," *California Globe*, May 13, 2024, https://californiaglobe.com/articles/no-climate-crisis-says-coalition-of-1600-actual-scientists

[26] David Perlman, "Dinosaurs in the Foothills?/First evidence of meat-eater in California," *SFGate*, June 20, 1997, http://www.sfgate.com/news/article/Dinosaurs-in-the-Foothills-First-evidence-of-3305272.php

[27] "Prehistoric Marine Fossils," *Fresno Bee*, December 25, 1980, p. E1.

[28] *The Columbia Electronic Encyclopedia*, 6th ed. "Sierra Nevada" (Columbia University Press, 2012), http://www.infoplease.com/encyclopedia/us/sierra-nevada-mountain-range-united-states.html; McNab, W.H.; Cleland, D.T.; Freeouf, J.A.; Keys, Jr., J.E.; Nowacki, G.J.; Carpenter, C.A., comps. 2005. Description of ecological subregions: sections of the conterminous United States. Washington, DC: U.S. Department of Agriculture, Forest Service. pp. 24-27.

[29] U.S. Department of the Interior, *Lassen Volcanic National Park*. 1973.

[30] "California Coast a geologic ripoff," *Fresno Bee*, December 11, 1980, E7.

[31] "Mono cones seen likely to erupt", *Fresno Bee*, December 11, 1980, E7

[32] "Mammoth find at landfill," *Madera Tribune,* May 12, 1993, 1.

[33] George C. Page Museum, *The La Brea Story and the History of Man* (Los Angeles: Los Angeles County Museum of Art, 1978); "La Brea Woman," Los Angeles Almanac 25 Years! (accessed February 2, 2024), https://www.laalmanac.com/history/hi02v.php

Chapter One FURTHER READING

1.   Arax, Mark. "The Ghost of Tulare Lake", accessed April 21, 2023, https://mark-arax.com/the-ghost-of-tulare-lake/

2.   Christopher, Ben. "California loses congressional seat for first   time,"   Cal   Matters,   May   6,   2021, https://calmatters.org/politics/2021/04/california-congress-census/

3.   Hok, Soreath. "It's Got a Memory: Tulare Lake's return tests human changes to the land." KVPR, April 6, 2023, https://www.kvpr.org/local-news/2023-04-06/its-got-a-memory-tulare-lakes-return-tests-human-changes-to-the-land

Chapter 2: Prehistoric California

<u>Origins and Generalities</u>

Until quite recently nothing complimentary was written about California's aboriginal peoples, referred to now as in the past as California Indians. The only positive adjective that Spanish missionaries could apply to them was "numerous," while Spanish secular officials, less-charitably, saw the natives as rustics compared to what they were familiar with in the Gulf region, Mexico, and Peru. To the Anglo-American settlers who had fought Indians on the western borders for two centuries they were subhuman "diggers,"[1] so named because they were wrongly assumed to be like the natives in the Great Basin who scratched the earth with sticks for edible roots, a people who could be killed when they got in the way, as we will see in Chapter 9. What inspired this shared Spanish and American attitude towards the California Indians? Compared to other North American Amerinds, California's aboriginals were in fact deficient. They were not civilized like Mexico's Aztecs, nor politically or militarily organized like the Iroquois of the Northeastern woodlands. They did not build as the Pueblo Indians of New Mexico and Arizona. They did not farm like the Cherokee of the Southeast, nor work with wood or stone as was the custom with the Salish of the Pacific Northwest. What, then, occupied them? As will be seen, excepting the Yurok, Kashaya, and Mojave peoples, not much. For over 15,000 years (nearly 60,000 generations) they left their environment as they found it. And therein lies the source of much of today's admiration and previous generations' contempt for them.

In 1492, of an estimated 50 to 100 million Indians in North and South America, only about 130,000 were living in what

52

is now California. They were divided into 22 language families, speaking 135 dialects in about 1,000 different villages.[2] Thus, as often observed, prehistoric California had the greatest concentration of language families in the world (one for every 7,241 square miles [18,755 sq km], an area slightly larger than modern Riverside County). Most ancient Californians were members of one of three linguistic families: the Penutians, Hokans, and Shoshoneans. The 57,000 Penutians included the Maidu and Wintun of the Sacramento Valley, the Miwok in Marin and the Sierra foothills, the Yokuts of the San Joaquin Valley and the Costanoans of the area from the Golden Gate to the Salinas River. The 37,500 Hokans, noted for their basketry, included the Pomo in Sonoma, the Karok, Shasta, and Yana of the Cascades, the Washo around Lake Tahoe, the Esselen, Salinian, and Chumash of the area from Big Sur to Santa Monica Bay, and finally the Yuman of extreme southern California. The 23,500 Shoshoneans, related to tribes in the Great Basin, included the Paiute of northeastern California, the Mono of the Owens Valley, the Tübatulabal, Panamint, Ute-Chemehuevi, and Serrano of the Mojave Desert and Death Valley, the Gabrielino of Los Angeles, and the Luiseño-Cahuila of the area from the San Gabriel River to the Salton Sea. These tribal names often were merely that group's term for "The People".

In the White Mountains northeast of Bishop hunters ascended the slopes of the Owens Valley as early as 1300 BC, and hunter-gatherers appeared around AD 600. By AD 1300 these had displaced the hunters. They, in turn, left, but their destination has not been traced. Many possible reasons have been suggested for why they left, including the extreme cold of the mountains. While they lived there the men would go out hunting, building rock walls to hide behind, and then flinging rocks at the mountain sheep with throwers called atlatls. By AD 900 the atlatls were replaced by bow and arrow, scaring the mountain sheep into higher plateaus where it would be too cold to follow for long.[3]

Where they came from and when they arrived in California are two questions which have never been conclusively answered - nor have most theories on these matters been disproven. Probably after crossing the prehistoric land bridge between Siberia and Alaska, they ultimately migrated to California via the Yukon River, the Liard River system of Canada, the Fraser Plateau, and the passes and valleys between the Coast Ranges and the Cascades. Archaeologists have deduced this route from studies of glacial advance and retreat across the top of North America. The earliest Asian migrants (who, however, bore no resemblance to the Java or Peking Men, extinct humanoids once thought to be the "missing link"), probably found themselves brushed aside by later and larger groups speaking a common tongue and finding in California a haven apart from the mainstream of traffic which continued down the Rockies and Great Plains to Mexico and beyond. Dr. Alfred L. Kroeber (1876-1960) calculated in 1923 that they attained in California a population density of 16.8 persons per square mile (6.5 per square kilometer).

Archaeologists and ethnologists nevertheless have theorized that the presence of many distinct languages is typical of very early times. If that is correct then California settlements must have been present in the very remote past, for California's 135 different dialects among 130,000 people represents the greatest concentration of different tongues in a comparable area anywhere in the world. Unfortunately, the oldest sites discovered in California are only about 15,000 years old - not terribly ancient (North America's oldest site, found in Oregon in 2019 is slightly older, and the world's oldest human sites in East Africa are 2-3 million years old).

A link to Siberia seems to have been found by Otto J. von Sadovszky (1925-2004). In 1985 he published his findings that compared the tattoos and certain rituals of a tribe in Siberia with the Northern Californian Indians. In addition, he traced certain words to a people in Siberia called the Ulagans. The Ulagans lived at the source of the Ob River at the present-day Russian-Kazakhstan-Mongolian border. To the Ulagans, for example, the word for a chin tattoo is *jet-ki* and among the Miwok the same chin tattoo is called *jet-ku.*; another example is *hule-m* (ashes, to the Ulagan) and *kulya*, a Miwok word from Yosemite meaning burned pine nuts (ashes).[4]

As late as 2003 National Geographic presented evidence that predecessors of those who came from northeast Asia via Alaska came from Southeast Asia, people who had migrated into Australia and reached the Americas 1,500 years before those from Siberia. The primary evidence is in the slender-faced skulls found in Baja California.[5]

Indian remains on many private property sites have long disappeared, but state park lands in California contain a rich cultural heritage dating back thousands of years into prehistory. It is generally accepted that no place in the world has a longer, richer, and more diverse past, just as no other place in America had such linguistic diversity. The complex record of this human history is contained in a myriad of archaeological deposits, rock art sites, ancient villages and trails, campsites, resource procurement areas, cemeteries, and sacred sites. These archaeological resources are the fragile and irreplaceable vestiges of California's ancient past.

One of these sites is at Torrey Pines State Reserve in San Diego County. Four dozen clusters of fire-affected rock and burned soil were noted there. Another dozens of these fire-affected rock features was also reported. These features have been interpreted as hearths or "roasting platforms" for the processing of Torrey pine seeds and other edible plants. A whole valve of a Washington clam (*Saxidomus nuttalli*) shell from the depth of two to three feet (61-91 cm), and a single piece of charcoal from the one to two feet depth level were found. The results of Carbon-14 testing of samples give dates of AD 345 to 670 for the shell sample and AD 1395 to 1470 for charcoal samples.

Another strange site is in Tulare County by Tyler Creek at California Hot Springs, south of Porterville. Nearly three dozen "tubs", depressions in the rocks about 3.5 feet (1 m) deep have been known to the public for a century and a half. Whether these were used for storage, fermenting grains, or even bathing is a matter of scholarly speculation, although most scholars lean toward fermentation.[6]

Camp sites of the Diegueños of southern California are only about 4,000 years old, those in Kern County's Buena Vista Lake area and Oak Grove (near Santa Barbara) are about 3,000 years old, and the shell mounds which once dotted Alameda County's shoreline revealed tools dating back 5,000 years; in 2024 the city of Berkeley restored one of the shell mound sites (a parking lot) to the Ohlone people. In 1950 a Nevada cave gave up some shell beads from a species native to the central coast that were at least 9,000 years old. Found in 1978, a set of 54 footprints bore witness to a family stroll through the cottonwoods then lining the Mojave River near Riverside 4,300 years ago. These are the oldest prints found to date in North America![7]

Though ethnologists list 21 language families, there were probably only six cultural areas: Northwest, Central California, Southern California, Colorado River, Great Basin, and Northeast. Dr. Kroeber, who exhaustively studied the California Indians early in the 20th century, observed that in at least four of these cultural areas at least one tribe held the best areas for food gathering and, we may assume, were relieved from the continuous pressure of gaining a livelihood. Thus, they could devote some of their leisure time to further develop some aspect of culture such as ritual or ceremony, creating and devising necessary implements (their material culture), or warfare.

**

"In the land of Dreams / Find your Grown-up Self / Your Future Family"

- Wintu song

**

Northwestern Tribes

The Northwestern tribes shared many characteristics with coastal natives as far north as the Gulf of Alaska. Living in a rain forest environment, their settlements were clustered on the ocean coast or along salmon-rich lower rivers navigated in laboriously shaped and hollowed-out redwood log canoes. Their dwellings were rectangular with gabled roofs and split plank walls. Society (especially among the Yurok of the Klamath River and the Hupa of the Trinity River) was based on the amount of wealth possessed. Unlike the rest of California, where all land was held in common, an individual Northwest Indian might own the exclusive gathering rights to a particular oak grove's acorn crop or the sole right to fish salmon from a certain pool. A man's social status was based on ownership of many red-headed woodpecker scalps, large, chipped knives or blades made from black or red obsidian, or rare furs such as the skin of the white deer. Excellent craftsmen, compared to other prehistoric Californians, their tools and weapons were always neatly made and decorated with intricate carvings.

This emphasis on wealth-as-status naturally affected family life. A more affluent girl's property value for marriage was impaired if she bore a child out of wedlock. Subjected to abuse from her family and public disgrace she would choose abortion if possible; among the Yuroks the preferred method was to place hot stones on the abdomen and dispose of the child in the river. Of course, girls from poorer families had less to lose by conceiving out of wedlock.[8]

The Yuroks had a highly developed and precise legal system. In it, wealth was status: every possession, privilege, injury, and offense had an exact property value. Every invasion of privilege or possession - regardless of technicalities such as accident, intent, ignorance, malice, or negligence - required compensation. In those cases, only two things mattered: the fact of the damage and the amount of property that could be assessed. Wealth was involved in various ways; if, for example, one struck a rich man's son, mentioned the name of a dead rich man, or insulted a man richer than oneself all were common grounds for a damage claim to be levied. If the defendant could pay the damages, then the matter was settled permanently and irrevocably. On the other hand, an insolvent defendant would become the plaintiff's slave. If the defendant was able to pay but refused to, then he risked death.

Dr. Robert Heizer (1915-79), a noted student of California, Great Basin, and Southwestern Indians, describes a case that is typical of the Yurok law. It seems that a Yurok who had been born out of wedlock, and therefore lacking family connections, once burned over a hillside. Since this was a common practice for keeping brush back, encouraging seed grasses to grow and providing the deer with grazing land, there was nothing illegal about the burning itself. However, a rich man from a neighboring village had hidden some valuables in a bush on that hillside. The owner of the now-incinerated treasure demanded and got compensation. The defendant, with no wealth of his own nor rich relatives to borrow from, became the rich man's slave.

Wars were rare and were simple blood feuds marked by an occasional ambush, capture of a woman, or burning of a house rather than conventional battles. These feuds might drag on for a long time until public opinion demanded that the two sides settle it. Go-betweens would meet and present damages; if these were agreed on, both sides would pay. Strange to our way of battling and war-making, the one who achieved the most killings, burnings, or insults - in other words, the winner - had to pay more.

Archaeologists studying in that area made an interesting discovery in 1993 when a state forester came upon an outstanding petroglyph site in a remote section of the Eel River Canyon in Trinity County. This was originally the territory of the Wailaki, who lived there for over two thousand years. There are two panels of petroglyphs which display elaborate, multiple, superimposed elements representing six styles.

The largest and most elaborate rock art panel occurs on a vertical surface of a large schist boulder at the north end of the site. It is partially within a rock shelter but also extends outside it on a fully exposed vertical rock surface. This grouping contains an amalgamation of "pecked" abstract curvilinear figures (so called because they seemed to have been tapped by a woodpecker) overlaid by a multitude of both shallow- and deeply-incised lines. Numerous examples of superimposition indicate that the two styles of incised line petroglyphs were carved into the rock after the pecked designs were created. The panel is dominated by numerous large, pecked, abstract curvilinear motifs formed by tightly clustered pecking, probably made by punch and hammerstone. These figures include long wavy lines, zigzags, circles, dots, linked circles, linked diamonds, "tally mark" designs, deeply incised lines, and other more abstract shapes. A second, moss-covered grouping of weathered petroglyphs occurs on the opposite side of the same boulder. These figures include grooved circles, cup-shaped figures, and several deep linear grooves. Part of this panel was buried a foot (30.5 cm) below present ground surface.

Central Tribes

In the Central California cultural area lived the most populous tribes in the state, sedentary peoples who stayed in the same villages for countless generations. Travel was usually on foot (even after the Spaniards introduced the horse) and was for trade between coastal, valley, and foothill tribes. In this way the natives got desirable items from far away. It is an anthropological paradox that the absence of sharply definable traits is what gives a cultural unity to these peoples. Food was abundant - oak groves producing more acorns than could be gathered, vast seed-bearing grasslands, fish-filled streams and lakes, huge herds of elk and deer, and flocks of ducks.

Compared to the Northwest tribes, wealth was unimportant with these Central peoples. Land was held in common by the village (though defended if trespassed on by outsiders), tools and weapons were simple and lacking in ornamentation, and funerals were potlaches of deliberate and ostentatious wasting of valuable goods to express mourning. Their dwellings varied from half-buried earth-covered houses in the Central Valley to the cone-shaped lean-tos made of long bark slabs in the Coast Range and Sierra foothills. In the High Sierra they didn't build permanent dwellings because this area was a sort of summer vacation spot away from the hot valley.

These mountain and valley peoples left many rock holes - tubs actually, for they are about three feet (91.4 cm) across and four feet (1.22 m) deep. Some believe that they were used to make a kind of alcoholic beverage from the fermented fruits in the area while others believed they were used for communal baths because of the nearby creeks and springs.

Abortion and infanticide were common among these tribes, being used by the Pomo as population control and, in some cases among the Maidu, to ward off evil spirits. Maidu twins and their mother were killed and a baby whose mother died in childbirth was killed. In the case of a childless woman, the Pomo believed that a "baby rock" a phallic-shaped geological feature that had acquired this name, would help conception.

The Pomo, like many other Indians in western North America, believed that an individual in search of power ought to seek an appropriate portal through which to access the supernatural world. These portals were geographic features, such as rock crevices, caves, springs, pools, and mountain tops. Rocks appear to have been considered the primary frontier separating the actual and supernatural worlds.

One of these Pomo rituals, which may have involved a belief that the petitioner's spirit moved through rock, involved the petroglyph boulders known as "baby rocks." The spirits of future children dwelled in these rocks and were born to parents who followed the proper ritual. The wilderness was full of power capable of affecting human fertility, and certain springs, trees, gopher mounds, rocks, mud, and snakes could cause pregnancy. In addition, a female effigy made of clay, and called "Earth Woman," was given to sterile women to insure conception. Apparently, the powers affecting fertility resided beneath the surface of Mother Earth.

A childless woman fasted for four days before visiting the baby rock alone. The fact that she went alone, and after fasting, thus inducing a certain degree of sensory deprivation, suggests that she may have sought an altered state of consciousness at the petroglyph boulder. If the spirits of the unborn children resided in the rock, the carving of petroglyphs on it may have been intended to allow one's spirit entrance into the rock for the purpose of negotiation.

Other aspects of family life were also at variance with Judeo-Christian cultural practices. Among the Yokuts and Miwok a man might have wives in several villages, one in each, thus insuring peace among those communities. While a woman had no right in theory to reject a suitor selected by her father, the rejected suitor would usually bow out to save face. Superstition surrounded menstruation, since bleeding without the infliction of a wound and often occurring at the same moon phase were inexplicable phenomena.

The Yokuts treated a boy's initiation into manhood with a ceremony consisting of long, moralistic sermons about courage and loyalty followed by the boy's drinking an extract of the hallucinogenic jimson weed which might produce pleasant or terrifying visions. Less pleasant was the custom of the Yuki of Mendocino County, who initiated a boy by shoving a long, chipped obsidian knife down his throat to cause bleeding.

Most ritual ceremonies among these tribes were held in spring. The Yokuts had their Rattlesnake Ceremony, in which shamans captured several deadly reptiles, publicly handled the snakes, and were believed through rituals to confer immunity from snake bite on the villagers. The snakes' venom had been secretly milked, after which the villagers observed the shamans bitten with no ill effects. The Maidu celebrated their victories of the previous year by tying their war prisoners to a pole and shooting them to death with arrows. On the other hand, the major religious cult known as the Kuksu Cult, held its secret ceremony in winter. Members dressed in elaborate feather headdresses to represent various gods.

The Kashaya, who lived on the Sonoma coast, measured time according to the seasons and had observed long since the relationship between the sun, moon, and earth, and how sun and moon affected the earth and its inhabitants. During the summer they moved to communities along the coast where they gathered food from the sea. In the late fall they moved back inland to their main village sites atop the ridges where shelter was available in the cold winter months. Ceremonies marked the arrival of new fruits, salmon, the ripening of acorns, migration of deer and significant social events.

One of the most important rituals involved food gathering. Usually, the Ohlone of the Bay Area ate acorn mush but during the annual seed harvest in the Oakland hills, seeds would be gathered from shoulder high grasses, fresh greens would be collected, such as clover, poppy, tansy-mustard, melic grass, and mule ear shoots, and there would be treats like roasted grasshoppers and berries from the hills. The women would gather the seeds, greens, and berries for the tribe, while men - in a division of labor that marked their way of life for thousands of years - would hunt for meat and fish.

A modern anthropologist working with those Bay Area peoples, Malcolm Margolin (1940-), found that the coastal regions were once wetter than today, with tule marshes covering the coastline and water easy to strike just a few feet below the surface. The Indians would move from spot to spot as the environment supplied or failed to supply basic needs.[9]

Margolin described this people's virtues as well as their failings. Living in a symbiotic relationship with nature, having strong family and tribal ties, and sharing whatever they had were very positive family traits. They could also be quarrelsome and superstitious. Deformed infants were killed, as were twins, while a shaman deemed unfriendly would also be killed.

Family life among the Kashaya involved strong, warm, and close emotional relationships. Each village group constituted of any number of extended families, who, with the immediate family, provided protection, moral support, and identity to individuals. Relationships between children and adults were loving, and bonds were tight. Children enjoyed a good deal of latitude in their behavior. Codes of personal responsibility and family honor were strongly encouraged. Relationships beyond the group were discouraged. Significant personal events for each Kashaya were celebrated with ritual and ceremony which integrated the natural, supernatural, and human worlds.

Also, the Kashaya excelled in the arts and technologies. They created a wide variety of tools, utensils, basketry, and objects of personal adornment which reflected a high degree of technical knowledge, design, and artistic ingenuity. Their baskets, some of which were sufficiently water-tight for food preparation, was a ritual art that achieved extraordinary respect by the early 20th century, as it incorporated stone, bone, shell, horn, fibers, and feathers in unique designs.

The religion of these peoples was animist. An example of Miwok creation stories concerns the mastering of fire, something that most ancient peoples viewed as a theft from the gods. They believed that when the world was cold and dark, and needed light and fire, Little-White-Footed-Mouse went and stole flame from another place. People from the other place chased him, and he hid the fire in the buckeye. The fire shot up into the air and became the sun. Some of the fire remained in the trees, so that The People always knew that if they rubbed buckeye and cedar together, they could make a fire. Where grass seeds were an important food, the Indians burned fields annually to remove old stocks and increase the yield.[10]

Southern Tribes

The Southern California cultural area embraced the southwest portion of the state. Living along the ocean front and the Channel Islands the Chumash and Gabrielino peoples fed their large population on fish and mollusks captured in nets thrown from their unique canoes. These canoes were made of many small planks of wood lashed together with cords passed through drilled holes and caulked over with asphalt.

**

"When a god dies...he should hear no weeping."

- Cocopa song

**

These were the peoples who worshipped Chinigchinich, a benign god/demon. He was too lofty to be impersonated, so the ritual costumes of his followers were very simple. He used animals as messengers, and if a person sinned against him, an animal - spider, puma, or rattlesnake - would be the instrument of punishment. In the Chinigchinich cult rituals, there was a constant reference to the human soul, to mystical concepts, cosmology, and a strong symbolism of death.

From the work of John Peabody Harrington (1884-1961) of the Museum of the American Indian we know that these people believed that "animals had once been people and had attained their various form by a slow process of evolution" descended from the "first people." Harrington, a linguist and ethnologist who specialized in the California Indians, was noted for the massive volume (nearly 700 feet [213 m] of space) of documentary material in the National Anthropological Archives of the Smithsonian's Museum Support Center in Suitland, Maryland. As a linguist he was probably the only recorder of some languages, such as Obispeño (Northern) Chumash, Kitanemuk (Antelope Valley), and Serrano. He was also very secretive, deliberately hiding many of his notes from colleagues, the Smithsonian finding over six tons of boxes stored in warehouses, garages and even chicken coops all over the West.[11]

Along the Colorado River lived the most warlike, agricultural, sexually promiscuous, and traveled of California Indians - the Mojave. Thinking of their area as a country (unlike the highly individualistic Northwest Indians) they developed a strong military spirit which regarded a man's most glorious moment to be when he was engaged in mortal combat. Victory was treated as an enhancement of the tribe's spiritual power. War was organized, but the entire tribe did not necessarily participate. It was left to a soldier class to handle the bloodletting - usually of the Papago and Pima, who lived a 15 days' walk away in Arizona. These soldiers were the ones who had dreamed in boyhood that a war-power had been bestowed upon them. Despite the honor of warfare these soldiers were never allotted special food or housing.

The Mojave and their Yuma neighbors were the only California Indians to depend on farming for a livelihood, raising beans, pumpkins, melons, and corn. To store this food, they made excellent pottery and lived in houses made of mud-plastered willows.

Their use of courtship for unbridled sex rather than for marriage meant that promiscuity was institutionalized among them. They had no conception of chastity. Women were treated with greater respect the more willing and available they were as sex partners, yet abortion was not practiced, infanticide was rare, and twins were honored as clairvoyant gifts from the sky.[12] Marriage occurred when a young man bought his intended bride from her father for one or two horses. The couple would build a house, over which the wife was supreme. Children were raised by both parents but if there was a divorce they usually stayed with their mother. Those born out of wedlock, a natural consequence of the promiscuity, were not discriminated against.[13]

The Mojave traveled widely, acting as middlemen in a trade system which exchanged cotton blankets and stone axes from the Pueblo peoples of Arizona with Pacific coast seashells. They made trading expeditions into other peoples' territories - to the sites of San Diego, San Gabriel, Santa Barbara, and Bakersfield; when Fray Francisco Garcés visited the San Joaquin Valley in 1776 he came from the Colorado River with a Mojave trading party.

Lesser Tribes

The Great Basin cultural area, including the eastern deserts of California, was an extension of the tribes found in the deserts as far east as Utah. These Indians, such as the Panamint and Chemehuevi, knew the secrets of how to make the apparently barren desert a food source and thus stave off ever-threatening famine: how to find water, convert unpalatable cactus into food, and collect small game such as rats and rabbits. Having few belongings since they had to roam constantly, they carried whatever they possessed - usually no more than rabbit skin clothing, rabbit-catching nets, a few baskets, bows and arrows. With their chronic hunger and poverty when compared to other California peoples, the Great Basin natives were the least materialistic and had the simplest culture of any North American Indians.

The Northeastern California cultural area was occupied by the Modoc and Achomawi tribes. A simple culture prevailed, for the population was thin, the country was not overly productive, and people spent most of their time hunting and root-digging. Having almost no free time, they never developed imposing rituals or ceremonials. Their simple homes were the half-underground dwellings found in Central California. An interesting example of the Achomawi use of sparse resources was in trapping sucker fish using stone traps. By 1993 archaeologists had found ten stone traps at different spots along the Tule River.

The traps utilized the flow of cold water springs emerging from the lava and the propensity of bottom-dwelling suckers to seek these areas. A massive outer wall in deeper water formed an impoundment, connecting two points of land. Water depth might be two or three feet (61-91 cm), and the stone wall was built up to the lake level using three courses of lava stones or more. A central opening measuring about a foot is designed to allow suckers to enter. It was closed with a keystone or a log, dip net or canoe prow. The outer wall and opening served to concentrate the spring outflow as it entered the lake, making a strong current to carry the spawning suckers.

As evening approached, preparations were made for sucker fishing. Nets and spears were readied. A few hours after sunset the sucker fish would appear. There was a general prohibition against loud or drunken behavior when harvesting suckers. This was serious business and proper care was advisable lest high winds or rough water be encountered.

Loud noises were thought to scare the fish and produce bad results. The men would approach cautiously, the harvesting directed by an elder who owned rights to a particular trap. The first order of business was to close the outside enclosure opening. A special board or stone might serve this function. If canoes were used, one might be placed in the opening to block escape of the fish to deeper water. At this point torches would be lit to reveal the fish. A large trap might contain several hundred. The leader typically struck the first fish, then other men would carefully wade in and spear them, tossing selected specimens up on the bank. Young boys aged ten or twelve might be allowed to spear suckers with their own equipment. Others would gather them in baskets. Women might also join in, scooping out fish with their hands or using spears or basket scoops. The catch was loaded into baskets or gunny sacks in the boats.

When an adequate supply was taken, the trap was reopened, and fish were allowed to resume spawning. Occasionally, it would be left closed until the following day, but great care was taken to allow the spawn to be successful. It was not unusual for an expedition to take one hundred fish or more from a given trap. Individual specimens might weigh 4 to 7 pounds (1.8-3.2 kg). As many as three or even six trips might occur during the spawning season, depending on the availability of fish and water conditions. The fish were cleaned by gutting and scaling with the heads attached. They were then sun-dried or smoked over a wooden frame. The catch would be shared with relatives and sometimes traded to neighboring groups for venison or acorns. Once dried, the fish would last for several months.

The Horizon Cultures

Middens are the spots where Indian villages once existed.

At a midden, the earth is usually darker in color because of charcoal from ancient fires, food remains such as seashells or animal bones, lost or discarded tools and weapons, human feces, trash accumulating from day-after-day living, and graves. A site occupying a favorable position regarding water, food, and drainage may have been occupied by many peoples over many generations. Archaeologists have worked for years in California middens to uncover evidence of Indian life, with much success.

Among the Central California culture, for example, people have been traced back ten thousand years. In the Delta region Dr. Heizer led University of California workers who studied occupation and burial sites going back four thousand years. They published their findings in 1949, having found three successive cultures.

**

"Walowtah the Cloud Maiden, sang: This will be the last song / Of our people, the First People / In this, the first World"

- Achomawi creation myth

**

The most ancient of these cultures (c. 2000 BC) they called the Early Horizon. This culture was apparently concerned with burial ritual, for corpses were invariably laid head to the west. Most of those whose remains were found in these graves appeared to have died naturally. The graves contained shell beads, weapon points, and other useful items.

Then, about 1500 BC, came the Middle Horizon people. Many of these were warlike, for their skeletons contained embedded stone implements such as arrowheads and spear

70

points. No material possessions were found in these graves, so they were probably passed on to heirs, in keeping with the emphasis on wealth which probably developed at this time. Corpses were buried differently than in the case of the Early peoples - knees drawn up and arms folded against the chest, unless the more common practice of cremation disposed of the body. The Chumash of the Central Coast around Morro Bay relied heavily on fishing and harvesting shellfish. Their village at the Back Bay site plus a stabilized sand dune at Los Osos left many samples of their culture.[14]

The Middle Horizon people were succeeded by the Late Horizon about AD 500 and endured until the white conquest twelve hundred years later. They continued the funeral practices of the Middle people and wide-ranging trade relations were evident.

Since all prehistoric California's archaeology is rather static – never changing, offering nothing startling or unique in dating or measuring the relationships between cultures - it is a safe conclusion that what is now California has been occupied for over ten millennia by Indians who lived much as those first seen by the Spaniards.

The California Indians have borne a reputation for being lazy, superstitious, having obnoxious habits (such as the Bay Area's Ohlones' picking off and eating their body lice), and keeping filthy dwellings. Nevertheless, the Indians, by virtue of original possession and age-old use of the land, were (according to Dr. Robert Heizer, "as much an element of the natural background of modern California as the forests, lakes, mountains, wildlife and climate." They live on in the names of 13 of the 58 counties. Their names are given to four of our most scenic spots (Lake Tahoe, the Mojave Desert, Yosemite National Park, and Mt. Shasta). A score of Franciscan missions was established to teach the natives the Catholic religion, Indian skeletons are found in modern earth-moving, which attends nearly all building improvements, and there are thousands of spots where one can see evidence of Indian occupancy in acorn mortar holes in rocks and arrowheads lying on the surface of ancient campsites. These reminders are the heritage of former Indian occupancy and an enduring part of our heritage.

Unfortunately, a large part of this heritage is disappearing as time takes its inevitable toll and new construction overtakes many relics of the past.[15] Progress does not have to be stopped, but careless disposition of this prehistoric heritage must be replaced by a policy of respectful removal of discoveries to museums, known Indian burial grounds and other dedicated sites.

Chapter Two END NOTES

[1] "Indians to Discard 'Digger' Label for Term 'Meuwk',"
Oakland Tribune, April 17, 1924, p.11.

[2] The population is estimated because there were no censuses taken. See James W. Davidson and Mark H Lytle, *After the Fact: The Art of Historical Detection*, (Boston: McGraw-Hill, 2005), pp. 131-134. Language family refers to groups of languages with common origins and marked similarities, such as French, Italian and Spanish in the Romance family; Bulgarian, Russian, and Serbo-Croatian in the Slavic family; Burmese, Chinese (both Cantonese and Mandarin), and Tibetan in the Indo-Chinese family.

[3] "Long-lost tribes studied at Davis," *Fresno Bee*, September 18, 1986, p. C4.

[4] Otto von Sadovszky, "Siberia's Frozen Mummy & The Genesis of California Indian Culture," *The Californians*, 3:6 (November-December 1985): 12; von Sadovszky's work, *The Discovery of California: a Cal-Ugrian Comparative Study*.

(Budapest: Akadémiai Kiadó, 1996).

[5] Sze Wei, "The Pericúes – the Mysterious Lost Tribe of Cabo," May 31, 2021, https://www.diveninjaexpeditions.com/pericues-los-cabos-history/ ; Susan Hallett, "PEI's Indigenous Culture Explored in New Exhibition." *Epoch Times*, October 21, 2014, https://www.theepochtimes.com/peis-indigenous-culture-explored-in-new-exhibition_1033608.html

[6] "The Great Indian Bathtub Mystery," *Fresno Bee*, July 21, 1974, p. B1.

[7] "Footprints from 2,000 BC," *Fresno Bee*, September 2, 1978, p. A3; Anser Hassan, "Berkeley restores Ohlone land to Ohlone hands in largest give-back in CA history," ABC 7 News, March 13, 2024, https://abc7news.com/shell-mound-ohlone-tribe-berkeley-parking-lot-sogorea-te-land-trust/14520567.

[8] Ronald Genini, "Abortion and the California Indians: Myth and Reality," *Natural Family Planning*, 3:3 (Fall 1979), p. 254.

[9] Meg Betts, "Recreating the Ohlone Indians: our predecessors by 5,000 years," *The [Oakland] Montclarion*, December 13, 1978, p. 15.

[10] Davidson and Lytle, *After the Fact*, p. 129.

[11] "Indians Believed Man Became Animal," *Oakland Tribune*, March 1, 1924, p. 9; Cf. Kay Sanger and Tom Sanger, *When the Animals were People: Stories Told by the Chumash Indians of California*, (Banning: Malki Museum Press, 1983); Lisa M. Krieger, "Long gone Native languages emerge from the grave: Millions of cryptic notes from linguist John Peabody Harrington," *San Jose Mercury-News*, December 23, 2007, https://www.mercurynews.com/2007/12/23/long-gone-native-languages-emerge-from-the-grave/; Wikipedia contributors, "John Peabody Harrington," *Wikipedia, The Free Encyclopedia*, https://en.wikipedia.org/w/index.php?title=John_Peabody_Harrington&oldid=1155125328 (accessed March 3, 2024).

[12] Genini, "Abortion and the California Indians," p. 255.

[13] William J. Wallace, "Infancy and Childhood Among the Mohave Indians," *Primitive Man*, 21:1-2 (January-April 1948), p. 21, https://doi.org/10.2307/3316262

[14] C. Michael Hogan, "Los Osos Back Bay," *The Megalithic Portal* (2008), http://www.megalithic.co.uk/article.php?sid=18353.

[15] Rasa Gustaitis, "The West's prehistory is being lost." *The [Oakland] Montclarion*, September 24, 1980, p. 12.

Chapter Two FURTHER READING

1.   Bishop, Ellen Morris. "Ancient Nez Perce village site yields oldest date of human habitation in North America," Nez Perce Waallowa Homeland, September 30, 2019, https://www.wallowanezperce.org/news/2019/9/30/ancient-nez-perce-village-site-yields-oldest-date-of-human-habitation-in-north-america

2.   California, State of. Native American Heritage Commission. Tribal Atlas Pages. https://nahc.ca.gov/cp/tribal-atlas-pages/

3.   Devereux, George. "The Sexual Life of the Mohave Indians." *Human Biology*, 9:4, (1937): pp.498-527.

4.   "Mohave Indian Obstetrics: A Psychoanalytic Study," American Bishop, Ellen Morris. "Ancient Nez Perce village site yields oldest date of human habitation in North America," Nez Perce Waallowa Homeland, September 30, 2019, https://www.wallowanezperce.org/news/2019/9/30/ancient-nez-perce-village-site-yields-oldest-date-of-human-habitation-in-north-america

5.   California, State of. Native American Heritage Commission. Tribal Atlas Pages. https://nahc.ca.gov/cp/tribal-atlas-pages/

6.   Devereux, George. "The Sexual Life of the Mohave Indians." Human Biology, 9:4, (1937): pp.498-527.

7.   "Mohave Indian Obstetrics: A Psychoanalytic Study," *American Imago*, 5:2 (July 1948), pp. 95-139, https://www.jstor.org/stable/26301199Imago, 5:2 (July 1948), pp. 95-139, https://www.jstor.org/stable/26301199

Chapter 3: To the Rim of Christendom

**

"Know that, on the right hand of the Indies, there is an island called California, very near to the Terrestrial paradise."

- Garci Ordoñez de Montalvo, 1510

**

Columbus

For 2000 years, waves of invaders had swept over the Iberian Peninsula, each wave leaving its mark - Celts who left their red-haired and blue-eyed genes, Greeks and Carthaginians who altered the diet by introducing wine and olive oil. Romans, whose Latin language provided 75% of the Spanish lexicon still in use today, introduced ideas of statehood, empire and (much later) Catholicism; and Visigoths, whose Germanic language left almost no trace on the Spanish language except for some proper names and words associated with war. For their part, the Moors, as these last invaders who came from Morocco were called, introduced a notable vocabulary into Spanish along with their concept of a woman's place in society (e.g., retaining maiden surname and owning her own property - unlike the customs in Muslim countries today).

In January 1492, the Castilian troops of Queen Isabel - wife of Fernando (Ferdinand) of Aragón - occupied Granada and ended nearly eight centuries of intermittent Catholic-Muslim warfare. This had been the *Reconquista* (reconquest), one of the medieval conflicts, later known as the "Crusades," that marked the ten centuries of Christian Europe's fight to repulse and to defend itself from constant Muslim jihad (holy war) incursions, which in Western Europe had advanced as far as Tours, France, in 732. With this *Reconquista* complete, the Spanish rulers could turn their attention to the Italian, Christopher Columbus (1450-1506).

It was a time for new adventures for a new kingdom, as Spain was becoming a nation. After the battle of Tolosa in 1212 the Moors were confined to Granada and five Catholic kingdoms occupied the remainder of the peninsula – Portugal, Navarre, Castile, León, and Aragón. Portugal became a separate entity while Castile and León were united a century later, and Aragón became a Mediterranean trading kingdom with its great port of Valencia. With the marriage of Fernando II (1452-1516) of Aragón and Isabel I (1451-1504) of Castille in 1469 Spain was united in its present form, and never again would invaders leave their stamp on it. This unification was merely de facto; it would become de jure in 1516. Isabel had died in 1504 and left Castile to their mad daughter, Joanna of Castile (1479-1555), with Fernando as her regent due to her insanity. The Castilian nobles rejected Fernando and replaced him with Joanna's husband, the Burgundian Hapsburg son of the Emperor Maximilian I, Philip the Handsome (1478-1506), as Felipe I of Castile. When Felipe died Fernando took back the regency. Joanna would succeed her father on his death in 1516 but was imprisoned in Tordesillas due to her insanity, and the throne passed to her son Carlos (1500-58, ruled 1516-56). The Hapsburg family would rule Spain until 1700.

For ten years, Columbus had sought official backing for an expedition to find a quicker, cheaper trade route to China, a route that Spain (rather than the Muslim Turks or the Italian cities of Venice and Genoa) would dominate. He received three ships and set out to prove that such a route existed.

He did not attempt to prove that the earth is round: Everyone who cared already knew that it was, and this fact had been known since Empedocles and Anaxagoras deduced it from observations of the earth's shadow during a lunar eclipse in the 5th century BC. In the 3rd century BC Eratosthenes calculated its circumference by geometry.

Columbus's voyage was primarily a commercial enterprise, combined with a desire for personal fame and to spread Christianity. In August 1492 he set sail, and, after a pause in the Canary Islands, reached the Bahamas after 70 days. Where he landed was disputed for centuries. Was it Watling Island (Columbus' San Salvador) or one of three other places, including the uninhabited Samana Cays? Watling Island was the accepted site for historians until the National Geographic Society determined, after a five-year study in 1986,[1] that it was Samana Cay, 65 miles (105 km) southeast of Watling Island.

From there he sailed southwesterly into the West Indies, following native directions to Cuba, whose aboriginal term (Cibao) he thought to mean Cipango (Japan), "in which they [the Bahama natives] say there are ships and mariners, many and very great." This exaggeration was only the first time that the Spaniards would be led astray in their searches by their own wishful thinking and the locals' exaggerations. He reached Cuba, which he named Juana for the Infanta (heir to the Spanish throne), and when its coast appeared Columbus thought he had reached China. Sailing east, his mixture of fact, fancy and credulity identified Haiti as Japan. (The native word for stony mountains, cibao, was misheard as Cipango, the medieval name for Japan). From there he went home to a triumphant reception, taking with him some plants, birds, and natives to show the royal court.

In three later voyages, Columbus discovered Puerto Rico (1493), Jamaica (1494), and Venezuela (1499), and touched the already discovered Caribbean shorelines of Costa Rica and Panama.

In the next two centuries, Portugal, France, England, Holland, Sweden, Denmark, and Russia would stake out claims to portions of the American continent, but for the time being, Spain had the Western Hemisphere to itself. The thought of this expansive realm inflamed the Spanish heart. An unbounded optimism and curiosity about the new lands opening before them was an underlying inspiration for the Spanish art and literature of the time. A nation which had sent its younger sons into battle against the Muslims/Moors to carve out estates denied them by the laws of primogeniture (according to which the oldest son inherits everything) saw a new chance for those among their younger sons who would not be priests. A nation sporadically at war for eight centuries and faced with a large, unemployed army now had a place to use these soldiers. A nation which identified with its Catholic faith was now handed a commission by Spanish-born Pope Alexander VI (1431-1503, reigned 1492-1503) to spread Catholicism among the heathen. And a nation that, like all the successor states of the Roman Empire, had inherited the forms of imperial power, could now flesh out those forms and carry on the imperial tradition.

In 1494, Columbus established the town of Isabel on the north coast of Española (now Haiti and the Dominican Republic). Two years later he moved his headquarters to Santo Domingo, on the south coast. This first colony would be the proving ground for Spanish colonial experimentation. Though today's citizens of the Dominican Republic call theirs "the land Columbus loved," it gave him many disappointments, for little gold was found and no food farms, warehouses or missions took root. He was removed as governor, yet his experiences had a great effect on the Spanish Empire's development: He led the first entrada, a formal entry into pagan lands to take possession, he defeated the first native uprising against the white man (thereupon demanding tribute in treasure or goods), and he introduced the encomienda system – a form of slavery - which parceled natives out to the Spaniards for labor. Though apparently a failure when judged on his scant individual achievements, he had created a basis for subsequent conquest of richer territories.

The man who replaced Columbus as governor was himself replaced after a few years, and Santo Domingo became a sturdy and profitable colony. Spaniards arrived to establish ranches, farms, and mines, the native Arawaks died off at shocking rates, and West African slaves, usually kidnapped by neighboring tribes or sold by their own tribes, were imported to labor. Sugarcane and the familiar European fruits and vegetables, as well as fowl and livestock, made Santo Domingo a paying enterprise, but its chief function was to provide horses and supplies for later invasions. As the bolder men left for the other islands, Florida and South America, Santo Domingo was left to those who were content to develop plantations and ranches. When Columbus's son Diego assumed power in 1509 his power was limited by an audiencia, resembling a modern county board of supervisors. Though he was officially governor for nearly twenty years, the island came to be ruled by the Dominican friars. Despite its prestige as the first colony, Santo Domingo sank steadily in importance as history's spotlight shifted to Cuba, then to Mexico and Peru.

**

"Oh, what a troublesome thing it is to go and discover new lands"

- Bernal Díaz de Castillo, 1576

**

Cuba

Columbus had sworn that Cuba was a part of the mainland but in 1508 it was circumnavigated, and so proven to be an island. Interest in Cuba as a source of gold and labor increased, and many settlers on Española (Hispaniola) made plans to conquer it. With the king's approval in 1511, Diego de Velásquez (1465-1524) sailed with about 300 men from Española and established the first colony on the island. Unfriendly Indians were crushed within two years by two of Velásquez's lieutenants, Hernán Cortés (1485-1547) and Pánfilo de Narváez (1470-1528). Nearly all the conquerors had been in America long enough to employ, apparently without pangs of conscience, wantonly cruel methods to terrorize the people. Horses, steel armor plate and swords, crossbows and gunpowder gave them an undisputed military edge, and by 1515 the island was subjugated.

That same year Velásquez was able to ship enough stolen Indian gold to the king for the *quinto*, or royal fifth (of the goods) to the Crown. To give Cuba a sound economic base, Velasquez introduced grain, vegetables, fruit, sugar, cattle and hogs, introduced the *encomienda* system and provided free transport from Santo Domingo.

Meanwhile, on Tierra Firme (as Central America was then called), Alonso de Ojeda and Diego de Nicuesa were granted permission, in 1508, to settle the Caribbean coast. Ojeda (1468-1515), who had distinguished himself in the battle to take Granada thanks to his agility and familiarity with all

80

types of weapons, was a colorful, tough, and deeply religious man noted for almost reckless bravery and a contradictory nature: vindictively cruel, yet softhearted toward the poor, extremely courteous with women, quarrelsome and a duelist. He began with a settlement at the place where modern Panama and Colombia meet. His colony was soon called Darién, while Nicuesa settled in Panama

The elements turned the experiences of these colonies into a horror story. Beset by hostile Indians, land crabs, flies, mosquitoes, crocodiles, and jungle cats, the 900 Spaniards were reduced to a few dozen within a year. In 1511, Ojeda gave up and became a monk, while Nicuesa went insane and was put to sea by mutinous troops (the Santo Domingo, the ship he was given, was lost at sea). Darién became a city, and, as it was customary to name their leader (or *adelantado*, frontier governor) these settlers named Vasco Núñez de Balboa (1475-1519) *adelantado* and authorized him to proceed in the king's name.

Balboa, a stowaway fleeing creditors in Spain, had originally joined Ojeda in Santo Domingo. A tall, rugged, blond Castilian, he easily dominated his unruly men and made sincere friendships with the Indians. Soon his colony was comfortable and he undertook to investigate reports of a great western sea - along with the usual legends of mountains of pearls and powerful kingdoms deeper in the interior. In September 1513, he set out with a large party of Spaniards and native guides and porters, magnificent hounds, and not a single horse. Penetrating the trackless swamps and jungles they came to a mountainous ridge bisecting the isthmus. The only memorable incident was their coming upon a colony of native homosexuals, whom the Spaniards massacred by having the dogs tear them apart. Approaching the crest of a ridge Balboa went ahead alone and became the first European to see the Pacific Ocean from the east. In a moving ceremony the Spaniards took possession of the "South Sea" for King Fernando, erecting a cross and taking the usual affidavit of all the participants that the discovery had occurred on that date, September 25, 1513.

Back in Cuba, Governor Velásquez was contributing to his colony's decline by sending expeditions to the American mainland, thus depleting his colony of industrious workers and skilled leaders. Voyages in 1517 and 1518 had reported on the Mayan cities of Yucatán and the rumors of still greater wonders in the interior. While waiting for royal permission to begin the conquest of the mainland, Velásquez was aced out by his bold and unscrupulous lieutenant, Hernán Cortés, who looted the slaughterhouse for meat to carry with him and sailed away across the Gulf of Mexico.

Cortés

**

"Glory, Gold and God"

- Cortés

**

A 34-year-old lawyer who had been in the Indies since he was 19, having become *alcalde* (mayor) of Santiago (Cuba's capital), Hernán Cortés, in May 1519, landed at Tabasco and stayed for a short time to get some idea about the land and its people. The natives, awed by the strangeness of the Spaniards, their weapons, and animals, nevertheless fought and defended their land. He defeated them and won them over, receiving presents such as the young woman Malinche (renamed Doña Marina, c1496-1529), who became the conquistador's interpreter-mistress and bore him a son, although Cortés had

82

a wife in Spain. Sailing to another spot on the coast he formally freed himself from Velásquez's control by founding the city of Veracruz and establishing a *cabildo* (town council), which in turn elected him captain general and chief justice, empowering him to conquer Mexico in the name of King Carlos I (better known to history as Emperor Charles V). He then destroyed his ships to prevent desertion and gave his men the choice of following him and possibly coming back rich or staying on the coast to be slaughtered by the natives. (Like Napoleon, Cortés is credited with many dramatic exhortations at critical moments, which may have been apocryphally written into the record afterward.)

Cortés then set out for the interior, relying sometimes on force, sometimes on amity, but always careful to keep disturbances to a minimum. The Tlaxcalans, a nation in a state of chronic war with the Aztec rulers of Mexico, resisted Cortés at first, but once defeated they became his most faithful allies. One can safely imagine that having been undefeated until Cortés' arrival they sensed his excellent potential for defeating the Aztecs, and that, as his allies, they could share in the fruits of conquest.

The Aztec emperor, Moctezuma II (c1466-1520) had ruled an empire stretching from coast to coast since 1502. An organizational genius, he had built up a gigantic political, military, and religious bureaucracy centered on his capital of Tenochtitlan. The Aztecs were the latest, and cruelest, rulers of a highly advanced civilization that had evolved 3,000 years earlier and reached an apogee in the 1,700 years before the Spanish conquest. Their civilization, began with the Teotihuacanos in the Valley of Mexico, the Olmecs at Monte Albán in Oaxaca, and the Maya in the south, followed then by the Zapotecs, Mixtecs, and, finally, about AD 1325, the Aztecs from the northwest area of Nayarit. Each of these had conquered the prior occupants. While pursuing conquests they found time for producing monumental architecture and excellent ceramics, sculpture, and murals, while developing a very sophisticated knowledge of astronomy and mathematics, as well as scientific farming and a written pictograph language. Arriving at the concept of the zero cipher even before the Hindus in the fifth century or its arrival in Europe via Arab mathematicians in the 12th century, and developing the world's most accurate calendar, these accomplished Middle Americans still had not made any practical use of metals, nor had they stumbled on the use of the wheel – except for children's toys.

Religiosity was a trait common to all these peoples, religion being the center of their lives and culture. The Aztec pantheon consisted of approximately 250 gods, goddesses and spirits governing all aspects of life, some gentle and benign, others cruel. Huitzilopochtli, the god of death and war, was one of the four most important. He demanded blood sacrifice wherein victims' hearts would be ripped out and offered to him. On one of his feast days thousands of young people of both sexes from conquered tribes would be sacrificed at the Temple of the Sun, their blood running down its steps.

A brave warrior, but cursed with indecisiveness, a fatal flaw in any ruler, Moctezuma was unsure how to react to the advent of the Spaniards. Some of his advisers told him to wait and see what course to pursue while others counseled a quick attack; his predecessor and uncle, Ahuitzotl (ruled 1486-1502), would likely have descended on the Spaniards in a quick and powerful strike, but he had been replaced after a head injury drove him mad. To complicate the situation, Moctezuma held Cortés in awe because of the prophecy of the return of the benign god and cultural hero of legend, the fair-skinned, red-bearded Quetzalcoatl. His return, prophesied

84

since ancient times as coming from the east with amazing magic, would occur in the Year of the Reed (coincidentally AD 1519) and would result in Quezalcoatl's replacing Huitzilopochtli, the severe chief deity of the Aztecs. Besides this parallel of the Spaniards' arrival with ancient prophecy, Cortés's large ships, mounted armored soldiers and guns caused Moctezuma some very natural concern, and he responded by sending many gold objects to Cortés, hoping to keep him away from the capital. These gifts only served to whet Cortés's appetite, and in November 1519 he entered Tenochtitlan with a Spanish-Tlaxcalan army. The emperor, believing Cortés to be Quetzalcoatl - a role Malinche's tales helped her lover to perform - received him with the greatest honor. He never surmised that Malinche had instructed Cortés in Quetzalcoatl's history nor passed on whatever plots she overheard being concocted, so that the Spaniard seemed prescient. Cortés's soldier-chronicler, Bernal Díaz (c.1495-1584), vividly portrayed the capital's wealth and the emperor's magnificence as well as the horrors of its human sacrifices.

Cortés decided to seize the emperor and rule the country through him, achieving both a political and a religious conquest. When news arrived that a small Spanish fort at Veracruz had been destroyed and its soldiers massacred, Cortés went immediately to seize Moctezuma. From there he went on to Veracruz, seized the rebel chief and burned him at the stake. By this time, he felt his position secure enough to unlock the now-powerless Moctezuma's chains. It did not matter that Moctezuma still wore the crown. It was Cortés who wielded the staff of power. For the moment, the emperor's subjects were unaware of this.

Meanwhile Governor Velásquez, smarting from what Cortés had done to his plans to explore and conquer Mexico, had sent Narváez to arrest Cortés, who left to intercept him, leaving a garrison of 80 Spaniards under Pedro de Alvarado (1485-1541) in the capital. Despite the governor's orders, Cortés got the upper hand by showing Narváez samples of Aztec wealth and convincing him to ally with Cortés.

Alvarado knew that the Aztecs were going to hold a religious ceremony, but he had been informed that the Indians would use it as an excuse to attack and sacrifice the garrison. Alvarado decided to strike first that night, June 30, 1520. The garrison committed an irresponsible aggression against the Aztecs during their ceremony, and they were thereupon besieged by the angry natives. The Aztecs were determined to drive out the Spaniards and their Indian allies. When Moctezuma tried to induce his people to cease their revolt, he was stoned to death by his own people when he appeared on a balcony to try to pacify them. They blamed him for the presence of the Spaniards. As the uprising continued, approximately 800-1,000 Spaniards and 2,000 Indian allies were drowned in Lake Texcoco, tortured or killed outright. The Spaniards, unable to swim in any case, fled into the lake with their armor stuffed with looted gold plates, and tortures included having molten gold poured down their throats. This became known in Mexican history as *La Noche Triste* (the Sad Night).

Driven from the city in *la Noche Triste*, the survivors retreated, only to turn back again and defeat the Aztecs a week later. Hearing of this, Cortés returned in haste and was welcomed by his Tlaxcalan allies. He regrouped, subdued neighboring territories, and, after a stubborn siege which the Aztecs resisted with arrows and stones from the flat rooftops and hand-to-hand combat in the narrow streets, captured and destroyed Tenochtitlan almost to rubble in August 1521. This victory marked the fall of the Aztec Empire, and when a new urban center (Mexico City) rose over the still-smoldering ruins of Tenochtitlan, a Catholic cathedral was built on the stones of Huitzilopochtli's temple where so many thousands had been sacrificed in the previous half-century.

Cortés's success was due to a combination of six factors: the aid of Malinche and her vital skills as an interpreter (whose role led to her name's becoming synonymous in Mexico with treachery), the hatred of the conquered tribes for their Aztec overlords, Moctezuma's religious beliefs and indecisiveness, Cortés's personal qualities of leadership and diplomacy, European arms and horses, and smallpox introduced by one of Cortés's black slaves (whether intentionally or inadvertently continues to be debated.)

Once in control of central Mexico, Cortés dispatched men southwest into Oaxaca. The following year Cortés sent Alvarado into Guatemala while he went into Honduras. In 1526 Francisco de Montejo (1479-1553) conquered Yucatan. The lower part of Central America had been conquered from Panama, and soon Panama became the base for the conquest of the Inca Empire in Peru. Meanwhile, Cortés had appeased Velásquez by reimbursing him for his personal losses from the earlier treacheries when Cortés took the governor's men and supplies from Cuba and turned Narváez into a supporter.

Spanish Government

Until Cortés sent an embassy to Charles V, the emperor had been largely disinterested in his American holdings, which while vast and intriguing, offered little wealth. Upon the conquest of Mexico, with its immense riches and millions of hard-working Indians, Charles and his government took a sudden interest in the New World. He and his advisors understood that before royal power could be imposed on Mexico, officially known as *Nueva España* (New Spain),

Cortés's power would have to be curtailed. While he was in Central America, Cortés's enemies - who were not necessarily Charles's friends - took control. In 1524 the Conqueror's power over finances was taken over by the setting up of a *Real Hacienda* (royal treasury). He went to Spain to plead his case in 1528, but in his absence, legislative power was assumed by an *audiencia*. The emperor in fact received him well, making him Marqués del Valle de Oaxaca, and Cortés then threw himself into the work of organizing the land, studying its resources, and pushing forward the work of exploration. His enemies, however, worked through the Council of the Indies, the colonial law-making body in Madrid, to thwart him, ordering his goods seized and his servants arrested. Again, he went to Spain where Charles received him with marks of honor, but he returned to Mexico nearly stripped of authority. In 1535 the emperor appointed Antonio de Mendoza (1495-1552), the Conde de Tendilla, one of the empress's chamberlains (and fourth choice for the post) as the first viceroy of New Spain.

In this role as vice-king (a position unknown in the English colonies), Mendoza and his 61 successors would be the personification of sovereignty, the direct representatives of the Spanish national head, and would always form an independent and truthful channel of information. Set high above the crowd of adventurers who swarmed to America, the viceroy was selected from among the unquestionably loyal Spanish nobles, was permitted to engage in no business in his colony and was removable at royal whim. The viceroy was assisted by an *audiencia* in his capital, consisting of four or more *oidores* (appellate judges). Subordinate *audiencias* were later established at Guatemala (1543), Guadalajara (1548), and Manila (1583). With the older audiencia of Santo Domingo, the viceroy of New Spain held titular sway over Mexico, Central America, Venezuela, the West Indies, the

Philippines, the Mariana Islands, the Caroline Islands, and parts of the present-day United States. The colony was divided into provinces and ruled by governors; these were first subdivided into smaller units entrusted to *corregidores* or *alcaldes mayores* (appointed local administrative and judicial officials). The only institutions permitting any self-government were the *cabildos* (elected town councils). However, composed of American-born Spaniards (creoles), the cabildos had little authority.

After the Inca Empire, stretching from present-day Colombia southward to Chile and eastward to Bolivia, was conquered by Francisco Pizarro (c1471-1541) in 1532, a new viceroyalty was established in Lima in 1551. All Spanish holdings in South America, with the exception of Venezuela, were governed from there. In 1717 Nueva Granada was set up as a viceroyalty centered on Bogotá, taking in the present-day countries of Colombia, Ecuador, Panama, and Venezuela. In 1778, at Buenos Aires, another viceroyalty was created, the Río de la Plata, including present-day Argentina, Bolivia, Paraguay, and Uruguay.

In Mexico, Mendoza was challenged by both Cortés and Cortés's enemy Nuño Beltrán de Guzmán (1490-1558), conqueror of Zacatecas, governor of both Pánuco and Nueva Galicia, and president of the audiencia, but both acceded to Mendoza's authority. He crushed a savage Indian uprising, forced the *encomenderos* (who owned Indians) to moderate their treatment of the natives, and promoted agriculture. A new mining frontier was attracting a rush, and the Church was firmly rooted (having started slowly, but then spreading deep and wide after the reported apparition of the Virgin of Guadalupe in 1531.) Most of the Aztec leadership had been killed off in the Conquest, but Church-run schools were operating, and royal authority was everywhere acknowledged.

Mendoza preferred manipulation and diplomacy to force, though he never shrank from the latter. His success was rewarded by promotion to viceroy of Peru, the first appointed there, in 1551. He would have little chance to carry on his good work, however, for he died the next year.

Since no European nation had had previous experience with empire, each had to develop its own policy by trial and error. The entire Spanish Empire would be subject to evolving imperial policy. Later colonies - such as California – would similarly incorporate earlier structures while pioneering new ones.

As this was a New World, there would be a new social structure. A semi-rigid class division eventually embracing sixteen categories developed. At the top were the *peninsulares*, those born in the Iberian Peninsula; from them would come the rulers. The second group were the *criollos* (creoles), those born in the New World of Spanish parents; thus, a family might include peninsular and creole siblings, depending on where their mothers were at the time of their births. This happenstance caused not a little resentment among siblings born into families whose locations or relocations affected their status, the peninsular granted a higher one than creole offspring. The third and eventually largest social category were the *mestizos*, those born of a Spanish father and an Indian mother. Far below them were the *indios* (the natives), and lower still the *mulatos* (Spanish father and African mother), the *zambos* (half Indian and half African), and the *negros* (African slaves) at the bottom of the rung. People could and did cross lines eventually via intermarriage and the need for colonists in new territories, but inevitably an offspring's status would be lower than the father's and higher than the mother's, depending on how remote he or she was from peninsular or creole. In this system of racial hierarchy, or castes (or *sistema de castas*), the *mestizos*, who formed the majority of the population, had fewer rights than the minority elite-born European *peninsulares* and the minority colonial-born white *criollos*, but more rights than the now minority *indio*, *negro* and *mulato* populations.

Spain's imperial philosophy was simple: the colonies were regarded as royal, not national, property. Accordingly, the crown-controlled taxation, church appointments, and frontier advances. Another characteristic of the Spanish Empire was the prominent role of the Catholic church: Absolutely orthodox in their Catholic faith, the Spanish monarchs wanted to make Spanish America orthodox as well, and churchmen would be counted on to evangelize, teach the rudiments of Spanish culture to the Indians, and run educational and charitable institutions.

Likewise, Spanish imperial Indian policy was simple yet sensible. In the Roman Empire many individuals of diverse cultures that came under Roman sway had aspired to be Romans, and imperial policy encouraged this aspiration. Spain copied this Roman policy towards its colonial peoples. The Indians would be made Spanish. They would be taught the Spanish language, the Catholic religion, basic Spanish customs, and they would be given Spanish names. They would be encouraged to live in villages on a Spanish pattern and might be racially fused with the Spaniards by intermarriage. This policy was poles apart from the English one of extermination of conquered peoples, and at variance with the Anglo-American dislike of interracial marriage, but it had a practical basis as well: There were simply not enough Spaniards to fill the colonies, so the natives themselves could serve as colonists. Another practical reason for keeping the Indians alive was that they would do the work, whether as slaves of the first conquerors or, in later centuries, under mission discipline, or, in more recent times, in debt peonage. In the Spanish world, the Indians were regarded as inferior humans with souls to be saved, while in the Anglo world the Indian was despised as subhuman and killed if inconvenient.

Another feature of colonial policy was that of the *pueblo*, or town. In the early history of the United States, individuals advanced the frontier by clearing a homestead. In the Spanish Empire the preferred unit of advancement was an entire town with its people.

The Church came with the conquerors and established an episcopal bureaucracy even before the pope could confirm it. With the first conquistadores the Church established sees within boundaries that it chose. This turned out to be a disaster in Cuba, where natives destroyed the churches in the first three bishoprics, so the Church willingly let the crown's representatives take care of establishing sees and building churches. The diocese of Mexico, including what would be the viceroyalty, was set up in 1540, and became an archdiocese six years later; in 1579, Manila was separated from it the archdiocese of Mexico. In 1779, the diocese of Sonora, covering the entire northwest of the viceroyalty, was set up under the archbishop of Mexico. The first archbishop was the Franciscan Juan de Zumárraga (1468-1548), who had taken up the task without confirmation from Rome in 1528; Pope Clement VII (1478-1534, reigned 1523-34) was a prisoner of Charles V during the 1527 sack of Rome and unable to dispatch Zumárraga, who went across the ocean on the orders of Charles. Six years later he returned to Spain and was consecrated bishop, going back to Mexico to take up his duties. An educated man who established a printing press office, published books, set up schools and colleges, Zumárraga nevertheless destroyed many of the idols, temples, and hieroglyphics he found in the belief that they interfered with the conversion of the natives. He also presided over 131 trials of people accused of heresy, idolatry, and sorcery, sentencing some of these to burning at the stake; this was long before the official Holy Office of the Inquisition was established in Mexico City (1571). It was to then Bishop Zumárraga that the seer of the Guadalupan apparitions, Juan Cuauhtloatizin (Juan Diego, 1474-1548) brought word of his experience and of the instructions he perceived in the visions of 1531, which he clearly understood to be from the Virgin Mary and intended for the bishop.

Baja California

A millennium before Columbus (AD 458), Hwui Shan, a Buddhist monk from what is now Afghanistan may well have reached the west coast of North America with five other monks. He wrote an account of voyaging in a boat which had the misfortune of being blown from the Chinese coast by a great storm, and that he kept going eastward until he reached land, about 21,000 li away (one li equaling 1/3 of a mile or 1/2 of a kilometer). He called the land Fusang and described natural features such as the coast redwoods, the Grand Canyon, and artifacts such as totem poles, dwellings made of sun-dried mud blocks, and the huge stone faces in Central America. His accounts of the Aleuts and the people of central Mexico, the flora and fauna, could only have been written by an observer. That his account survives proves that he returned to China. Evidence beyond his written account includes Chinese coins and stone anchors found on the coast of Baja and an iron spear head with Chinese characters found at Bolinas.[2] However, as in the case of the Vikings or others on the East Coast, nothing came of these pre-Columbian visits, so the glory of discovery remains with Columbus. That others failed to open the new world to the old, a feat accomplished unquestionably by Columbus, should end the perennial debate about whom to credit with the historically significant discovery of these new lands.

After Mexico and Peru had been conquered and their vast wealth exposed, explorers set out to find "Otro Méjico" because of fanciful ideas that had enjoyed credibility in Europe for a generation. The Fountain of Youth would give eternal youth to the one who drank from it (though how youthful was never specified), the Amazon Island was a kingdom of beautiful warrior women, the Terrestrial Paradise (the Biblical Garden of Eden) was alleged to be there, and the Seven Cities were part of a kingdom of golden cities. These were only a few of the mythical places sought.

The men who went searching in this geography of dreams, risking lives and wealth, were not idle dreamers. On the contrary, they were hard-bitten realists. What motivated them, fantasy or reality? Before the conquests of the Aztecs and Incas, such concentrated wealth had been undreamed of. Once these places were revealed to the Old World, the notion that other, previously-undreamed-of, territories existed seemed possible as well. After all, it was a New World.

Another sought-after place was the Strait of Anián, or Northwest Passage. In 1519 Ferdinand Magellan (1480-1521) had started on a round-the-world voyage for Spain. Sailing southwest across the Atlantic to the tip of South America and into Balboa's South Sea (which he named the Pacific Ocean) he crossed it to Guam and to the Philippines, where he was killed in an intertribal battle. His pilot, Sebastián Elcano (1476-1526), continued the voyage across the Indian Ocean, around Africa and back to Spain in 1522. Had anyone still doubted the roundness of the world after Magellan's voyage, that doubter would have to have been invincibly ignorant.

Mapmakers believed that the world is in perfect balance, so that if a water passage exists below America, then a water passage must exist above America. Such a passage does exist, in the Canadian Arctic, but is useless due to its being mostly covered by sea ice throughout the year and almost completely in winter. Though then unknown, such a passage above or through North America was drawn and labelled on maps as Anián, and for three centuries explorers vainly sought this shortcut to Asia.

After Cortés had conquered Central America, he turned to the Mexican Pacific coast. In 1527, he built four ships to undertake this conquest, but as they were about to sail a royal order arrived diverting them to the Moluccas (now part of Indonesia). The ships, under Alvaro de Saavedra, were to assist two explorers from Spain who had been shipwrecked. They were unsuccessful. Two of the ships disappeared, and one of them may have been shipwrecked in Hawaii according to a native tradition. Saavedra reached the Moluccas, was unable to fulfill his mission and died in October 1529 on the way back.

In 1533, Cortés was able to send an expedition to sail north under Diego Becerra. The expedition had hardly left Mexico when a mutiny broke out and the leader of the mutineers, Diego Fortún Ximénez, killed the evil tempered and arrogant Becerra and took the ships to a little bay which he named La Paz. Fortún was himself killed by the Indians there.[3] The others made it back to Mexico and reported pearls at La Paz. Lured by the tantalizing reports of pearls, Cortés finally made the voyage to Baja in late 1535. He found the voyage difficult, taking a month because of storms. (Today the ferryboat from Mazatlán to La Paz takes nineteen hours.) The Indians were hostile, and the find of pearls was not impressive. He named the bay Santa Cruz, and the water was later called the Sea of

Cortés. Supply problems, the fierceness of the Indians, and the poverty of the land led him to abandon the settlement after a few years.

As the conqueror of Moctezuma's empire, Cortés naturally felt that he was the proper person to investigate any new attractions. As noted, Viceroy Mendoza disagreed and tried to stop him at every opportunity. This would continue until 1541, when he returned to Spain and lived out his last years embittered at what he considered the perennial obstruction of his ambitions by Mendoza.

Cibolá

In 1536 two travelers arrived in Mexico City with a wondrous tale. Alvar Núñez Cabeza de Vaca (c1488-c1560), a Spaniard, and Estevanico (c1500-39), a black Moorish slave, had been part of Pánfilo de Narváez's expedition from Cuba to Florida in 1529. Exploring the northern rim of the Gulf of Mexico they had been shipwrecked on the Texas coast and spent the next seven years moving toward Mexico. They were enslaved by one tribe, and, escaping, lived among others as traders and medicine men. When they arrived at Culiacán, they paused to tell their tales of wealthy cities in the north, and then went on to Mexico City to report to the viceroy. What they reported was that they had heard of - though not actually visited - Cibolá, the Kingdom of the Seven Cities.

This aroused a good deal of interest in the capital and the viceroy put his secretary, Francisco Vásquez de Coronado (1510-54), in charge of an expedition to go north to find and conquer Cibolá. Coronado, Mendoza, and many rich men in Europe and America invested in it. An elaborate retinue - 225 mounted cavaliers, 62-foot soldiers, 800 Indians, 1,000 black and native slaves, herds of horses, oxen, cows, sheep, swine, droves of laden mules - were assembled. To report on the

96

exact location, Coronado sent the illiterate Estevanico with a Franciscan friar, Marcos de Niza (c1495-1558). Estevanico went ahead, and for a time hugely enjoyed being lionized by the Indians. His fortune turned, and they suddenly killed him because of advances he made to their women. Sobered by this misfortune, Friar Marcos steered clear of the natives, but claimed that he had reached Cibolá, whose stone houses of two, three and four stories were ornamented with gold and turquoises. With that endorsement, Coronado set out with high hopes in 1539. Up the west coast of Mexico from Compostela to the present site of Nogales, northeast to the Little Colorado River, then east they went. They found no Seven Cities of gold or even silver; instead, they found the Zuñi villages, a collection of mud huts, whose only gleaming must have been sunshine on their white-washed adobe. The Seven Cities increased in number but decreased in splendor. The blue-blooded cavaliers, who hailed from many countries, hurled such curses at Fray Marcos that one chronicler wrote, "I pray God may protect him from them." Fray Marcos was sent back to Mexico in disgrace.

Coronado continued his search. One detachment of his men found the Hopi villages, while another discovered the Grand Canyon, whose scenic beauty failed to compensate for the tales of Fray Marcos. Aside from its lack of golden civilizations, it seemed to be the actual geographic end of the world. Coronado himself led an expedition east along the Rio Grande. There he wintered among the aloof Pueblo Indians, eating the food plundered from the native villages in expeditions to the southern Rockies and the Grand Canyon.

In Texas Coronado was lured north to Quivira (probably in Kansas) by a Wichita Indian whom he called "El Turco" (The Turk) because "he looked like one" from his headgear.[4] Quivira was a land whose cities were encrusted with gold and precious stones, where the "ordinary dishes [were] made of wrought plate, and the jugs and bowls were of gold." Since El Turco was willing to go along with the Spaniards, Coronado felt he could trust him, so he struck northeast across present-day Oklahoma to Kansas and found only a few ragged Wichita villages. El Turco's motive was to lure the Spaniards into the interior, where they might become lost and die. When Coronado found out El Turco's intention, he had him garroted and then turned back to Mexico. Bedraggled and dispirited, the expedition, depleted to 100 men, returned to Mexico in 1542.

Because of the high expectations and original lavishness of his venture, Coronado's failure was regarded as particularly reprehensible, but he remained as governor of Nueva Galicia until 1544, retiring then to Mexico City where he died ten years later. Although he returned to Mexico empty-handed, he had added to New Spain the area from Arizona to Kansas and proven that the continent to the north of Mexico was very wide. It would take many years before anyone would take that wind-swept wasteland seriously. The land held little interest for Spain, and Mendoza soon received orders to stop wasting money on useless expeditions.

Still Mendoza was not convinced that all the northern lands were barren. When the Spaniards sent out an expedition by land it was accompanied by a sea expedition, in the belief that one or the other would achieve the goal. While Coronado was looking for Cibolá by land, four sea expeditions set out. Cortés sent the first of these, and Mendoza the others.

In 1539 Cortés sent Francisco de Ulloa (?-1540) to find Cibolá. He sailed to the head of the Sea of Cortés (later called the Gulf of California), turned south, and became convinced that what was thought to be an island was a peninsula. He rounded the peninsula and went about halfway up the Pacific side to Cedros Island before returning. After this expedition Cortés went back to Spain, where he remained the rest of his life, to the unconcealed joy of Mendoza. Malinche, now known as Doña Marina, having died, their son, don Martín Cortés, called "the first Mestizo," married and had a son who became the principal judge of Vera Cruz. Hernán had two other illegitimate children by native women, including one by a daughter of Moctezuma. He married twice and had two sons and four daughters by his second wife.

Returning to Spain in 1541 Cortés was unable to obtain an imperial audience until he audaciously jumped onto the imperial carriage and demanded one. When the emperor demanded to know who he was, he replied, "I am the man who has given you more provinces than your ancestors left you cities." Impressed, the emperor allowed him to join an expedition against the Muslim stronghold in Algiers. Putting in a claim for some imperial reimbursement for his expenditures in the successful conquest, he was given the runaround for three years and retired to Mexico in some disgust. Soon falling ill, he died wealthy but embittered, leaving his numerous children, legitimate and illegitimate, well provided for, and prevailing upon the pope to legitimize their "natural" (illegitimate) status.

In 1540 Mendoza sent Hernando Alarcón up the inner coast of the Gulf between Baja and the Mexican mainland to rendezvous with Coronado, who sent Melchor Díaz, who had charge of the expedition's livestock, to meet him. Alarcón sailed as far as the Gila River's mouth on the Colorado, which he named the Buena Guía. The first European to see California from the east, he went on to explore the Colorado River a few months before García López de Cárdenas, one of Coronado's officers, discovered the Grand Canyon. López de Cárdenas was unable to descend to the river because of the sheer cliffs, remaining on the south side of the rim and finding himself forced to return to Coronado's camp. Meanwhile, Díaz had crossed the Colorado River (which he named Río del Tizón, for the Indians' campfires, the "Charred Stick River") into Baja and went on a short expedition, probably to the Imperial Valley, likely seeing the geothermal springs at the future site of Calexico. When the two failed to meet, Alarcón sailed back to Mexico as his ships were "being eaten by worms," leaving a cache of supplies plus a letter explaining his role and actions. When Díaz arrived at the spot where they were supposed to meet, the Indians reported the cache and letter.

Díaz suffered a mortal wound in an accident. He had hurled a lance at dogs attacking his sheep and, unable to stop his horse's momentum, he was accidentally impaled in the groin and died 20 days later. Unlike other conquistadores, Alarcón treated the natives humanely, and, in the words of Bernard de Voto (1897-1955) in his *Westward the Course of Empire* (1953), "The Indians had an experience they were to never repeat; they were sorry to see these white men leave." Pedro de Castañeda, the chronicler of the Coronado expedition, described Díaz as "a hard worker and skillful organizer and leader. He inspired confidence in his companions and followers, and always maintained the best order and diligence among those who were under his charge."[5]

In 1541 Francisco de Bolaños was sent out by Mendoza, but got only as far as Punta Abreojos, below Cedros Island, and then returned south to Cabo San Lucas, the tip of the peninsula. Though Ulloa and Alarcón had gone much farther Bolaños's voyage is of importance because he named California.

A popular novel published in 1510 was *Las Sergas de Esplandián* and its author was Garci Rodríguez de Montalvo.

Esplandián was a knight who had many breathtaking adventures with evil knights, wizards, monsters, and similar beings. One of his adventures was the invasion of the Amazon Island, ruled by the beautiful Queen Calafia. This all-black female warrior island, filled with multiple dangers for any man so bold as to think he could set foot on it, was a natural challenge for someone like Esplandián. He took the queen prisoner and somehow won her love. Her land, described as an earthly paradise, thus provided the name for Bolaños's anchorage, and was probably a tongue-in-cheek designation. Today Cabo San Lucas is a luxury resort area, but as recently as 1950 it was nothing but a windswept, rocky spot with little to appeal to any but hermits, should they have chosen to live there.[6]

In 1542, Juan Rodríguez de Cabrillo, a Portuguese sailing for Spain, was sent to find Cibolá, and thence to sail north along the coast until he reached China and then reconnoiter in the Philippines. On June 27, 1542 he left Navidad (later Acapulco), sailed north and took possession at "Cabo del Engaño," whose exact location is disputed: Punta San Antonio? Punta Baja? Cape Disappointment? It was there that he heard of Coronado's men to the east. On September 28, 1542, he discovered San Diego Bay and was thus the first European known to have touched California. He later discovered the Channel Islands and the Bay of Smokes (Los Angeles), so named because the Indian campfires' smoke hung over the harbor hemmed in by the mountains around the basin – just as modern smog is inconveniently confined there. He went on to Point Concepción and then to San Miguel Island, where he broke his arm, some claim, in a storm-related accident: a mast had fallen on him and caused a compound and complex fracture. According to others he got into a fight with the Indians on San Miguel and suffered a broken leg, which became infected. Despite the pain, he ordered the voyage to continue and went as far as the Rogue River in Oregon. Passing Monterey Bay, he never actually sails into it, but he "takes possession" of the region for Spain from the decks of his ship, naming it "Bahía de San Pedro". Delirious by the time they reached the Rogue, he lost effective command to his pilot Bartolomé Ferrelo (1499-1550), who ordered a return to San Diego. On the way back Cabrillo died from the infection in his arm (or leg) and was buried on one of the Channel Islands.

Cabrillo had conferred names on most of the prominent coastal sites, but later mapmakers and explorers renamed them: San Miguel became San Diego; San Salvador, Santa Cruz; San Lucas, Santa Rosa; Isla de Juan Rodríguez, San Miguel; Puebla de las Canoas, Ventura; Dos Pueblos, Rincón Point; Sardinas, Gaviota; Cape Galera, Point Concepción; Bahía de San Pedro, Monterey Bay; and Bahía de San Francisco, Drakes Bay. The names of Cape Mendocino, bestowed in honor of the viceroy, and Cape San Martín are to the present the same they received from Cabrillo.

As to the Rogue River, Mendoza believed that it must be the Strait of Anián, but it was so far north that it would be no threat to Mexican security to leave it alone for the moment. The expedition had no immediate impact since Spain made nothing of his claims for two centuries.

The Philippines and the Manila Galleons

In 1555, Charles V abdicated and retired to a monastery. His empire was divided between his brother, Ferdinand I (1503-64), who inherited the German Hapsburg lands, and his son Felipe II (1527-98), who received Spain and its empire. Felipe would rule until 1598 and began with an order to expand Spain's imperial frontiers. In Mexico this meant a northward thrust, and in 1562, Francisco de Ibarra (1539-75) was sent into Nueva Vizcaya (later the Mexican states of Durango and Chihuahua) to establish control and protect the silver miners from Indian attacks, to convert the Indians there to Catholicism, and to find new silver veins. What the Spaniards wanted, and more than that, what the crown wanted for the new lands, was conversion to Catholicism. One motive of this campaign was to create a spiritual army to overwhelm the Protestant Reformation's world-wide effect by sheer numbers. Meanwhile, it was the search for silver that led the way to New Mexico and California.

The Philippines, claimed for Spain by Magellan forty years earlier and named for the Spanish prince by Ruy López de Villalobos (1500-44) in 1541, provided a new interest for settling California. In 1565 Miguel López de Legaspi (1502-72) had crossed the Pacific from Mexico, passing through the Marshall Islands, establishing Spanish control on the island of Cebú. He was ordered to "discover the return route to Mexico with all possible speed." His pilot, the friar-seaman Fray Andrés de Urdaneta, (1498-1568) was with him when he set out from Cebú in June, and he followed the "Great Circle" route northeast past Japan, using the Japan (or Kuroshio) and Humboldt currents. Previous pilots had failed because of contrary winds and currents but Urdaneta succeeded by finding the Great Circle's Japan current. From Japan Urdaneta crossed the Pacific, sighting land at San Miguel Island, then heading southeast to Acapulco. The voyage had taken 129 days and cost twenty lives, though none from scurvy because Urdaneta had put in a supply of legumes and coconuts to last for nine months.[7] Though difficult, the voyage was proven possible.

A speedier route between Spain and the Philippines would have taken ships around Africa, but the Treaty of Tordesillas (1494), by which Spain and Portugal, with papal sanction, divided the new lands between them (ignoring England and France), made the Indian Ocean Portuguese. Contact between Spain and its South Pacific colonies would have to go through Mexico. The merchants of Mexico jumped at the chance to get in on trade with the Far East, seeking wealth from silk, chinaware, wax, and spices - but mercantilist Spanish policy dictated that merchants in the mother country should not have to compete with colonial merchants, and the king restricted contact to one vessel per year between Manila and Acapulco. For 250 years, the Manila galleons skirted the California coast from Cape Mendocino to Cabo San Lucas, and in all that time only 23 were lost to pirates or the weather; in October 1974, the wreckage of one was found in the Channel Islands.[8]

Because this trade was so profitable, it was imperative that a port of call be located where inbound ships could pause for the scurvy-ravaged crew to recuperate, to take on fresh food and water, and to overhaul their ships. Such a base could also be used to provide protection against foreign pirates. The California coast was a logical location for such a port.

For its part, the Philippines were governed as part of the Viceroyalty of New Spain. The local states were consolidated and natives were moved into different new towns, enabling the missionaries to convert most of the lowland natives. The missionaries also founded schools, a university, hospitals, and churches. For defense the Spanish built and maintained a network of military fortresses throughout the archipelago. Legaspi had claimed the island of Guam in 1565, but Spanish colonization did not begin for another century, with the arrival of missionaries in 1668. Tensions over the missionaries, who were initially welcomed, erupted into a mostly guerrilla war in 1670-95, resulting in the establishment of Spanish rule from Manila. Guam became an important stop for the Manila galleons.

In the 16th century, Spain was the greatest country in Europe, and its greatest enemy was the England of Elizabeth I (1533-1603, reigned 1558-1603). Religious differences had led to trade differences, and these to military encounters, which would end with the defeat of the Spanish Armada in 1588. In 1577, Francis Drake (1540-96), an English seaman, set out on what would be the second voyage around the world. He sailed into the Pacific, hitherto a Spanish lake, sacking undefended towns in Chile, Peru, and Mexico, capturing the Peru-to-Panama silver ship, stealing tons of Spanish treasure. In June 1579, he spent a month in Marin County, where he repaired and provisioned his ship, the *Golden Hind*, exchanged presents with the Indians while many of his men fathered children with the Indian women, and claimed the area for England with the name of Nova Albion. As with other English explorers under Elizabeth this was not a colonial venture but a trading expedition. The English were not interested in colonies at that time. When they would become interested in the next century, the colonies would be on the Atlantic coast of North America, closer to the mother country than had they been planted in the far-away Pacific.

**

In 1936, some picnickers at Greenbrae (near San Quentin) found an object that would be known as the Brass Plate. It bore an inscription that appeared to identify it as the one Drake had placed to give notice of his discovery and claim of the land. Another story has it that a chauffeur found it at Drakes Bay, but that he threw it away as junk, and that a young man who stopped to rest after changing a flat tire near Point San Quentin picked it up. In 1974, a 16th century English six-pence piece was found near Novato; Drake's log noted that such a coin had been inserted in a hole in the plate. Historians disputed the plate's authenticity for nearly 40 years until

October 1974, when it was proven to be a forgery, surprisingly dated at least 30 years before its discovery. About the same time the hoax was discovered, the *Golden Hinde II* set out from Britain for a voyage to San Francisco, where it was welcomed in March 1975.[9]

Why and by whom the fraud was perpetrated is still a mystery. Theories as to its origin range from the shenanigans of a British author to a University of California fraternity's hijinks. Sir Arthur Conan Doyle (1859-1930), creator of Sherlock Holmes, once visited California and enjoyed himself at Mount Tamalpais in Marin County. Besides creating absorbing fiction, he apparently also perpetrated several hoaxes, one of which may have been the Brass Plate. Others say that four friends in the E Clampus Vitus fraternity at the University of California, Berkeley, created the Brass Plate as a practical joke to fool Spanish borderlands historian Herbert Eugene Bolton (1870-1953), who had long sought the plate. In any case, the Bancroft Library, which once displayed the Brass Plate with pride, now keeps it in the basement.[10] Charles L. Scamahorn (1935-) has investigated and reported on several Conan Doyle fakes since 2005. He asserted that metallurgical and chemical tests, plus close analysis of the letters and other markings on the plate, proved it a fake, implying that Conan Doyle was the fraudster.

**

Of more interest is the location of Drake's anchorage. Did he enter San Francisco Bay? If so, was he the first European to see the great bay, or did he remain outside the Golden Gate at what came to be called Drakes Bay? It would seem from the research of Robert Power (1926-91), a restaurateur at the Nut Tree (operated 1921-96) in Vacaville and a trustee of the California Historical Society, that Drake did indeed enter San Francisco Bay. The evidence is at least impressive if not conclusive: an unauthenticated map drawn by Drake of the islands in the Bay as they appear from Point San Quentin, Drake's descriptions of the flora and fauna of the Bay side of Marin (as opposed to what he would have found on the ocean side of Marin), and the improbability of not finding the entrance during an entire month spent in the vicinity. Power's extensive collection of Drake material formed the nucleus of the Drake 400 Exhibit in the City of Plymouth, England, in August 1977; the Exhibit's catalog was presented to Queen Elizabeth II (1926-2022, reigned 1952-2022) and Prince Philip (1921-2021).[11]

Oliver Seeler (1934-2019) was a musician and scholar who has spent many years analyzing what he considers misinformation about Drake. He has minutely examined The World Encompassed, a narrative of the voyage published in 1628, based on the accounts of the ship's chaplain, a Church of England priest, Francis Fletcher (c.1555 - c.1619). Seeler refuted many of the arguments concerning the Golden Hind's anchorage, the impossibility of snow in June, and sexual contact between the crew and the Indians. His work sifts through what he claims is four centuries' accumulation of errors ranging from innocent mistakes to outright fraud. Seeler, as a professional historian, refused to accept at face value the interpretations of primary sources made by earlier examiners. However, his work is also open to scholarly criticism for defying tradition in asserting that Drake's anchorage took place in Oregon or Washington or even Vancouver Island rather than in northern California.

On October 17, 2012 the United States Department of the Interior settled the matter by designating the Drakes Bay Historic and Archaeological District a National Historical Landmark.

In any case Drake's voyage was seen as a potential threat

to Mexican security and to the galleons. Something would have to be done to keep future invaders out. Finding the Strait of Anián headed the list of options. The authorities continued to believe in the strait, though experienced seamen had long doubted its existence except when talking to their credulous political superiors, on whom they depended for their livelihood.

Other English corsairs (as pirates were then called) followed Drake into the Pacific and wreaked havoc on Spanish shipping and towns, robbing and burning ships, and torturing and killing prisoners. Among these corsairs were Thomas Cavendish (1560-92) in 1586 and Richard Hawkins (1562-1622) in 1593-94. All of these used the harbors of Baja as lurking-places. Of Cavendish it was written by a chronicler that his "savage cruelties made even the monkeys bitterly rue their coming to the isthmian [Panama] coast."

In 1587, Francisco Gali, the captain of the galleon *Nuestra Señora de la Esperanza*, with a Filipino crew, was ordered to find the Armenian Islands ("Islas Ricas de Oro y Plata," rich islands of gold and silver, also known as "las Islas del Armenio"), a fictional grouping somewhere between Japan and Canada. He died following the Great Circle eastward. Pedro de Unamuno, who replaced him as captain, briefly sought these islands but concluded that they were fictional. He opted to make for North America instead. Exploring the California coast, he reached Pillar Point (37o30'), sailed south and anchored, penetrating inland at Morro Bay. However, he was driven off by Indians. When the viceroy heard of his rout, he ordered that no more attempts be made to land in that vicinity. As for the Filipinos (known as Luzon Indians) in the crew, these, whose names are unknown, were the first documented Asians to land in North America.[12]

Felipe II had inherited the throne of Portugal (as Felipe I) in 1580, as he was the grandson of Manuel I (ruled 1495-1521), and Spain would hold Portugal for the next 60 years, a confluence of powers that brought many Portuguese to explore alongside the Spanish.

Eight years after Gali's and Unamuno's voyage, Sebastián Rodríguez de Cermeño [sometimes spelled Cermenho] (1560-1602), a Portuguese, reached the rank of galleon captain, being given the *San Augustín*. He was ordered to find the Armenian Islands along the usual route from Manila. He concluded, as had Unamuno, that the islands were non-existent, and, like his predecessor, opted to head for North America. He stopped at Drakes Bay to take refuge from a storm - a grievous mistake, as it turned out. The galleon sank and the treasure it carried was lost. To return to Mexico and whatever awaited them the crew had to use the ship's launches and leapfrogged along the coast, touching the Farallon Islands, the future sites of Santa Cruz and Monterey, the Channel Islands, and several points in Baja. He and his men achieved a mapping of the coast (except for the Golden Gate) not improved on until Vizcaíno in 1602, but Cermeño was bitterly criticized for losing the *San Augustín*. He suffered ethnically motivated criticism, for his Portuguese origin made him a target for quick negative judgments by the Spanish.

While the California coast was being explored to find a protective base for the galleons, interest in New Mexico continued. In 1595, Juan de Oñate (1550-1626) was commissioned by the king to occupy New Mexico and establish new missions. In April 1598, he crossed the Rio Grande near present-day El Paso, went up the river valley to the Pueblo Indians and founded Santa Fe de Nuevo México. He searched unsuccessfully for silver mines. The Pueblos for the most part were welcoming, but the people of the mesa-top sky city of Acoma resisted his demands for goods and killed his nephew in a skirmish. He besieged Acoma, took it, and retaliated cruelly, killing or maiming and enslaving the entire village. In 1601, he went east into Texas and the Central Plains looking for Quivira and had major encounters with the Apaches. In October 1604 he went to the Colorado River and reached the Gulf of California to locate a port by which New Mexico could be supplied rather than by the laborious overland route from New Spain. No suitable place was located, so he returned to Santa Fe four months later. In Santa Fe, his restive settlers, angry about his harsh governance, became difficult to deal with, and the Franciscan missionaries reported his cruel treatment of the Acoma people and other natives. After a less than successful assignment as colonial governor he was removed for cruelty to the settlers and natives in 1606 and exiled from New Mexico, moving to Spain a few years later.

As Oñate was trying to establish control in New Mexico Sebastián Vizcaíno (1548-1624) went in search of coastal pearl fisheries, perhaps in cooperation with Oñate's efforts in the north. The voyages planned for 1595 and 1596 failed because of fires and drownings, but in 1602, he sailed from Cabo San Lucas to Point Reyes. He had been ordered by the Viceroy, the 5th Conde de Monterrey (1560-1606, served 1595-1603), to proceed directly north to explore the coast and not to look for pearls until his return voyage. From what he saw he praised the climate and the Indians, describing them as gentle and peaceable, docile, generous, and friendly, but not very adept at making themselves understood. He also thought some of the coastal tribes were lazy for using pelicans to catch their fish: They would break one wing of a pelican and tie it to a stake, and others would help it by catching fish and bringing a share to the crippled bird. The Indians would then gather the fish. Fray Andrés Asunción, the expedition's chaplain and chronicler (ships often carried a priest for these tasks), reported that the coastal Indians were friendly and generous with their supplies, but that their petty thievery "beat the gypsies in cunning and dexterity."

Vizcaíno's fleet, consisting of three ships, the *San Diego*, the *Santo Tomás*, and the *Tres Reyes*, sailed past Carmel Bay, and on December 16, 1602, rounded Point Pinos and entered the harbor. They went ashore the following day and pitched the church tent under the shade of a (now long-fallen) oak whose branches touched the tidewater, "20 paces from springs of good water in a ravine." (The oak's location was about where the Lighthouse Avenue tunnel leading from Monterey to Cannery Row emerges today at Cannery Row.) Most of the sailors were suffering from scurvy, and sixteen had already died. In the shadow of this historic tree, Fray Asunción celebrated the first recorded mass north of San Diego.

The morning of December 17 was foggy, but the fog cleared as mass ended. After mass it was decided to send one of the vessels back to Mexico to carry the sick and to report on the expedition's progress, unfortunately not realizing that those with scurvy did not need more sea travel. Later that day the party set up camp on the shore and remained in the area until January 3, 1603. The party worked on the ships, and on December 29, the *Santo Tomás*, carrying the sick, as well as news of the expedition, was dispatched to Acapulco. The voyage was one of great suffering; only nine of the crew of 25 survived.

After the *Santo Tomás* departed, the remaining crewmen turned their attention to readying the remaining two vessels for the voyage north, an effort hampered by cold weather. Fray Andrés recorded that on Christmas Day the mountains near the port were covered with snow, and New Year's morning found the water holes frozen "to the depth of a palm." By Friday, January 3, 1603, most of the chores were completed, and Vizcaíno, Fray Andrés, and ten arquebusiers were able to explore inland to the southeast. About three leagues away they discovered another port, with a respectable river descending from snow-covered mountains -- Carmel Bay and the Carmel River. They spotted elk, but they were unable to kill any. This cold weather may have had something to do with the Little Ice Age, a period of bitter winters and mild summers that affected the Northern Hemisphere between the mid-14th and early 19th centuries, although this cannot be verified in the absence of settlements and written records; we know that the Little Ice Age did affect southern Mexico and the northern Rocky Mountains.

They encountered no people but saw a village about a league away. When they investigated, they found it deserted, and speculated that the inhabitants had taken refuge in the interior to escape the cold. It is generally thought this was the village of Tucutnut, about a league from where Carmel Mission was subsequently located. This is the only village mentioned. The Monterey Peninsula area apparently was uninhabited in January 1603. Vizcaíno, however, reported that the land was thickly populated with "numberless Indians", and that a great many came several times to their camp at Monterey. He comments that they indicated by signs that there were many settlements inland.

They sailed at midnight that night, never to return.

As church scholar, Msgr. James Culleton (1898-1978), summarized the effort:

> Vizcaíno had been sent to find a good port. He located but two worthy of any name and he pictured one of them as perfect. To attract the Church, he peopled Monterey with numberless ideal Indians though he saw but one deserted *rancheria*. To entice colonists,

he spoke of much fertile land while he stood on sand overlooked by mountains. While numb with cold he wrote that the climate was like Seville's. . . So untrue was this picture that Portolá and Crespi [in 1769] failed to recognize the place.[13]

Vizcaíno thought Monterey Bay the best Pacific port and named it for the viceroy, the Conde de Monterrey. Besides renaming Monterey he also permanently renamed San Diego, Santa Catalina, San Buenaventura, Santa Barbara, Point Concepción, Point Pinos, Carmel, and Point Reyes; in most cases naming the spot for the saint's day or religious feast day on which it was reached. (For example, on December 4, 1602, the feast of St. Barbara, he reached Santa Barbara.)

Having arrived at Point Reyes the Vizcaíno group spent some time in Drakes Bay (which the Spaniards knew as Puerto de San Francisco) and then went north. As the weather turned colder and foggier, and more of his men sickened, Vizcaíno turned back. Although under orders to go as far as Cape Mendocino, they reached as far north as 41o or 42o. Neither Vizcaíno nor Asunción left much useful information about the coast above Point Reyes.

Back in Mexico Vizcaino reported to the viceroy, who was very pleased with his report and chose him as captain of the next year's galleon. King Felipe III (1578-1621, reigned 1598-1621), although rather indifferent to government or the Empire, awarded Vizcaíno money and promoted Monterey to the viceroyalty of Peru. The new viceroy, the Marquis of Montesclaros (1571-1628, served 1603-07), desiring to quash as much as possible of his predecessor's administration, ignored his suggestions for settlement, reasoning that by the time the galleons reached Monterey Bay they were in the home stretch of the trans-Pacific voyage, and in no need of a stopping place so far north. In addition, he cancelled

Vizcaíno's appointment as galleon captain, never bestowed a monetary award ordered by the king, and even hanged Vizcaíno's cartographer, whom he falsely accused of forgery. As a result, Alta California was shelved for 170 years, during which time the frontier advanced up the Mexican coast, into Arizona, and over to Baja California, coming only a step or two away from the future state of California.

The Jesuit Province

In the 17th century, the preferred unit of frontier expansion was the mission. Travelers in California, Arizona and northwestern Mexico are inclined to think of the mission as merely a church and some little amount of surrounding land set up to be permanent. However, the mission on the Spanish frontier was a self-sufficient yet temporary economic unit. It had many duties: to congregate the Indians in a pueblo, to teach them the Catholic religion and the Spanish language, and to teach them a trade and the customs and rudiments of Spanish life. Whether this was good or bad is irrelevant; the old days were gone forever, and the Indians had no choice but to adapt if they were to survive. The Spanish kings were devoted to the Church, and mission expenses were lumped with the upkeep of presidios (military forts) in royal bookkeeping. Only temporary, the missions were to be replaced in a generation or two by a parish church and native-born clergy, mission lands having been given to their converted natives.

There were several reasons that missions were chosen over other forms of settlement, and the location of the missions was planned and deliberate. Wherever possible they would be built by the sea so that they could easily supply ships that came to port there. The Spanish kings hoped that someday there would be powerful cities and harbors in the colonies. To support the cities, which would buy and sell things, they had to have farms to produce things. They decided to create a series of farms along the coast. Each would be a day's ride or hard walk apart. In that way, it would be easy to trade and sell goods, and relay information. Many were placed along native trails because the Spanish knew that the Indians always made their trails near fresh water and fertile soil, two things that the Spanish needed for successful missions. Another reason for building them along native trails was to make recruiting people even easier.

The only problem with their plan was a lack of labor. With few Spanish people in the area, there would be very few to work the farms, so the labor of the missions fell to the Indians, who did not speak a European language, and had dark skin and a very different way of life. The Spanish viewed their way of life as inferior, particularly before their conversion to the Catholic faith. Clearly, working on the missions was not optional, and the Indians became slaves or prisoners since they could not leave, but the priest-Indian relationship was feudal in that the mission priests would protect them from other Spaniards and hostile tribes.

The missions included more than a church. There were also a rectory, Indian quarters, granaries and storerooms, workshops for carpentry, blacksmithing, weaving, and the making of pottery, candles, and soap. On surrounding land there were corrals, irrigated fields, and grazing land.

The missions were designed by the padres and built by the Indians they hoped to convert. Each mission was unique in a few ways, but they all had the same basic plan: a large, four-sided building with a patio in the center. The church was usually placed in one corner of the square, always the tallest and grandest structure. All the rooms in the square building faced the patio. The back was reserved for the unmarried native women who worked in the kitchen. The other three sides contained rooms for the two priests of the mission, workshops, a kitchen, storage rooms for food, and the mission office. The rest of the Indians lived outside the mission walls in huts. Surrounding the mission were the vast fields used for growing crops and feeding livestock.

In addition to the actual missions the missionaries also established *visitas*, subordinate mission stations with a church and inhabitants, operated under the mission system but without a resident priest. They were to contribute to the missions' upkeep with animals and crops, and in return the mission priest would visit these outposts and perform his religious duties.[14]

In Mexico, as a rule, the Indians who were brought to the missions seemed to prefer living as neophytes under the padres' supervision and control rather than in their former barbaric state. This may have been due to the security and protection of human life which the priests imposed, for practices such as abortion, infanticide, human sacrifice, and killing the old and infirm were absolutely prohibited while protection from enemy raiders was provided.

A three-pronged mission movement north began by the end of the century: up the west coast by the Jesuits, and into the central plains and the northeast by Franciscans.

The area that is today Sinaloa had been conquered in 1531 by Nuño de Guzmán (1490-1558) and a force of over 10,000 men who defeated a force of 30,000 Cahita warriors. He then built an outpost at San Miguel de Culiacán. Sinaloa then became part of the *gobierno* (government) of Nueva Galicia. Indian wars continued to break out but by the 1620s these had ended.

In 1591 a Jesuit province was created to embrace the west coast from Nayarit to the Gila River, carrying the frontier one step from California. The first mission was at San Felipe in Sinaloa, with 2,000 converts the first year, which the 30-year-old Father Gonzalo de Tapia had made with his humor, courage, and ready speech. Two other priests soon joined him. Three years later Father Tapia became the first martyr on the frontier when he was killed on the Fuerte River by a shaman, Nacabeba, whom he had caught stealing according to one account, while another alleged that Nacabeba and several other Indians were whipped at *alcalde* Manuel de Maldonado's orders for refusing to adore the cross and accept Spanish acculturation. This induced the authorities to send a guard under Captain Diego Martínez de Hurdaide (1564-1626), noted for being bowlegged, to protect the priests. To ensure continued protection and hoped-for conversions, a presidio was built in Sinaloa in 1595, and Captain Martínez de Hurdaide was put in command of it from 1599 until 1626.

Little by little the frontier was pushed north. By 1600 there were 10,000 converts and eight missions, and by 1624, 100,000 converts. By 1646 there were 35 missions along the coast, each caring for about three or four Indian villages. By 1680 the Catholic mission frontier stretched from Monterrey (in Nuevo León) to the Conchos River (in Coahuila), swept northward to include the numerous Franciscan stations in New Mexico, and reached the Pacific at the Sonora River. Behind lay a land of civilized and Catholic convert natives, ahead a land of unsaved souls that lured the missionaries farther inland. To the northeast the road was blocked by the hostile Apache, but to the north and northwest lay the domain known to the Spaniards as Pimería Alta. There, the missionaries first entered the American Southwest.

In the vanguard was an Italian-born priest who almost singlehandedly won a new domain for Spain. Fray Eusebio Kino (1645-1711), a man "merciful to others but cruel to himself," a fine scholar who arrived in 1681 requesting an assignment to the frontier. He was sent to the Sonora borderland in 1687.[15] Fray Kino built the mission station of Dolores high on the San Miguel River, and threw himself into the task of winning heathen souls, founding a mission chain along the Altar and Magdalena rivers. Fray Eusebio was never content so long as unsaved humans or unexplored lands lay before him. A tough man, he frequently visited his Indians, sometimes riding 75 miles (120 km) a day and averaging 25 miles (40 km) daily in the saddle. A priest, he was also a cattle king, with a long list of accomplishments beyond that: He planted garden crops and orchards and established pack trains to connect the missions with the older settlements. In 1691 his evangelizing wanderlust carried him into Arizona where, along the Santa Cruz and San Pedro valleys, he found natives eager for the Gospel. There, among the rising Canelo Hills, the thickets of oak, the towering mountains and the broad sweep of the valley, a mission was built, and cattle ranches were established to ensure a food supply. In 1700 Father Kino led a party northward to lay out the mission of San Xavier del Bac, near today's Tucson.[16] Other missions - eventually a total of 20 - were established, and cattle ranches and farms followed as settlers moved in. Between projects he baptized Pima, Papago, Sabaipuris, Cocopah, Yuma and Maricopa Indians, and organized an effective defense against the Apaches. Over all these he ruled with benevolence, while maintaining a deep interest in exploration. He made a total of fourteen journeys of several hundred to a thousand miles each, either alone or with a few companions - especially the faithful soldier, Juan Manuel Manje (1670-1727?) - and on his death in 1711 left a series of excellent maps which remained the standard for the Pimería region for 150 years. Padre Kino's cause – the investigative process leading to sainthood – is advancing in Rome.[17]

After Vizcaíno's voyage, the only interest anyone had in Baja was in its pearls. There were at least four licensed expeditions and numerous unlicensed ones. Poachers took the risk to avoid paying the *quinto* (the 20% tax). The records of the six representative ones show less than illustrious results.

In 1611 the king gave Venetian native Tomás de Cardona a monopoly on pearls in the viceroyalty. His agents started in the West Indies and in three years had gotten to Acapulco. His nephew and agent Nicolás de Cardona would supervise the explorations in the Gulf of California.

In 1615 Juan de Iturbe, working for Nicolás, reported his belief that California was an island, in agreement with Cortés and Oñate but contrary to Ulloa. This belief was understandable for someone who had not gone up the Gulf as Ulloa and others had, for the bay of La Paz is at least a hundred miles (160 km) from the Mexican mainland.[18] Though the expedition was profitable, Iturbe lost a good portion of his pearl take to the Dutch pirate Jan Spilberg (1568-1620), who had come into the Pacific and raided towns on the Mexican coast, capturing Cardona's pearl ship San Francisco at Zacatula.

The Dutch as allies of England were generally hostile to Spain, against whose tyranny they had rebelled, and pirates such as Spilberg preyed on Spanish shipping routinely. The harbors of Baja offered good hiding places from which to attack the galleons. These Dutch pirates were called "pichilingües" (or "chest-speakers") because of the guttural sound of their speech.[19]

In 1627 Martín de Lezama, Vizcaíno's son-in-law, began building a pearl-fishing ship at San Blas but was defeated by swarms of mosquitoes. In 1632-36 Francisco Ortega took many pearls and was able to alert the authorities of the presence of "pichilingües."

In 1644 Pedro Porter y Casanate (1611-62) was able to warn the Manila Galleon of the "pichilingües," picking up a few pearls on the way back. In 1648 he planned to fish for pearls but encountered many bureaucratic problems regarding his pearl fishing licensing in Spain and Mexico. He managed to overcome them with the support of the viceroy. Another major setback was the loss of one of his two ships in a fire, so he accomplished very little in Baja aside from exploration of the gulf and the west coast, for which Felipe IV (1605-65, reigned 1621-65) named him admiral. Though his service in Baja was not stellar, he had a long list of accomplishments in the royal service, being considered an expert in naval matters whose works were published in Spain and England. In 1656 he was promoted to governor of Chile.

Bernardo Bernal de Pynadero (1630-?), the licensee in 1664 and 1666, made one of the richest hauls in pearls because of his cruelties. The Indians were enslaved and forced to dive for pearls under a quota system that carried the punishment of maiming by severing of hands or feet. When "pichilingües" attacked they were beaten off. His men then quarreled over the division of the treasure, and some ended up killing each other. The Audiencia of Guadalajara impounded his ships temporarily, but he sailed again in 1667 or 1668 without any significant incidents. On his return to Spain, he was charged and investigated for cruelty to the natives but apparently eluded punishment.

Francisco de Lucenilla received the license in 1668, but his attempt failed when the paltry haul did not justify the expense. After his return, voyages to California were temporarily suspended.

Historian John Caughey (1902-95) sums up the century

and a half of pearling:

> That pearl fishing at the "Island of California" far
> exceeded the revealed record is likely. Known facts
> include use of Negro as well as Indian divers; trade
> with the Indians, though most of their pearls had been
> spoiled by fire; some finds of excellent pearls,
> including one valued at 4,500 pesos; interference by
> Pichilingues and rumors of Pichilingues. The pearlers
> accomplished no more than temporary and
> interrupted residence on the scene.[20]

In 1683 Isidro Atondo y Antillón (1639-?), the governor of
Sinaloa (whose authority extended to Baja), went with Padre
Kino the cartographer to La Paz for pearl fishing and
colonization. The expedition failed after two years because of
Indian hostility (with memories of Pynadero still fresh) and
land scurvy. Kino, however, would add fresh evidence to the
debate over California as an island.

In 1699 Kino went from Pimería to Yuma, on the east side
of the Colorado River. There he saw shells used for money
that were of the same type he had seen at La Paz when he was
with Atondo. La Paz and Yuma are about 1,200 kilometers
apart and on opposite sides of the water. When he saw the
Colorado River from the Santa Clara Mountains in Arizona,
he knew that it was a river and not part of the ocean. These
discoveries convinced him that Baja is a peninsula.
Nevertheless, belief in the island was shown on maps until
1746, which name the water separating the island from the
mainland Mare Rubium, or Red Sea.[21]

Despite the presence of pearls, Baja had been an
unqualified failure. No settlement attempts had succeeded, so,
as a last resort, the Spanish crown gave Baja to the Jesuits. To
sweeten the deal, for Baja appeared to be a white elephant, the

Jesuits were given various privileges.

In 1697 Italian-born Padre Juan María de Salvatierra (1648-1717) was sent to the peninsula after working in Chihuahua and Sinaloa for a dozen years, and he started a mission at San Bruno, near Isidro Atondo's fort. Later, he moved his mission headquarters to Loreto, which became the capital of the Californias. By the time he died in 1717 he had founded five other missions (San Francisco Javier de Viggé-Biaundó, San Juan Bautista Malibat, Santa Rosaliá de Mulegé, San José de Comondú, and the Visita de San Juan Bautista Londo). In the next few years other missionaries joined him: Padres Francisco María Picolo (1654-1729), Juan de Ugarte (1662-1730) and Jayme Bravo.

He was not Father Kino missionizing over long distances, converting, studying, building, and planting, so what accounted for his success? Maize porridge. As in a later century Catholic and Protestant Christian missionary in China attracted Chinese by free rice (hence the phenomenon of "rice Christians"), and just as church soup-kitchens, in the U.S. mostly, until recently, required transients to hear a sermon before they got a bowl of soup, so did Father Salvatierra with the Indians of lower Baja. Some authorities report that the natives had a mostly shellfish diet while others say that they were accustomed to an unpalatable mixture of varying ingredients known as we-wish; maize porridge was a major step toward a more enjoyable diet for them and perhaps more nutritious as well.[22]

As soon as he landed in Baja, he began to recruit Indians to help build his missions, rewarding the workers with porridge and withholding it from those who refused to work. The latter demanded some of the porridge, but Salvatierra held his ground and refused to pay for no work. When the non-working Indians became violent, Salvatierra had his soldiers fire on them from their swivel gun. Both the Indians and the Spaniards were surprised when the gun exploded. The next day the Indians returned, seeking peace. Father Salvatierra had scored his point, and from then on, the work of mission building and conversions would be easier.

There were other instances where he proved his mettle. Once, when Indians attacked, he went out to reason with them. Arrows were shot at him but lodged in the folds of his robe. Another time he and a companion were saved when arrows meant for them struck the pavilion housing the image of Our Lady of Loreto, patroness of the Baja missions. On a third occasion he was called to baptize a dying Indian and lost his way. He gave free rein to his mule, and it took him to the *rancheria* where the dying man lived.[23]

Fr. Salvatierra left Baja for Mexico City to take up the duties of Provincial Superior of the Jesuits in 1704, but returned to Loreto when his term was up in 1707. In 1717 he was called back to Mexico City by the viceroy to provide material for a history of California which had been ordered by King Felipe V (1683-1746, ruled 1700-46, except for January-September, 1724). He was sick but made the journey anyway, sailing across the Gulf, but upon reaching Guadalajara he died.

Salvatierra was succeeded by Father Ugarte (1662-1730), the missionary at San Javier. Ugarte was a promoter for the Pious Fund of the Californias, a charity for the support of missions to which many wealthy individuals in Mexico, Central America and Spain contributed in life or provided for in their wills.[24]

Father Ugarte first arrived at Loreto in 1701, and the next year he went to Mission San Francisco Javier de Viggé-Biaundó, which had been abandoned in 1701 because of the hostility of the fierce Waicuri Indians. He started by overawing them when he began attacking, with no terrible consequences, one of their sacred rocks. He then put some to work cutting timber for a ship, *El Triunfo de la Cruz*. He used the *Triunfo* to explore the coast to find new mission sites or to learn more of the geography; for example, in 1720 he sailed from Loreto to La Paz and founded a mission. In 1721 he sailed again in the *Triunfo* to the head of the Gulf to try to settle the question: peninsula or island?

The bravery he exhibited when he first arrived was shown on other occasions, as when he quelled an uprising by grabbing the two ringleaders by their hair and cracking their skulls together. He also started agriculture in the peninsula with successful crops at Mission San Javier (which had a history of crop failure), and his successful methods spread to other missions, along with stock raising.[25]

San Javier had become his home, and by the time he died in 1730, the number of missions had grown to fourteen. In 1720 La Purísima Concepción de Cadegomó, Nuestra Señora del Pilar de La Paz Airapí, and Nuestra Señora de Guadalupe de Huasinapi were founded, followed by Santiago de Los Coras and Nuestra Señora de los Dolores del Sur Chillá in 1721, San Ignacio Kadakaamán in 1728 and Estero de las Palmas de San José del Cabo Añuiti in 1730.

In 1732 the king separated Sinaloa y Sonora from Nueva Vizcaya and in the following year Manuel Bernal Huidobro was made governor of the new province. This would lead to some problems as Huidobro had no love for the Jesuits.[26]

In 1734 a rebellion broke out led by Chicori and Botón, two *zambos* (black-Indians) who were angered when the priests tried to suppress polygamy. Two priests, three soldiers and 27 Catholic convert Indians were killed in the south until

124

Captain Estevan Rodríguez Lorenzo (c.1665-1746) took about two dozen soldiers and Indian allies from La Paz into rebel territory, though he was unable to crush the revolt. As the rebels spread north, Rodríguez was recalled to Mexico, and the missionaries concentrated their forces at Loreto.

Another native, Gerónimo, became the rebel leader, and had some successes. The rebels, however, numbering about 600 by this time, really went too far in trying to capture the Manila galleon. The galleon put into the harbor to replenish supplies and 12 men were sent ashore. The rebels captured them and tried to lure the rest of the crew ashore so that the ship could be taken. They failed, but this attempt prompted Governor Huidobro to come over from Sinaloa with an army of soldiers and Yaqui Indian allies to crush the revolt, although Gerónimo escaped immediate punishment. The area remained unpacified for eleven years until a measles epidemic wiped out most of the rebellious natives.

Following the ancient Roman example, the Spanish created vast networks of roads which were designated *caminos reales* (royal roads), routes that communicated to the different regions governed by the crown, always under the protection of the army.

During and after the conquest, roads were constructed in New Spain that received the same designation. A letter written by Padre José Echeverria on February 10, 1730, to the Marquis of Villapuente tells him that with respect to roads that were passable, in California in only thirty-four years more progress had been accomplished from the beginning of the conquest than in Spain during the preceding two centuries. El Camino Real, the "Royal Missionary Road of the Californias" began with the establishment of the Mission Nuestra Señora de Loreto in 1697. The corridor continued southward to the region of Los Cabos, and northward, crossing the present border with the United States. 126 years later the Camino was finally finished, reaching Sonoma, California.

The Jesuit need for roads was apparent as soon as they consolidated their first religious center at Loreto and began their travels to convert bordering native communities. The first written consignment document to build a road was in 1698, and in 1699 a road crossing the Sierra de la Gigantea westward to establish Mission San Javier was laid. From this beginning, the road was extended with the establishment of each mission northward and southward. The roads connected the mission centers and water sources, and crossed lands presenting as few obstacles as possible.

The last six Jesuit establishments were founded in 1733-1767: Santa Rosa de las Palmas (Todos Santos, 1733), San Luis Gonzaga Chiriyaqui (1740), Santa Gertrudis (1752), San Francisco Borja (1762), the Visita de Calamajué (1766), and Santa María de los Ángeles (1767).

Despite this growth on paper, after over a half century of mission colonization, Baja was barely self-supporting. Apart from the missions' success in evangelizing the native populations the missions were a failure insofar as they did nothing to stimulate further advances. The Jesuits were supposed to make the missions self-supporting, but they continued to rely on the Pious Fund and the royal treasury. "Grow or die," a motto of successful capitalism, seems to have been a natural law of the missions as well.

In 1700 the frontier threat from the French movement toward Texas from Louisiana was somewhat diminished upon the death of the last Hapsburg king of Spain, the insane and impotent Carlos II (1661-1700, reigned 1665-1700), and the coronation of the grandson of Louis XIV (1638-1715, reigned 1643-1715), the Bourbon king of France. Carlos might have been insane, but he was not stupid. No one – not even the English – had done so much to hurt Spain as Louis XIV, but Carlos knew that if the Bourbons controlled Spain they would protect its empire. Philip, Louis' grandson, duly became Felipe V. A general European war broke out, the War of Spanish Succession (1701-14), to prevent this consolidation of power for the Bourbons: France and Spain (with Bavaria, Cologne and Mantua) fighting England, the Dutch Republic, the Holy Roman Empire, Piedmont-Savoy, Prussia, Portugal, and the Hapsburg adherents in Spain. In the end, though, the principal provisions of Carlos II's will prevailed. Austria got Spain's European possessions, Felipe received the Spanish Empire and Spain, but renounced his inheritance to the French throne. This arrangement preserved the balance of power in Europe but had little effect on the Americas, except that the Bourbons had replaced the Hapsburgs as imperial masters.

The Bourbons introduced a more efficient governing system, with a new functionary: the *visitador* (an inspector-general with nearly unlimited powers).

With both France and Spain ruled by the same family, war between them was practically unthinkable, a peaceful state of affairs formalized by a document known as the "Family Compact". French styles and ideas, popular all over Europe, became the way upper-class Spaniards thought and dressed. Among the popular French thinkers, the philosophes such as Voltaire (1712-78) and Jean Jacques Rousseau (1694-1778), religion was anathema *("Ecrasez l'infâme,"* Voltaire declared. "Crush the infamous thing," the "thing" in question being the Catholic faith. The Catholic church was especially hated, and the Jesuit Order, as the brightest priestly order in that church, was detested. Hatred of the Jesuits stemmed from their wealth and suspicion of their influence through royal court connections.

In the 1750s, Portugal and France expelled the Jesuits from their kingdoms and their overseas empires, and in 1767 Spain followed their lead, accusing the order of mismanaging its missions in Paraguay and of hoarding vast treasures. Under pressure from these monarchs and Austria, Pope Clement XIV (1705-74, reigned 1769-74) suppressed the order throughout the world in 1773, although non-Catholic countries such as Russia and Prussia ignored the ban, not allowing a papal edict to be published in their countries, so allowing the Jesuits into their realms.

In 1814 Pope Pius VII (1742-1823, reigned 1800-23) restored the order throughout the world.

Carlos III's *visitador*, José de Gálvez (1720-87), was entrusted with the expulsion task in New Spain. He sent Gaspar de Portolá (1716-86) to carry it out in Baja. Portolá gently removed the sixteen Baja Jesuits from their twenty missions with little native resistance. In other parts of the empire, notably Mexico City and Paraguay, troops had to suppress angry pro-Jesuit demonstrators. Their Baja missions were given to the Franciscans.

The northwest push had halted but not for long. A new threat to Mexican security loomed in the north - the Russians.

Chapter Three END NOTES

[1] "Columbus actually landed 65 miles from San Salvador" *Fresno Bee*, October 9, 1986, p. A16.

[2] Lindsey Williams, "Buddhist Monks Discovered America Before Columbus." LAL Archives. October 11, 1998, http://www.lindseywilliams.org/index.htm?LAL_Archives/Buddhist_Monks_Discovered_America_Before_Columbus.htm~mainFrame. Frank Cliff, "The Chinese Discovered America," *Oakland Tribune Magazine*, March 4, 1923, p. 6.

[3] James H. McClintock, *Arizona, Prehistoric, Aboriginal, Pioneer, Modern: The Nation's Youngest Commonwealth Within a Land of Ancient Culture*, vol. 1, (Chicago: S.J. Clarke, 1916), p. 8.

[4] Tom Smith, John S. Bowman, Maurice Isserman, *Discovery of the Americas, 1492-1800*. (New York: Infobase Publishing, 2009), p. 116.

[5] Ralph Emerson Twitchell, *Leading Facts of New Mexican History*, vol. 1, (1912; Santa Fe NM: Sunstone Press, 2007), p. 178n.

[6] Rose Marie Beebe and Robert M. Senkewicz, *Lands of Promise and Despair: Chronicles of Early California, 1535-1846*, (Berkeley: Heyday, 2001), 9-11; "Now the jets get you quickly to Cabo San Lucas for the superb big-game fishing and so much else," *Sunset*, (October 1977), p. 82.

[7] Juan José Sánchez Arresigor, "From Asia to America: Conquering the Pacific," *National Geographic History*, (August-September 2015), p. 19.

[8] "Clues to Ancient Galleon Off L.A.", San Francisco Chronicle, October 14, 1974, p. 23.

[9] "Historian Says Golden Hind Visited SF, Not Drakes Bay", *Fresno Bee*, September 23, 1973; "Drake Plaque Called Hoax" *San Francisco Chronicle*, October 11, 1974, p. 1; "New Clue to Drake Landing", San Francisco Chronicle, November 9, 1974, p. 3; "'Golden Hinde II' Begins Voyage to San Francisco", *California Historical Society Courier* (abbreviated *CHSC*), (October 1974), p. 8; "Golden Hinde Blows Into SF For Big Welcome", *Fresno Bee*, March 10, 1975, p. 1.

[10] Harold Gilliam, "The Mystery of Sir Francis' Bay Visit" *San Francisco Examiner and Chronicle*, March 25, 1979, World, p. 39.

[11] "Robert H. Power Escorts Queen Elizabeth to Drake 400 Exhibition," *CHSC*, (November-December 1977), p. 6.

[12] Eloisa Gomez Borah, "Filipinos in Unamuno's California Expedition of 1587", *Amerasia Journal*, 21:3 (Winter 1995/1996), pp. 175-183.

[13] Gary Breschini, "Vizcaíno's Exploration of Monterey Bay 1602-1603," pp. 8-9, www.mchmuseum.com/Vizcaino.html

[14] "Baja California Mission Visitas," www.Vivabaja.com/missions3/.

[15] Ray Allen Billington and Martin Ridge, *Westward Expansion: A History of the American Frontier*, 6th ed. (Albuquerque: University of New Mexico Press, 2001), p. 71.

[16] "Arizona Missions Take Visitors Back in Time," *Fresno Bee*, February 8, 1976, p. C6.

[17] Kino Heritage Society: Sainthood Cause, (accessed September 5, 2015) http://padrekino.com/index.php/kino-heritage-society/cannonization/

[18] A legend grew up around "the Pearl Ship of Juan de Iturbe," according to which the ship, about the size of one of Columbus' caravels, was blown by winds to the Imperial Valley and now rests at the bottom of the Salton Sea. Charley Clusker's 1862 attempt to find it was the subject a television documentary that no longer is available on American Heroes Channel's "The Lost Ship of the Mojave Desert." Other references are Kristin Scharkey, "5 Facts about the lost ship of the desert: What we actually know," *Palm Springs Desert Sun*, December 2, 2019, https://www.desertsun.com/story/desert-magazine/2019/12/02/5-facts-lost-ship-california-desert-what-we-know/3981175002/ and Boo Difley, "The Lost Ship in the Desert," DesertUSA, https://www.desertusa.com/desert-activity/lost-ship-desert.html. While this legend circulated widely, it is groundless as the vessel returned to Mexico.

[19] There is another theory that the word has nothing to do with Dutch pirates. Leeds's Singing Organ-Grinder, "Pirates and Kleinecke's etymology of 'pidgin,'" November 15, 2004 (accessed February 8, 2024) https://elorganillero.com/blog/2004/11/15/pirates-and-kleineckes-etymology-of-pidgin/

[20] John Caughey, *California: A Remarkable State's Life History*, 3rd ed., (Englewood Cliffs NJ: Prentice-Hall, 1970), p. 43.

[21] "When California Was an Island," *Oakland Tribune*, August 5, 1923, p. 4W.

[22] Anent diet cf Peter Masten Dunne, "Salvatierra's Legacy to Lower California," *The Americas*, 7:1 (July 1950), pp. 42-43, Los

Cabos, "8 Facts about the Pericues Tribe that populated Los Cabos," July 30, 2018, (accessed February 7, 2024) https://www.visitloscabos.travel/blog/post/8-facts-pericues-tribe-populated-los-cabos/#:~:text=6%20%2D%20Their%20primary%20diet%20was,%2C%20agave%2C%20and%20wild%20plums, and W. Michael Mathes, "History 165:History of the Spanish Borderlands" (lecture, University of San Francisco, San Francisco, CA, Fall 1967).

[23] This story reflects a pivotal moment when St. Ignatius of Loyola, founder of the Jesuits, argued with a Moor encountered on the road to Monserrat. After the Moor expressed doubts about the perpetual virginity of Mary, and the two had parted company, Ignatius brooded over whether to seek revenge on the man. Arriving at a crossroads, he left the decision as to whether to seek blood revenge up to his mule, letting the reins go slack. The mule took the road away from the Moor's destination, which Ignatius took as divine guidance away from such revenge.

[24] In 1902 an old but friendly dispute between the United States and Mexico over the disposition of the Fund provided the first case heard by the Hague Tribunal (the U.S. had inherited the Catholic church's claim when California was taken from Mexico); Baron d'Estournelles (1852-1924), a strong advocate for the Hague Peace process, begged President Theodore Roosevelt (1858-1919, served 1901-09), a man the world believed to be an advocate of violence, to breathe life into the Court. The president told John Hay (1838-1905), his secretary of state, to find something for the Court, this case was dug up and the Mexican government agreed to have it heard. Barbara Tuchman, *The Proud Tower: A Portrait of the World Before the War 1890-1914* (New York: Macmillan, 1966), p. 273.

[25] Thomas Sheridan, *Empire of Sand: The Seri Indians and the Struggle for Spanish Sonora, 1645-1803*. (Tucson: University of Arizona Press, 1999), p. 124n.

[26] Harry Crosby, *Antigua California: Mission and Colony on the Peninsular Frontier, 1697-1768* (Albuquerque: University of New Mexico Press, 1994), p. 199.

Chapter Three FURTHER READING

1.   Dunne, Peter Masten. *Black Robes in Lower California.* Berkeley: University of California Press, 1952.

2. Fouché, Gyladys. "North-West Passage Is Now Plain Sailing." *Guardian*, August 28, 2007. https://www.theguardian.com/environment/2007/aug/28/climatech ange.internationalnews.

3. *Probaway*, "The fake Drake Plate was created by Conan Doyle," March 8, 2009. https://probaway.wordpress.com/2009/03/08/the-fake-drake-plate-was-created-by-conan-doyle/

Part 2: The Beginning of Civilization (1769-1847)

Chapter 4: Planting the Colony

The Russians

In 1581, Ermak Timofeevich (c1532-84), a Cossack land-pirate and mercenary for the powerful Stroganov trading family, went east across the Urals into Siberia with 840 men and began the Russian conquest of that land. Other Cossack hetmen (military and administrative commanders) followed, and by 1649 they had founded Okhotsk at the juncture of the Okhota and Kakhtuy Rivers on the Pacific. The warlike Chukchi people, who live at the tip of Siberia, were annexed, but not conquered, in the next century.

In 1714 Peter the Great (1672-1725), who reigned 1682-1725, sent a party of shipbuilders to Okhotsk so that the furs in Kamchatka could be accessed faster than by land. In 1728 Vitus Bering (1681-1741), a Dane sailing for Russia, discovered the strait named for him. In 1741 he commanded a second expedition to the Pacific with two new ships, the *Sv Piotr* (*St. Peter*), which he captained, and the *Sv Pavel* (*St. Paul*), captained by Aleksei Chirikov (1703-48). They discovered Alaska, landing at Kayak Island in the Aleutians. Bering became ill and unable to command his ship, the St. Peter, and his men returned to Kamchatka. In the Commander Islands group near Kamchatka the St. Peter was wrecked in a storm, and Bering died, probably of heart failure (though it was long believed to have been from scurvy) on the island named in his honor. His surviving crew reconstructed the St. Peter and brought sea otter pelts to Petropavlovsk (in Kamchatka), stimulating the demand that lured fur traders to the new coasts. Chirikov went on to discover Alaska's Aleksander Archipelago, though he was prevented from doing much exploring due to the loss of both of his longboats.

Russian fur hunters, known as *promyshlenniki*, led by Stepan Glotov (1729-69) first landed on Unalaska, in the Aleutian Islands, in 1759. Relations with the Aleut natives turned sour in 1763-66 when they destroyed four Russian ships (the *Zacharias and Elizabeth*, the *Holy Trinity*, the *John*, and the *Adrian and Natalie*), killing 300 Russian hunters, some by ruse luring them into an attack and others by direct attack as they slept. Captain Ivan Solov'ev (sometimes Soloviev) returned to Unalaska and directed the massacre of hundreds of natives. The Russians then established their first permanent post in the Aleutian Islands, Unalaska, in 1774. Their next post was set up in 1784 at Kodiak, closer to the mainland. By then the relationship between the Russians and the Aleuts were peaceful but hardly amicable: The Aleuts understood that the Russians would have to be appeased if a repeat of Solov'ev's revenge was to be averted, so they became the Russians' hunters along with those from Russia. After all, the Aleuts' harpoons were better suited to seal hunting than the Russians' muskets.

The Russians enslaved the natives for marine hunting since they preferred hunting land animals. On some islands the Russians got along with the natives, on others not, but the Aleuts became dependent on a barter economy as they desired Russian goods. Those who were enslaved had no choice, but others hunted for furs to trade for goods, soon depleting the animals with the result that more posts were established down the coast, through the Inside Passage and on to what became British Columbia.

In 1759 Father José Torrubia (1698-1768), a former missionary in the Philippines whose interests spanned from religion to history to fossils, researching material for the official Franciscan history of Mexico, received in Rome, from the Imperial Academy in St. Petersburg, a published report detailing Bering's voyages and an accompanying map that showed the passage between Asia and North America. The implication was alarming: The Russians could sail to California and threaten Spain's holdings in Mexico. In Rome, he composed a report, I *Moscoviti nella California* (*The Muscovites in California*), opening with "Whoever imagined? Who said so? How could it be? How are they going to get there?"

When the royal court in Madrid was apprised of the report, the Spanish ambassador in St. Petersburg was instructed to investigate, "with the greatest cunning and deceit," Russian attempts to sail to America." The fears resulting from the ambassador's findings spurred the Spanish government's determination to occupy the coast north of the Baja peninsula.

Gálvez and the "Sacred Expeditions"

Carlos III (born 1716, ruled 1759-88) was the greatest of the Spanish Bourbon kings. He reformed the royal government, reduced taxes, created a police force, encouraged industry, modernized education, and gave Spain an efficiency it had not seen in over a century. He introduced the offices of *intendente* (intendant) and *visitador* (inspector) into the colonies, which extended efficiency to the empire as well as throughout the "mother country", as Spain was called by its colonials, la *"madre patria."*

The *visitador* was a sort of inspector-general appointed by the king and charged with investigating the administration of the viceroy and other officials. At the end of the inquiry, or *visita*, the *visitador* sent a report to the king on the official's honesty and competence. A favorable report would usually result in a reward of some type, while an unfavorable report could lead to removal of the official.

José de Gálvez was the greatest *visitador*. A man of the middle class, he had learned French from his wife and thus was able to rise to a high post in the Foreign Ministry. In July 1765, he arrived in New Spain with unlimited authority to investigate charges of decreased royal rents, while at the same time he approved expanding royal expenses against the viceroy, Joaquín de Montserrat, the Marqués de Cruillas (1700-71). He found that the charges were true. The king removed Cruillas and the following year replaced him with General Carlos Francisco de Croix, the Marqués de Croix (1699-1786). Croix was an amiable man with a slight drinking problem, but thanks to the reforms introduced by Gálvez, the viceregal government moved ahead with an efficiency previously unknown. Among Gálvez's reforms were the firing of many dishonest customs officials and the establishment of a state tobacco monopoly that generated much tax revenue. Croix introduced the lottery into Mexico (to this day a highly popular aspect of popular Mexican culture), established a college of surgery in Mexico City, peacefully settled a silver miners' strike, built special schools to teach more Indians Spanish, and built a defensive castle at Vera Cruz. However, he also supported and promoted the Inquisition, suppressed any protests against the expulsion of the Jesuits, shutting down a literary-scientific journal and executing protest leaders.

Gálvez was rigidly loyal to the king, highly effective, a superb organizer, and respected by his subordinates. On the other hand, he was cruel, proud, deceitful, hypocritical, and overbearing. On one occasion he spoke with a prisoner who was condemned to death and whose sentence he had no intention of commuting, promising the condemned that he would pray for guidance. The man was hanged the next day. When he expelled the Jesuits from New Spain, he silenced popular protest with the edict that it was "the sole duty" of the people "to obey" and that they must "speak neither for nor against the royal order, which had been passed for motives reserved alone for the sovereign's conscience!"

When the Jesuits were expelled, he determined to shore up the Northwest to prevent the feared Russian encroachments, and he received the king's permission to do so. Delighted, Gálvez made plans with Croix to pacify the frontier and to settle San Diego and Monterey Bays. He proposed new settlements and troop concentrations, and a *captaincy* (a military territory) over Nueva Vizcaya, Sinaloa, Sonora, and the Californias, with its headquarters at the junction of the Colorado and Gila Rivers. A captaincy was almost the equivalent of a viceroyalty, yet still part of a viceroyalty. It had the benefit of more local control. Before captaincies could be established - in fact the ambitious project was never to be - the area would have to be pacified. The Pimas and Seris were in revolt, and Colonel Domingo Elizondo (c1710-83) was sent with a large force to crush them.

Meanwhile Gálvez decided to visit the west coast port of San Blas, a heavily silted and very small harbor he wanted developed to aid Elizondo's campaign. From there he sailed over to Loreto to meet with Portolá, Captain Fernando Rivera y Moncada (1725-81), who was in charge of the presidio, and Fray Junípero Serra (1713-84, canonized a saint of the Catholic church in September 2015), in charge of the missions. Gálvez stayed in Baja for ten months, supervising some marginally successful mining and pearl fishing activities.

With help from Portolá and Serra, Gálvez was able to organize two colonizing parties with unusual speed. One, composed of soldiers, settlers, and Christian Indians, was under Portolá and Serra, and would be sent overland from Loreto. The second, composed of three ships (the *San Carlos,*

San Antonio and *San José*) would carry additional colonists and supplies from La Paz. Called "the Sacred Expeditions" they would rendezvous at San Diego Bay, move on to Monterey Bay, and there in the wilderness plant the white emblazoned flag of Spain (the familiar red and gold was not adopted until 1785) together with the cross of Christ.

The Franciscan missionaries were drafted to convert Alta California while still technically responsible for Baja California until the Dominicans fully took over. The peninsula missions were wretched, yet were expected to assist (as older settlements) in the founding of new ones in the north. Accordingly, Gálvez requisitioned from them altar furniture, vestments, foodstuffs, tools, and livestock.

The first two ships above-named, little more than packet boats, had been built to transport troops to Elizondo. Both - especially the leaky *San Carlos* - needed to be made seaworthy, so Gálvez supervised the repair and reloading, "often," Hubert Bancroft notes, "lending a hand in the stowing of an unwieldy package, greatly to the encouragement of his men," in a friendly competition of speed with the expedition leaders. As Dr. Caughey notes, "things hummed because the visitador had both authority and enthusiasm."

On January 9, 1769, the *San Carlos* set sail, captained by Vicente Vila. On January 25, the *San Antonio* sailed to Cabo San Lucas, leaving for the north on February 15 with carpenters and blacksmiths, under Juan Pérez. Both captains were experienced at sea, Vila as a naval pilot and Pérez in the galleon trade.

The first land expedition, under Captain Rivera, consisted of 25 soldiers, three muleteers, and 42 Christian Indians. Attached to Captain Rivera as chaplain was Fray Juan Crespí (1721-82). The Indians were to act as interpreters and models for the northern tribes to follow in accepting the drudgery of heavy work and assistance to the Spaniards. Having gathered 400 animals, Rivera moved to the then-northernmost mission, Santa María de los Ángeles, but found insufficient pasture. Going on to Velicatá, situated at latitude 30°N, about halfway between Mission Santa Gertrudis and San Diego Bay, he started north on March 24. Two weeks earlier, on March 9, Portolá had started from Loreto, accompanied by Serra, ten soldiers, two servants, and 44 Christian Indians. On May 14, they reached Velicatá and founded the mission of San Fernando de Velicatá. The next day, Portolá set out on Rivera's route.

The San José never arrived. It sailed from Loreto on June 16. According to one account, it sank on the way north; according to another, it sank after being storm-driven back toward Cabo San Lucas.

Having seen the Sacred Expeditions off, Gálvez, in March, went to Sonora to take personal command of the Pima war. The Pima revolt, which had broken out in 1751, had reduced the civilized population by 86%, the settled ranches from 125 to just two, and mining settlements by more than forty. Elizondo was never able to fight the Indians, for they fled into the fastness of the mountainous Cerro Prieto, but Gálvez was determined to crush the Pimas and Seris because Sonora and Arizona were rich areas that would serve as a land link between Mexico and California. His intent was thwarted when the king and his secretary of the Indies ordered that an amnesty be offered, though few accepted it.

The frustrations of defeat led Gálvez into a deep depression that drove him mad. He made nonsensical proposals: a canal from Mexico City to Guaymas for deep-water ships and the enlistment of monkeys from Guatemala as soldiers. He "ordered" the royal treasury to give every soldier

140

whatever the latter requested, had visions of St. Francis of Assisi, burned his clothing, lectured the Indians while naked, and at different times imagined himself to be Frederick the Great, St. Joseph, Bishop Juan de Palafox y Mendoza (1600-59, historian, viceroy, and scientist), Moctezuma, and more, including God. In the spring of 1770, he returned to Mexico City, where a change of scenery was credited with restoring his sanity. His severe break from reality followed by a surprising return to sanity was ascribed to a condition he had had all his life, a malady that would lead to his death.[1]

He went on to greater achievements, returning to Spain in 1772, becoming the governor of the Council of the Indies, in which position he oversaw some major changes in governmental structure to expand areas of settlement and stimulate the economy. In order to provide for more efficient local administration he subdivided two of the viceroyalties and created a new viceroyalty out of the third – the commandancy-general of the Internal Provinces as part of the viceroyalty of New Spain, the captaincy general of Caracas as part of the viceroyalty of New Granada, and the viceroyalty of La Plata out of the viceroyalty of Peru. He established the Royal Company of the Philippines to compete with the Dutch and British East Companies and consolidated all the colonial records into the *Archivo General de Indias*. He also established a uniform excise tax on the importation of African slaves and allowed limited free trade among the Spanish colonies. As part of the Bourbon administrative reforms he introduced the office of *Intendencia* (Intendency) to supervise the treasury and tax collecting, and to promote agriculture and general economic growth. He also solicited contributions for the American Revolution, since Spain was participating in that war against Great Britain. Clearly his transitory mental breakdown in the Pima war did not have a deleterious effect on his career.

Northwestern Mexico was finally pacified when some of Elizondo's men found a rich gold placer near Altar in the Sonoran Desert. A rush brought in 2,000 miners within a few months, outnumbering the hostile Indians, their sheer numbers reducing the danger of attack. In 1775, Captain Bernardo de Urrea (1710-77) built the first settlement there, a military fort he called Santa Gertrudis del Altar.

In retrospect, the Sacred Expeditions were a dramatic success. However, the participants doubtless felt otherwise. The *San Antonio* arrived on April 11, and the San Carlos, which had started out first, arrived on April 29. The *San Antonio* had passed San Diego Bay because of faulty maps, going up to the Channel Islands before Pérez realized his mistake and dropped south. All on board (except the friars) were sick or disabled, but no lives had been lost. The *San Carlos* was not so lucky, as 24 of the 26-man crew had died of scurvy, while both survivors were disabled with the same malady.

At San Diego, the illnesses increased. An earthen enclosure was built "close to the beach, on the east side of the port," recalled engineer and cartographer Lieutenant Miguel Costansó (1741-1814) in his diary, translated as *The Narrative of the Portolá Expedition of 1769-1770,*

> "And mounted with two cannon. Some sails and awnings were landed from the vessels and, with these, two tents suitable for a hospital were made.... [But] medicines and fresh food. . .
> were wanting. The surgeon, Don Pedro Prat, supplied this want as far as possible, with some herbs. . . [but] needed them as much as his patients, for he was all but prostrated by the
> same disease as they. In the barracks the cold made itself severely felt at night, and the sun by day:

extremes which caused the sick to suffer cruelly. Every day, two or three of them died. . ."

The Rivera party arrived on May 14, all in good health, though their journey had not been pleasant. It had been marked by bad-tasting water in the arid areas, drenching storms that slowed down his livestock as they broke new trails, and desertion of their Indians when frightened by the local savages. Yet their self-pity vanished when they beheld the arrival of their comrades from the two ships. After a day's rest, their officers decided to move the camp closer to the river. The new camp was transferred to "a hill of moderate height, where it was possible to attend with greater care to the sick." There, at Presidio Hills, in San Diego's Old Town, Rivera founded - without fanfare - the San Diego Presidio.

Portolá reached San Diego ahead of most of his party on June 28, and the rest of the group arrived on July 1, all in good health. All four expeditions having reached San Diego, possession was formally taken in a ceremony in which Serra said Mass, all joined in singing the *Te Deum*, salutes were fired, and the flag was raised. Two days later, the Presidio was formally re-founded, and on July 16 Serra founded the mission of San Diego de Alcalá, the name given to the harbor by Vizcaíno 167 years earlier.

Gaspar de Portolá, leader of the Sacred Expeditions and California's first governor (Wikimedia Commons)

St. Junípero Serra, founder of the first nine missions
(Wikimedia Commons)

Thus were the expeditions reunited at San Diego, but many of the individuals who had started from Baja California were missing. Of slightly less than 300 men who had started out, only 126 remained, and almost half of those were now unfit for service. Of every five who had set out, only one remained strong enough to go on. . . Such was the heavy toll on that first band of pioneers.

To Monterey and San Francisco

To Gálvez had decreed that the Expedition should "explore and settle if it be possible, the port of San Diego," but had specified that Monterey was the main objective. Accordingly, Portolá sent the San Antonio back to San Blas for supplies and men, the crewless San Carlos was left at anchor, Serra was instructed to help Dr. Prat nurse the ill and comfort the dying, so it fell to Portolá to take about sixty men to begin what was to be his "march of the skeletons" north.

On July 14, two days before Serra founded his San Diego de Alcalá mission to convert the naked natives with the help of cheap trinkets, Portolá's march began. Leading the way were Sergeant José Ortega (1734-98), the great scout, with other scouts. In the main party were Portolá, Pedro Fages (1734-94), six Catalan volunteers (one of whom was Antonio Yorba), Costansó as map maker and architect, Fathers Crespí and Francisco Gómez, and 125 Christian Indians. Near the rear was the pack train of 100 mules and seven muleteers, followed by Captain Rivera and the rest of the soldiers. These soldiers were known as *soldados de cuera*, or "leather-jackets" because of their multi-layered deerskin coats which could turn arrows except at very close range. Among the soldiers were many whose families would become famous in California history: Pablo Antonio Cota (1744-1800), Juan José Robles (?-1781), José María Soberanes (1753-1803), Pedro Amador (1739-1824), Juan Bautista Alvarado, Bernardo Alvarado, José Raimundo Carrillo (1749-1809), Guillermo Carrillo (?-1782), Francisco (?-1781) and Gerardo Peña, Juan Bautista Valdés, Juan Ismerio Osuna (1746-90), Ignacio Lugo, Mariano Verdugo (1746-1822), and Juan Puig. At the rear were some friendly Indians who drove the herd of spare horses and mules.[2]

Their progress was terribly slow, taking a day to cover a little over two leagues. Costansó's diary describes their problems:

> "With so great a train and so many obstacles, through unknown lands and on unused roads, the marches could not take long. Not mention other reasons that made it necessary to halt and camp early - the necessity of reconnoitering the country from day to

146

day in order to regulate the marchers according to the distance between watering places, and consequently to take the proper precautions.... Stops were made, as the necessity demanded, intervals of four days, more or less, according to the extraordinary hardships occasioned by the greater roughness of the road and the straying of the animals. . . that had to be sought by their tracks. At other times, because it was necessary to accommodate the sick when there were any - and there were many. Skittish pack animals were the most dreaded enemies because they would stampede at the sight of a coyote or fox, a bird flying past or a dust devil. Then their fright would make them run leagues, throwing themselves over precipices and cliffs, defying human effort to restrain them. . . and those that were not killed by falling over a precipice, or lamed in their headlong race, are of no service for a long time.... However, this expedition suffered no serious detriment on this account."

**

"At sunrise the Indians came welcoming us, one behind the other, singing and dancing."

-Fray Pedro Font, 1776

**

Watching for the *San José*, which had sailed from Mexico but had not arrived, the band hugged the coast by a route that continued from Loreto, a road soon to be known as *El Camino Real*. This classic California road was the route later followed by the railroads and U.S. 101. Most of the way pasture and water were plentiful and the numerous Indians friendly, albeit greedy for the Spaniards' cheap trinkets. In the first stage, from San Diego to the Río de los Temblores (Santa Ana), the

Spaniards travelled fifteen days, arriving on July 28. Passing the future site of Mission San Luis Rey, Fray Crespí described the valley as so beautiful and green that it seemed to have been planted. Gifts were exchanged - beads in return for hemp-fiber fish nets. The women were

> "Modestly covered, wearing in front an apron of threads woven together which came to the knees, with a deerskin in back. To cover the breasts they wear little capes made of rabbit skins, of which they make strips and twine them like rope. . . but all the men go as naked as Adam in Paradise before he sinned. . just as though the clothing given them by nature were some fine garment."[3]

At the Santa Ana River a sharp earthquake was felt. "It lasted" according to Crespí, "about half as long as an Ave Maria, and about ten minutes later it was repeated, though not violently." Costansó explained that one of the natives, whom he took to be a "priest" began "with horrible cries and great manifestations of terror to entreat the heavens, turning in all directions and acting as though he would conjure away the elements." He might have been kept quite busy, for as the band crossed the Los Angeles plain, aftershocks - whose frequency amazed the Spaniards - were felt. After they crossed the Los Angeles River (near present day Santa Monica) on August 3 the earthquakes were left behind. While still on the Los Angeles plain the scouts saw marshes of boiling and bubbling pitch which Crespí speculated would be sufficient to caulk many ships. These were the asphalt beds at La Brea.

The natives told them that a shoreline passage would be impossible, so they turned northward through Sepúlveda Canyon and entered the San Fernando Valley. Going down past the future site of Santa Paula on August 13, they began to move along the coast of the Santa Barbara Channel, where they spent two easy weeks following the shoreline. The natives were hospitable, bringing seeds and honeycombs. At the present site of Ventura, they reached a large native town of 400 people who "presented us with a quantity of bonito fish, it had as good a taste and as delicate a flavor as that caught . . . on the coasts of Granada." Farther along the coast they watched some natives constructing pine wood canoes and named the place *Pueblo de Carpintería*.

Occasionally along the Channel, the natives serenaded the visitors all night long with pipes and whistles. There ensued an intense inter-village rivalry over the presents and feasts they would give the Spaniards. This proved to be a mixed blessing for the visitors, for on August 20, the:

> "Dances lasted all the afternoon, and it cost us much trouble to rid ourselves of the people. They were sent away, charged with emphatic signs not to come in the night and disturb us; but it was in vain, for as soon as night fell they returned, playing on some pipes whose noise grated on our ears. It was feared that they might frighten the horses so Portolá went out and gave them some beads and implored them to go, telling them that if they came again to interrupt our sleep they would not be welcome and we would give them an unfriendly reception."

This worked.

They noticed that among the Channel Indians, polygamy was permitted only for chiefs and that there was a class of male transvestites. On August 26, the party reached Point Concepción and there, in the village of the lame chief (*Ranchería del Cojo*) Crespí recorded that "these heathen

149

have European beads, and when asked they said they got them from the north." Proceeding up the coast, they passed Morro Bay on September 8.

Five days later they camped at the foot of the very rugged Santa Lucía mountains near the present Monterey-San Luis Obispo County line. Steep cliffs overhanging the sea convinced Portolá that the hardest part of the trek would be there. He decided to make camp and sent Rivera and eight scouts to find a way over the barrier Crespí described as "inaccessible not only for men but also for goats and deer."

Several days later, the scouts returned having found a way up the steep slopes along San Carpoforo Creek. For two weeks they toiled, preparing a path by roadwork through the mountains, crossing the many arroyos, and finding more ranges that hid valleys and sea. They continued to the north and northeast for about fifty miles (80 km), across the Nacimiento and San Antonio rivers, and down Kent Canyon to the Salinas River, which they reached at the site of King City on September 26.

On the 29th, they reported many antelope, and in a grove in the bed of the Salinas River encountered a group of Esselen Indians who apparently were engaged in a communal hunt.

The scouts thought they could see the ocean but found that it was farther along. When they returned to camp, they reported that "the river emptied into an estuary which entered the canyon from the sea; that the beach, bordered by sand-dunes, had been seen to the north and south, the coast forming an immense bay; and that, to the south, there was a low hill covered with trees like pines which terminated in a point in the sea."

Traveling six days after they came down from the Santa Lucía, they approached the shore in breathless anticipation.

On October 1, the party reached the area now known as Blanco, along the Salinas River between Marina and Salinas, probably about four miles (6.5 km) from the beach. There they camped for six days in a grassy plain near the river to rest and explore. On arrival, Portolá, Crespí, and five soldiers immediately went downstream to the mouth of the river, and from a small sand hill (Mulligan Hill, about 60 feet [18 m] in height) viewed Monterey Bay. Vizcaíno had written of a "fine harbor" and the scouts' reports seemed to confirm the achievement of their primary goal. Strangely, they did not recognize it. Caughey, citing Robert Louis Stevenson, accounts for this by comparing Monterey Bay to a fishhook, curving down from the north with the Point of Pines as the barb and the port the small area behind the barb; reconnoitering on horseback (unlike the bay's discoverer, Vizcaíno), Portolá not only could not see its full merits, but he also couldn't recognize it. Later he wrote to one of Gálvez's secretaries that "although the signs whereby we were to recognize the port were the same as those set down by Vizcaíno in his log, the fact is that, without being able to guess the reason, we were all under hallucination, and no one dared assert openly that the port was indeed Monterey." He concluded that the port must be farther north.

Officers and missionaries held a council of war in which they decided to continue the march to find the port and the supply ship *San José*, which was supposed to meet with them at Monterey. Throughout October the expedition, whose members were experiencing more cases of illness, was beset with doubts as to their location.

On to the north they went, crossing the Pájaro River (named for a large bird the Indians had captured, killed, and stuffed with straw.) On this expedition, they were the first white men to see the coastal redwoods. Crespí described these immense trees as very tall with a ruddy trunk and brittle wood resembling cedar but very different in odor. Costansó wrote that they were the largest, straightest, and tallest trees he had ever seen. Since nobody recognized these trees, Crespí named them from "their [red] color" - *palo colorado.*

Once they passed the site of Soquel, the sick started to recuperate slowly. Fewer men were falling from their mules and having to be carried on sidesaddles. By the third week of October the sick were pretty much restored to health. On October 30 they reached Half Moon Bay, in the lee of the Montara Hills, which they called Rincón de las Almejas because there they had gorged on mussels. The next day they left their camp and followed the scouts up Montara Mountain. From there they could see the Gulf of the Farallones, the Farallones, Point Reyes, and "San Francisco" (Drake's) Bay. The latter they recognized immediately, for Admiral José González Cabrera Bueno's (c1670-c1733) 1734 navigator's handbook (*Navegación especulativa y práctica*) had it made it better known than any other point on the north coast. Thus, "it seemed to us beyond all question," wrote Costansó, "that what we were looking at was the port of San Francisco [*sic*] and thus we were convinced that the port of Monterey had been left behind."[4] Crossing Montara Mountain, they pitched camp at San Pedro Point, to rest and debate what course to take.

Ortega was sent ahead to try and reach Point Reyes within three days. On the next day, November 2, food being nearly exhausted, some hunters struck into the hills northeast of the camp looking for game. The chase led upward until presently they came out on a clear height and beheld a great quiet harbor to the east and north. They returned to camp greatly excited about "this great arm of the sea, as far as they could see, to the southeast." If Drake was not the first white man to see it 200 years earlier, these hunters were the first to report a glimpse of San Francisco Bay.

A few hours later Ortega returned reporting that his way to Point Reyes was cut off by an almost landlocked estuary, so close to one another stood the two pillars of its gate, protecting the inland sea from the ocean. The Indians near the Golden Gate, which Ortega and later Spaniards called "la boca," had told him that two days' march to the north there was a ship in a harbor. Hungry and hopeful the explorers believed that this was the San *José* or perhaps the *San Antonio* with provisions. Accordingly, Portolá decided to push on and find the ship and a land route to Point Reyes. Since the way north was blocked by the Golden Gate, he decided to go around the bay by swinging south.

On November 4, the party topped Sweeny Ridge to the east of their San Pedro camp and saw spread out before them the great Bay of San Francisco. In hindsight, this date may be the most significant for the Portolá expedition, but only Crespí sensed its importance: "In a word," he wrote, "it is a very large and fine harbor, such that not only all the navy of his most Catholic Majesty but those of all Europe could take shelter in it." Costansó described seeing "a large arm of the sea, or extremely large estuary, which they assert may be four or five leagues in width in some places, and in others two." Portolá, however, could only think of the alleged ship supposedly two days away; in his diary he entered that "they had found nothing" - apparently feeling that the bay was an obstacle to further northward advancement.[5]

That afternoon, Ortega was sent out with eight men to find the roundabout route. From the vicinity of Palo Alto, they explored the bay's southern extremity as far as what today is Hayward. From there they saw the Golden Gate and the Islands of Angel, Alcatraz, and Yerba Buena. On November

10 they returned to the Palo Alto camp, having found neither port nor ship. The next day Portolá convoked a council and requested that his officers and the priests vote in writing. The decision was made to turn back and search for the Port of Monterey behind them.

On the way south, Monterey was identified, and on November 28, they passed through the Del Monte Forest. They erected two crosses, one near the Carmel River and the other near the shore of the bay, and camped at San Jose Creek (Monastery Beach). On November 29, they made camp at Point Lobos while local explorations were made to find the port of Monterey. Twelve days later they concluded that Vizcaíno's port was a hallucination and decided to return to San Diego. There was abundant food for the animals, but little for the explorers. They could find neither fish nor game and were forced to eat sea gulls and pelicans. On November 30, a group of Rumsen Indians from the interior visited bringing pinole and seeds. The following day a mule was killed for food, but not everyone would eat it. To make matters worse, the weather was bad, and snow began to cover the hills. The dejected party decided to return to San Diego. They plodded wearily south, and during the last dozen days butchered and roasted one of the weak old mules each evening, entering Serra's camp at last on January 24, 1770, "smelling frightfully of mules."

**

"The Devil lies on heavy hearts."

-Spanish proverb

**

A Poor Outlook

They approached San Diego with justifiable misgivings. Conditions had not been very good in July when they had started north, and now conditions were terrible. More men had succumbed to scurvy. The Indians had not only rejected Serra's overtures but had attacked the camp and stripped clothes from invalids before being driven off. Portolá and his party were exhausted from their journey. The *San José* had not appeared, and the *San Antonio* had not returned from Mexico. This last problem was the worst, for the colony had barely been surviving on geese, fish, and such food as the otherwise hostile Indians would trade for clothing.

In addition to these practical daily problems there were others: The site for the mission at Point Reyes was blocked by the "Estuary of San Francisco" (now known as San Francisco Bay), and Monterey apparently had no harbor. In short, the outlook for California was grim.

Finally on February 10, 1770, Portolá sent Rivera back to Velicatá with forty men to get any available supplies and the cattle left behind. This would also reduce the number of hungry mouths at San Diego for the present. He would not return until July. In the six weeks after Rivera's departure privations were severe and there was talk of abandonment of the little colony. Portolá had resolved to hold out as long as possible because his reputation would suffer were he to give up.

Portolá's wise, courageous leadership did much to preserve the colony, but the man of the hour was Serra, whose faith held the colony together. "What I have desired least is provisions," he wrote. "Our needs are many, it is true; but if we have health, a tortilla, and some vegetables, what more do we want?. . . If I see that along with food hope vanishes I shall remain together with Fray Juan Crespí and hold out to the last breath."

Though neither Costansó nor Crespí mention it, Fray Francisco Palóu (who was not there at the time) in his *Life of Serra*, published 17 years later, asserts that on March 11, Portolá set March 20 as the deadline for the arrival of a supply ship, or San Diego would be abandoned. According to the charming story, Serra and Crespí began a *novena* (a nine-day period of prayer and devotion) to invoke divine assistance. On the evening of the 19th - the final day of the novena and the day before the projected abandonment - the *San Antonio* was sighted, though it did not get into port until four days later. As historian Herbert Bolton has it, "to the eyes of the friars... and to the discouraged Portolá, the white sails of the *San Antonio* cleaving the clear blue twilight must have seemed as the wings of some heavenly visitant, more beautiful than ever ship before had spread to the beneficent wind." The critical situation is not exaggerated; the colony could not have held out for much longer without the supplies brought by the *San Antonio*.

In accordance with human nature, the colonists promptly forgot the pains of the previous months. Over Pérez's protests, Portolá sent the *San Antonio* to Monterey on April 16 while he marched north with the remaining sixteen able soldiers the next day. On May 24, they made rendezvous, Pérez seeing that this was the good port described by Vizcaíno.

On June 3, 1770, the mission and presidio of San Carlos at Monterey were formally established near the spot where Father Ascensión had said Mass for Vizcaíno's crew under a spreading oak tree. Portolá's task was accomplished, whereupon in accordance with his instructions he invested Fages with the government of the province. On July 9 Portolá and Costansó sailed with Pérez on the *San Antonio*, reaching

156

San Blas on August 1. Pérez and Costansó hurried to Mexico City, arriving on the 10th with news of the success. Viceroy Croix, in a special compliment to Gálvez, ordered the church bells rung and flags flown to mark the 300-league advance of the frontier. He then ordered a special High Mass of Thanksgiving at the cathedral, which was attended by the entire viceregal court.

Alta California was born!

Viceroy Bucareli

Rejoicing was premature. Would the infant colony survive? It was hardly robust, the breast of Baja California was nearly dry, it was surrounded by hostile life forces, and within the infant's body the organs were not functioning harmoniously. Nevertheless, it did survive and reach a rich maturity. How?

When Pedro Fages was appointed governor, or more correctly, *gobernante*, someone in charge of a region but subject to an official governor, in this case Felipe Barry (c1714-84), governor of the Californias at Loreto. It was the highest office he had yet attained. A 40-year-old Catalan, like the older Portolá, he had been an officer since 1762 and had fought in the Seven Years' War. Sent to Veracruz to join Elizondo's campaign in Sonora, he was reassigned to the Sacred Expedition in September 1768. At the time he replaced Portolá he was inexperienced in matters of command. He was high-strung and irascible, frequently clashing with fellow officers and alienating his troops to the point of provoking some desertions.

Rivera arrived at San Diego with the livestock from Velicatá , but hearing that he had been passed over for *gobernante* by the much younger (by 20 years) and lower ranking (lieutenant rather than captain) Fages, he petulantly refused to go to Monterey despite Portolá's orders. Rivera, a *criollo* (a Spaniard born in the New World), found it hard to deal with others of the same status, but he was fond of his soldiers and they of him, a grace in him that balanced some of his bad points. In 1772 he retired from military service.

Serra was incapable of compromise. Fifty-seven years old in 1770, he had been ordained a priest while still a teenager and became a professor of philosophy at a Spanish university where Francisco Palóu (1722-89) and Crespí were among his students. Serra was known as a bright, articulate scholar-- apparently a moving speaker and a clear, precise writer--but he did not remain long in academic life. He went to Mexico in 1749 and trained at the College of San Fernando for missionary work. Short, zealous, stoic, he began his California career at an age when most men dream of retirement.

As neither Serra nor Fages was inclined to compromise, a break soon occurred between them. In 1771, Matías de Armona (1731-96), the new governor at Loreto (although he never visited Alta California), prohibited building any new missions because of the lack of soldiers – a total of 43 in Alta California. Fages, as Portolá's successor, felt that he had inherited Portolá's powers (subject to the governor at Loreto) and, therefore, that he had something to say about the time and place for building new missions. After all, he was responsible for their defense and supplying. Serra, on the other hand, insisted that Fages have nothing to do with the activities or functions of the friars but only with the soldiers of the mission guard.

Spanish missionaries administering the first baptisms in Alta California near San Diego. [Public domain] via Wikimedia Commons

**

"We rejoiced to see so many pagans upon whom the light of our holy faith was about to dawn."

-Palóu, 1782

**

Accordingly, Serra continued to establish mission sites. San Carlos was moved from Monterey to the Carmel Valley because of the priestly fear that the general rowdiness of the soldiers would influence the impressionable natives and because the soil nearer to the Carmel River seemed more receptive to crops. In 1771, Mission San Antonio de Padua was situated in the Valley of the Oaks and was the first to have an Indian present at its founding, no doubt attracted by the sound of the bell Serra had hung from a tree and vigorously rung. Later that year, Mission San Gabriel Arcángel was founded near the mosquito-infested swamps of the San Gabriel River, but the murky water overflowed its banks and carried out to sea many of the logs intended for the first church. In September 1772, a 13th century French bishop, St. Louis of Toulouse, was honored by the establishment of Mission San Luis Obispo de Tolosa.

Serra was not pleased with the guard. Rather than the tough, disciplined Catalan volunteers Fages had originally led to Alta California, most of the soldiers were Mexican convicts. Without wives, they soon looked amorously upon native women. Pretending to go hunting, their prey was usually women, and these amorous attentions usually constituted gang rape. Shortly after the founding of San Gabriel in 1771, some soldiers lassoed a chief's wife, her husband shot an arrow at the guilty leader of the pack of soldier rapists, the chief was killed and beheaded by them, and an Indian revolt broke out. The soldiers were a further problem to the missions since, bored and tired, they often deserted. Usually, however, they returned, because escape to Mexico was out of the question, and life among the natives was too dangerous. Yet, these morally scrofulous, rough-natured soldiers were vital to the missions. Franciscan Mission historian Zephrin Engelhardt concluded that "[i]n truth, the guards counted among the worst obstacles to missionary progress. The wonder is, that the missionaries nevertheless succeeded so well in attracting converts."[6]

Missionization itself was a failure in the beginning. Despite rapid successes in other parts of the Spanish Empire, the California missionaries were faced with a dearth of baptisms - indeed, by 1773, with five missions established, less than 500 Indians had been baptized, of whom only 462 were still alive, among them but 124 adults. Little wonder, then, that Serra's superior in Mexico City, Fray Rafael Verger (1722-90), felt that it was an exaggeration to call them missions. He had opposed the venture, predicting its failure, but had assented when compelled by Gálvez. His was now a triumphant "I told you so" attitude.

One reason for the early failure of missionization was that the priests had nothing to offer the natives. Faced with a royal mandate to cut expenses to overcome the national deficit, the viceregal government did not provide sufficient trinkets for the natives (for their part, California and San Blas in 1768-73 had cost the government 570,000 pesos, but the only return was 150,000 pesos from the salt mines at San Blas). Unlike the Indians of Baja California, the natives of Alta California had an abundance of food, so the priests could not use it as an inducement. As for religious instruction, the Indians were utterly indifferent as they were satisfied with their animist beliefs and saw no reason to change.

The Spaniards did not share in the Indians' abundance of food: As at Plymouth, Quebec, and Jamestown the first colonists faced hunger. The first two seasons saw small plantings of beans, wheat, and corn saved by late spring rains; but in 1772, normal conditions prevailed and, in the absence of irrigation ditches, the crops failed. Knowing very little about California's soil or farming they rarely got more in return for their seed than more seed; by 1773, only Mission San Gabriel had a productive farm. Baja California could provide no more, and the shipments from Mexico were irregular and slow. In 1772, when the tardy supply ships went only as far as San Diego, Fages (already called "El Oso" because of his habitually angry disposition), organized a bear hunt in the vicinity of San Luis Obispo. This famous bear hunt saved Monterey from starvation until pack trains could arrive from San Diego. It also helped to select San Luis Obispo as a mission site later that year; the region demonstrated that it could provide food in an emergency and the natives were grateful for the killing of the bears.

It was not, of course, only food that was scarce. Manufactured goods, domestic animals and settlers were all in short supply. Nothing - not even a piece of ribbon or a nail - could be manufactured in California. In 1773, there was only one blacksmith and one forge in Alta California. These were at Monterey, and in any case, there was very little iron to work with. Animals, both for food and as beasts of burden, were in short supply; they could be used for milk production, but their lives were not expendable, and many pack animals were needed to transport supplies from San Diego or Monterey to the three inland missions. By 1773, there were only 616 animals at the five missions. As for settlers, only 61 soldiers, 11 friars, and an occasional mechanic on government business constituted the European-derived population in 1773. Although Serra gave lip service to the idea of building towns for the Spaniards after the Indians were civilized, he and the other friars opposed every such move in order to protect the Indians and to maintain their own influence in the province.

Gálvez had retired in 1771 and returned to Spain, making the explorers' hold less secure. He was the only powerful Spaniard in Mexico who demonstrated interest in California. His departure was followed by a warning from the new viceroy, Antonio María de Bucareli (1717-79), to Madrid, that Alta California - because of its marked failure - might have to be abandoned.

In September 1772, Serra and Fages clashed over the priest's wish to establish Mission San Buenaventura. Unable to persuade the *gobernante*, the *padre-presidente* took the extraordinary course of going to Mexico City over the *gobernante's* head to see the viceroy. In mid-March 1773, he was granted an audience.

Bucareli had been an army engineer and governor of Cuba prior to becoming viceroy in 1771 and was to be one of the best of the 62 viceroys in Mexican history. In appointing him, Carlos III trusted him so implicitly that he increased the viceregal salary to 80,000 pesos ($300,976 in 2023 US dollars) and gave him the right of *patronato*, by which friends and relatives could be appointed to government posts. A charming man, popular with the Mexicans, he gave the country some basis for future industrialization by establishing cotton and woolen factories; many of these were disgusting sweatshops but helped many fortunes to be made and allowed a small middle class to develop. He - not the Church authorities - organized many charitable institutions, notably poorhouses, lending agencies for victims of usury, and mental asylums. A realist in trade matters who knew that mercantilism put unnecessary constraints on the economy, he allowed a system of imperial free trade which resulted in less smuggling and more revenue for the king.[7]

The king had ordered the Californias be given "special attention," but Governor Armona had suggested that Alta California be abandoned as too expensive. Serra's arrival was timely. The priest, apparently alone in his optimism for Alta California, proceeded to convince Bucareli that the mission to Alta California was of the greatest value for the crown. Though no record of their conversations exists, Serra - appearing, in the words of a chronicler, "old, infirm, . . .and shabby" - did present his arguments in a *Representación* of 32 clauses.

Rejecting the idea of continuing the status quo, Serra itemized improvements needed in allowances and delivery of supplies, urged that blacksmiths, carpenters, and six *peones* (farm laborers) be assigned to each mission, proposed enlarging the mission escort to between 10 and 20 soldiers each, and urged that a land route be opened with Mexico. He reported that the natives were amazed at the absence of women among the settlers and suggested that a land-and-livestock grant be made to any Spaniard who married a baptized native woman. He asked that certain specific decisions be left to the clergy and suggested that Fages be replaced by Ortega.

After consultation with his council, Bucareli granted some of Serra's wishes. The extra guards and the *peones* were not forthcoming, but Fages was removed and replaced by Rivera, who was called out of Guadalajara retirement. He arrived in Monterey in late May 1773 and formally took command of the province while Fages was assigned to a garrison in Guadalajara. Ortega was commissioned a lieutenant and put in charge of the San Diego Presidio.

On July 8, 1773, Bucareli completely reversed his position of six months earlier, an about-face which must have seemed to Serra an answer to prayer, by issuing a *Reglamento* which, expanded in 1779, constituted the law of California for many years. In summary, the 42 paragraphs of the *Reglamento* of 1773 required seven things:

(1) The missions were to be expanded.

(2) The Indians were to be converted and civilized, for, Bucareli predicted, the missions would become great cities, and sites, land parcels and street design should be planned accordingly.

(3) Records were to be kept and sent annually to Mexico City and Loreto.

(4) An annual supply ship was to be sent from San Blas.

(5) The coast was to be explored to checkmate the English and the Russians.

(6) To minimize troubles concerning soldierly lust for native women, only married soldiers with their families were to be sent to Alta California.

(7) San Francisco Bay was to be explored and settled as soon as possible.

So armed with the Reglamento of 1773, Serra returned to Monterey early in 1774.

While he had been in Mexico City there had been some changes in the mission system as well as additional exploration.

When the Jesuits were expelled, the Franciscans had been given the missions of Baja California. The Dominicans had wanted a share of those missions but were cut off by the Franciscans. However, when Alta California was penetrated, the Franciscans could not dispose of Baja California fast enough because of poor prospects, so in 1772 the provincials of the two orders in Mexico City divided the California missions between them, at the approximate boundary which later divided the two Californias politically. North of Velicatá, the only Franciscan-built mission in Baja California, the Dominicans built seven new missions in the next quarter century; by 1830 they had built eleven. Unlike the Franciscans or Jesuits, the Dominicans had less experience as missionaries, for Bancroft notes that they "were harder masters. . . exacting comparatively excessive labor and administering severe punishments." More than one Indian revolt in the peninsula was due to this mistreatment.

At the time of the transfer, Fray Palóu, who had been in charge of Franciscan efforts in Baja California, moved to Carmel with half a dozen Franciscans, including Fray Francisco Fermín de Lasuén (1721-1803.) At the Carmel Mission, Palóu began building a new church to replace the inadequate mud hut erected by Serra. The new structure was built of logs and planks with a tule-thatched roof. Fages enlarged the herd of livestock with 29 horses and mules, and

Palóu, an excellent gardener, enlarged the vegetable patch lettuce and artichokes. (The artichokes of today's Monterey are descendants of those plants.)

In 1771, Fray Francisco Garcés (1738-81), a missionary from San Xavier del Bac who had made several journeys to the Gila-Colorado area, crossed the Colorado at Yuma in search of new mission sites. He blazed a trail across the Colorado Desert to within sight of the San Jacinto Mountains. This virtually waterless trail was known as *El Camino del Diablo* (the Devil's Road); today it is followed by Mexican Federal Highway 2 from Sonoyta, Sonora, and on the American side by a dirt road through the Barry M. Goldwater Air Force Range to Interstate 8 at Wellton, Arizona.

Fages, searching for army deserters in 1772, charted a new route northward. Heading east from San Diego to the desert, he turned north along El Camino del Diablo through Paso de Buena Vista (Tejon Pass) into Antelope Valley and on into the San Joaquin Valley. Earlier that year he, Crespí, and some soldiers went up the eastern shore of San Francisco Bay to find a way to Point Reyes. Eventually they were blocked by the Carquínez Strait, discovering the San Joaquin River and, in the distance, the Sacramento River. Turning eastward they reached a point near the site of Antioch where they decided to return to Monterey. Seeking a shorter route, they crossed the Santa Angela Plain, and, via the San Ramon and Amador Valleys and Mission Creek, they crossed their outward trails near the site of San Jose. The details for this exploration are found in the diary Fages composed for Bucareli; it was translated in 1937 by Herbert Priestley (1875-1944) but forgotten until found in the Bancroft Library in 1971 by Theodore Treutlein (1906-86).

Despite his originally negative attitude toward California, Bucareli certainly recognized the area's strategic value for

Mexico against the Russians. Having been governor of Cuba when Spain entered the Seven Years' War, he had experienced the humiliation of defeat when the English captured Havana. It also taught him the value of buffer areas against foreign enemies.

Spain's 16th and 17th century colonies had been established for their own value. But as the 18th, century European rivals began to crowd into the *terra incognita* separating Spanish colonies from theirs, Spain decided to create buffer colonies to protect the older, more valuable territories from encroachment. Thus, in 1762, Florida was garrisoned to protect the Silver Fleet (also known as the West Indies fleet, its galleons carrying goods across the Atlantic from Mexico to Spain), Texas was planted to ward off French activities in the Mississippi basin (1680), Uruguay was designed to block the Portuguese drive southwest from Brazil (1624), and Louisiana was accepted from France after the Seven Years' War (1763) to shield New Spain from English expansion.

If the province of Alta California was to survive, coastal exploration and an overland trail from Mexico were necessary. Coastal voyages designed to sniff out the Russians were established. They were also motivated by Bucareli's concern about English activities. Renewed English interest in discovering the Northwest Passage, as represented by Captain James Cook's (1728-79) second voyage (1772-75), pushed Bucareli to act. As a result, Spain could claim priority in the exploration of most of the coast up to Alaska.

In 1773 Portolá's naval commander, Pérez, was ordered to sail to 60o N., the supposed Strait of Anián (or Northwest Passage.) Scurvy and the local storms kept him from getting past 55oN. He coasted the Queen Charlotte Islands without recognizing them as islands, and then was forced to turn back. On August 7, 1773, he anchored in Nootka Sound, San

Lorenzo to him, and gave Spain the claim that predated Cook by five years. The regional fogs kept him from seeing any actual entrances or from checking the imaginary ones those fanciful cartographers had placed there.

Two years later Pérez was back as the chief pilot of Bruno Hezeta's (1743-1807) expedition of two ships, the *Santiago* and the *Sonora*, one of whose commanders was Juan Francisco de la Bodega (1744-94). In 1774, Pérez had taken the Santiago north but had not been able to get as far as originally ordered. This time it was a success. They stopped at Trinidad Bay in northern California, where formal possession was taken in Carlos III's name. They proved that the Juan de Fuca inlet was just as fictitious as its discoverer. On July 14, north of Gray's Harbor on the northwest coast, they anchored and became the first Europeans to walk on that soil. At another stop hostile Indians killed half of one of the ship's crews. Hezeta, disgusted, wanted to return to Mexico before bad weather and scurvy made their appearance.

Bodega, determined to reach 60°N, as ordered, had other ideas. His pilots helplessly allowed their undermanned ship to drift in the night fog, and managed to reach 58°N. Hezeta and Pérez, with a sick crew, went only as far as Nootka before turning south. Running along the shore when the fog dispersed enough to allow them a view of the coast, Hezeta on August 17, 1775 "discovered a large bay, to which [he] gave the name of Assumption Bay." Unable to land, for "if we let go the anchor, we should not have had men enough to get it up," he lay to, but the night currents swept him far out to sea. He had marked on his map and described two bold headlands that were temporarily named Cabo San Roque and Cabo Frondoso, "the mouth of some great river, or of some passage to another sea. . . .." Temporarily named Entrada de Hezeta it would be unrecognized for another seventeen years, until

Captain Robert Gray (1755-1806), master of the *U.S.S. Columbia*, rediscovered it and renamed the river for his ship and the two capes Disappointment and Adams.

On his return from the north, Hezeta attempted to enter San Francisco Bay through the Golden Gate, but failed.

Juan Manuel de Ayala (1745-97), who was originally assigned to sail with Hezeta and Bodega on the *Sonora*, was put in charge of the Monterey-bound ship *San Carlos* when its captain, Don Miguel Manrique, went insane at San Blas before the *Sonora* and *Santiago* could sail. The plan then ordered Ayala and the *San Carlos* to join the *Sonora* and *Santiago* and sail north together until they reached Monterey. At Monterey, Hezeta and Bodega continued north while Ayala took on supplies before continuing to San Francisco Bay, which he was to explore.

On July 27, 1775, the *San Carlos* left Monterey and a week later arrived off the Golden Gate. However, things did not go as planned. The insane Manrique "had left loaded pistols about his cabin, and one of these accidentally exploded, wounding Ayala," who then had to conduct most of his exploration of the Bay through subordinates. During the next evening (August 5) the little ship successfully passed through the strait and anchored near the present North Beach. Stories about Sir Francis Drake notwithstanding, Ayala and his subordinate, José Cañizares, attained the honor of making the first recorded entrance into San Francisco Bay through the Golden Gate.

For 44 days, the crew of the San Carlos explored the Bay thoroughly, going to the mouth of the San Joaquin River, taking soundings, and naming geographical points. Two of the names have survived: Angel Island, where the ship anchored while the crew explored in a launch, and Pelican Island (better known as Alcatraz, the *Isla de los Alcatraces*).

Ayala returned to Monterey on September 19, and soon departed for San Blas. No longer could anyone confuse San Francisco and Drake's Bays. In his report to the Viceroy, Ayala wrote of San Francisco Bay that it was

> "the best I have seen in those seas from Cape Horn north.... It is not one port, but many, with a single entrance.... Not only does it offer fine proportions to the sight, but also there is no scarcity of good water, wood and stone for ballast. Its climate, though cold, is entirely healthful, and is free from the annoying daily fogs experienced at Monterey. To all these advantages must be added the best of all, which is that the heathen Indians of the port are so faithful in their friendship and so docile in their disposition that I was greatly pleased to receive them on board."[8]

Chapter Four END NOTES

[1] Donald E. Chipman, "GALVEZ GALLARDO, JOSE BERNARDO DE," *Handbook of Texas Online* Uploaded on June 15, 2010. Published by the Texas State Historical Association, accessed September 29, 2015, http://www.tshaonline.org/handbook/online/articles/fga53.

[2] Bill Mason, "The Garrisons of San Diego Presidio: 1770-1794," *Journal of San Diego History*, 24:4, (Fall 1978), accessed July 12, 2015, http://sandiegohistory.org/journal/1978/october/garrisons/; Ron Filion, "California Spanish Genealogy – California Census 1775," accessed May 9, 2023, https://www.sfgenealogy.org/doku.php?id=california_bay_area:dat abases:california_census_1775; Granville Hough, and N.C. Hough, *Spain's California Patriots in its 1779-1783 War With England During the American Revolution,* accessed May 9, 2023, https://www.southcoastsar.org/borderlandstudies/BOOK_1.PDF

³ Herbert Eugene Bolton, *Fray Juan Crespi: Missionary Explorer on the Pacific Coast 1769-1774* (Berkeley: University of California Press, 1927), p. 139. This volume includes the Crespi diary of the Sacred Expedition and is duplicated at https://babel.hathitrust.org/cgi/pt?id=uc1.$b233487&view=1up&seq=9

⁴ *Publications of the Academy of Pacific Coast History*, Volume 2. University of California, 1911. By which they meant Drakes Bay.

⁵ "Route of Discovery", *San Francisco Sunday Examiner & Chronicle*, Sunday Punch, October 15, 1978 for a description of the route for tourists.

⁶ Zephyrin Engelhardt, *San Juan Capistrano Mission* (Los Angeles: Standard Printing, 1922), p. 10.

⁷ For three centuries European countries' economic policies had been joined to their diplomatic policies – a belief that all external activities should benefit themselves. Thus, trade should be for the country's advantage and tariffs should be imposed to keep the balance of trade to the nation's benefit. When colonies were established, they were expected to benefit the mother country and not compete with it. Trade was to be with the mother country exclusively and not even with the mother country's other colonies. To obtain desired goods, colonial people often engaged in smuggling, despite the risks, and deprived the mother country of the revenue that would have gone to it had the trade been legal. By Bucareli's time, economic thinkers were pointing out the disadvantages of mercantilism – as opposed to the benefits of free-trade - and enlightened rulers were abandoning it. This was Bucareli's motive for liberalizing trade law. Henry William Spiegel, *The Growth of Economic Thought* (3rd ed.), (Durham NC: Duke University Press, 1991), pp. 93-118, and Murray Rothbard, "Mercantilism in Spain," Mises Daily Articles, April 28, 2022. (Accessed May 8, 2023) https://mises.org/library/mercantilism-spain

⁸ Charles E. Chapman, *A History of California: The Spanish Period* (New York: Macmillan, 1921), p. 280.

Chapter Four FURTHER READING:

1. Bolton, Herbert E. *Pageant in the Wilderness: The Story of the Escalante Expedition to the Interior Basin, 1776*. Salt Lake City: Utah State Historical Society, 1950.

2.   Breschini, Gary S. "The Portolá Expedition of 1769." Monterey County Historical Society, 2010. Accessed July 5, 2015. http://www.mchsmuseum.com/portola1769.html.

3.   Farebrother, David L. "Alta California: Portolá Expedition." Facebook. February 10, 2024. https://www.facebook.com/portolaexpedition

4.   Fireman, Janet and Servin, Manuel. "Miguel Costansó: California's Forgotten Founder". *California Historical Society Quarterly,* 49:1 (1970), pp. 3-19. Abbreviated *CHSQ*

5.   Frost, Orcutt William, ed., *Bering: The Russian Discovery of America.* New Haven: Yale University Press, 2005

6.   Gibson, James R. "Russian Expansion in Siberia and America," *Geographical Review* 70:2 (1980), 130. Cited in Claudio Saunt, *West of the Revolution: An Uncommon History of 1776.* (New York: Norton, 2014), p. 36.

7.   Hough, Granville and N.C. *Spain's California Pioneers in its 1779-1783 War With England During the American Revolution.* Accessed July 12, 2015. http://www.cagenweb.com/monterey/books/Spain's%20California%20Patriots.pdf.

8.   Howe, George. "The Voyage of Nor'west John," *American Heritage* 10, no. 3 (April 1959): pp. 65-80. Accessed April 18, 2015. http://www.americanheritage.com/content/voyage-nor'west-john

9.   Linehan, Paul. "Jose Torrubia" *Catholic Answers* https:www.catholic.com/encyclopedia/jose-torrubia (accessed August 5, 2022).

10.   Priestley, H. I. *José de Gálvez, Visitador-General of New Spain,* 1765-1771. Berkeley: University of California Press, 1916.

11.   *Publications of the Academy of Pacific Coast History*, Volume 2. University of California, 1911.

12.   Santa Clara Valley History. Early California:Miguel Costanso's Diary of the Portola Expedition. Accessed March 3, 2015. http://www.scvhistory.com/scvhistory/costanso-diary.htm.

Chapter 5: Outpost of Empire (1775-1821)

The Anza Trail

The viceroy had ordered an annual supply ship from San Blas, although numerous people had suggested that a land route was preferable. Father Verger had recommended increasing the number of pack animals in the new missions, Serra and Palóu favored a route from New Mexico, Costansó had little use for Bucareli's designs at San Blas and pointed out that a Sonora route was the best idea, and José de Areche (1731-89, fiscal [treasurer]) of the Audiencia of Mexico) supported the idea of a Sonora route as cheaper than the sea route. To all these requests, Bucareli politely turned a deaf ear.

It was two Sonora men, Captain Juan Bautista de Anza (1735-88) and Father Garcés, whose recommendation to the viceroy was heeded because it offered a concrete plan.

Fray Garcés, 26 years old in 1774, had established friendly contacts with various Arizona tribes, including the Papago, Pima and Yuma. With the Pimas he had achieved great success by using colored banners - mild blues and whites emblazoned with the Virgin Mary on one side as a depiction of the joys of Heaven, the reverse depicting in stark reds and blacks the Devil to detail the pains of Hell. This appealed to the Pimas and resulted in many conversions. Learning that the Pimas and Yumas were enemies he decided to make peace between them, and, setting out along the eastern flank of the Gila Range, headed west along the desert before turning south to the Gila River ten leagues above its mouth. Late one night in August 1771, he reached the Yumas and was warmly welcomed by their chief, Ollyquotquiebe, later known as

Salvador Palma.[1] After two months of exploratory wanderings he explored the Gila and Colorado, touching the sites of Pilot's Knob, Ogden's Landing, Heintzelman's Point, San Jácome, Cerro Prieto, Yuba Springs and Lake Maquata. This difficult journey by a lone man on horseback took him "about 300 leagues" (approximately 1,255 km or 780 miles) until he returned to Caborca. He had traversed the Yuma desert in two places, trailblazing from the head of the Sea of Cortés to Alta California, a feat Kino had unsuccessfully attempted, and on his return, he crossed the terrible Colorado desert via El Camino del Diablo.

Anza, three years older than Garcés, was, like his soldier father before him, a seasoned Indian fighter. Reputedly fierce in battle and someone the natives would challenge only at their peril; he was also fair and just in his dealings with Indians and always preferred to settle disputes peacefully. As the captain at Tubac, he was one of Fray Garcés's parishioners. Having been an unsuccessful candidate for the leadership of the Sacred Expedition, Anza repeated the offer to pioneer a route to California in May 1772, after Garcés returned from his trek. Garcés had seen a ridge beyond the Colorado which was probably the ridge behind San Diego, so the desert must be narrower than supposed. "In view of this," he explained to the viceroy, "this Reverend Father and I concluded that the distance to Monterey is not so enormous as used to be estimated, and that it will not be impossible to compass it." He concluded by requesting Garcés's company should the plan be approved.

Captain Juan Bautista de Anza (via Wikimedia Commons)

Bucareli did approve and Anza was ordered to find a way from Mexico to the California settlements via Sonora (which then included southern Arizona). Years earlier Kino had made known the way from San Xavier del Bac to the foot of the Gila Range, and now Garcés had opened a trail across the Yuma and Colorado deserts; Anza would have to find the way over the California mountains to connect with Portolá's trail to the coast.

On January 8, 1774, Anza set out from Tubac on this first

task accompanied by Garcés, Fray Juan Díaz, and a runaway from San Gabriel called Sebastián to serve as guide, plus 30 other men, 140 horses, and 65 head of cattle. In a month they reached the Gila via Sonoyta and were well received by Chief Palma, whom Anza presented with a new suit of fine clothes and a golden badge of office under Spain (to the Indians such gifts were validation of their extant and workable native structures of government, but to the Europeans, bestowing such items was merely an act of patronizing). Leaving many of the animals with Palma and a few muleteers, he crossed the Colorado on March 9, keeping to the south of modern Interstate 8, and camped in California. From their campsite just above the later boundary line they continued southwest until they reached Anza's Laguna de Santa Olaya, south and west of the Colorado; beyond lay hostile tribes and treacherous sand dunes blocking the way into what is now southeastern Imperial County. Undaunted, Anza determined to cross this forbidding waste, but the dunes forced him to retreat to Santa Olaya, reaching it on February19. After resting among friendly Indians, they resumed their trek on March 2, and reentered California a week later, camping between Yuha Well and the modern border with Mexico. The next day they rested while Anza opened wells "distilling an abundant supply of most beautiful water," naming them Pozas de Santa Rosa de las Lajas (wells of St. Rose of the flat rocks), later altered to Yuha Well, in a basin between modern Dixieland and the border. On March 10 their last desert camp was made at the junction of the San Felipe and Carrizo creeks, which Anza called the San Sebastián, in honor of their guide. Later it was renamed Harper's Well, at the western wall of the Colorado desert. On March 16 they climbed the pass he named San Carlos, coming up from the San Jacinto Mountains and the Borrego Valley along what became State Route 71. Two days later they reached a leafy cottonwood grove on the

San Jacinto River and camped. On the 20th they turned left passing the sites of Moreno and Riverside in Sycamore Canyon. There they encountered friendly Indians who ferried them across the Santa Ana River. Following the old Indian trail along present-day Euclid Avenue between Ontario and Upland, Anza reached Mission San Gabriel at sunset on March 22 and was given a joyous reception.

Resting for three weeks to await supplies to take them to Monterey, Anza and his men went up into the San Fernando Valley to the Los Angeles River and westward into the mountains past present-day Glendale. They generally followed modern U.S. 101's route with campsites in Russell Valley, Goleta, the mouth of the Santa Ynés River, and Mission San Luis Obispo (where Anza met with Serra returning from Mexico and regaled him with tales of the desert crossing.) Anza and his party traversed the Santa Lucía over the Cuesta Pass to the site of Paso Robles, at the Nacimiento River, and finally crossed the San Antonio River to a welcome at Mission San Antonio de Padua. During a rainstorm they made a final stop at the site of Gonzalez, and on April 19, reached Monterey. Within two weeks they had returned to San Gabriel and began their trek across the desert, reaching Tubac on May 26. As Bolton assesses it, "for full 600 miles (965 km) he was a trail blazer. His journey to and from Monterey covered more than 2,000 miles (3,220 km). To go to Mexico City to report his work to the viceroy and return to his post involved a horseback ride of an additional 3,000 miles (4,828 km). He had earned his title of 'the hard-riding captain.'"

Having proven the feasibility of the land route, Anza organized an expedition of 240 colonists and more than 1,000 livestock. From a recruiting station at San Felipe in Sinaloa and from the rendezvous at Horcasitas, on the Sonora River (for civilians) and at Tubac (for clergy), they set out on

October 23, 1775. Garcés, along with Fray Pedro Font (1737-81), the short, chunky missionary at San Jose de Pimas (at present-day La Colorada) and Fray Tomás Eixarch (1744-c1790), from Tumacácori, comprised the clergy.

On the road from Horcasitas to Tubac, an Apache horse-stealing raid enlivened the journey, as did the tribulations of inexperienced muleteers who were kept busy reinforcing the packs. On the day after leaving Tubac, the party suffered its only casualty: the wife of one of the sergeants died in childbirth - ironically, and sadly, because Anza, who had pledged to use only "modern" medicines, refused to allow the midwives to employ what he considered "superstitious" native herbs known to control bleeding. Her infant son survived and became the father of a large family in California. Two other infants were born along the way, one at Coyote Canyon (Riverside County.) He is considered California's first *non-Indian* native son, Salvador Ignacio Linares (1775-1807).

When they reached Yuma junction, Palma gave them a warm welcome, supplying them with melons and helping them to cross the Colorado. The old ford was no longer passable, and it was too cold for swimmers to guide the rafts, so Anza found another ford with water three to six feet (91 cm-1.8 m) deep that allowed them to cross half a day later. A little girl was swept away when a rider deviated from the proper course, but a soldier stationed below the spot rescued her. Father Font, dizzy from ague, was carried across between two mounted natives, and Garcés, who could not swim, was carried across, stretched out between three Yumas.

On the California side they put up a little cabin and stocked it with food for Garcés and Eixarch, and then headed toward Santa Olaya. There, at the edge of the desert, Anza ordered a rest for several days, then divided the party into three groups to travel at one day intervals. On December 11 Anza led the first party, and two days later Lieutenant José Moraga (1741-85) started out with the third party.

Rather than desert heat they encountered snow. The third day was particularly rough, with a 35-mile (56 km) trek though bitter cold to Santa Rosa, where they made camp with very poor fires. Moraga was so exposed to cold that for some time he was deaf. Anza's first party passed San Sebastián and camped without water in the Borrego Valley; the next night, with only a little water at San Gregorio, some of the cattle stampeded and many were lost - a particularly frustrating event especially since they were so near the end of the journey.

On Christmas Eve they camped at Coyote Canyon, and it was here that little Salvador Linares was born. Forgetting their misery, the colonists spent their first California Christmas singing, dancing, and over-imbibing the aguardiente Anza issued. On Christmas morning they remained because of the baby, so Font took the opportunity to scold his hung-over flock for their overindulgence and to wish them a happy Christmas.

From there they journeyed through rain and sleet up Coyote Canyon, camped just below the Royal Pass of San Carlos, then crossed the divide. On New Year's Day, 1776, they spent an arduous day crossing the turbulent Santa Ana, losing more cattle and spent the night on San Antonio Creek, near present Ontario. Two days later they received a warm welcome at San Gabriel.

Though still over 400 miles (644 km) from San Francisco Bay, they counted their journey practically completed. Unfortunately, they could not go on immediately. On the night of November 4, the unconverted Indians gave vent to their

179

hatred of Mission San Diego by making a surprise attack. Thirty-five-year-old Fray Luis Jaume (or Jayme), trying to calm the savage mob of over 600 by walking toward them with his hand extended in his usual blessing "Love God, my children!" was brutally slain, being stabbed repeatedly, shot with 18 arrows, disemboweled and having his face pulverized. Also killed were the two guard soldiers, and the mission buildings were destroyed. Anza, Font and 17 soldiers joined Rivera in a journey to San Diego to punish the killers.

A number were caught by now-Lieutenant José Ortega, the commander of the San Diego Presidio. Following Rivera's orders, Ortega ordered the prisoners whipped in the style of "the law of Bayonne" whereby they would be forced to sit on the ground with a pole placed in the crook of their knees, their arms pulled under the pole, and their wrists bound together around their legs, thus leaving them at the mercy of the one wielding the whip. This continued as rumors of further rebellions circulated and Indian ringleaders were captured, including one Diego, who was Rivera's godson, for several months. When Bucareli heard of this, he approved the punishments but decided against executions, much to Rivera's disapproval.

Rivera used the uprising as an excuse not to obey Bucareli's orders to assist Anza in establishing a new settlement in the Bay Area. Rivera, who with Palóu, had planted a cross on Point Lobos above Seal Rocks in 1774, disapproved of the site for a colony or a mission. Another cause of delay was the desertion of five muleteers who started back to Sonora with the 25 best horses. Moraga, in hot pursuit, overtook them at Santa Olaya, recaptured the cattle that had stampeded at San Gregorio and returned the deserters to the San Gabriel calabozo.

At San Gabriel there was a severe supply shortage, so Anza

left for Monterey on February 21,1776, taking only half his party and leaving the rest to follow with the cattle. His route was much the same as that of 1774, and he arrived at Monterey on March 10. After a day of rejoicing, Serra escorted the travelers into his Mission San Carlos. Anza had become sick, but, obedient to his orders, he insisted on pushing north before fully recovering.

On his way north he took Font and 13 soldiers, leaving the rest of his people at Monterey until final arrangements for their migration could be made. He went via the Salinas River and the Gabilán Mountains into the Santa Clara Valley, to the Arroyo de San Jose Cupertino, and then up the Peninsula, passing through the present sites of Burlingame, Millbrae, and Daly City before reaching San Francisco on March 27. On the Peninsula, near Crystal Springs Lake, Corporal Robles shot an immense bear whose skin was preserved as a gift for the viceroy.

On March 28 Anza selected the site for the Presidio of San Francisco, and on June 27, Palóu arrived and chose the site for Mission San Francisco de Asís, near a little stream which he named the Arroyo de Nuestra Señora de los Dolores (Our Lady of Sorrows.) Having made his selection, Anza marched around the southern end of the Bay. In the East Bay he vainly searched for the white and bearded Indians Crespí had found in 1772, chalking it up to a harmless mistake on Crespí's part. Unable to detect any current at Carquínez Straits they concluded that this body of water must be an inland, freshwater sea. Marshes blocked further progress east, so Anza returned to Monterey, cutting across via the Livermore Valley, the tick-infested San Antonio Valley, and the Gilroy Valley.

It had been Anza's hope to conduct the colonists personally to San Francisco, but Rivera's dilatory and obstructionist policies delayed him. On April 14 he turned command over to Moraga and started south with two pairs of cats to be used against problem mice at San Gabriel and San Diego. Rivera, half-crazed with anger that the San Francisco project was moving forward despite his disapproval, hurried north from San Diego to confer with Anza. Here began a power contest: Meeting just south of Monterey, exchanging hardly more than a salute, and going on in opposite directions; then Rivera retracing his path to catch Anza, having to cool his heels when Anza refused to communicate except in writing, then Anza having to cool his heels at San Gabriel. Moraga and Rivera exchanged a few letters while they were both at San Gabriel but came to no agreement concerning San Francisco. Rivera seems not to have cared that the settlement *had* been ordered by the viceroy. Anza then made a fast ride to Mexico City to see the viceroy, taking one companion and making the trip in two weeks. Bucareli issued a new order, and this time Rivera was forced to comply.

Moraga, joined by Palóu and another priest, led the settlers - who wept because they missed Anza - to the chosen site. There, on September 17, 1776, the presidio was founded, and the mission was dedicated 22 days later. This outpost of empire, San Francisco, "was at least on the map," in Bolton's words. He lauds the achievement:

> Anza, Font, Moraga and Palóu had placed a 'sign of occupation' at the portal, and a nucleus of civilization on the shores of the harbor of harbors. The city by the Golden Gate is their monument. The genius and devotion with which Anza served his country in this time of need made him a distinguished figure. His performance of the strenuous tasks to which he was assigned revealed him in his true proportions - a man of heroic qualities, tough as oak, and silent as the

desert from which he sprang.... His achievement was a significant factor in the long contest of European peoples for the domination of a continent.

In a similar vein Gary Kurutz (1948-) of the California Historical Society summed up this event with praise for:

> These rugged settlers [who] left their homeland in Mexico in the hope of finding a better life in California. They were the first to come to California as a result of an organized, promotional campaign. After the long trek, those that stayed in California formed the nucleus of great Californio families, ranchos and pueblos. Such names as Bernal, Moraga, Pico, Peralta, Pacheco, Berryessa, and Vásquez remind us of the heroics of those original colonists.[2]

Surveying the site Father Font wrote two prophetic entries into his journal for the of March 27 and 28, 1776. In these he described with great vision the future potentialities of this "Harbor of Harbors" and the city that would one day be located on what would one day be known as the Golden Gate. He also gave it its first name, "the yerba buena," from the mint plants that abounded, a name that stuck until the Gold Rush.

**

Captain Anza went on to become governor of New Mexico. While there, he approved the journey of Fray Francisco Atanasio Domínguez (1740-1805) and Fray Silvestre Vélez de Escalante (1750-80) to find a land route from New Mexico to Monterey. Escalante, the more famous of the two because his journal described the expedition, was first stationed at Laguna pueblo in New Mexico, and then was assigned to minister to the Zuñi. Domínguez had been sent to

New Mexico to inspect the missions there. In June 1776, Domínguez summoned Escalante for the journey to California. Eleven New Mexicans were chosen to join them, the most important being the Spanish-born artist and cartographer Don Bernardo Miera y Pacheco (1713-85).

Escalante and his band did not reach the Pacific coast, but their explorations in the Great Basin, progressing for 70 days from late July to October through a largely uncharted area between the Rockies and the Sierra Nevada, brought them in a round trip from Santa Fe to the future sites of Durango (Colorado), then in Utah, to Vernal, Provo, Cedar City, St. George, and Oraibi.

Escalante enjoyed Miera y Pacheco's company, but Domínguez was less than pleased with the artist, perhaps a matter of clashing personalities. In any case, Miera y Pacheco's maps of the area were the greatest result of the expedition, since Domínguez published them along with a report in 1778.

**

Anza's obstructionist foe, Rivera - unable, like Fages, to maintain good relations with Serra - was removed as gobernante in February 1777 because of conflicts with the priest and disobedience to the viceregal orders relative to San Francisco. Ten months earlier the king had ordered that Monterey be the capital of the Californias; accordingly. Colonel Felipe de Neve (1728-84), governor of the Californias from March 1775, moved from Loreto to Monterey, and Rivera was promoted to the newly-created office of lieutenant governor of the Californias in residence in Loreto.

Neve, aged 49 when he arrived in Monterey, had been a soldier since he was sixteen, and had served with Portolá in

Europe and in Mexico. A very capable administrator, dedicated to duty despite a chronic illness, he was very aloof, and would gain the respect - but little more - of his soldiers. His wife had remained in Spain, and sadness at her absence may have appeared as cool aloofness to his associates.

At the same time Governor Neve arrived at Monterey, a new administrative district was created. Against Bucareli's wishes the frontier provinces of the North and West (that is, from California to Louisiana and what is now northern Mexico) were grouped into a new entity called the Provincias Internas, with co-capitals at Arizpe (in Sonora) and Monterrey (in Nuevo León) under a captain-general. Madrid's ultimate intention was to create a new viceroyalty after the territory had become sufficiently cohesive. Bucareli naturally saw this as a degradation of his own power and a threat to subdivide the viceroyalty the way Peru had been partitioned into three (New Granada in 1717 and La Plata in 1776). In command of the Internal Provinces was General Teodoro de Croix (1730-92), nephew of the former viceroy.

One of the reasons Bucareli lost direct control of the north was that he had been incapable of crushing the warlike Comanches and Apaches who harassed the colonists of Chihuahua year after year. General Croix, in an alliance with the Comanches (who, it was hoped, would calm down as a result of the alliance), determined to force the Apaches into an ambush on the Rio Grande in order to exterminate them. It would have worked had Spain not found itself embroiled in the war of the American Revolution. Spain, it appeared, had no time to think about what it could only view as savages on an endless frontier.

Governor Neve's reign saw a great deal of growth. The first two pueblos, San Jose and Los Angeles, were organized, since Neve hoped that they would be the core of a system to rival the missions and win military domination over Alta California.

In 1777 Neve appointed Moraga to establish a settlement on the Guadalupe River two and one-quarter miles (3.6 km) from Mission Santa Clara. He was to take with him nine soldiers of "known agricultural skill, two settlers, and three laborers." On November 29 it was founded about one and one-half miles (2.4 km) from the center of the present city of San Jose, where the Guadalupe Parkway crosses Taylor Street. The next year it was moved three miles (4.8 km) to where its downtown is located today.

A few years later, on September 4, 1781, in a location "45 leagues from the Presidio of San Diego, 27 leagues from the Presidio of Santa Barbara, and about one and one-half leagues from Mission San Gabriel, el Pueblo de Nuestra Señora la Reina de los Angeles del Río Porciúncula was founded in the name of the king in the plaza now bordered by North Main Street, Bellevue, New High Street and Sunset Boulevard.[3] It is one of history's comic touches that such a small pueblo had such a long name while, as one of the largest cities in the world today, it is popularly known as "L.A.," short for Los Angeles. Fourteen civilians and 59 soldiers - poverty-stricken Sinaloans - constituted the founders, and they had to be quarantined because of smallpox. The plaza was about 200 feet wide by 300 feet long (61-91 m), established with building lots around it and planting fields beyond, the latter to be parceled out as the pueblo grew. Neve read a proclamation, a modest parade was held, and a lone cannon was fired. Then, before returning to Monterey, Moraga placed Corporal José Vicente Feliz (or Félix) (1741-1809) in charge as "little father of the pueblo" (in effect the first mayor of Los Angeles). Among the original settlers was six-year-old Antonio María Lugo (1778-1860), who would become one of California's most affluent ranchers.

In June 1779 Neve issued a *Reglamento* which formed the basis for governing California during the Spanish period, approved by Bucareli in 1780 and by the king in 1781. Though not all his proposed legislation, for example single-friar missions and use of military escorts by the friars except when called to hear confessions, was fully implemented, his administrative ability was sufficiently appreciated to get him promoted to inspector-general the same year, and in 1782, to commander of the Internal Provinces.

Rivera had been ordered to enlist settlers for Los Angeles, and with difficulty had gathered eleven families (44 persons) and 17 soldiers as well as 960 head of cattle. Having to recruit as far south as Guadalajara, he began the march to the Colorado. There he reached the two little settlements - La Concepción and San Pedro y San Pablo - that had been founded in 1780 by Croix in a less-than-favorable conditions. Meeting some soldiers from Monterey, he sent his married men ahead. Four days later, July 18, 1781, Rivera paid for his old anti-Indian prejudices: He was a careless disciplinarian who did not restrain his company from antagonizing a group of Yumas, and his gifts for Palma - who had kept the trail open and always received fine goods in return - were inexcusably cheap. On July 17 the Yumas had attacked the two tiny missions, enslaving the women and children and killing all the men except Garcés and 32-year-old Fray Juan Antonio Barreneche, who were spared until two days later when they were clubbed to death against Palma's orders. Rivera and his soldiers, unaware of the excitement a few kilometers distant, were massacred on the 18th. A total of 131 would fall.

This mass slaughter ranks as one of the worst frontier disasters in the history of the United States. Neve refused to permit *Alférez* (Second Lieutenant) Cayetano Limón (c. 1745-

?), from San Gabriel, to avenge it. Croix sent Fages from Sonora to recover bodies and ransom prisoners.

It is tempting to blame Rivera for the tragedy. He had done much for the colony, and his inglorious end, for which he bore some measure of guilt, beclouds his reputation. Yet Croix and Neve chose to include Garcés and Anza in the blame, maintaining that the latter had underestimated the danger at Yuma; as a result, he lost the governorship of New Mexico. The chief blame, however, rests with Croix; he delayed establishing settlements, boasted of "economies" in Indian presents and presidial guards, and, providing an example of the Peter Principle (promulgated by Laurence Peter and Raymond Hull in the 1960s, according to which one is promoted to the level of one's incompetence), he was eventually promoted to viceroy of Peru.

The Anza Trail was rendered useless, never to be restored. Yuma hostility would preclude further immigration by way of it, and California's only connection with Mexico would now be by the very unsatisfactory sea route from San Blas. California's prosperity, growth, development, and political attachment to Mexico - all flourishing during the preceding half-dozen years - were impaired. For the future, growth would have to come from within. In retrospect, the Yuma Massacre would make it easier for the United States to take California 65 years later. When the Spanish founded San Francisco and checkmated the British and Russians, they ensured that no powerful nation would move in on California. When California was cut off from Mexico, its Mexican loyalties would weaken, making it within six decades a ripe plum for another great power, the United States of America.

**

"...a beautiful country, a warm climate, an abundance of grain and cattle -- and nothing else."

-Doña Concepción Argüello, 1806

**

A Tranquil Period

The 40 years following the Yuma Massacre saw California grow gradually but well because of the institutions introduced and developed by Gálvez and Bucareli. The governors, who had previously been at Loreto, now resided at Monterey and presided over affairs in both Baja and Alta California. The first dozen years of settlement had been filled with momentous events - the Sacred Expedition, the discovery of San Francisco Bay, Anza, Bucareli and Neve, the first pueblos and the Yuma Massacre. Starvation, shipwreck, and constant Indian hostility added to the mystique of those exciting times. In contrast, the next four decades were generally peaceful, and therefore much less spectacularly heroic. In popular history these decades have become the "good old days," a romantic and idyllic period that provided the setting which no doubt would have been recognizable to Californians of those days (recognizable, despite many anachronistic touches) for stories such as Helen Hunt Jackson's *Ramona* (1884) and Johnston McCulley's *Zorro* (1919). A very well-known figure from California's entertainment industry in fact had family connections that linked California's idyllic four decades to a recognizably modern California: Leo Carrillo (1881-1961), an actor best remembered for his role as sidekick to "The Cisco Kid" in a 1950-56 television series. His great-great-grandfather was José Raimundo Carrillo (1749-1809), who had come with Portolá, and who was married to Tomasa Ignacia Lugo (1762-1816) by Father Serra in 1781.

189

Nevertheless, this four-decade period was not uneventful. Some of the most colorful figures of the state's local history walk across the stage at this point, including the pair of lovers in California's most famous love story, which will be covered later in this chapter.

The major area of California's growth was on the central coast until the arrival of the Americans.

Cattle raising, beginning with the few dozen the Sacred Expedition brought, and increasing with Anza's party, became the economic mainstay for many years to come. By 1800, the estimate of 153,000 head of cattle and 61,000 horses - most belonging to the missions - was not far off the mark. As the number increased, it became increasingly difficult for the colonists to care for them without help. The priests, responding to this need, violated Spanish law and taught their Indians to ride, rope, brand, skin, and dress cattle. These skills were disseminated among them in the 1770s, despite Spanish fears that they would apply riding skills to uprising, and by the 1780s, a generation of Indian *vaqueros* had come into existence, many Indian boys equaling in skill their Spanish and Mexican teachers.

The large area from Los Angeles to Monterey, including the Channel Islands, provided a perfect nest for pirates or foreign enemies. The Chumash were still resistant to Spanish conquest. Accordingly, in March 1782, Mission San Buenaventura and the Presidio of Santa Barbara were founded, and in 1787, Mission La Purísima Concepción. The first settlers at Santa Barbara were the military families who had escaped the Yuma Massacre.

The Church

Eventually there would be 21 Franciscan missions,

intelligently located, prosperous, well-run and with a good Indian compulsory-labor supply. Their growth was slow, but once an area was brought under control, real progress was made. Serra built the first nine missions in four phases: San Diego and San Carlos (1769-70), San Antonio, San Gabriel, and San Luís Obispo (1771-72), San Francisco, San Juan Capistrano and Santa Clara (1776-77), and San Buenaventura (1782). The original Mission San Francisco probably stood at the present-day intersection of 18th and Church Streets near a willow-edged swamp called Laguna de Dolores (thus it is known as Mission Dolores), but the priests found that the soil was too damp and soft, so in 1782 they laid the cornerstone on Dolores Street between 16th and 17th Streets. 360 miles (580 km) to the south of Mission Dolores, Mission San Fernando had become a thriving industrial center supplying hides and shoes, tallow and soap, cloth and blankets, as well as wine, olive oil, and iron work to other missions or the pueblos. Its *convento* took thirteen years to construct (1809-22), a corridor with 21 Roman arches, four foot (1.22 m) thick adobe walls and the original grilles from the original mission building. On the Central Coast, under the direction of Fray Pedro Benito Cambón (1738-c.1792), an expert in irrigation, agriculture and building whom Padre Serra left in charge of the new Mission at San Buenaventura, a seven-mile-long (11 km) aqueduct was constructed to bring Ventura River water to the Mission. With plentiful water the Mission was able to maintain flourishing orchards and gardens, which were described by English navigator George Vancouver as the finest he had seen.[4]

Mission San Carlos Borromeo de Carmelo, Serra's favorite and the mission headquarters, as it would have looked before secularization, painted by Oriana Day (1838-86), the second artist to paint all 21 missions. (Via Wikimedia Commons)

According to historian Charles Lockwood (1948-2012) as many as 1,500 Indians lived and worked at the Mission Dolores, tending the animals, planting, and harvesting, grinding grain in the two mule-powered grist mills, and sewing clothing for themselves and the soldiers. Their religious instruction does not seem to have been very transformative, for they gambled among themselves for weapons, tools, ornaments, even the food they planted in their private gardens. And after Sunday Mass, they often painted their bodies black, red and white and put on their native headdresses and ornaments, much to the consternation of the padres.[5]

**

Today Mission San Juan Capistrano is beautiful, old, and romantic. There one can hear the tolling of its centuries-old bells and walk down its timeworn paths. Its serenity and peace amid lush gardens and cool fountains, cloistered by old adobe walls, offers visitors seclusion from the sounds and sights of a busy world just a few hundred meters away. This quiet is interrupted twice a year, near St. Joseph's Day (March 19), when cliff swallows return from their wintering in Corrientes, Argentina (about 6,000 miles [9,650 km] distant) to their mud nests at the mission, and near St. John Capistran's day (October 23) when they leave on their southern trek.

**

Neve did not get along with Serra any better than Fages had. Again, it was a battle of two strong-willed men. Neve, with the backing of the bishop of Sonora, wanted to replace the missions with the custodia. This policy would continue the Franciscans' religious authority over the Indians but would remove their constant control. Missions were intended to be temporary, lasting at most two generations, after which they would become parish churches as the missionaries headed to the frontier. However, Neve's attempt came before the first mission was even ten years old, and Serra successfully fought the change.

Probably smarting from his loss to Serra, Governor Neve made another move on the priest's power. Serra, as the highest Church official in California had taken on the duties of the hierarchy, including the administering of the sacrament of Confirmation. In the Catholic church, only a bishop can administer that sacrament, which confers the fullness of the Holy Spirit initially given in Baptism. Since Serra was not a bishop, Croix as the commander of the Internal Provinces had not approved his right to administer the sacrament. Neve took the opportunity to suspend Serra's right to administer Confirmation. While the Catholic church in Spain was closely tied to the government, the crown did not presume to exercise strict control over church matters, so Neve was probably overstepping his limits. Serra did not argue with Neve, nor did he appeal to the civil or church authorities in Mexico City; instead, he sent an appeal to Pope Pius VI (1722-99, reigned 1775-99), who, as head of the Catholic church, approved Serra's right to administer all sacraments and function in place of a bishop until one should be appointed. Because communications were so slow in the 18th century, the pope's approval didn't come until two years after Serra had sent in the appeal – at about the same time Croix granted authorization after Neve had presented *his* complaint about Serra's non-compliance with the order to suspend administering Confirmation.

In 1782 Neve stepped down as governor, to be promoted to commander of the Internal Provinces.

In August 1784 Serra died at the age of 70. Born on the island of Mallorca he had entered the Franciscan seminary at seventeen and had been sent to Mexico in 1749. He had been a missionary half his life, spending the last 15 years in California. Most of his time in California, he was in a great deal of pain from an ulcerated leg (caused by an insect sting) that never seemed to heal. His age and his poor health make his achievements even greater. A brave and unselfish man, often called the Father of California until the 1980s, he had always been highly regarded by Californians of all faiths as paramount among the first settlers. As the unsympathetic Carey McWilliams (1905-80) wrote in 1946 "Not one of the numerous Pope-baiting fundamentalist pastors of Southern California has ever objected to the community-wide adoration of the Missions."

Though many unfairly blame Serra for certain abuses of the Indians, among these, corporal punishment, confinement to the mission and forced labor, Serra tried his best to prevent ill effects, believing that the overall system would benefit the Indians. While it is true that the mission system seems harsh, we must remember we are looking at it from a twenty-first century perspective. When one realizes the mentality of the time and the attitudes then prevailing towards previously unimagined and often shockingly cruel cultures encountered by explorers, California's indigenous peoples might well have been subject to widespread extermination, as occurred in the case of U.S. treatment of such populations. The missionaries saw themselves as responsible for the conversion and care of the souls of the natives for their salvation, a care that encompassed their physical and economic well-being. Anti-Serra critics' complaint that Indians were whipped fails to take into account that such punishments were once seen as mild – the proverbial "slap on the wrist" - though by today's standards slaps on the wrist would likely be actionable. In January 2015, Pope Francis (1936-, reigning since 2013) decreed that Serra would be canonized later that year. In the opinion of a *Los Angeles Times* columnist, "his virtues outdistance his sins," perhaps the most tepid praise one might accord Serra. In September 2015 Serra became a saint of the Roman Catholic church, in the first canonization to take place in the United States.[6]

The Indians obtained a reliable food source, thanks exclusively to the missionaries. They learned new trades that would serve them well. Most importantly, from the Catholic perspective of the time, their souls were saved in the only way possible, living and dying as baptized Catholics. The Catholic principle *Extra Ecclesiam nulla salus* ("There is no salvation outside the Church"), under which the missionaries labored, has undergone development over the centuries, and it has been reformulated. Suffice it to say that the missionaries of California's founding era were motivated to suffer extreme labors and hardships for the sake of people they considered to be eternally lost without remedy if they were not received into the *Church.*

Junípero Serra personally oversaw the planning, construction, and staffing of each mission from his headquarters at Carmel. From Carmel he traveled on foot to the other missions along the California coast to supervise mission work and to confer the sacrament of Confirmation. Biographers estimate that, still bothered by a leg infection that had started soon after he arrived at Vera Cruz in 1749, Serra walked more than 24,000 miles (38,625 km) in California alone-- a greater distance than the journeys of Marco Polo (1271-95) and Lewis and Clark (1804-06) combined. (These explorers, however, mainly relied on conveyances other than their feet.) He kept steadfastly to his watchword, *"Siempre adelante, nunca hacia atrás."* ("Always go forward, never turn back.")

The mission president succeeding Fray Junípero Serra was Fray Fermín de Lasuén. Under Lasuén, the number of missions doubled. He added San Juan Bautista, Santa Cruz, Soledad, San José, Santa Bárbara, and La Purísima Concepción. The number of *neophytes* more than doubled, and Serra's missions - originally grass huts - were rebuilt, in what we refer to today as "mission style," of lumber-reinforced adobe. Mission San Francisco was completed in 1791 with adobe walls four feet (1.2 m] thick providing stability and insulation, thanks to Fray Cambón.[7]

In 1793 Lasuén undertook the building of Mission Carmel, as Serra had hoped. Native sandstone (easy to work until it starts to harden on contact with the air), quarried from the Santa Lucía Mountains, was used. Lime plaster (from burnt seashells) covered walls. An arch, a Moorish-style tower, and floors of burnt tile graced this beautiful structure, which took four years to complete. The mission's prosperity reached its height under Lasuén: 927 Indians and good crop reports marked the year 1794.

Because Serra had left Monterey and moved to Carmel, in 1794 Lasuén built the Royal Presidio Chapel with Indian labor. The Indians were under the direction of Manuel Ruiz, a Mexican master stonemason who had also directed the construction of Carmel Mission. At the time the chapel was at the southeast corner of the Presidio and helped to form the twelve-foot stone wall of the plaza (today at 500 Church Street, Monterey).

Under the auspices of Franciscan master craftsmen, the various missions made many long-lasting improvements. At Santa Cruz, in 1794, a horizontal water wheel mill was built, and in 1816, Fray José María de Zalvidea (1780-1846) designed what became known as El Molino Viejo at San Gabriel. Ten-inch-thick (25.4 cm) beams hewn from pines and sycamores hauled down from the San Gabriel Mountains, with walls ranging from 3 ½ to 5 ½ feet (1.06-1.67 m) were erected with earthquakes in mind, as were two massive buttresses to the east wall's corners. Although built for utilitarian purposes, beauty was not neglected. According to architectural historian Rexford Newcomb (1886-1968):

> "The simple proportions of this staunch old structure are admirable and the building reflects in every detail the good taste of the padres whose architectural creed seems always to have been simplicity, strength, and beauty." [8]

Every mission had a library. In addition, there were collections of musical instruments including organs, brass, string, and woodwind. Choirs and orchestras, some significant in size and competence, were favorably mentioned as early as in the 1780s and 1790s by foreign visitors. Of the 142

Franciscans who served in California, six were the primary promoters of church music, notably later Mission President Fray Narciso Durán (1776-1846), who arrived at Mission San Jose in 1806 and almost immediately set to work teaching his neophytes to read music and creating a 30-piece orchestra with some locally made instruments. In 1813 he produced the first of ten large format choir books for their use. To spread their appeal, he supervised a scriptorium at Mission San Jose to produce manuscript music books for the other missions. Other priests helped in this project, notably a student of native languages, Fray Felipe Arroyo de la Cuesta (1780-1840), to whom is owed a manuscript with settings of texts in the Mutsun Indian language. Formally-trained choirmaster Fray Florencio Ibáñez (1740-1818) wrote a *Pastorela* in 1801, A "shepherds' play" produced widely throughout California.[9]

The most prolific trained musician among the Franciscans was Fray Juan Bautista Sancho (1772-1830), whose copies of over forty works he brought to California in 1804 included sacred plainchant and polyphony, as well as opera arias that could be adapted to mission use such as Pietro Metastasio's (1698-1782) *Artasere* (1730), which evolved into use at a solemn piece by the imposition of two contrafactum texts (*Laudate Dominum*, from Psalm 116, and *Iam auditur celum*). Sancho's best original works are his *Misa en Sol* and *Misa de los Angeles*. Father Sancho spent his entire career in California at Mission San Antonio, and besides musical contributions also co-wrote a *Interrogatorio* which reported on the condition of the natives, their social customs, their music and even their flora. He also compiled vocabularies of several of their languages.

Affairs in Spain

Carlos III, the greatest of the Spanish Bourbons, the king

who ordered the settlement of Alta California, died in 1788 after a 29-year reign. A believer in enlightened absolutism, that is basing laws on rationality while retaining absolute power as monarch, he tended toward religious toleration, freedom of speech and press, and the right to hold private property. He also promoted education, science, and the arts. With the assistance of his prime minister, the Conde de Floridablanca (1728-1808) he had tried to rescue Spain and its empire from decay through such far-reaching reforms as weakening the power of the Church and its monasteries by promoting science and university research, facilitating trade and commerce, modernizing agriculture, and avoiding wars. Though never achieving a successful handle on finances, having to borrow constantly to meet expenses, his reforms did not survive him, and Spain relapsed into the decline that had begun with the defeat of the Spanish Armada two hundred years before. Historian Stanley Payne (1934-) opined that he "was probably the most successful European ruler of his generation. He had provided firm, consistent, intelligent leadership. He had chosen capable ministers…. [and his] personal life won the respect of the people."

One reason that his reforms did not take root was his successor, his 40-year-old son, Carlos IV. Unlike his father, he preferred diversions such as hunting (for which he was nicknamed El Cazador ["the Hunter"]) to affairs of state. An amiable, pious, and simple man, he left these to his wife, María Luisa and Floridablanca, to deal with. In 1792 Floridablanca's political and personal enemies forced him from office and replaced him with the Conde de Aranda, a man with liberal leanings, who was in turn replaced by Manuel de Godoy (1767-1851), Queen María Luisa's lover. Godoy, given the title of "Prince of Peace" by Carlos, tried to keep Aranda's policy of peace with France even after the French Revolution began in 1789, but when the Revolution turned bloody in 1793 and executed the king's cousin, Louis XVI, Spain declared war on Republican France and formed an alliance with Portugal. In 1795 France forced Godoy into an alliance and a declaration of war against Britain. Spain remained an ally of France until the British naval victory over the French and their Spanish allies at Trafalgar in 1805, at which time it switched sides and became an ally of Britain until Napoleon's victory over Prussia in 1807 led Godoy to renew the French alliance. All this switching back and forth made Carlos IV a less than trustworthy ally.

Meanwhile, there was a movement in the country to remove Carlos and replace him with his son Fernando (1784-1833), who favored an alliance with Britain and the ouster of Godoy, his rival for power. The country was suffering a lengthy catalogue of woes: economic troubles stemming from the loss of food imports from its American colonies after the defeat at Trafalgar, the rumored relationship between the queen and Godoy, Godoy's willingness to make an alliance with atheist France against Christian (if Anglican) Britain, and his sexual indiscretions in the court. Godoy's allowing Napoleon to station 100,000 troops in the country, combined with Carlos' ineptitude and strong support for Godoy, were further strikes against him. All these factors together caused the monarchy's prestige with the public to plunge. Fernando and his followers ("*los fernandistas*") thought the moment was right for a coup to overthrow the king in 1807, which, however, came to nothing.

In March 1808, riots and a popular revolt broke out in the town of Aranjuez, where the royal family and Godoy were staying. Soldiers, peasants, and townspeople attacked Godoy's quarters and captured him, then forced Carlos to dismiss him and two days later to abdicate in favor of Fernando, who became Fernando VII.

Napoleon, pretending to resolve the conflict, invited both Carlos and Fernando to a meeting in Bayonne. Both men were afraid of the emperor's power, especially since they would be completely at his mercy in France rather than at a location in Spain. Well might they have mistrusted Napoleon, for he forced them both to abdicate and transfer power to him. The emperor then named his brother Joseph as king.

While they might have inspired some conversations among the officers and priests, these dramatic events in Spain and Europe in general did not affect California directly until Napoleon installed his brother as king of Spain. Threats of war never materialized while they were occupying European and American attention. Life went on as it had in the far away province.

The Governors After Neve

In 1782 Pedro Fages was reappointed governor of California and served for nine years. In 1785 his wife, Doña Eulalia Fages, 29 years younger than her husband, arrived at Monterey, and so began a six-year period of marital conflict that would keep the governor occupied.

Doña Eulalia was a young lady of refined background who could not abide the poverty and roughness of a frontier province. Upon her arrival with their little son, the populace did its best to welcome her, but she soon started a campaign to get her husband to leave his post for a more comfortable one in Mexico City. Fages wrote to his mother-in-law that Eulalia was constantly bickering with him over his governorship; she wanted him to give up his lucrative and honorable position, but he refused. She later accused him of adultery with an Indian girl he had rescued from slavery on the Colorado River, an accusation for which she had no real evidence. Fages enlisted the help of the padres at San Carlos while he had to go south on business, sending her to live with them. Enraged, she flatly declared that the devil might take her before she would live with him again. Force had to be used to get her to the mission and while there she subjected the priests to the outbursts of her fury. In return they made empty threats of flogging and irons. With the intervention of an old friend a reconciliation was eventually reached: she admitted being wrong about the adultery with the Indian girl, but she continued to agitate - albeit quietly - for her husband to leave California. She embarrassed him by writing to the audiencia in Mexico City to have him reassigned because of "health problems." Learning of this, he wrote to a friend to intercept her letter. Undaunted, she tried several more times to get him to resign, and finally won; after nine years as governor he was recalled, whereupon she immediately sailed with the children to San Blas, although he could not follow for a year. During those years, however, she was an angel of mercy to wounded soldiers and sick people in the vicinity.

The next governor was José Roméu, who served for about a year, becoming governor at Loreto in April 1791, and moving to the new seat of government, Monterey, in October. He had been with Fages in the Sonora Indian war, but now sickness kept him from instituting seriously needed financial reforms. He died in April 1792 at about age 50.

Upon Roméu's death, José Arrillaga (1750-1814) became governor, serving the longest of any Spanish or Mexican governor of California (1792-94, 1800-14). A career soldier from Spain who spent six years in the campaign against the Seris and Pimas, he had been *appointed* comandante of the presidio at Loreto in 1783, going on to become governor. When he arrived at Monterey in 1793, he requested help from the other presidios to fortify Alta California, and after failing to build a fort at Bodega Bay, oversaw the building of fortifications at the Castillo de San Joaquín, on the site of the present Fort Point in San Francisco. At the time it was a high white cliff where Anza had first planned a presidio. However, Roméu's adobe brick fort was built on the cliff to protect the Presidio, which had been built in a sheltered valley about 1.5 miles (2.4 km) southeast of the location Anza had selected.

During Fages's second administration, Roméu's administration, and then Arrillaga's first administration, Spain was generally at peace. Spain had been involved in the war of the American Revolution, which ended in 1781, and would not go to war again until the war with Revolutionary France began in 1793. Consequently, foreign visitors were welcomed to California. The two most important were Jean François de Galaup, the Comte de la Pérouse (1741-88), a French naval officer sailing around the world with the ships *Astrolabe* and *Bussole* for his government on an expedition for political, scientific, geographic, and commercial purposes; and Sir George Vancouver (1758-98), an English admiral exploring the North Pacific on the *Discovery* for his government. La Pérouse, the first foreigner to visit since Drake, stopped at Monterey for a month in September 1786, and Vancouver, who consistently called California "New Albion" to emphasize Drake's English claim, stopped there four times (May 1792, May and October-November 1793, and November-December 1794).

Reportedly, although there is some dispute, La Pérouse observed the only historical eruption of Mt Shasta on 7 September 7, 1786, while sailing south from Alaska. (According to the US Geological Survey this was probably a small eruption where the magma nearly reaches the surface and interacts with groundwater, as its last over-the-surface eruption occurred about 3,200 years ago).[10] He stopped at San Francisco long enough to create an outline map of the Bay

Area, "Plan du Port de St. François," which was reproduced at Map 33 in L. Aubert's *Atlas du Voyage de la Pérouse* (1797). Arriving at the Monterey presidio on September 14 he was welcomed by Governor and Doña Eulalia Fages (the two being at peace for the moment) and Fray Fermín de Lasuén as French allies. For 10 days his geologists and botanists collected specimens and made drawings, and he observed the fertility of the region, visiting the pueblos, ranchos, and missions. In his posthumously published four volume *Voyage De La Pérouse Autour Du Monde* (1797) he observed that the Spanish would not develop the province rapidly, and that furs were the only promising source of wealth. While he reported the high ideals of the missionaries, especially Lasuén, he made critical notes about the mistreatment of the Indians at the missions, as well as their failure to rapidly convert the natives into the Catholic religion as well as civilizing them. From California he sailed west to China, Japan, Russia (where he fortunately dispatched his logs across Siberia via the French consul at Kronstadt to Paris); then on to Tonga, Samoa, Botany Bay, ending with shipwreck and death by drowning in the Solomon Islands.

The respective presidio commanders at Monterey and San Francisco, José Darío Argüello (1754-1827) and Hermenegildo Sal (before 1756-1800), welcomed Vancouver on his four visits, and he became the first foreigner to visit inland sites (Santa Clara) in a viewing of the missions that took him to Monterey and San Diego. Vancouver's fine maps (on which he honored two of his hosts by putting their names on Points Fermín in San Pablo Bay and Sal on the Santa Barbara County coast) and good accounts of the Spanish settlements, mission program, and commercial prospects appeared in his three-volume work, *A Voyage of Discovery to the North Pacific Ocean and Around the World 1791-95*, published in 1798.

Between these two foreigners another visitor was welcomed, this time an Italian in the Spanish Navy, Captain Alejandro Malaspina (1754-1810), who arrived at Monterey with the corvettes *Descubierta* and *Atrevida* in September 1791 while on a royal commissioned scientific expedition (1789-94) to explore the Pacific coast and determine whether there was a Strait of Anián. The expedition mapped much of the west coast of the Americas from Cape Horn to the Gulf of Alaska, crossing to Guam and the Philippines, and stopping in New Zealand, Australia, and Tonga.

Fages having retired and departed, Malaspina was welcomed by Lasuén and Argüello. During his fifteen-day stay, his two artists made charts as well as pictures of Indian and Spanish life while he collected artifacts and recorded information about the local flora, fauna, and human culture. In the crew of one of the corvettes was John Green, the first American known to have landed in California; he died and was buried at Monterey.

Upon his return to Spain Malaspina was received at court, was promoted, and began arranging the publication of his reports. However, he became a victim of a political conspiracy, being accused of "becoming too friendly with the ladies of the court," as Dr. Caughey puts it. He was banished from court and imprisoned for six years until pressure from Napoleon secured his release and his return to Italy. The more likely reason for his problems was his joining a conspiracy to overthrow Prime Minister Godoy. As a result, the seven-volume account of his voyage, *Viaje político científico alrededor del mundo por las corbetas Descubierta y Atrevida, al mando de los capitanes de navío, don Alejandro Malaspina y don José Bustamante y Guerra, desde 1789 a 1794*, which had been put into the archives in the interim, was not published until 1885.

He noted the natural beauty of Monterey but vehemently denied its suitability as a port for the Manila galleon. Fog-shrouded, rocky, and exposed, the bay required special accommodations for use: Ships needed to rely on cannon fire from the presidio to guide them into it. Three anchors were lost in the process. On the missions Malaspina took Lasuén's word, and so reported favorably.

Diego de Borica (1740-1800), the inspector of presidios in Chihuahua, was the governor sandwiched between Arrillaga's two terms (1794-1800). Spain was again at war, so the harbor defenses were strengthened. The third pueblo, Branciforte (named for the viceroy), was founded in 1797 by soldier colonists across the San Lorenzo River from Mission Santa Cruz. This one would not be like other pueblos, for it would be under military rule. It did not prosper, although its failure is hard to explain, since Borica ordered a better settlement plan than that used at San Jose or Los Angeles. Each settler was to receive an adobe house (unlike the tule huts used at the other pueblos) as well as the usual subsidies (a musket, a plow, a few animals, and a little money). The adobe houses would be an advantage because, at the other pueblos, settlers couldn't build better houses without neglecting their crops. Within three years, Branciforte had a population of 66, but the settlement was later abandoned. Today Branciforte Plaza and sites of similar name around Santa Cruz recall the effort to establish the secular pueblo, Branciforte, but there is no trace of the old pueblo itself. Homes built on the site were annexed years later to the city of Santa Cruz.

Borica's term was also notable for two other reasons: convict colonists and California's first schools.

Throughout the 18th century and well into the 19th, the debtors' prison was an unfortunate part of the criminal justice system throughout the western world. Debtors were not

206

violent criminals but people who could not pay their bills. Their imprisonment benefited no one. The debtor could earn no money while in prison to repay the debt, the creditor got nothing back (and in fact, through his taxes, paid to keep the debtor locked up), while society temporarily lost the benefit of having a useful worker. Usually, the debtor's wife and minor children lived in the prison. Gradually various nations began to abolish debtors' prisons as impractical and inhumane. The United States abandoned them only in the 1830s.

There were many such prisoners in Mexico, men with various skills who were down on their luck. Borica encouraged sending these debt convicts to California as settlers, in consideration of which their debts would be forgiven. Among the first group of 26 were hatters, miners, carpenters, bakers, a shoemaker, a saddler, a silversmith, a trader, a tailor, a laborer, and three unskilled men. At various places, such as San Francisco, they were to teach their trades to the natives as part of their sentence. There some (though not all) were able to establish new lives for themselves and go on to be the founders of families which later became prominent: The son of José María Pérez, for example, became a judge; Felipe Hernández became the *alcalde* of Branciforte and the grantee of Laguna de Calabazas; José Hernández became the grantee of Los Gatos. Orphan children, 60 boys and 60 girls, were sent as well, and were adopted by various families.

At San Jose, Borica established California's first school. The parents tried to ignore the order to send their children to school because they needed them for work, and they perceived no need to be literate. Borica, however, felt that "if the young are not educated, the country, in place of making progress, will necessarily be forced to retrograde, a thing which it is the duty of the authorities to prevent at all costs."

The schoolroom was long, badly lighted, dirty, and dilapidated. The pupils, generally children between seven and ten, were seated on rough benches. Education was no more than memorization of a catechism book. The teachers were retired army sergeants and order was maintained with a *disciplina*, a sort of cat-o'-nine-tails, a form of discipline and instruction then common all over the world. Years later, General Mariano Vallejo (1808-90) humorously recounted that on one occasion the pupils rose up and gave the teacher a taste of his own medicine, driving him out of the room, so that he had to get help to re-establish control. Nothing was done to the little rebels, he surmised, because the pueblo's *alcalde* probably recalled what a dance with the *disciplina* had been like in his own youth.

For some strange reason the mission priests took no part in this public education, a surprising fact since they were all well-educated and some highly cultured. Some priests did teach privately, for their personal satisfaction in imparting knowledge, favoring guards or children of Spanish descent. In one case a friar became so interested in his soldier pupil's progress that he arose at all hours of the night to instruct him while the soldier took his turns on sentry duty, and with the ramrod of the man's musket traced in the ashes of the guardhouse fireplace the letters of the alphabet.

Unlike the first governors, Arrillaga and Borica got on very well with the missionaries, seldom interfering with their plans. Borica encouraged the addition of new missions to fill the gaps between the older ones and argued for their location inland. Consequently, he authorized Lasuén to explore the areas between the older missions to find spaces for at least five new ones. It was his plan to convert all Indians west of the Coast Range, and thus reduce the needed number of guards, since the missions would be near enough to each other for mutual help and support.

Six new missions were established as part of this program: San José de Guadalupe, San Juan Bautista, San Miguel Arcángel, and San Fernando Rey de España between June and September 1797; San Luís Rey de Francia in June 1798, and Santa Inés Mission in September 1804. Eventually two more would be built: San Rafael in 1817 (as a health spa for Mission Dolores) and Mission San Francisco de Solano in 1823 in Sonoma. With the completion of Santa Inés, it was fair to say that the entire area west of the Coast Range from San Diego to San Francisco was spiritually occupied. With each mission about 30 miles (48 km) apart, citizens, missionaries, and government officials could now travel comfortably from one end to the other of this 500-mile (800-km) road and enjoy the hospitality of the missions at each night's stop rather than having to carry loads of provisions and sleep in the open. Horses and pack animals were plentiful and could be traded for fresh animals the next morning if the traveler so desired.

Borica stands out as one of colonial California's greatest governors: able, progressive, always open to new ideas and eager to promote the province's defenses, culture, agriculture, and settlement. In addition, he was reputed to be a very pleasant man who loved to joke, and who was ably assisted in social matters by a lovely wife and daughter. A merciful and just man, he would never order the execution of an Indian criminal, even a murderer, believing them to be a primitive people as incapable of serious guilt as children, and preferring to give them a sentence of imprisonment and hard labor.

In 1804, during Arrillaga's second term, Alta California became a separate province. The system that had existed since 1775, with a governor in Monterey and a subordinate lieutenant governor at Loreto, had proven too cumbersome in view of the distance and slow communications. Arrillaga remained as governor of both Californias for two years until Felipe de Goyoechea (1747-1814) was appointed governor of Baja. Also of note during his term were the suppression of Indian uprisings at San Gabriel and San Jose. Death ended his term in 1814.

The Russians Arrive

The arrival of the Russians eclipsed in importance all other events during Arrillaga's time in office. It had of course been the presence of Russians in Alaska that had inspired the creation of California as a buffer colony to protect Mexico from Russian encroachment.

Count Nikolai Rezanov (1764-1807) had gone to Siberia in 1793 as a representative of the Shelikov-Golikov trading company, for whom his father had worked as a civil servant. In this capacity he had visited China and observed the trading practices of the British East India Company in Guangzhou [formerly Canton.] He determined to help organize Shelikov-Golikov as an operation with privileges from the Empress Catherine (1792-96, ruled 1762-96) similar to those the East India Company had enjoyed from the British government. In 1796 the Russian empress signed the charter for the company, but died shortly thereafter, and was succeeded by her mildly insane, eccentric, generous, but vindictive son Paul (1754-1801, ruled 1797-1801). Dealing with Paul seemed hopeless, but Rezanov's charm, which had worked so well with Shelikov that he married his employer's daughter and became his business partner, overcame the czar's idiosyncrasies, and Rezanov received the imperial signature on a ukase (a Russian imperial decree with the force of law) establishing the Russian-American Company with a 20-year monopoly on the fur trade in the Pacific coast of North America above 55o. The czar, his son Alexander, and Rezanov were among the minority partners since Shelikov held a majority of shares. Rezanov, who had done most of the work to get the charter, received the title of "High Representative in the Capital," or plenipotentiary. At first the Company worked Alaska at a profit, but soon shortages of food and furs caused it to lose money.

In 1805 Rezanov went to New Archangel (now Sitka), Alaska's capital. He found the reports of starvation to be true, the colonists' blue skin and falling teeth sure signs of scurvy. He was surprised at their lack of industriousness, since they had failed to grow any vegetables, or even milk their cattle. Rezanov saved New Archangel by buying food from a passing American ship, the *Juno*, although Rezanov knew this was but a stopgap measure, Alaska would have to depend on a constant food source, so he decided to establish trade relations with California in defiance of Spanish law.

Spain, like the other European colonial powers, practiced mercantilism, according to which colonies existed to help the mother country. Any colonial business that threatened competition with a business in the mother country was forbidden, as was any direct foreign trade by a colony; in many cases colonies of the same nation could not even trade with each other, but only through the mother country.

Rezanov, undaunted by foreign laws, sailed south and arrived at San Francisco Bay in April 1806. He entered the Bay by rushing past the Castillo de San Joaquin which guarded it, "even at the point of receiving a few cannon balls," recalled the ship's engineer, while ignoring the shouted demands for identification and orders to drop anchor, until the ship was safely in the harbor and could not be fired upon. After a quiet standoff, the Russian officers were allowed to come ashore. Since none of them spoke Spanish, and none of the Spanish officials spoke Russian, the language barrier was crossed in Latin between one of the mission priests and Rezanov's jovial engineer, Georg Heinrich von Langsdorff (1774-1852).[11]

Governor Arrillaga came from Monterey to take charge from the Presidio commander, José Argüello. Neither they - nor Rezanov - wanted to risk a war; after all, with changes in European alliances with or against Napoleon, they couldn't be sure whether Russia and Spain (nations they knew had been at peace the last time any news arrived) were now allies or enemies. Meetings were polite but formal. The Spanish sensed that the Russians in Alaska were desperate for food and consequently were less inclined to sell them any, likely regarding the Russians as ants at a picnic - uninvited guests.

Thus, began Early California's most famous love story.

Rezanov had not been successful in his quest for trade. The Presidio commander had a lovely 15-year-old daughter, Concepción Argüello. Langsdorff wrote of her that

> She was distinguished for her vivacity and cheerfulness, her love-inspiring and brilliant eyes, which pierced his inmost soul, and her exceedingly beautiful
> teeth; for her pleasant and expressive features and for a thousand other charms. Yet her manners were perfectly simple and artless. Beauty of her kind one may
> find, though seldom, only in Italy, Portugal, and Spain.[12]

His first wife having died in childbirth in 1802, the charming Rezanov courted the young girl. He was sophisticated, good-looking, and rich, qualities that cast her into a state of total infatuation. Her parents' objections were finally overcome, Governor Arrillaga consented, and they became engaged. Since she was a foreigner, a Russian noble would have to get the czar's permission to marry her, and Rezanov would set out to do that.

Now that he was practically a member of the family, doors that had been closed to him suddenly opened, and in May, Rezanov sailed for New Archangel with a cargo of beef and grain. He was to traverse Russia to meet with Czar Alexander I (1777-1825, ruled 1801-25) and then return to claim his bride. In the fall he sailed to Okhotsk but on his way across Siberia he became ill at Krasnoyarsk, fell from his horse, struck his head, and died.

Concepción waited for his return, not knowing why he did not come back. She turned down other marriage proposals and became a nun. For 35 years she didn't know if he had jilted her, had only toyed with her affections, died, been refused by the czar, or changed his mind. In 1841, at a formal dinner in Monterey honoring Sir George Simpson, the retiring head of the Hudson's Bay Company on a world tour, she was informed that Rezanov had died before reaching the czar. She could finally rest, knowing that she had not been trifled with.

Had he genuinely wanted to marry her? His status would have soared had his dreamed-of alliance between Spain and Russia resulted. On the other hand, one of his American crewmen, John deWolf (1779-1872), considered Rezanov arrogant, cruel, and unfriendly, and commented in reference to marital plans after the Rezanov engagement, "His Excellency failed to make any arrangements for the future."[13]

While nearly all California historians support the 1841 date for her learning of her fiancé's demise, the National Park Service, which today owns the Presidio, gives another version. In its account, his young fiancée learned of Rezanov's demise in 1811, a mere five years after he sailed. According to this version, one of Rezanov's junior officers brought her the locket she had given him. According to the junior officer, the count's last words were of her.

Nootka Sound

Spanish claims to the coast north of Bodega Bay were being seriously challenged by the British as well as the Russians, and this challenge had its genesis at Nootka Sound, an inlet on Vancouver Island's west coast. Juan Pérez had first reached the island in 1774, followed four years later by Captain James Cook (1728-79). Cook's journals were published in 1784 and aroused great interest in the fur trade. A flurry of exploratory expeditions was undertaken by all three nations, and Nootka Sound became the most important anchorage on the northwest coast. Pérez had claimed it for Spain, but no Spanish settlements resulted. Cook had not claimed it for Britain but publicized the potential wealth in furs. Following up on Cook's report, John Meares (1756-1809) arrived in 1788 with two ships, the *Felice Adventurero* and the *Iphigenia Nubiana*, bought land on Friendly Cove from Maquinna, a chief of Nootka Indians, and built a small trading post. Esteban José Martínez (1742-98), in 1788, on a voyage to Alaska, learned that the Russians were planning to erect a fort on Nootka Sound and reported this to the viceroy, Manuel Antonio Flores (1722-99), who then ordered him to occupy Nootka Sound and make it clear that Spain was establishing control of the area. In May 1789 Martínez arrived with the warship *Princesa* and the supply ship *San Carlos*, and built British Columbia's first settlement, Santa Cruz de Nuca, protected by Fort San Miguel. Nuca, as it was informally known, consisted of houses, a church, and an infirmary. When he arrived, Martínez found two American ships, the *Lady*

Washington, commanded by Robert Gray (who would discover the Columbia River), and the *Columbia Rediviva* under Gray's superior officer John Kendrick (1740-94.) The latter vessel had been there since the previous November. In what was considered a formal act of possession, Martínez ordered the ships and the fort to fire cannon salvos; Grey and Kendrick's ships fired salutes in return, and this was interpreted as recognition of Spanish possession. During the summer, several British and American fur trading vessels arrived at Nootka, but the Americans, upon being warned, withdrew. Thomas Hudson, the British captain of the *Princess Royal*, was ordered by Martínez to leave, but a few hours later another British vessel, the *Argonaut* under James Collnet (1753-1806) pulled into the harbor and was becalmed. Martínez seized the *Argonaut*, imprisoned Collnet, and put his Chinese crew to work improving Fort San Miguel. Two American ships that arrived after Martínez's establishment of a Spanish claim, the *North West America* and the *Fair American*, were also captured by Martínez for violating Spanish sovereignty.

Eleven weeks after Martínez arrived, the viceroy ordered Nuca and the fort to be abandoned, and Martínez to return with the captured ships and their personnel to San Blas. Upon arrival, the two American ships were released without much fanfare, and no crisis developed between the United States and its ally in the War of Independence.

In October a new viceroy was appointed, the 2nd Conde de Revillagigedo (1740-99), a man as determined as his predecessor to extend and hold Spanish claims as far as possible. Martínez, who had left Nootka because of the former viceroy's orders, was held responsible for abandoning the area and was replaced by Bodega, now the naval base commander at San Blas. Bodega departed at the head of the largest naval force to sail north to date. In early 1790, Nootka Sound was re-occupied by the Spanish under Francisco de Eliza (1759-1825), a veteran of a naval war with Algiers and the siege of Pensacola during the American Revolution.

By this time the news of what had transpired reached London and was reinforced by Mearnes, who trumpeted the Spanish perfidy in dealings with a British subject who had lawfully purchased land from the natives, as well as the illegal seizures of British vessels. Anti-Spanish feeling spread in Britain, providing an opportunity for the Prime Minister, William Pitt the Younger (1759-1806), to increase his popularity and prestige. Pitt demanded Britain's right to trade in any Spanish colony it desired, Spanish laws to the contrary notwithstanding. This was indefensible according to international law, as Pitt well knew, but the public supported it, and British warships appeared at Nootka. Spanish warships were already there, and it looked as if war would break out.

Much depended on the role of France. The French Revolution had begun, but Louis XVI, Carlos IV's cousin, was still very much in power, and his military and naval forces were still intact under his rule. Would France support Spain and present a major problem to Britain in the Pacific? When the National Assembly voted against French participation in such a war, Floridablanca realized that Spain was unlikely to emerge victorious, and so negotiations opened that resulted in the Nootka Conventions of 1790 and 1794. Vancouver, Malaspina, Bodega, and even Maquinna participated in the talks, while changes in European alliances in the wake of the French Revolution shifted each country's stance and interests. In March 1795, both nations agreed to abandon Nootka Sound, allow each other to visit, and prevent any other nation from establishing a base there.

This was the end of Spanish expansion. In the words of

eminent California historians Rockwell Hunt (1868-1966) and Nellie Van De Grift Sánchez (1856-1935), "It was Spain's first step backward; its ancient glory was beginning to dim."

The Interior

Throughout the five decades of Spanish rule in California, Spaniards generally avoided the Central Valley, entering it only for punitive reasons: to catch army deserters, fight Indian raiders, or capture Indians who had run away from the missions. Some scouted for possible mission sites, but these brief forays came to nothing.

Fages, going to Monterey from the Bay Area in 1772, then leading a pursuit of army deserters from San Diego over the Grapevine (Tejón Pass over the Tehachapis), saw the floor of the San Joaquín Valley as a "labyrinth of lakes and tulares [areas abounding in tules, a type of bulrush native to California]." Garcés in 1776 went from San Gabriel to the San Joaquín Valley over Tejón Pass, passing the sites of Arvin and Bakersfield, and suspected that he had reached the headwaters of the San Joaquín River. At the same time Anza went to the San Joaquín's mouth. In 1804 Fray Juan Martín found the village of Bubal on Lake Tulare and suggested missionaries be sent in his wake. In July 1806 Lieutenant Francisco Ruiz (1754-1839) and Fray José Zaldivea (1780-1846) went from Santa Inés into the Visalia region and found several friendly Yokuts bands before returning via Tejón Pass.

The explorer who really opened the interior to the awareness of the coastal settlements was Gabriel Moraga (1765-1823). Starting as a lieutenant in 1805 and becoming a colonel by 1820, Moraga participated in 46 expeditions (according to his service record), naming several interior waterways either to honor aspects of Catholic faith or for natural features - Mariposa Creek, and the Kings, San Joaquín,

Merced, Calaveras, Tuolumne, Feather, and Sacramento Rivers.

Late in 1804, Moraga entered the southern San Joaquin Valley. On January 5,1805, he reached the Kings River and camped there for two days. The 6th of January being the Feast of the Epiphany, the day to honor the Magi, popularly referred to as kings, Moraga named the river El Río de los Santos Reyes - and the name, in English and abbreviated, remains.

Moraga, a lieutenant stationed at Santa Cruz, made four more expeditions into the Central Valley in 1806, 1808, 1810 and 1813. He was the son of a pioneer of the Anza expedition, José Joaquin Moraga, and was unquestionably Spanish California's foremost Indian fighter and explorer.

In early September, 1806, Arrillaga ordered the Monterey commandant to dispatch Moraga inland with Fray Pedro Muñoz as chaplain and diarist.[14] In late September, the party of 27 left San Juan Bautista, traveled northeast to cross the San Joaquín near the present Merced-Madera County boundary, and then turned north. The name Mariposas was applied to a nearby stream because of the multitude of butterflies, one of which greatly irritated a soldier by getting into his ear. These were probably the same little yellow butterflies that plague drivers each summer on Interstate 5 and Highway 99. The next day, September 28, they crossed "a famous river with many timid gentiles [non-Christian natives]," the Merced. This, the first large stream crossed, was considered the best place in the region for a mission. The Tuolumne was also discovered and named at this time.

From here they went northwest to the Calaveras River, still called the Río de la Pasión from an earlier, cattle-retrieving expedition. The Indians were timid, and though they sometimes followed the party up into the Sierra, friendly relations were rare. Nevertheless, a few natives (about 192 of 5,300 contacted) expressed a desire for baptism. Beyond the Calaveras River, a great language variation among the Miwoks from the dialects they had hitherto dealt with made further communications impossible.

Throughout early October, the party split between a group on the Valley floor and one in the mountains. Camping at the site of Millerton they explored the San Joaquín for a great distance upstream and down. Here they heard still-unfounded rumors of visits of soldiers from New Mexico 20 years earlier, believed by Moraga to be a patrol of Escalante's men; more likely it was a punitive party from the south. They went to the Kings, explored branches of Kaweah Creek near Visalia, and pronounced this a suitable mission site. Then they crossed the Tulare and the Kern, and climbed Tejón Pass on November 1 toward Mission San Fernando, completing their journey after 43 days.

In the fall of 1808 Moraga penetrated the northern portion of the San Joaquin Valley and went as far north as Nevada County. On this expedition he explored the lower course of the Merced and the Stanislaus waterways, naming the Stanislaus River for two Polish saints, one from the 11th and the other from the 16th century, whose feast days coincided that day. He named the Calaveras River for the large number of human skulls and bones found beside it, which he credited to a tribal battle.

Going into the Sacramento Valley, Moraga camped on the lower Feather River, which he named for the large quantity of bird feathers floating south on it. He crossed the Feather and explored the Sutter Buttes, "a mountain range in the middle of the valley," and turned west to cross the Sacramento. On the opposite shore he traversed modern Yuba County, naming the region *"Uva"* for the numerous wild grapes along its riverbank.

In 1810 Moraga made two trips into the San Joaquin Valley, whose main river he did not name until an 1813 journey in pursuit of Indian runaways. These two exploratory ventures were not to prove as spectacular as those of 1806 and 1808.

The first expedition was in August, when eleven men went north from Mission San José to the mouth of the San Joaquín. They went upriver about 80 miles (130 km), until they were stopped by the muck, and then west through Pacheco Pass to Mission San Juan Bautista. On this trip they killed many bears and deer, caught plenty of salmon and trout, and made a few minor treaties with the Yokuts villages. They reported that there was no spot suitable in the area for a mission.

In September Moraga was in the Bodega region because of the Russians had established a settlement there, leading a second in October. At the head of a force of 83 soldiers and mission Indians he captured a group of 30 runaway Indians on the San Joaquín. Completing this task, he crossed the San Joaquin River in the vicinity of the Merced and Tuolumne and made a new tour of the Merced region. This area, although the best of any region Moraga had seen in the years of exploring the Central Valley, did not (because of alkalinity) seem as favorable for a mission as had been reported in 1806.[15]

Sketchy reports described the Valley's terrain as "broad, rich and extremely fertile uplands... shaded with oak groves, and a grassy sward beneath, with many plants in bloom... Issuing from the woods... there were open prairies partly covered with bunch grass, the timber reappearing on the rolling hills of the River... In the usual belt of evergreen oaks... we passed elk, running in bands over the prairie and... along the left bank...immense droves of wild horses."

220

After Moraga's tours only a few minor penetrations were made. In October 1814 Sergeant Juan Ortega and Fray Juan Cabot with 30 soldiers entered the south San Joaquín Valley and went to Bubal on Tulare Lake. They were welcomed, and Cabot baptized several villagers, including an old woman who requested it because of her advanced age and fear of dying unsaved. After a few days they went to a village that was not at peace with that of Bubal and, though met with force, defeated Bubal's enemy and crafted a lasting peace between the two villages.

Cabot wanted to go on to Roble de Telume because of earlier expeditions which had reported its usefulness as a mission and presidio site. Ortega, however, had other plans, so they went to Ranchería de Tache, where their arrival caused the villagers to run away in fear. Like his predecessors, Cabot praised the Kings River country. Crossing the Kings, they returned over the mountains to Mission San Miguel after an eleven-day tour.

In May 1816 Fray Luis Martínez of Mission San Luis Obispo traveled along the Kern River.[16] Though he came in peace, the Indians fled before him. Eventually, however, their terror subsided, and many agreed to be baptized, but refused to be transported to the coast. On this tour Martínez encountered several Indian wars and found the land and water poor for settlement purposes.

In 1817 Fray Narciso Durán, later mission president, accompanied Lieutenant Luis Argüello (1784-1830) on an exploratory trip to the various channels of the Sacramento River, passing the site of the city of Sacramento. In 1819 another Spanish expedition into the Visalia region was undertaken by Lieutenant José Estudillo, in an attempt to suppress hostile Indians. In his report he was emphatic that a presidio was necessary in connection with any mission built in that country, where the Indians were both numerous and hostile.

The last expedition to carry the red and gold Spanish banner into the Central Valley was that of 1820 when a cavalry detachment went to the Arroyo de las Garzas (in Stanislaus County) to retrieve runaway Indians and a soldier who had deserted and settled there.

Early it had been apparent that the situation of the runaways who engaged in various depredations on the coastal settlements could only be controlled by a series of inland missions. By 1814, however, the Mexican War of Independence had paralyzed the missions by withholding military aid while requiring them to pay for the troops they needed, which however, were not sent. Despite this frustrating situation, Mission President Fray José Señán (1760-1823) in 1814 called for a mission in Telame (the Tulare region, bounded roughly by Dinuba, Lemon Cove, Allensworth, and Huron), as an advantage for both church and state. Señán argued that it would be ideal, since reports indicated that the natives desired baptism.

In 1815, Señán was succeeded by Fray Mariano Payeras (1769-1823), who made similar pleas for the establishment of inland missions, especially since the coastal missions were so far from the interior. He pointed out that expenses would be small.

He didn't get them then, nor did he when he asked for funds for the purpose in 1817. In 1820, having lost hope for the Telame mission, he warned that the result would be "a new Apachería" - referring to the Apache ferocity which prevented settlement in Arizona. The faith recently introduced would die, he warned, since it wasn't rooted well and would not be passed on. After 1820, Payeras' hopes for an interior mission skipped the Valley entirely and centered - though with equal failure - on southeastern California. He was promoted to the office of commissary prefect for the diocese of Sonora in 1820, and Señán returned to Carmel as mission president.

The hot semi-desert Central Valley summers and cold, swampy winters militated against an agricultural base for a proposed mission, while the lack of suitable timber made sturdy buildings impossible. Thus, from the Payeras' standpoint, the Telame remained "a republic of Hell and a diabolical union of apostates."[17]

Today one of the few reminders of the Spanish period in the Central Valley is a road. Originally called *El Camino Viejo* (the Old Road), today it is generally followed by S.R. 33 and I-5, running along the western foothills. Since it was unpatrolled, and passed through uninviting country, it was usually used only by those seeking to move fast or avoid the authorities. An interesting story about El Camino Viejo concerns two runaway lovers.

A young couple from Chile, whose parents disapproved of their match, had eloped to California, thinking that destination as far as they could get from the bride's father. When they arrived at Los Angeles, they heard that a warrant had been issued for their arrest and decided to go to Fort Ross, where they would be safe from Spanish law. The coastal route would be watched, so they headed into the interior and up El Camino Viejo to the Bay Area, at last reaching the Russian outpost. The journey in the interior was anything but pleasant. Swamps, wild animals, and hostile Indians kept them on the lookout. When their cartwheels began to creak, they feared the noise might draw Indians, so in the absence of grease, she tore parts of her dress to pack in between the wheels and the axles. The story ends happily with both families embracing the marriage.

The Earthquake of 1812: California's First Recorded Natural Disaster

In 1812 the coast along the northwestern shore of the Santa Barbara Channel was part of the Rancho del Refugio, a tract of ranch land that had been given to the first *comandante* of the Santa Barbara Presidio, upon his retirement. It was a favorite place for American smugglers to trade their goods for otter pelts. These American smuggling ships traveled between the Spanish-controlled coasts of southern and central California, the Russian-controlled coasts of Alaska and northern California, and the Hawaiian Islands (then known as the Sandwich Islands). On the morning of December 21, 1812, a Boston ship, the *Charan*, alias the *Thomas Newland*, commanded by Capt. Isaac Whittemore, was lying at anchor not far from Gaviota Pass, engaged in smuggling with the happy collusion of the padres. Otter skins, tallow and hard dollars meant a nice little business in 1812. While thus riding at anchor, the captain and crew were witnesses to an astonishing natural event: The sea was observed to draw back all at once and return in an immense wave which came roaring and plunging to the shore, tearing over the beach, "fit to crack everything to pieces," according to a witness. This earthquake-generated tsunami wave penetrated the lowlands of the gulches a mile (1.6 km) from the shore, a terrifying sight to behold.[18]

That ship afterwards got 1,800 otter skins to the Sandwich Islands, but a few days afterwards she was captured by the British man-o-war *Cherub*, whose presence in those islands was connected to the United States' and Britain's engagement in the War of 1812. It was subsequently taken as a prize to London.

At the time of the earthquake of 1812, whose strength was

estimated to have been 7.1 on today's Richter scale, 999 Indians, two priests, and a handful of soldiers resided at Mission La Purísima. These missions were working ranches: At the time of the earthquake, Mission La Purísima had 4,000 cattle, 12,000 sheep, 1,150 horses, and grew wheat, corn, beans, and wine grapes.

On that December day when the earth shook and a tsunami tidal wave hit the coast, Father Payeras reported that it

> "entirely destroyed the church [of La Purísima] and vestry, buried under the walls the various images and paintings, and ruined the greater part of the furniture. Some of the work shops went down ... One hundred houses of neophyte Indians and the community kitchen,
> the walls of which were an adobe and a half thick, and roofed with tiles, have become inserviceable. The garden walls of adobe, covered with tiles, have collapsed or threaten to fall. ..." [19]

He concluded his account with the hope that "Experience may teach us the best method of constructing other buildings."

Father Señán, perhaps alluding to the tearing of the veil of the Temple at the Crucifixion (Matthew 27:1, RSV), gave a fuller account of the damage: "As a result of the ruinous events we have

> to build anew the churches of Missions San Fernando and Santa Barbara. ... Mission San Gabriel suffered somewhat. At Missions Santa Inés and San Buenaventura quite, some time will be required to repair the damage which I consider annoying to describe in detail. Concerning the last named mission I will say only that the tower partially fell and that the

wall of the sanctuary was cracked from top to bottom. ..."

At Mission La Purísima the bells rang out without the aid of a bell ringer, and in a few minutes the mission was "reduced to rubble and ruin presenting the picture of a destroyed Jerusalem." At that time every Indian left the island of Santa Rosa: The waters had receded from the island several hundred meters, which so alarmed the Indians that, fearful that the island was about to be engulfed, they departed and were settled in bands of three or four hundred at the several missions. For some, we may speculate, it was not difficult to see the power of the priests in this abandonment. Had they made dire predictions of Biblical-proportion heavy punishment in case the islanders remained stubborn? If they had, then it was natural that the superstitious natives saw this earthquake as the first of a series of fatal catastrophes. If they had not made such predictions, in any case the fearful Indians sought refuge where they had previously refused to venture. As it is unknown if such threats were made it makes for interesting speculation.[20]

This migration of formerly independent Indians to missions fortuitously completed the task begun under Neve to secure the Channel Islands for Spain.

Chapter Five END NOTES

[1] Natalie Zappia, "The One Who Wheezes: Salvador Palma, the Colorado River, and the Emerging World Economy" http://cpb-us-el.wpmucdn.com/sites.ucsc.edu/dist/f/482/files/2017/08/SocialBio.Zappia.pdf

[2] Gary Kurutz, "The Anza Expedition: Great Overland Journey", *CHSC*, (April 1976), p. 6.

[3] "L.A. 200!: A Special Issue Celebrating Our Bicentennial," *Los Angeles Herald Examiner, California Living Magazine*, August 31, 1980, p.12.

[4] San Buenaventura Mission, "The Old Mission Basilica San Buenaventura", (May 2023), accessed May 10, 2023, https://www.sanbuenaventuramission.org/history/mission-history

[5] Charles Lockwood, "The Changing Moods of Mission Dolores," *San Francisco Sunday Examiner & Chronicle*, March 29, 1981, p. 40. The Serra Chapel at Mission San Juan Capiistrano is the oldest surviving building in California; teams of indigenous Acjachemen (known as "Juaneños) built it and the first mass was celebrated in 1783. The magnificent golden altar is thought to be around 330 years older and came from Barcelona, but wasn't installed in the chapel until the early 20th century. https://www.thediscoverer.com/blog/the-oldest-building-in-all-50-states/X72PXKdLaAAGbifz?uym_source=blog&utm_medium=email&utm_campaign=1581354581

[6] Robert Barron, "Why Francis wants to go ahead with Serra canonization: Extraordinary model," *California Catholic Daily,* September 12, 2015, http://cal-catholic.com/?p=20417

[7] The mission style came from the missionaries' familiarity with the churches and other religious buildings they saw in Spain, combining Romanesque and Baroque features while adapting to the local needs. An enclosed courtyard, using massive adobe walls with broad unadorned plaster surfaces, limited windows and doors, low-pitched roofs with projecting wide eaves and non-flammable clay roof tiles, with thick arches springing from piers. The exterior walls were coated with white plaster, which with wide side eaves shielded the adobe brick walls from rain. Other features included long exterior arches, an enfilade of interior rooms and halls, and semi-independent bell gables, while the more prosperous missions boasted curved gables on the principal façade with towers.

[8] Kurutz, "El Molino Viejo", *CHSC*, (Fall 1979), p. 6.

[9] "Unearthing California's Mission Music," You Tube video, 7:46, posted by KCET Online, February 8, 2013, https://www.youtube.com/watch?v=iJImToF47xM. A pastorela is a comic musical play with a rural setting originating in the Middle Ages. Copying the medieval miracle plays the Franciscans used

them from the 16th century as a catechetical tool and involved most of the audience. This one taught the Seven Deadly Sins with the Christmas story as a backdrop. It is still performed in alternate years at Mission San Juan Bautista, adapted by American playwright and screenwriter Luis Valdez (1940-). México desconocido, "¿Qué son las pastorelas navideñas?" http://www.mexicodesconocido.com.mx/las-pastorelas-en-mexico.html; Lily Dayton, "El Teatro Campesino keeps Christmas tradition alive with 'La Pastorela,' *Monterey Herald*, November 24, 2011, http://www.montereyherald.com/general-news/20111124/el-teatro-campesino-keeps-christmas-tradition-alive-with-la-pastorela.

[10] USGS, Eruption History by Mt. Shasta, https://www.usgs.gov/volcanoes/mount-shasta/eruption-history#:~:text=Mount%20Shasta%20erupts%20episodically%20with,surface%20about%203%2C200%20years%20ago.

[11] Bancroft, *History of California*, vol. 2, pp. 67-68.

[12] U.S. Department of the Interior, Presidio of San Francisco, "Concepcion Arguello & Nikolai Petrovich Rezanov: A Presidio Love Story," http://www.nps.gov/prsf/learn/historyculture/love-story.htm.

[13] Howe, "The Voyage of Nor'west John," p. 72.

[14] Pedro Muñoz, *The Gabriel Moraga Expedition of 1806: the Diary of Fray Pedro Muñoz*. Ed. by Robert Cleland. (1946; repr., Whitefish MT, Kessinger: 2008).

[15] Originals of Gabriel Moraga's service sheet are in the De la Guerra Collection in the Santa Barbara Mission Library.

[16] Fray Martinez's legacy at San Luis Obispo included the famed 1818 mission bells made by Manuel Vargas of Lima, and the iconic five-arched campanile built to hold them. He was both a paternalistic pastor and a genuine protector of the rights of the natives against the greedy newcomers, and foreign visitors regarded him as a generous host and a good businessman. Dan Krieger, "Mission San Luis Obispo priest pays a price for speaking his mind." *San Luis Obispo Tribune*, July 23, 2016 https://www.sanluisobispo.com/news/localnews-columns-blogs/times-past/article91548757.html

[17] Genini, "The Red and Gold in the Great Valley: The Story of Spanish Exploration of the San Joaquin Valley, 1772-1820", *Fresno Past & Present*, 16, no. 4 (December 1974), pp. 1-5; Annie Mitchell, "King of the Tulares," *Presses of the Visalia Times-Delta*, 1941, pp. 24-25, cited in National Park Service History, "Spanish Exploration of the Kaweah River Basin," September 8, 2008, http://npshistory.com/publications/corps/terminus-reservoir/sec5.htm

[18] Proceedings of the California Academy of Sciences (1864), p. 133.

[19] Santa Barbara Earthquake History, "The 1812 Santa Barbara Earthquake: Mission La Purisima." U.C. Santa Barbara, (2006), http://projects.eri.ucsb.edu/sb_eqs/1812/payeras.html.

[20] Frederick Caire Chiles, *California's Channel Islands: A History* (Norman: University of Oklahoma Press: 2015), p. 56; Eugene Wheeler and Robert Kallman, *Shipwrecks, Smugglers and Maritime Mysteries* (Oxnard: Pathfinder Publishing, 1994), pp. 20-21; H.W. Henshaw, quoted in Anthropological Records, California Linguistic Records, v. 15, no. 2, in George Pararas-Carayannis, "The Santa Barbara, California, Earthquakes and Tsunami(s) of December 1812," (1967), , http://www.drgeorgepc.com/Tsunami1812SantaBarbara.html

Chapter Five FURTHER READING:

1.   Bancroft, Hubert Howe. *History of California*, vol. 1, chaps. 14-36, vol. 2:chaps. 1-29.

2.   Blackburn, Jim. "What 'No Salvation outside the Church' means" *Catholic Answers Magazine*, May 2010. http://www.catholic.com/magazine/articles/what-no-salvation-outside-the-church-means.

3.   California Department of Parks and Recreation. "Missions of the Californias." (2016), http://www.parks.ca.gov/?page_id=22679.

4.   California Department of Parks and Recreation. "San Juan Bautista State Historic Park." (2016). http://www.parks.ca.gov/?page_id=563

5. "California Earthquakes – Reminiscences of an Old Trader on our Coast" *San Francisco Bulletin*, March 16, 1864, cited in "The 1812 Santa Barbara Earthquake: Tsunami." http://projects.crustal.ucsb.edu/sb_eqs/1812/tsunami.html.

6. "The California Missions On-Line Project." http://www.mrgarretson.com/missions/missionlinks.html.

7. Díaz, Josef. "The Art and Legacy of Bernardo Miera y Pacheco: New Spain's Explorer, Cartographer, and Artist," *El Palacio*, Winter 2013. https://www.elpalacio.org/2013/12/the-art-and-legacy-of-bernardo-miera-y-pacheco/

8. Dutton, Davis. *Missions of California*. New York: Ballantine, 1972.

9. *Encyclopædia Britannica Online*, s. v. "Jean-Francois de Galaup, comte de La Perouse," http://www.britannica.com/biography/Jean-Francois-de-Galaup-comte-de-La-Perouse.

10. Engelhardt, Zephyrin. "Mariano Payeras" *Catholic Encyclopedia* (1913). Vol. 11. https://en.wikisource.org/wiki/Catholic_Encyclopedia_(1913)/Mariano_Payeras .

11. Engelhardt, *San Juan Capistrano Mission*. Los Angeles: Standard Printing Co., 1922.

12. Galbraith, Edith. "Malaspina's Voyage Around the World." *CHSQ* 3, no 3 (October 1924): pp. 215-37.

13. Farris, Glenn. "Indian Family Housing at Mission San Juan Bautista." California Department of Parks and Recreation. (2016) http://www.parks.ca.gov/?page_id=22731.

14. Geiger, Maynard. *Franciscan Missionaries in Hispanic California, 1769-1848*, Ibañez, Florencio. A Biographical Dictionary, The Huntington Library, San Marino, 1969.

15. Gill, Antoni. *J. B. Sancho: Pioneer Composer of California*. Palma: Universitat de les Illes Balears, 2007.

16. Hunt, Rockwell and Van De Grift Sánchez, Nellie. *A Short History of California*. New York: Thomas Crowell, 1929.

17. Griffin, William and Julia Ortiz. *Spain and Portugal: A Reference Guide from the Renaissance to the Present*, s.v. Charles IV. Facts on File (2007).

18. McWilliams, Carey. *Southern California: An Island on the Land.* 1946. Reprint, Santa Barbara: Peregrine Smith, 1973.

19. Medina, Rosendo "Fray Francisco Garces" *Kern County Historical Society* 57, no.4 (Winter 1986).

20. Mission San Juan Capistrano. "The Mission San Juan Capistrano." (2016). http://www.missionsjc.com/history-preservation/history/.

21. Mount Shasta Annotated Bibliography. Chapter 4. Early Exploration: Lapérouse Expedition, 1786.

22. National Park Service. Tumacácori National Historical Park Arizona, "Pedro Font." http://www.nps.gov/tuma/learn/historyculture/pedro-font.htm

23. Orfalea, Gregory. "Sainthood and Serra: His virtues outdistance his sins." *Los Angeles Times*, January 24, 2015. http://touch.latimes.com/#section/-1/article/p2p-82616856/

24. Orser, Mary Beth, Amanda Whitman, *It Happened in Soledad.* Soledad: Community Action Team of Soledad, 1996.

25. Payne, Stanley G. *History of Spain and Portugal*, vol. 2 (1973). The Library of Iberian Resources Online. http://libro.uca.edu/payne2/payne16.pdf

26. Pethick, Derrick. *The Nootka Connection: Europe and the Northwest Coast, 1790-1795.* Vancouver: Douglas & McIntyre: 1980.

27. Rawls, James. "Napa County Beginnings". Paper presented at the Annual Meeting of the California Historical Society, Napa, CA, March 25, 1977.

28. Russell, Craig H. *From Serra to Sancho: Music and Pageantry in the California Missions.* New York: Oxford University Press, 2009.

29. Saunt, Claudio. *West of the Revolution: An Uncommon History of 1776.* New York: W. W. Norton & Co., 2014.

30. Stoddard, Charles W. *In the Footsteps of the Padres*. San Francisco: Robertson, 1902.

31. Vancouver, George. *A Voyage of Discovery to the North Pacific Ocean and Round the World 1791-1795*, edited by W. Kaye Lamb. London: Hakluyt Society: 1984.

32. Van De Grift Sanchez, Nellie. *Spanish Arcadia*. Los Angeles: Powell Publishing Company, 1919.

33. Weber, David. *The Spanish Frontier in North America*. New Haven: Yale University Press, 1992.

34. Weber, Tricia Anne. "The Spanish Missions of California." (2006). http://www.californias-missions.org/.

35. Yenne, Bill, *The Missions of California*. San Diego: Thunder Bay Press, 2004.

Chapter 6: A Mexican Province (1821-46)

The Mexican War of Independence

Joseph Bonaparte (José, 1768-1844), Napoleon's brother who had been popular as the king of Naples, had replaced Fernando VII in 1808 and was immediately unpopular with the Spanish public. Though actually an abstemious man, he was labeled "*Pepe Botella*" for alleged heavy drinking. His arrival sparked a revolt in reaction to new ideas and institutions, which began the Peninsular War, with Britain and Portugal joining with Fernando's guerrilla supporters. With his brother's support he maintained a tenuous, nominal control over the country.

He lost no time in appointing new officials to his American colonies, but these were generally rejected by the Peninsular and Creole patriots who considered Fernando their legitimate king. In New Spain there was abundant confusion about who was in charge: With Fernando out after his abdication at Bayonne, who was king? Certainly, loyalists were not going to accept José as an illegitimately crowned ruler imposed by a foreigner. Who then? Logically, when the legitimate ruler is not present, then the successor would be the viceroy, in this case José de Iturrigaray (1742-1815), who had served since 1803. Iturrigaray was perceived as friendly to more liberal ideas, unacceptable to the conservative Audiencia in the capital, so he was forcibly removed in September 1808 and bundled off to Spain as a possible traitor. Seeing itself as the guardian of Fernando's presently nonexistent authority, the Audiencia then chose the viceroy.

Between September 1808 and Fernando's restoration in

1814, five men served as viceroys of New Spain: Pedro de Garibay (September 1808-July 1809), Archbishop Javier de Lizana y Beaumont (July 1809-May 1810), Pedro Catani (May-September 1810). Don Francisco Javier Venegas (September 1810-March 1813), and Don Félix María Calleja del Rey (March 1813-September 1816). All of these were rigidly loyal to Fernando.

The French had shattered the Bourbon government in Spain and tried to replace it with a more efficient one. Most of the public would have none of it, and numerous feuding *juntas* sprang up all over the country. Soon realizing that there would have to be some unity to fight the French and utilize British aid, the *junta* formed in the city of Cádiz was chosen as the official one. Patriots who assembled at Cádiz in 1812 drew up a constitution making Spain a parliamentary liberal monarchy. Fernando promised to abide by its terms upon his restoration. By 1814 the Spaniards, with British help, had expelled the French from Spain, and Fernando came back. Soon, however, he broke his promises about the 1812 constitution and made Spain once again an absolute monarchy.

José had not been acceptable to any of the regions of his new empire.

In Mexico, what would become the fight for independence began with Father Miguel Hidalgo (1753-1811) a few days before the installation of Venegas in September 1810. Hidalgo was a member of a liberal book club in the town of Dolores. The books they read and discussed were products of the French Revolution that preached freedom from absolute rule, looking to both the United States and France for inspiration. The tug of war resulting from the political confusion created an opportunity for Hidalgo to make his move: He called on the people to rise, and they followed him in a bloody liberation

234

of a large part of Mexico. The Indians were probably indifferent to whoever sat in the viceregal palace, but they most certainly responded to the part of Hidalgo's *Grito* (Call for Independence) that called for "Death to the *Gachipines*! " (the *peninsulares*)[1] His followers began with the slaughter of a large group of people who had taken refuge in the granary in Guanajuato - something the soon-to-be-defrocked priest was unable to control. His success was short-lived. as the creoles and many of the mestizos were alienated by this gratuitous violence. Spanish troops captured and executed him in 1811.

The fight was taken up by another priest, José María Morelos (1765-1815), who organized a well-armed force that captured Acapulco in 1813 and proclaimed Mexican independence. His plan was to establish a republic in which all races were equal, end the special privileges of army and Church, and break up large estates into small farms for the people. Most of the Creoles did not want Morelos' social and economic reforms, and, turning against him, threw their support to the viceroy. The Spanish forces began winning important victories in 1814, and the next year Morelos was captured and shot. The fight for independence was carried on by only a few small bands in the mountains as the criollos and *peninsulares* united behind King Fernando VII.

Fernando was less than worthy of this popular loyalty. As Stanley Payne summarizes his reign

> "He proved in many ways the basest king in Spanish history. Cowardly, selfish, grasping, suspicious and vengeful, [he] seemed almost incapable of any perception of the commonwealth. He thought only in terms of his power and security and was unmoved by the enormous sacrifices of Spanish people to retain their independence and preserve his throne."

In 1820 a liberal revolt in Spain forced Fernando to accept the Constitution of 1812. Fernando submitted but in 1823 French forces (now serving his restored Bourbon cousin Louis XVIII [1755-1824, ruled 1814, 1815-24]) invaded to restore his authority. Immediately, Fernando broke his word about accepting the Constitution and granting an amnesty to the rebels, and lashed out against his foes, executing 30,000 and imprisoning 20,000, a move that disgusted his French rescuers and his dwindling Spanish supporters. The duke of Angoulême, who led the French forces, made known his protest of Fernando's actions by refusing to accept the Spanish decorations Fernando offered him for his military services.

The initial liberal victory alarmed the conservatives in Mexico, who feared that reforms in the colony would soon follow. To prevent such reforms, conservative leaders who had supported the viceroy decided secretly to bring about independence in their own way.

The conservatives persuaded the viceroy to send their military leader, Agustín de Iturbide (1783-1824), to crush the revolutionaries who were now led by Vicente Guerrero (1782-1831). Instead, Iturbide and Guerrero agreed in February 1821 to make Mexico independent under the Plan de Iguala: The Mexican nation would be organized as a constitutional monarchy under a suitable European king, and the Catholic religion would hold a spiritual monopoly in the country, its clergy supported by the government. *Peninsulares* and *criollos* would be treated equally in the new country. The novel government attracted wide support, only a little armed conflict took place, and Mexico became independent by the end of 1821. The various groups who had fought for independence had been united only by opposition to the Spanish government, and they soon began to quarrel among themselves. Conservatives wanted one of Fernando's relatives to become king of Mexico, liberals wanted a republic like the United States, while a third group wanted Iturbide to take over. Iturbide seized power and was declared Emperor Agustín I in 1822. There is no escaping the irony that a conservative colony had gained its independence from an only temporarily liberal mother country.[2]

Fighting against Spanish rule went on in Spain's colonies in South America as well. As it became clear that there would be no reversal of independence, international recognition started to be granted: The United States in early 1822 recognized Mexico as well as Peru, Gran Colombia, Chile, and the United Provinces of Río de la Plata; Britain waited until 1825, and within a few more years more followed. Although Fernando and his successor (Isabella II, reigned 1833-68) refused recognition of Mexico until 1837 (Spain would not recognize Honduran independence until 1894![3]) by 1825 Spain's once great empire in the Americas was reduced to the islands of Cuba and Puerto Rico.

During these years California did not revolt because it was isolated, Spain had been good to it in a paternalistic way, and the priests and military officers were loyal to Fernando. In any event, most of the people had no doubt as to the outcome. After 1810 the supply ships from San Blas stopped coming, and the last Manila Galleon sailed in 1815, but California survived because the mission crops were well established and there existed a profitable - if illegal - trade with the Americans and Russians.

The last governor under the king of Spain was appointed in 1815, Pablo Vicente de Solá (1761-1826). His arrival in Monterey was feted elaborately. The welcome was to be short lived. He had a haughty demeanor, convinced of his own superiority to the Californians whom he considered

237

incompetent and untrustworthy based on his Spanish birth and education. Such airs soon made him unpopular with the people. Initially furious about the Russian presence and the extensive smuggling, he tried to extinguish foreign military and commercial interests in the province, but economic need soon led him to wink at the illicit trade with the Russians and the Americans. As governor, his greatest accomplishment was the foundation of schools at each of the four presidios and two pueblos.

California's only military involvement in the Latin American wars of independence occurred in November 1818, when the Argentine privateer, Hippolyte de Bouchard (1785-1843), with two black-painted ships, sacked Monterey for a week, forcing Solá and his advisers to flee into the interior. He likewise sacked San Juan Capistrano, but spared Santa Barbara because three of his men had been captured at Refugio where they had pillaged José Ortega's rancho, and they would be hanged if he attacked. When the viceroy heard of this raid, he sent 200 troops to guard California for the future. 100 were good cavalrymen, and the rest were considered *cholos*, low-class fellows serving as infantrymen, who arrived in August 1819 to scant welcome having been flushed out of Mexican prisons.

In 1819 the United States and Spain signed the Adams-Onís Treaty, which defined California's northern border at 42oN (as well as those of Nevada and Utah.) In 1803 the United States had bought Louisiana from France. Louisiana's borders were rather fluid, including parts of Texas and a claim to Oregon. Spain claimed all of Texas and had a claim on Oregon as well. Florida was involved too, the Spanish believing that part of the Louisiana Cession by France to Spain in 1763 had included part of it. American General Andrew Jackson (1767-1845) had invaded Florida in 1818 to wipe out nests of Indians who were raiding into Georgia, since the Spanish authorities could not control the raiding. To settle the dispute over the boundary, the two nations agreed to a fixed boundary by which the United States gave up any claim to Texas, and Spain ceded its claim to Oregon (as well as Florida) to the United States.

When word reached Monterey that Iturbide had become emperor of Mexico, Governor Solá convoked a junta in Monterey which pledged allegiance to the Mexican empire in April 1822. The Spanish red and gold was gone, replaced by the Mexican eagle on red, white and green stripes.

**

"If California ever becomes a prosperous country ."

-Richard Henry Dana, 1840

**

The Early Mexican Period

When the *junta* at Monterey voted California into the Mexican Empire it called for elections for a delegate to the Mexican Congress. Iturbide's commissioner to California, Father Agustín Fernández, described as a "rosy-cheeked, jovial, gaily dressed priest, a *bon vivant* who spent money freely and borrowed as freely, with an unclerical fondness for wine, women, and gambling that greatly scandalized the friars,"[4] ordered that even the mission Indians be allowed to vote, and Solá was chosen. Fernández then persuaded the provincial legislature, the *diputación*, to choose Luís Argüello (brother of Concepción) as governor.

While Argüello was governor (1822-25), an attempt was made to move the mission from San Francisco to the healthier climate at Sonoma, but Mission Dolores stayed put, and a new

239

mission - the last, called San Francisco de Solano - was built at Sonoma.

In spring of 1824, an Indian revolt broke out at the three Central Coast missions: Santa Bárbara, Santa Inés and La Purísima. Argüello suppressed it.

In 1823 Iturbide was overthrown and a federal republic was created with General Guadalupe Victoria (1786-1843) as the first president. California was now part of the Mexican Republic, officially known as the United Mexican States. With the overthrow of Iturbide, the old order died, and for California the new era would be one of uncertainty.

Government by Revolution

California was no exception to the disorders that plagued all the newly independent Latin American countries. Spain had left those countries rich but had never given them the right of self-government. Consequently, the people had no political experience, and ambitious, corrupt, venal generals fought to seize power to get their hands on the treasury. There were civil wars between regions and parties, with frequent revolutions a predictable occurrence. Wars with neighbors over disputed territories whose colonial lines had been less-than-specific raged for a generation. The result was that the wealth left over from colonial times was dissipated, and these nations soon teetered on the edge of bankruptcy.

Mexico's history started off on the wrong foot, and Mexico has yet to overcome its poor start in life to realize its full potential as a world power.

In Mexico there were 21 presidents and dictators in only 22 years (1824-46). General Antonio López de Santa Anna (1794-1876) was the one responsible for bankrupting Mexico during that period. A unique man, one of history's most enigmatic, Santa Anna was a survivor. Vain and narcissistic, without loyalty except to himself, he betrayed his wife *and* his mistresses, the Church *and* its enemies, the political right *and* left. A thief, a forger, an embezzler, a liar, and an oath-breaker, he did have the ability to raise armies by his appeals to patriotic causes of one sort or the other. His survival is usually credited to his personal charm, for when sworn enemies such as Sam Houston (1793-1863) met him face-to-face their animosity evaporated; it was commonly said that he was like a snake who could charm a bird from its nest, and, even more, charm the bird into giving the snake its eggs.

President eleven times between 1833 and 1855 (for a total of only 2,175 days, or five years, 11 months and 16 days!), Santa Anna would often "retire" soon after an election and leave the rest of his term to a flunky or "fall-guy" who would so mismanage things that people would beg him to return and put things right.[5] One historian concisely summarized his place in history: "For nearly a quarter of century the public life of Mexico was dominated by as preposterous a figure as Latin America has produced, a unique dictator as little comprehensible now as he was to many contemporaries."[6]

During that period Mexico had two constitutions, 1824's federalist and 1834's centralist. The Constitution of 1824 gave the Mexican states and territories some local autonomy while that of 1834 required all matters of importance to be decided by the Mexican government, turning the states (including California) into governmental units resembling military districts. Zacatecas, Tabasco, Yucatán, and Texas revolted, declaring independence, and in the north, the Republic of the Rio Grande was formed, comprising Coahuila, Nuevo León and Tamaulipas, for several months in 1840. In August 1846, President José Mariano Salas (1797-1867, served August 5-December 23, 1846) restored federalism.

Alta California was not one of the states of the Mexican Republic. Because of its small population, it was referred to as a "territory." The centralist constitution reunited Alta and Baja California as the *Departamento de las Californias* (California Department) The *Californias*, though this move changed nothing politically, the capital remaining at Monterey. When the federalist constitution was restored in 1846, California again became a separate territory, a condition would soon be transformed by the American conquest.

In Mexican California the conflicts were between the larger, more densely populated southern districts and the smaller, more sparsely populated north. The north enjoyed the advantages of having California's capital and customs house. Politics never centered on ideas but on individual rivalries between men who were not far removed from one another in blood or cultural homogeneity. At the same time, many thoughtful Californians, soon to be called "*Californios*" rather than "*Mexicanos*," began to feel that independence from Spain was merely a prelude to independence from Mexico.

Many battles were fought between rival factions, but unlike typical armed conflicts in Mexico or the rest of Latin America, these were mostly comic-opera affairs, more for appearance than for bloodshed. One wit, scorning these frequent Mexican-standoff style battles between factions, threatened to bring his barber onto the battlefield while a fight was going on; the barber would shave him, and, if made nervous by the gunfire, might nick him, and thus some blood *might* flow at a battle. An unhappy exception to this occurred at the battle of Cahuenga in December 1831. A rebel, José Avila, the 41-year-old former *alcalde* of Los Angeles, accepted a personal challenge to combat from Governor Manuel Victoria (?-1833). Victoria sent his aide, 36-year-old Captain Romualdo Pacheco, to fight the duel. Avila and

Pacheco were killed, Victoria was wounded (and resigned), and José María Echeandía (for whom Avila was fighting) became governor.

Mexican governors were generally inferior to Spanish ones. The Spanish governors had been appointed based on merit, having earned their spurs in the royal service before being entrusted with the rule of a province. The Mexican governors, on the other hand, were usually appointed based on patronage, most often as a political payoff by Santa Anna or one of his underlings.

Echeandía (?-1871, served 1825-31, 1832-33), an army engineer, was a hypochondriac who moved the capital to San Diego because of his frequent colds.[7] He totally mismanaged the government. The first governor appointed under the Constitution of 1824, he had arrived intent on secularizing the missions but found the task difficult. He was also faced with a revolt led by his treasurer, José María Herrera (1794-?), and Joaquín Solís, a pardoned convict from San Blas, acting on behalf of Monterey soldiers who had not been paid for a long time. He put down the uprising only to face a new one led by Chief Estanislao (c. 1798-1838), a neophyte who had been baptized with the name of the Polish 11th century bishop and martyr Saint Stanislaus by Father Durán at Mission San José. Angry about something, Estanislao left the settlement and fled into the Central Valley in 1829, taking refuge with other Indians on what became the Stanislaus River. Soldiers were sent to bring them back, but they put up such stiff resistance that the soldiers left when their ammunition ran out and the heat became unbearable. General Vallejo was sent to accomplish the task with 100 well-equipped soldiers. Vallejo's men started a brush fire that drove the Indians out. A battle ensued, the soldiers killing many of the Indians regardless of sex or age, and the rebellion was ended.

Estanislao fled in the night to take refuge with Father Durán, who kept him at the Mission until the governor pardoned him. Vallejo regarded Estanislao's warriors with great respect as opponents, stating that it was only the superior arms and training of his forces that enabled them to win the battle.

Echeandía could not have been a happy occupant of his office with all the problems he faced: mismanagement of the government, unpaid soldiers, two rebellions, a failed attempt to initiate secularization, paranoia about foreigners, and his probably imaginary fragile health. It all contributed to numerous mistakes for which the public automatically and sometimes unfairly blamed him. Echeandía in time planned to resign. Instead, Manuel Victoria replaced him.

Victoria, an officer from Baja California, was appointed by the conservative pro-clerical government in Mexico City and served 310 days (January 30-December 6) in 1831. José María Padrés, an army officer from Puebla, had been appointed by the preceding, more liberal Mexican government, and, although not formally installed, had received an order from Echeandía to secularize the missions. Victoria overruled the decree, banished Padrés and others, and established a harsh, high-handed, and repressive regime. When he was replaced by Victoria, Echeandía joined forces with Abel Stearns, (1798-1871), Pío Pico (1801-94) and Juan Bandini (1800-59) to mount a southern revolt against the legitimate governor. He was successful in reestablishing himself in the south because of the Cahuenga excitement, although the *Diputación* appointed Pico governor for three weeks after the battle. At that point Agustín Zamorano (1798-1842), commander of the Monterey Presidio, the province's first printer and a friend of the slain Pacheco, proclaimed himself governor in the north. Thus, in 1832-33 California had two rival and probably equally legitimate governments. As for

Victoria, "he gave up office and fled to Mexico, where he disappeared from history as silently as he had entered it."[8]

This semi-comic situation was settled by the appointment of José Figueroa (1792-1835) as governor in 1833. Figueroa, a man of mostly Indian blood with much frontier experience as *comandante general* of Sonora and Sinaloa, was the best of the Mexican governors. He pardoned Zamorano and restored him to his post at the Presidio, bringing peace to the province. Zamorano was also appointed official printer, and with a new Ramage wooden screw press from Boston began issuing broadside advertisements and official pronouncements, the largest being the region's *Reglamento Provincial* (1834) and Figueroa's 188-page *Manifesto a la Republica Mejicana* (1835). To checkmate Forts Ross and Vancouver, he sent General Mariano Vallejo north of San Francisco Bay to build two new towns, Petaluma and Santa Rosa.

**General Mariano Vallejo (Courtesy of the California
History Room, California State Library, Sacramento,
California)**

At Petaluma, Vallejo eventually received a rancho of ten
leagues or about 44,000 acres (17,810 ha). He started building
houses, corrals, and other needed improvements. A
commanding site on a knoll overlooking Petaluma Valley was
chosen for the main building, but it was never completed. The
rancho was to be a hide and tallow producer, but it became far
more than a cattle ranch. Fine horses were raised there in large

herds, and as many as 3,000 sheep were shorn each year. Great crops of wheat, barley and corn were planted for local use and export, while beans, lentils and vegetables of all kinds were raised for daily use on their own tables. He saw the Wappo Indians as potential laborers and herders, and he saw the northern valleys as rich pasture for his horses, mules, and cattle.

Vallejo's vision, however, would cause problems for the Wappo. The encroachment of his animals reduced the supply of game and wild vegetables upon which the Indians depended for food, The Wappo and other tribes wanted to keep the Napa Valley as it had always been, but they failed to protect it and were forced to substitute mule and horse meat for venison, leading to a battle between the Vallejos and the Wappo. In one pitched battle some 2,000 Indians engaged in combat with troops under Mariano's brother, Salvador. "Vallejo's casualties were light. Two hundred Wappo died from saber and lance wounds." This foreshadowed what was to come, not by weapons but by disease: In 1838 smallpox hit, and, as Vallejo recalled, the Indians "died like bugs." [9]

During Figueroa's term the secularization of the missions began, and though the governor personally opposed the move, he carried out orders. The Mexican government had granted some of the mission lands to a group headed by Padrés and José María Hijar (?-1845), who had been appointed governor. About 250-300 colonists, including many skilled in different trades, qualified teachers, and farmers, were recruited to settle in California with promises of land grants, tools, animals, and the equipment they needed to start over in life. The government's purpose was to settle people to shore up defenses. However, while the group was sailing to California, a change occurred in the Mexican presidency from Padrés's friend (and one of the soon-to-be-conservative Santa Anna's temporary stand-ins, the liberal President Valentín Gómez Farías [1781-1855]), to the now-conservative Santa Anna. The governmental switch voided the grant and revoked Hijar's appointment. Santa Anna, meanwhile, sent a special courier on a record-breaking overland trip (reputedly faster than Anza's ride to see the viceroy in 1776), to tell Figueroa to stay in office. Padrés and Híjar wanted to settle the mission lands anyway, but Figueroa required them to settle in the northern frontier area around Sonoma. This they refused to do. The would-be settlers, having no prospects in all this shuffling, revolted. Figueroa sympathized with their plight but would have no disorder. Those who did not surrender immediately were caught and quickly bundled off to San Blas with their two leaders.

Governor Figueroa, described by C. Alan Hutchinson (1914-81) as "the most capable governor" of the Mexican period,[10] died at the end of 1835, and the next year saw four administrations in power. Nicolás Gutiérrez, his army commander, served as interim governor and moved the capital to Los Angeles, a pueblo of about 600 people. After a short time, Mariano Chico (1796-1850) was appointed by Santa Anna. He arrived under a cloud: A vaquero who had had an affair with the wife of a popular ranchero conspired with the wife to murder her husband and throw his body down a ravine. About 50 angry citizens captured and lynched the vaquero and the errant wife. Gutiérrez had been assured that they meant nothing subversive by this and were only reacting to a growing uncontrolled crime wave, but the new governor saw it otherwise. So began his troubles with the citizens. Chico made himself hated because of three arbitrary actions: He tried to arrest those who had taken part in the vigilante action, and who happened to be the leading citizens of Los Angeles, he persecuted Father President Narcíso Durán for not swearing allegiance to the Constitution of 1834, which gave the go-ahead to secularization, and he committed an unforgivable *faux pas* by forcing his mistress on the Monterey social set. For a man who, Bancroft writes, was "skilled in the art of gaining popularity," he became "a tyrant, a rascal, and a fool.... the object not only of hatred... but of ridicule."[11] After three months in office he was overthrown and sent back to Mexico. He left claiming that he was going to get army reinforcements to reestablish himself in power, but never returned. In Mexico he held other offices for Santa Anna: governor of Agua Caliente and *comandante* of Guanajuato. Gutiérrez was again left in charge, but he was soon overthrown by Juan Bautista Alvarado (1800-82).

Alvarado opposed the way the previous governors had looked to Mexico for direction and led the Californios in company with the American mountain man Isaac Graham (1800-63) and the army under José Castro (1810-60) to affect a sweep into power.

Since Alvarado was very popular in the north, he returned the capital to Monterey. He soon met opposition in the south: The Mexican Congress had named Los Angeles capital. This opposition intensified when Santa Anna appointed another Californio governor, Carlos Antonio Carrillo (1783-1852). Six opponents moved against Alvarado at Los Angeles, but he defeated them in a typical bloodless battle in 1837. He deported all the Mexican officials and proclaimed California free and independent, with the understanding that such independence would end should the Constitution of 1824 be restored. The flag Alvarado chose for California was blue with a white star. Eventually, however, this flag was replaced, in 1839, by the Mexican eagle, when Santa Anna finally recognized him as governor.

To mollify the south, he appointed a semi-independent sub-governor with headquarters at Los Angeles. He then ensured his own safety by deporting Graham and the other American and English supporters before they could turn against him and seize power. His disapproval of the way his uncle, Mariano Vallejo, was administering the missions in what is today the North Bay led to a family break, aggravated when the governor gave a large land grant to John A. Sutter (1803-80) as a potential curb to Vallejo. This internecine strife led to governmental disorder, and in 1842, after six years as governor, he grew weary of politics and retired.

Alvarado was replaced by Manuel Micheltorena (1802-53), a Santa Anna appointee. He arrived with 300 criminal *cholo* soldiers, many of whom were products of prisons, thereby insuring his unpopularity. He was told to exclude foreigners, especially Americans, but was unable to do so. Instead, he gave large land grants to certain favored Americans, such as John Marsh (1799-1856), Pierson B. Reading (1816-68), and others who had come overland to live here. He mismanaged the customs house and had other financial problems due to corrupt duty collectors. He promised to return mission lands and income to the Church but failed to do so. Angered by the robberies, rapes and murders committed by Micheltorena's cholo soldiers, his currying favor with the foreigners and his dependence on Santa Anna, the Californios revolted. Micheltorena was overthrown by Alvarado's friends José Castro and Pío Pico at the second battle of Cahuenga in February 1845. Some blood was shed at this battle, one side losing a horse and the other a mule.

By this time Mexican authority had become nebulous. From the time of the Yuma Massacre, California had had to develop on its own with only occasional spurts of interest from distant Mexico. The Spain of Carlos IV and Ferdinand VII could not consistently attend to a far-away colony, and the viceregal treasury was shrinking so pitifully that soldiers went unpaid for years at a stretch; General Vallejo considered it remarkable that they gave as good service as they did under the circumstances. When the supply ships stopped coming, people turned to smugglers for basic goods, which cast some doubt on the utility of the Mexican connection. With Santa Anna seated in the Presidential Palace, there were sporadic attempts to tighten Mexico's grip on California, but his attentions were more focused on Texas and problems at home, while the men he sent as governors and other officials were overwhelmingly unpopular; once they were driven out, there was no real attempt to restore them. Mexican power steadily ebbed, making California a low-hanging fruit ripe for plucking by the United States.

Pico served for a year and a half, until the American conquest. During his short term he set up his administration in Los Angeles but lacking decisive influence in the north he let Castro run the customs and treasury from Monterey. Pico was lavish in handing out land grants to Mexican citizens and foreigners alike. His conflicts with Castro kept him from accomplishing much and made it easier for the Americans to conquer California.

Secularization

Secularization, which was mentioned in connection with several governors, had always been the goal of Christianizing the Spanish Empire, and - on the surface, at least – it did not appear to be a major threat to the Church. Running the missions as small, paternalistic villages was never intended to be a long-term arrangement, and from the beginning was meant to give way to parish churches, local clergy, and extensive land holdings divided between government and Indians. The actual church buildings and rectories, plus a small lot for the support of the clergy, would remain in Church possession. In sharp contrast to Spain's objectives in the Christianizing of its empire, the Mexican Republic's intention was not to benefit the Church in any way, but rather to undermine it. Secularization was a four-point program: (1) The missions would become parish churches, (2) The friars would be replaced by parish priests (friars were members of an order while parish priests were secular clergy), (3) The Indian neophytes would be released from mission jurisdiction, and (4) The mission property would be converted into pueblos in which each Indian family would receive some land and livestock.

Three things lay at the bottom of this later secularization. The missions were unpopular in Mexico because most of the hierarchy was loyal to Spain, many abandoning their dioceses and fleeing to Spain with independence, and the liberals wanted to free the Indians from priestly control. The greatest impetus to secularization, however, was a practical one: the desire for rich Church properties. It was this lust rather than expectation of the mission-to-parish evolution that distinguished secularization in California from the original plan that had been followed for two centuries throughout Spanish America.[12]

There had been attempts at secularization in the 1820s but the adoption of *An Act for the Secularization of the Missions of California* in 1833 by the Mexican Congress was decisive. Figueroa issued a proclamation in August 1834 ordering ten missions to be secularized that year, six in 1835, and the last five in 1836. The law turned the missions into parish churches and stripped the missions of all lands except for that under the church building and rectory; friars would remain in charge until they could be replaced by available curates, or secular clergy. In 1844, Micheltorena disposed of all remaining mission property except that of Santa Barbara, which survived intact. The livestock was taken. Half of the land and livestock went to the government and half to the Indians.

This was a disaster for the Indians. Had it been postponed for a dozen years it might have worked, as many of the natives were unprepared for freedom. Having been taken from their aboriginal lives, having seen those ways destroyed, they were yet unprepared to face the new world into which they were thrust, like young children faced with the demands of adulthood. Many of them stayed on at the missions, demoralized hangers-on. Those who did take possession of their lands had no real concept of property ownership and were soon swindled out of their land by crooked Mexicans for a drink or a few coins. The land that was to be governed by lay administrators soon passed via land grants to the rancheros and other non-religious persons.

The mission buildings fell into ruins, often being turned into storerooms, inns, or barns. Eventually the church buildings were returned to the Catholic church by the American government.

Governor Figueroa's secularization proclamation also replaced the Spanish-born padres at all the missions north of Mission San Antonio de Padua with Mexican-born Franciscan priests. In response to this, Father-President Durán transferred the headquarters of the Alta California missions from Carmel to Santa Barbara, where it remained until 1846.

**

"A ranchero if he's lucky has a pair of pants and wooden stirrups and some good leather reins."

-Song

Pastoral California

By 1846 about 8 million acres (3,237,000 ha) had been granted to about 800 people. Though this amounted to an average of 10,000 acres (4,047 ha) per grantee, and many American newcomers resented the apparently unmerited bestowal of such lavish spreads, it was a realistic approach to cattle raising in a semi-arid land. These grants of land were presented by the Spanish crown either as a reward for loyal service or to attract settlers to an undeveloped area. The first grant, a small one near Mission San Carlos, was made by Governor Rivera in 1775 to a retired soldier, Manuel Butrón. Nine years later, land granting took off when Governor Fages issued grants to three retired soldiers: Juan José Domínguez (1736-1809) received the 43,000 acre (17,400 hectares) Rancho San Pedro, José María Verdugo (1751-1831) was granted the 36,000 acre (14,570 hectares) Rancho San Rafael from Arroyo Seco to Mission San Fernando, and Manuel Nieto (1734-1804) received the 300,000 acre (121,400 hectares) Rancho los Nietos, all of the land between the Santa Ana and San Gabriel rivers from the Santa Ana and San Gabriel mountains to the sea. It was required of each grantee that he build a permanent dwelling and farm or raise stock on the land, whose title remained with the crown, based on Roman law. The tremendous size of Corporal Nieto's grant was not without some controversy; Mission San Gabriel contested it on the grounds that it encroached on the southern end of the Mission's property, and won its appeal, Nieto's land being halved to 167,000 acres (67,580 hectares). In 1834 Governor Figueroa ordered it broken up into six portions to accommodate his heirs.

Outright grants began after independence, with about 50

preceding secularizations. In the thirteen years before the American conquest, over 600 grants were made, including 87 by Governor Pico to friends in 1846. The latter were assigned according to the Law of Colonization passed by the Mexican Congress in 1824. This law provided that an individual might petition for a square league (about 4,400 acres or 1,781 hectares) of irrigated land, 4 square leagues of land dependent on rainfall only, and 6 square leagues for grazing cattle, the legal maximum being 11 square leagues (48,000 acres or 19,420 hectares). To claim land, the petitioner had to request property in the public domain, define it verbally and with a *diseño* (a primitively drawn topographic sketch of the land), and show cause why he should receive it. Based on this application the territorial assembly would advise the governor, who was authorized to grant or deny each petition. These terrains were usually located near the coast, although the Colonization Law prohibited grants within ten leagues (30 miles or 48 km) of the shoreline without special permission from Mexico City.

So the *rancheros*, the great landowning families of Mexican California, were created: in the south the Carrillos, with 320,000 acres (129,500 hectares), the De la Guerras, with 326,000 acres (131,900 hectares), and the Picos, with 532,000 acres (215,300 hectares); in the north the Alvarados with two ranchos of 23,949 acres (9,692 hectares), the Castros with twelve amounting to 251,432 acres (101,800 hectares), the Peraltas with four amounting to 48,366 acres (19,570 hectares), and the Vallejos with three totaling 39,750 acres (98,221 hectares). Foreigners who agreed to become Mexican citizens and Catholics were also eligible, and many would avail themselves of that privilege, "leaving their consciences at Cape Horn," as a popular saying had it.

Those days of the great ranchos, California's romantic era,

with its reputed idyllic life, inspired future tales. Here was the setting of the "Zorro" tales and Helen Hunt Jackson's 1884 novel *Ramona*. Life was simpler, since it centered on huge cattle herds overseen by vaqueros who did not have to ride fences. Little labor was required, since only the cattle hides, known as "California Bank Notes" were valued by foreign traders. It was a time of long lives and light taxation, less pressure than in the United States or Mexico at the time, astonishingly large numbers of children born to the average family, and consequently less stress. The rancheros were famed for their open-handed charity and honesty, and many foreigners felt that if they must be thrown on any foreign shore, California would be the one to choose. As if copying the males of most species of birds, the men dressed in gaudy hues while the women, with their large families and plenty of housework, were attired in more sedate colors. Sports included grizzly-bear hunting with a sword, bull-and-bear fights to wager on and be entertained by, and fiestas for any social occasion.

Portrait of a mounted Californio ranchero in traditional clothing. (via Wikimedia Commons)

The great ranchos are nearly all gone. The Irvine holdings in Orange County were some of the last to go. One remains at Los Banos, Rancho San Luis Gonzaga, last owned by Paula Fatjo (1921-92), great-great granddaughter of Francisco Pacheco (1791-1860), who was granted 150,000 acres over several years on both sides of Pacheco Pass in 1833-44. A San Francisco debutante, she moved onto the property in 1948. The year after her 1992 death, her will deeded 6,900 acres to the California Department of Parks and Recreation, which became Pacheco State Park.[13]

Thanks to Nellie Van De Grift Sánchez's magnificent book, *Spanish Arcadia* (1919), we can understand what this period was like.

Otter, Seal and Whale Hunters

Foreign intrusions on California had begun in the 1780s and 1790s with La Pérouse and Vancouver, and in later years world interest in the North Pacific expanded. Non-Spanish visitors - officially welcome or not - increased, a semi-illegal California trade developed, and California became cosmopolitan. When Mexico became independent, its new government opened California to world trade.

La Pérouse and Vancouver had reported to their respective colonizing nations that the only thing of value in California was fur. With the great demand for fur in clothing and hats in aristocratic fashion of the 18th and 19th centuries, trappers could market furs in China and the Western World for prices that fetched $300 for a virgin pelt and $25 for a scratched, worn-out pelt ($9,007-$751 in 2023 dollars).[14] If the hunters did not squander their earnings, their California-gained wealth, typically amassed in a short time, would make them affluent men who could easily return to the United States as plutocrats.

The Spanish had been bartering with the Indians for otter pelts since their first settlements in California, trading them in China. The native Californians had long been familiar with the sea otter (*Enhydra lutris*), using them for food, clothing, bed coverings, and as a medium of exchange for trade with inland tribes. The fur, obtained by hunting the animals close to shore in small rafts, was used for ceremonial attire, especially capes and skirts.

The first steady contacts with California by the English-speaking world were made by the Boston Men. Their story begins with the arrival at Monterey in 1796 of the sailing ship appropriately named *Otter*, under Captain Ebenezer Dorr. This group of American merchants and traders were dubbed the Boston Men, regardless of their place of origin, since Boston was known as the United States' main port. With the stopping of the San Blas ships and the Manila galleons, these men were welcome as they brought needed supplies. The Boston Men came in search of otters, and in about twenty years made the land otter almost extinct along the northwest coast. In 1801 about 18,000 pelts were marketed, and in 1810 about 10,000, but after 1820 no more were taken. This traffic gave Americans their first knowledge of California. Americans who came overland, like George Nidever (1802-83), George Yount (1794-1865) and William Wolfskill (1798-1866), also hunted the otters until the 1840s, when new fashions made otter skins and furs less desirable.

In the 1820s, American whalers, needing a port to rest and to provision before their long trip back to the States, (as residents of U.S. territories and other jurisdictions referred to the United States of America) appeared at Monterey. The gray whales and humpbacks, hunted for their blubber ("whale oil"), migrated annually through the coastal waters, and at the same time California afforded a good area for trade, supplies, and repairs on long voyages that took ships to the Arctic and far out into the Pacific. The American whalers generally preferred Hawaii because of the rum, women, and climate, but some did stop in California. Their numbers grew in the years that California was becoming Americanized.

Fort Ross

The Russians with their Aleut hunters in Alaska had

depleted the Aleutian Islands of fur seals, so Rezanov recommended trading posts in Oregon and California. In 1808 Alexander Baranov (1746-1819), the chief manager of the Russian American Company and governor of the Russian Colonies in America (1799-1818), sent Ivan Kuskov (1765-1823), his senior assistant, to Bodega Bay to try to build a post. Kuskov purchased land from the Kashaya Pomo tribe, and according to one account the entire area was acquired from the natives for "three blankets, three pairs of breeches, two axes, three hoes, and some beads." It was chosen as the most suitable location for a settlement site due to its harbor, plentiful water, good forage, and a nearby supply of wood for the necessary construction.

In 1812 Kuskov built Fort Ross with 180 Russians and Aleuts, mainly Kodiak islanders who did most of the hunting using *bidarkas* (hunting kayaks) and atlatls (sling shots, **Chapter 2**). This site was also relatively far from the San Francisco Bay area. In fact, it was several months before the Spanish authorities at Yerba Buena became aware of the development at Fort Ross, and by then it was too late, since the fort was completed, well-armed, and vigilantly manned.

A view of Fort Ross in 1828 by A.B. Duhaut-Cilly. From the archives of the Fort Ross Historical Society (via Wikimedia Commons)

The structures were built of redwood using joinery techniques typical of the maritime carpentry of the time. A wooden palisade surrounded the site, in much the same configuration as seen today, including two blockhouses complete with cannons. The interior of the stockade contained the two-story house of the manager, the officials' quarters, barracks for the Russian employees, and various storehouses. The chapel was added in 1824. Outside the walls were high-roofed cottages for the company laborers, a native Alaskan village of flat-topped houses, and the cone-shaped dwellings and ritual dance houses of the local Pomo Indians. There were several other important buildings outside the fort: a bathhouse, essential for any Russian community, a large windmill, and a large work building (60' x 80' x 100') (18.3 m x 24.4 m x 30.5 m), the tannery, and boat shop. Several 150–200-ton (136-181.5 metric tons) ocean-going ships were built at Ross in the early 1820s.

The Spanish traded with the Russians despite the illegality of trading with any but the mother country, in 1813 exchanging about $14,000 ($283,363 in 2023) in goods between Ross and Yerba Buena. By 1825 the Russians had wiped out the fur seals on the north coast with typical catches of over 73,000 per year between1810 and 1812. During those years they also reportedly took at least 5,000 otter pelts annually. So great was the impact of overhunting that in 1833 the Russians took only 54 seals, a catch so poor that seal hunts ended.

Like its British, American, Spanish, and Portuguese competitors, the Russian American Company was a profit-making company that hunted with no regard for the future of sea mammals. In California from 1803 to 1805, over 17,000 otter furs were taken. At times American trade ships worked together with the RAC, supplying the ships while the RAC supplied native Alaskan labor. The highest known catch of otters by Aleut hunters in one year was 9,356. The largest catch on record for a single voyage, 6,000 sea otter skins was by Captain John Suter's ship Pearl in 1808-09.[15] One of the ten Americans Baranov contracted with over the years was Captain Joseph O'Cain, owner of the brig *O'Cain*. O'Cain had been contracted to hunt otters along the Baja coast, took 1,800 and kept half of the take as his share. On the way back to New Archangel he went into San Francisco Bay where his hunters took 1,100 pelts and bought 700 from the Mission.[16] Kuskov reported that over 2,000 fur pelts were taken annually in the first few years at Ross. Hunting was practiced from Trinidad Bay in Humboldt County to Baja California. The Farallons and Channel Islands were said to be abundant. It is said that in the 35-year period that the RAC plied California waters, over 100,000 fur pelts were taken with the aid of British and American trade ships. Most of these pelts would end up in China via these same trade ships.

The RAC also hunted sea gulls along the California coast. These birds provided the main food for the hunters, and in what amounted to a war of extermination about 50,000 gulls a year were killed.[17]

**

The hunting of the elephant seal for oil on the Channel Islands and the islands off the Baja coast nearly wiped out the species by 1860. In the late 1890s Charles Haskins Townsend (1859-1944), a Smithsonian biologist, found a colony of less than 100 elephant seals on the Mexican island of Guadalupe and convinced the Mexican government to protect them. In 1911 the United States, Russia, Britain (for Canada), and Japan signed a treaty to protect the fur seals and the sea otters in the North Pacific. Fur seals, as of 2014, numbered 600,000, while California coastal sea otters numbered 2,944.[18]

**

When the furs gave out, Kuskov decided to make Fort Ross an agricultural supplier for Alaska. He started three farms but was unsuccessful. The land was poor for cattle, there were only enough vegetables and fruit for the locals, and only small amounts of butter and cheese were exported north; indeed, on only one occasion did the crop yield of vegetables and fruits exceed five exportable pounds (2.27 kg) for every pound needed for local consumption. However, the Russian colonists in northern California never fulfilled their agricultural goals due to coastal fog, gophers, mice, and lack of genuine interest on the part of men who saw themselves primarily as hunters. A century later it would be a different story: In 1922 Sonoma County would rank as second (after Santa Clara County) in plum production. [19]

Did Russians contribute anything to California? Several scholars, led by Foothill College professor Nicholas Rokitiansky (1912-96), have shown that they surveyed the Russian River, calling it *Slavyanka* ("Slavic Woman"), and gave Russian names to all its tributaries; they build the first shipyard in northern California; they may have named Mount Shasta ("Schast'ia," approximately the Russian word for happiness or fortune); and they catalogued the flower that would be the state's official floral representative - the Golden Poppy (*Eschscholtzia californica*).

Fort Ross's last commandant was a very colorful character, Alexander Rotchev (1806-73), who arrived in 1838 with his wife and children. In 1838 he built a new commandant's house, smaller yet more imposing than the original one, and probably far more comfortable. Rotchev was himself a well-known poet, writer, traveler, and translator - a master of five languages including Latin and Greek. His wife, the former Princess Helena Gagarin, was widely known for her beauty, charm, and wit. She was a favorite with all who knew her. A local Indian chief, Solano (c.1798-1851), tried to kidnap her, apparently because Rotchev would not agree to sell her as the chief's new wife. In the only recorded conflict between the Russians and the Indians, Chief Solano was punished when the Russians enforced Governor Rotchev's wishes with a display of military force. General Vallejo's son, Platón (1841-1925), recalled that the general had warned Chief Solano that the Indians would certainly face military reprisal in response to any such attempt, and that moreover they could not look to him for support, though he and Solano were friends. [20]

Princess Helena, one of the czar's nieces, had given up her position in high society, and her inheritance, to elope with Rotchev. Though they later separated (for reasons lost to history), they both agreed that their time at Fort Ross was the happiest of their lives.[21]

Travelers from all over the world visited Fort Ross. One of them, the very elegant and aristocratic French traveler and diplomat Eugene Duflot de Mofras (1810-85), visiting in 1841, was charmed by the Rotchevs' hospitality, commenting that their house was better furnished than that of Governor Micheltorena at Monterey. He was especially delighted by the Rotchevs' choice library, their supply of fine French wines, and the excellent piano on which Princess Helena played Mozart and other favorites.

In 1824 Russia and Britain signed a treaty whereby the Russians gave up their claims to Oregon, isolating Fort Ross. Relations with the Indians, with the exception noted, were good, but Russian relations with the Spaniards and Mexicans were very cool, although some trade was carried on, the missions even using Ft. Ross's blacksmith because of his skill.

When Mexican independence opened California to world trade, the goods the Russians might expect to export had lost value through market forces. Foreign ships bought up the local produce to such an extent that the Russians were finding their food supply threatened. In 1829 they had to send as far as to Chile for provisions. They determined to expand their territory from San Francisco Bay north to 42o and east to the Sacramento River, since they planned to bring several hundred serfs to operate hoped-for ranches in the Sacramento Valley, but this project could only be realized with Mexican consent, which was hardly forthcoming. The Mexican government insisted on Russian recognition in return for those land grants, but Czar Nicholas I (1796-1855, reigned 1825-55) refused to have anything to do with "revolutionaries." Nevertheless, the Ft. Ross Russians were determined to try, and in 1834 Baron Ferdinand von Wrangell (1796-1870), chief manager of the RAC and governor of Alaska, took over the negotiations, visiting Monterey. These talks came to nothing.[22]

The Russians now found themselves hemmed in on all sides as the missions at San Rafael and Sonoma and the pueblos at Santa Rosa and Petaluma were founded. With the decline of the fur trade, the isolation from Alaska, the failure of agriculture and the impossibility of expansion, the Russians were willing to leave for New Archangel and sent word of this to Vallejo in his capacity as Comandante of the Line (frontier military commander) in the North. Governor Alvarado announced this as soon as he learned of it, and the people of Monterey celebrated the end of the unwelcome occupation of their land. For his part, Rotchev opposed the move but had to go along with it. He wanted the Russians to stay because he believed that one day California would be a prosperous place.

One can only wonder what would have occurred had the Russians been a presence in California when gold was discovered seven years later.

Investigated by the RAC for mismanagement, Rotchev was dismissed from service. In 1849, taking advantage of the intense interest in the California Gold Rush, he published *A New Eldorado in California*, and returned to California for a short time in 1850.[23]

Although the presence of these uninvited foreigners in California for three decades had been galling to Hispanic pride, and one of Vallejo's primary tasks was to make things uncomfortable for them, he was generous in his appraisal of their stay. In his *Historia de la California,* he wrote:

> Upon saying farewell forever to these strangers who during So many years have been the nightmare of the governors of California, and even more so of the many comandantes, I must, in justice to the truth, set down as a positive fact that I do not recollect a single instance in which they have failed to keep their engagements or to give a frank and kindly reception to the Californians and Mexicans who visited their establishments. I am sure that I do not depart from the truth when I affirm that benevolence and loyalty were the inseparable motto of the Russians stationed at Ross and Bodega, just as honor was their guiding star.[24]

Vallejo took credit for pressuring them into evacuation, but other economic and political forces were at work. The general would have had no more success than anyone else in the previous thirty years had they not wanted to leave. They allowed Vallejo his fantasy as it cost them nothing. There was some question about what to do with the fort, and the RAC's officials considered everything from burning it down to dismantling it to selling it to an interested buyer. Ultimately, they sold the fort to John A. Sutter for $30,000 in 1841 ($1,110,322 in 2023).

Traders in Hides and Tallow

When the newly independent Latin American nations threw open their ports to world trade, the United States and Britain became major trade competitors. It was in hoping to secure this commerce that both the U.S. and Britain strongly supported keeping the new Latin American nations independent, the United States with its Monroe Doctrine and Britain with its navy. In California the generally friendly trade rivalry centered on hides and tallow.

In June 1822 two British traders, Scotsman Hugh McCulloch and Englishman William Hartnell (1798-1854), popularly known as "Macala y Arnel," arrived at Monterey and bought a three year trade monopoly from Father Payeras, the mission prefect (after 1819), for a dollar ($25.40 in 2023) a hide and 3/10 cent (eight cents in 2023) per pound (453.59 g) of tallow. A few days after this contract was negotiated, William Gale (1790-1841), an American agent for Bryant & Sturgis of Boston, who had first come in 1810 hunting seals (and whose wife, an Estudillo, would be the first Californio to visit Boston), arrived but waited until the British contract expired. Never letting an opportunity slip where he might undermine Payeras' confidence in the "Macala y Arnel," Gale managed to get the contract when it expired by offering Payeras a 15% increase in price. This semi-friendly rivalry seesawed for a decade, although Gale, called "Cuatro Ojos" (or "Four Eyes" because of his reputed "great staring eyes" magnified by thick eyeglasses) dominated after 1828. This trade war went on until secularization ended the virtual monopoly the missions had held on the product. After secularization ended the single contract between the missions and the traders, business was carried on with the ranchos under separate contracts.[25]

San Diego became the best hide-producing port, and the trading ships, carrying everything that Californios might want, were like floating department stores. The hides were taken to Boston, turned into shoes and boots, and then brought back to California to be sold at handsome profits. Some of these foreign traders stayed in California, marrying local girls and adopting local customs, Hartnell and Gale among them. Despite being inland, isolated, and inconvenient, Los Angeles was a prime customer for the Boston trading ships' cargoes of silk, shoes, furniture, and whatever else could be profitably carried.

Other traders did business with Hawaii, while still others conducted a triangular trade: manufactured goods to California, sea otter pelts from California, and trading them in China for Oriental goods to be taken back to Boston. Most hide business was, however, a matter of simple trade between Boston and California.

The best description of those days from an American perspective comes from the pen of Richard Henry Dana (1815-82), whose diary became *Two Years Before the Mast* (1840), the book that helped to end the practice of flogging on American ships and gave Americans one of their first sources of information about California.

A rich, cultivated young man from Massachusetts, Richard Henry Dana caught measles during his sophomore year at Harvard and lost much of his eyesight. In an attempt to regain it, he left his studies to live an outdoor life. In 1834 he signed on as sailor aboard the *Pilgrim*, a brig to California around stormy Cape Horn, and spent 16 months there (Jan 1835-May 1836), returning on the *Alert*. In his travels he came to know the various ports from Yerba Buena to San Diego from which his ships gathered hides, and in which they carried on trade or took on supplies.

Knowing Spanish, he got a good sense of California life, admired the grace of the people but also showed a contemptuous Yankee view of their idleness and love of ease and luxury, their sense of *no te apures* ("Don't worry!") and the infectious appeal of *mañana*. He did enjoy himself, as when he was a guest at the wedding of Alfred Robinson (1807-95) and Ana de la Guerra (1822-52), daughter of the richest family in Santa Barbara; he had been invited since the Alert was a Sturgis & Bryant ship and Robinson was its agent. He spent several enjoyable months ashore at San Diego's Point Loma curing hides and making friends. These good times were balanced by the drudgery of collecting the hides and tossing them down from the point to the beach, exemplified by an occasion when hides that had been caught in a cleft in the rocky cliff over which they were tossed had to be dislodged – a perilous, arduous task. Decades later that cliff would be named Dana Point in his honor.

His health restored, he returned to Harvard and completed his legal training. Having vowed to "redress the grievances and sufferings" of the American sailor, he wrote an article, "Cruelty to Seamen," for the *American Jurist* in 1839 and followed it with his popular and distinguished account in 1840. In 1859-60 he took a 14-month voyage around the world, stopping in California, where he wrote an appendix to his *Two Years Before the Mast*, calling it *Twenty-Four Years After*, a description of his nostalgic return.

The Hudson's Bay Company

The Hudson's Bay Company, whose initials some said stood for "Here Before Christ," had been founded in 1670 to trade for furs in British Canada. By the 1820s it had wiped out all rivals in Canada by cut-throat competition. In 1810 the Company established Fort Vancouver on the Columbia River and in the 1820s began sending trappers south into California's Central Valley along the Siskiyou Trail, starting with Finian McDonald and Thomas McKay. Those who went into California were known as the Umpqua Brigade because their jumping-off point was on the Umpqua River in southern Oregon. Most of these trappers, though working for a British company, were French-speaking métis.[26]

The Hudson's Bay Company's first trapper in California was Peter Skene Ogden (1794-1854) in 1826, and its first expedition into California was made two years later by Alexander Roderick McLeod (1782-1840), formerly with the North West Company, for whom the McCloud River was named. The next year McLeod went as far south as Stockton, having established the Siskiyou Trail, but lost most of his equipment in bad winter weather. McLeod was considered somewhat of a maverick by the HBC and had an obnoxious disposition. Nevertheless, he was respected as a translator, trader and fighter.[27] Ogden returned in 1829-30, leading a large brigade down through Idaho and Nevada, and advancing as far south as Needles before returning to trap in the Sacramento Valley. An expedition under John Work (died 1861) in 1832 and another under Michel LaFramboise (1793-1865), "[John] McLoughlin's troubleshooter" in 1832-33, were followed by annual parties traveling the Siskiyou and Trinity trails to hunt in the Central Valley.

La Framboise was the "Frenchman" of French Camp, their

headquarters near Stockton. Those who met him did not easily forget him. There are tales of his prowess in the histories of both California and Oregon. To Indian and white man alike he was "the Captain of the California Trail." His name often appeared in company documents as simply "Michel"; to the Americans he was "Big Mike," and the Russians, Californios, and Indians knew him well and respected him. The Indians were in awe of him because he was ruthless in dealing with them and knew more Indian languages than any other interpreter. The Mexican authorities from time to time issued orders to him, forbidding trade with the Indians and limiting his range, but they never exerted enough power over the area to enforce their decrees, and LaFromboise went on happily flouting their orders. Captain Charles Wilkes (1798-1877) of the United States Exploring Expedition met him at Champoeg (in Oregon) in the summer of 1841 and described him in his journal:

> In the morning we found horses waiting under charge of M. La Framboise who is in the employ of the Hudson's Bay Company and was very happy to see us. He originally came out in the ship Tonquin and was one of the party that landed at Astoria where he has resided ever since either in
> the employ of the North West Company or the Hudson's Bay Company. Michel is of low stature and rather corpulent, but he has great energy and activity of both mind and body and indominatable [sic] courage and all
> the vivacity of a Frenchman. He has traveled in all parts of the country and says he has a wife of high rank in every tribe, by which means he has insured his safety. From him I derived much information and to him all parties refer as possessing the most accurate knowledge of the country. He generally has charge of

271

a party, and was formerly engaged in trapping; but of late years passing through the country to California and back.[28]

Still, "Big Mike" was a realist in dealing with his brigade, and with life, and knew the limits of authority and loyalty. He decided to retire after his return in the fall of 1843. "I am," he said, "through the Mercy of God, come back safe because I gave way to my men; if I had assumed the tone of master, I would have been murdered by them. I will not venture again."[29]

A cache of arms, rifles and sabers long believed to belong to Hudson's Bay trappers, was found buried at French Camp, but these weapons were little likely to be theirs as sabers are not practical weapons for dealing with Mexican guns or Indian arrows. At the site of their camp at the confluence of the Sacramento and Feather Rivers (by the Buttes) where Work was camping with his brigade of about a hundred people, there remained for many years an old stone corral which they had erected.[30] On a ranch near Oakhurst is a woman's likeness carved in rock with the inscription "To J.M. 1841," believed to be a Hudson's Bay trapper's memorial to a loved one. Below Bakersfield is the town of Lebec, named for trapper Pierre Lebec, who was killed by a grizzly bear he had shot and wounded in October 1837. The tree near which he died and under which he was buried bore a carving attesting to the death. These are the few scattered mementos of the Hudson's Bay trappers in California.

In the late 1830s, the Company took an interest in expanding its ocean trade beyond the occasional ship calling at Monterey, Yerba Buena, San Diego, or Santa Barbara. In 1835 McLoughlin was informed in a letter from the Company that

"California trade should be pushed if it pays at all, it would afford freight to our country vessels, and a filling-up freight in the article of tallow to the homeward ships of the season."[31]

Five HBC ships, the *Columbia*, the *Cowlitz*, the *Cadboro*, the *Dryad*, and the *Prince Albert*, all carried on a lively trade moving salmon, lumber and flour from Honolulu to Fort Vancouver, sugar and manufactured goods from Honolulu to California, and beaver, wapiti, deer, and salmon to California.

In 1841, Sir George Simpson (1792-1860), the head of the Company, arrived at Monterey while on a pre-retirement trip around the world. It was he who told Concepción Argüello about Rezanov's death 35 years earlier. He was disappointed that Sutter had bought Fort Ross, but he gave approval to the opening of a store in Yerba Buena, buying it from Jacob Leese (1809-92), an American expatriate (brother-in-law to Vallejo) who had lived there for six years. Later Simpson would regret that decision, omitting any mention of the store in his memoirs, for it was unclear whether company officialdom wanted an active fur trapping enterprise, an agricultural reserve, or a store-based business, and for all his provincial greatness, Sir George could be petty. Glen Rae (1806-45), son-in-law of John McLoughlin (1784-1857), the Chief Factor at Fort Vancouver, was put in charge of it. Under Rae the store failed, for he was nearly blind and frequently drunk. Dishonest customers frequently cheated him with bad furs for good. He made two major mistakes - he backed with Company goods for credit the losing side in a revolution when Alvarado tried to overthrow Governor Micheltorena, and he carried on an affair with a local girl while his wife was pregnant with their tenth child. Ordered back to Fort Vancouver, he feared encountering his stern father-in-law and committed suicide in February 1845 in front of his family and servants. At about the same time, French Camp was abandoned. The store was sold at the end of the year at a loss of $2,926 ($118,445 in 2023 dollars], and in September 1846 the HBC left California for good. [32]

The Old Spanish Trail and the Mountain Men

In 1821 William Becknell (1787-1865) of Franklin, Howard County, Missouri, improved the Santa Fe Trail, the trade route that had been used by French traders from St. Louis to Santa Fe to make it usable by wagon trains. In 1829 what became known as the Old Spanish Trail was pieced together by Santa Fe trader Antonio Armijo, based in part on what Fathers Domínguez and Escalante had pioneered a half-century earlier, from the Santa Fe Trail and one of the routes known as the California Trail. Armijo started from Abiquiú, about 53 miles (85 km) north of Santa Fe. The Old Spanish Trail's several routes ran from Santa Fe to what today is Durango, Colorado, and continued through what today are Las Vegas and Needles to Los Angeles. Trading caravans consisting of twenty to 200 members, and twice as many mules loaded with goods, would leave from Santa Fe in December, get to Los Angeles in February, then leave Los Angeles in April to arrive back in Santa Fe by June, the schedule most favorable to accessing available water and avoiding heat. The traders who went over this two-part route brought manufactured goods by wagon from the United States; silver, sheep, wool blankets, serapes and rugs from New Mexico and Chihuahua; horses and Chinese silk from California. The traders themselves were not very welcome since many of the horses they exported from California were stolen from the ranchos with Indian help. They also engaged in slave trading, kidnapping women and children from Indian villages, and selling them as slaves to other tribes and

Mexicans.[33]

The mountain men were a group of young Americans who went west, combing every spot, in search of beaver pelts to take back to St. Louis. Their heyday was the thirty-year period prior to 1842. They were adventurous, usually illiterate, Southern-born, rough men who lived more like the Indians than not, often having an Indian wife. They worked for different companies based in St. Louis and generally ignored the territorial claims of either Mexico or the Hudson's Bay Company.

The highlight of the mountain men's year was the annual Rendezvous, a gathering of mountain men, Indians, and traders held at some pre-arranged spot in the Mountain West. There they would sell furs, talk about where they gone and what they had seen, meet the different company representatives, buy supplies and tools they needed, swap tales, get drunk, marry new Indian wives, and have a good time for about two weeks until it was time to resume their fur hunting lives.

The first of the mountain men to make contact with California - indeed his party was the first group of white and black men to reach California overland from the United States - was Jedediah Smith (1799-1831). Unlike most of his contemporaries, he was a New Englander, literate and cultivated. Smith, who had started as a trapper working for William Henry Ashley (1778-1838) when he was fourteen, had survived a massacre by the Arikaras and a grizzly bear mauling. He became a partner in the American Fur Company at the age of twenty when Ashley sold his shares to Smith, David Edward Jackson (1788-1837), and William Sublette (1798-1845). In 1826 he went south to trap in Utah and Arizona before being guided to San Gabriel by runaway Mission Indians. Though a Protestant foreigner, he was welcomed by the mission priests with gifts of food, wine, cloth, and lodging. He called Fray José Bernardo Sánchez (1778-1831) "the most Christian man I ever met" and named the entire Sierra Nevada "Mount Joseph." In return for his hospitality, he gave Fr. Sánchez a bear trap to catch poaching Indians in the orchards. [34]Whether it was ever used is unrecorded.

Upon asking Governor Echeandía for permission to trap, Jedediah Smith was jailed as a spy. A Boston shipper got him released when he promised to leave California as the way he had come. Having gotten out of the governor's sight, however, he rode into the Central Valley via Old Tejon Pass and trapped along the Kings and Stanislaus Rivers, going as far north as the American River. Unable to cross the Sierra Nevada because of deep winter snow, with over 1,500 pounds (680 kg) of beaver pelts destined for that year's Rendezvous at Bear Lake, he made the first west-to-east crossing of the Sierra by a white man via the 8,736 feet (2,663 m) high Ebbett's Pass in Alpine County. He added to that feat by crossing the Great Basin.

In 1827 he was once again in California despite losing ten of his eighteen men, killed by Mojave Indians on the Colorado River; two Canadian Indian women had been with the party but were taken by the Mojaves. At Mission San Gabriel he was again welcomed and continued north, stopping at Yerba Buena. At Mission San José, Father Durán was not as hospitable as Sánchez, and briefly jailed Smith to hold him for Echeandía, who was at Monterey. Oddly, since Smith had broken his promise to leave and not return, the governor freed him, giving him new orders to get out. He headed north to Oregon, being attacked by Umpqua Indians in a dispute over a stolen ax that resulted in fifteen of his nineteen men being killed. He reached Fort Vancouver where McLoughlin, angry that Indians had attacked trappers –albeit competitors –sent Alexander McLeod south to help him recover his horses, supplies, and furs. For that courtesy, Smith promised that the American Fur Company would confine its operations to east of the Great Divide. McLoughlin was so impressed by the quality of furs Smith dealt in that he started sending the Umpqua Brigade south to California in search of them.

In 1831, Smith was killed by Comanches in Kansas while seeking water for a party he was guiding on the Santa Fe Trail. When he did not return to the group, the party traveled on, hoping to meet him in Santa Fe. Some of them later found some of his possessions for sale by a Mexican merchant who claimed to have gotten them from the Comanches.

Another important trapper in California was James Ohio Pattie (1804?-50) who arrived with his father, Sylvester (1782-1828), in 1827. Three years earlier they had gone beaver trapping from the Missouri River to the Southwest and had been the first Americans to trap along the Colorado and Gila Rivers, claiming discovery of the Grand Canyon despite little evidence to support this claim. The two got into a bloody battle with the Mojaves. According to Pattie's account the Indians retreated before he and the surviving trappers could fire a shot. When the Patties arrived at San Diego, Echeandía jailed them as spies because they had not gotten permission to enter California. Sylvester died in jail, but the younger Pattie was released from jail during a smallpox epidemic because he possessed some vaccine they had brought for protection, and he agreed to serve Echeandía as a translator. He vaccinated 10,000 people at the missions, ranchos and settlements (including Fort Ross). When he asked for the pay Echeandía had apparently promised, the governor demanded that he become a Catholic to collect. Pattie refused and left California in 1830. The next year he published a book condemning

Mexican ownership of the region: *The Personal Narrative of James O. Pattie, of Kentucky: During an Expedition from St. Louis, Through the Vast Regions Between that Place and the Pacific Ocean, and Thence Back Through the City of Mexico to Vera Cruz, During Journeyings of Six Years, Etc.* In fact, the work was probably fictional, edited, or perhaps largely written by Timothy Flint (1780-1840), a New England minister and romantic novelist.[35]

The following description of Los Angeles is taken the book published by Pattie: "The houses have flat roofs, covered with bituminous pitch, brought from a place within four miles (6.5 km) of the town, where this article boils up from the earth. As the liquid arises, hollow bubbles like a shell of a large size, are formed. When they burst, the noise is heard distinctly in the town."

Penetrating every part of the West in pursuit of beaver fur, the mountain men became its propagandists and eventually guides for other Americans with many motives for going west: military and civilian, would-be miners, farmers, and railroad builders. Hundreds entered California and would play a role in its history for the next twenty or thirty years. Among them were Joseph Walker, J.J. Warner, Thomas Fitzpatrick, Kit Carson, Jim Bridger, Jim Beckwourth, and Ewing Young.

Walker (1798-1876) left Missouri and joined Benjamin Bonneville's fur hunting expedition into the Far West, which was probably a cover for gathering information for the military about the Mexican territory through which they were passing. Walker and his men were the first white men to make an east-to-west crossing of the central Sierra in 1833, and as recorded by one of the members of Walker's party, Zenas Leonard (1809-57), in his *Narrative of the Adventures of Zenas Leonard* (1839), the first to see Yosemite Valley during the great Leonid meteor shower of November 13, 1833. This unusually impressive event was seen over much of North America, and its spectacular abundance of meteors struck fear into many who saw it as a sign of the end of the world. Walker returned east over Walker Pass in the Tehachapi Mountains but returned to California later as an army scout and eventually as a settler.

Warner (1807-95), known variously as Jonathan Trumbull Warner, Juan José Warner, and John J. Warner, moved to California from Connecticut in 1831 to hunt and became a Mexican citizen. He received a large land grant, Warner's Ranch, northeast of San Diego. Later he would be a valuable player in the American conquest of California.

Fitzpatrick (1799-1854), known as "Broken Hand" because of a gun accident that had damaged his left hand, discovered South Pass in Wyoming with Jed Smith, and later would serve as a guide for wagon trains to Oregon and California.

Carson (1809-68) became a guide along the Santa Fe Trail in 1826 and three years later joined Ewing Young on a hunt that took him to California, where he remained for two years. A chance meeting with John C. Frémont would lead him into assisting the American conquest of California.

Bridger (1804-81) had joined with William Ashley going to the Upper Missouri as a trapper in 1822. In 1824-25, he became the first white man to see the geysers at Yellowstone and Great Salt Lake, its salinity convincing him it might be an arm of the Pacific. At the time many maps showed a fictional river, the Bonaventure, going from the Rockies to the Pacific, and, as with the Strait of Anian or the Northwest Passage, many – including Jed Smith – sought it. The legend's source was eventually determined to be the Humboldt River in Nevada, considerably shorter than the wished-for

Bonaventure. In 1830 Bridger and some others bought out Ashley and formed the Rocky Mountain Fur Company. In 1843, he and Louis Vasquez built Fort Bridger on the west bank of the Black Fork of the Green River to serve pioneers going to Oregon and California.

Beckwourth (1798-1867), a free mulatto from Virginia, went west to trap, joining Ashley's company as a wrangler in 1824, and became a trapper. There is evidence that the Rocky Mountain Fur Company encouraged the legend that Beckwourth was really a Crow Indian, the kidnapped son of a chief, to facilitate trade with that tribe. Gaining the respect of Jed Smith and Jim Bridger, he was always the first to volunteer for rescues or battles. The Snake Indians called him "Bloody Arm" after fighting alongside him against the Cheyenne. For his part, Beckwourth lived with the Crow for a dozen years, took an Indian wife (he had three other Indian wives), stole horses and scalped scores of enemy Indians. Later he became a trader on the Old Spanish Trail, moving stolen Mexican horses to the United States, going to California in 1848, and becoming a professional gambler in Sacramento. In 1850, he discovered Beckworth Pass (now State Route 70 in Plumas County), an Indian trail he improved into a wagon road over the Sierra Nevada, giving rise to Marysville.[36]

Young (1799-1841), from Tennessee, had moved to Missouri as a young man and in 1821 became the first Americans to travel on the Santa Fe Trail to initiate trade between New Mexico and the United States. The New Mexicans had not shown much interest in trapping beavers and other fur-bearing animals, so Young and others had an abundance to hunt, which he did for the next nine years; during the trapping season of 1827-28 he employed the young Kit Carson and eventually set up a trading post in Taos. In spring of 1830 he led the first group of Americans from Santa Fe to San Gabriel, traveling across the Colorado River and the Mojave Desert. After recuperating with the hospitable Father Sánchez at San Gabriel, they went on to Mission San Fernando Rey in the San Fernando Valley, then over the Tehachapis to the San Joaquin Valley, where they trapped along the Tule River. From there, they went up to the Sacramento Valley, encountering the HBC's Ogden. An official from Mission San José encountered them and got eleven of Young's trappers to help capture Indian runaways from the mission. Young went on to San Francisco Bay to sell pelts, afterward turning south to Los Angeles and back to Taos. Each year he took other expeditions to California. In 1834, at San Diego, he met Hall J. Kelley (1790-1874), a Bostonian Oregon promoter who convinced him to move up to the Willamette Valley, where he settled, much to McLoughlin's chagrin, as the HBC was trying to discourage American settlement. Of Young's activities in 1822-34, Western historian Joseph J. Hill (1884-?) wrote in 1923: "[a complete record] would give us a very full account of the fur trade in the Far Southwest during its most flourishing period." [37] Unfortunately, unlike so many mountain men, Young left no written memoirs.

Many of these, notably Bridger and Beckwourth, were famous tellers of tall tales often recorded in writing by interviewers and biographers and published numerous times since their day. Beckwourth greatly exaggerated his connections with the Crows and his military service. Bridger told of petrified forests with "petrified birds" as well as surviving impossible Indian attacks single-handedly. These yarns and others became part of American folklore.

**

"If I must be cast on the care of a stranger, let it be in

California."

-Walter Colton, 1848

**

Pioneers before 1840

Americans who came before the great American migration of 1841 were so relatively few that they have nearly all been accounted for in Bancroft's work. Between 1814 and 1840 about 475 foreigners arrived, mostly British and Americans. Most of these were welcomed. Those who came after 1822 generally had plans for commercial success. Most of these newcomers became Californians in nearly every aspect of their lives, marrying local girls, hispanicizing their first names, speaking Spanish, becoming Mexican citizens and Catholics, and following local customs as if they had been born California.

Among these, besides mountain men Beckworth, Walker and Warner, were John Gilroy, Joseph Chapman, William Hartnell, John Cooper, William Richardson, John Wilson, William Goodwin Dana, Abel Stearns, John Robinson, William Wolfskill, Thomas Larkin, Isaac Graham, John Marsh, Edward Turner Bale and John Sutter.

John Gilroy (1796-1869), British, was cast ashore at Monterey in 1814 by his ship captain because he was sick. Twenty years later, having married into the Ortega family, he was given a land grant (Rancho San Ysidro) where the town of Gilroy is today.

Joseph Chapman (1784-1849), American, had been impressed by the pirate Bouchard in Hawaii, but was probably one of the three crewmen from Bouchard's Santa Rosa captured during the attack on Refugio, a town north of Santa

Barbara, whereupon he deserted his ship. There are several variations to the story of how he came to be in California, but these are the ones he preferred: A noted craftsman, he settled down to make grist mills at several missions, helping to rebuild the one at earthquake damaged Mission Santa Inés. As a trained shipbuilder, another story goes, besides being a carpenter and millwright, he built the 60-ton schooner Guadalupe in 1831 at San Pedro for Mission San Gabriel.

In 1822, he was baptized a Catholic, married Maria de Guadalupe Ortega (1799-1865), the daughter of José Francisco Ortega, and helped to complete the roof of the Old Plaza Church (La Iglesia de Nuestra Señora la Reina de los Ángeles) in Los Angeles by leading a logging crew into the San Gabriel Mountains to cut timber for ceiling beams. Two years later he had prospered well enough to buy a house in the Los Angeles pueblo with some farmland on which he began the commercial growth of wine grapes in Los Angeles. He served as Jed Smith's translator when the trapper arrived at San Gabriel, and in 1831, became a Mexican citizen. Soon after that he moved with his family of eleven children to a Santa Barbara beach property that was later called Burton Mound. As with the accounts of how he came to California, there is some confusion over how he acquired that property, whether by grant from Governor Alvarado or purchased from Mission Santa Barbara. He sold it in 1840 to George Nidever (1802-83), a trapper who had first come with Walker, and moved to land in either Santa Barbara or Ventura counties.

William Hartnell had been a trader in Peru when he came with Hugh McCulloch in 1822 to buy the hide-and-tallow contract for his English employer, John Begg and Company. He married into the de la Guerra family and eventually had 25 children for whom he founded a school.[38] He was granted a rancho near Monterey with 8,000 head of cattle and a huge vegetable garden. He held various government posts under both Mexican and American rule (Alvarado's collector of customs, *visitador general* of the missions and appraiser of customs for one of American conquerors, Admiral Robert Stockton.) He was also an agent for the Russian American Company. His reputation was that of an honest, genial, and hospitable ranchero.

William Richardson (1795-1858) went to San Francisco from Britain in 1822 on the whaler *Orion*, received permission to stay, was baptized a Catholic, and married Maria Antonia Martínez, the daughter of presidio comandante Ignacio Martínez (1774-1848), adapting her given name as a middle name for himself, becoming William Antonio Richardson. General Vallejo appointed him captain of the port in 1835, a post he would hold for nine years. He built the first habitation – a tent, later a board house, in 1835, and an adobe in 1836 – in Yerba Buena, at the site of Grant Avenue between Clay and Washington Streets. In 1838 Governor Alvarado granted him the 19,752-acre (7,993 ha) Rancho Saucelito ("*little willow tree*")[39] after taking it away from an earlier grantee, José Antonio Galindo, as a penalty for the 1838 murder of José Doroteo Peralta. Rancho Saucelito was now officially in Marin County, and extended from the Pacific Ocean on the west, to Mount Tamalpais on the north, to Richardson Bay on the east, and included present-day Muir Beach, Stinson Beach, Sausalito, Tamalpais Valley, and Homestead Valley.

John Cooper (1792-1872), born British but raised in Massachusetts, captain of the American ship Rover, was Thomas Larkin's half-brother, arriving to settle in Monterey in 1826. He became a Catholic and a Mexican citizen, marrying one of General Vallejo's sisters. He became a prominent citizen through his triple careers of shipmaster, trader, and rancher.

John Wilson (1795-1861), British, was a shipmaster and trader who had operated in Hawaii and Peru when he arrived in 1826. He married Ramona Carrillo de Pacheco (1812-88), the widow of Captain Romualdo Pacheco (killed at Cahuenga), adopted her sons, one of whom would be a future governor, and had two children with her. His wife was a sister-in-law of General Vallejo. He settled at Santa Barbara and held offices under both Mexican and American rule. Through Doña Ramona and through his own acquisition, he owned several ranchos: Cañada de los Osos y Pecho y Islay, Suey, El Chorro, San Luisito and Huerta de Romualdo, a total of 44,602 acres (18,050 ha) all in San Luis Obispo County, and Los Guilicos, 18,834 acres (7,622 ha) in Sonoma County. Of him Bancroft states, "There were few of the old pioneers better known or more respected than Captain John Wilson."

William Goodwin Dana (1797-1858), an American from Boston who came to California in 1826 as the master of a trading vessel, was a distant cousin of Richard Henry Dana (though the families were estranged). He became a Catholic and a Mexican citizen, married Maria Josefa Carrillo (1812-83), Carlos Antonio Carrillo's daughter, in 1828 and eventually had 21 children. His main income came from the 37,888-acre (15,330 ha) Rancho Nipomo, near San Luis Obispo, granted to him by Governor Alvarado in 1837, and at Santa Barbara he was a minor government official under both Mexican and American rule.

Abel Stearns (1798-1871), another Massachusetts man, was the first known Jew to settle in California when he arrived in 1829. Stearns, nicknamed "Cara de Caballo" ("Horse Face"), had been a trader in Mexico for three years, where he was naturalized and became a Catholic. He had wanted a rancho in the Central Valley, but instead he settled at Los Angeles and became its leading trader, known for his shrewdness and hard-headedness. Soon after arriving he received a government concession to build a warehouse at San Pedro, the nearest seaport; it was to become one of California's four marine warehouses. He then established a stage line connecting San Pedro Bay with Los Angeles pueblo, and in 1831 built a three-story flour mill on North Spring Street, Los Angeles. In 1841 he married the eldest daughter of the very rich Juan Bandini, Arcadia Bandini (1825-1912), reportedly one of the most beautiful women in California, and received a sizeable dowry in land. They were childless. Bandini and Stearns had become friends and political allies during the 1831 revolt against Victoria, so Bandini had arranged the marriage. He was granted or purchased eight ranchos between 1842 and 1861, consisting of 200 square miles (518 sq km), and became the richest man in southern California from wine and hides. He was a leader in the revolts that overthrew Governors Victoria and Micheltorena. Arrested several times for smuggling to avoid the import taxes, he nevertheless became a minor government official under Mexican and American rule. In 1841 he sent the first shipment of California placer gold on record, a package of 1,843 ounces (52.248 kg) valued at $19 ($684 in 2023) an ounce (28.35 g), via Alfred Robinson, to the U.S. Mint in Philadelphia. [40]

Alfred Robinson (1806-95) was an agent for Bryant & Sturgis, who came to California in 1829 and in 1835 married into the De la Guerra family in the wedding vividly described by Richard Henry Dana in his *Two Years Before the Mast* (chapter 27). In 1846 he anonymously penned *Life in California*, one of California history's greatest primary sources for the time, adding to it as a supplement the account of the Indian religion in the Mission San Juan Capistrano area written by Father Gerónimo Boscana (1775-1831), *Relacion Histórica*, in 1814-26. [41]

William Wolfskill was a Kentucky trader who arrived in Los Angeles by way of the Cajon Pass and San Bernardino in 1830. Wolfskill pioneered the pack-train route that would later become the Old Spanish Trail. Settling in Los Angeles, he became a Catholic and a Mexican citizen, and built a schooner to trap sea otters in the coastal islands. In 1841 he planted one of the first orange groves in Los Angeles and became the largest grower in southern California. He also planted vineyards for wine, grew English walnuts, and helped introduce eucalyptus to California. His four brothers (John Reed, Milton, Mathus, and Sarchel) followed him to California and raised fruit and cattle on Rancho Río de los Putos (later Putah Creek) in Solano and Yolo counties, which had been granted to William by Governor Alvarado and which he later granted to them.[42]

Thomas Larkin (1802-58) was born in Massachusetts and lived in North Carolina before he went to California in 1832 to join his older half-brother, John B. R. Cooper (1791-1872), who had asked him to come to help in Cooper's business.[43] He sailed from Boston on the *Newcastle* bound for Hawaii and then California with stops at Yerba Buena, Monterey, and Santa Barbara. On shipboard he met and began an intimate relationship with an American woman, Mrs. Rachel Holmes (1807-73), who was going to California with her daughter to join her Danish sea captain husband. When they reached Monterey, they boarded at Cooper's house and soon learned she was pregnant with Larkin's child. She moved to Santa Barbara, and on April 13, 1834, their son, Thomas Oliver Larkin, Jr., was the first American child born of American parents in California. A few weeks later, Mrs. Holmes received news that her husband had died in 1833 at sea. Larkin sailed to Santa Barbara, and in June they were married by the U. S. consul to the Sandwich Islands on board the American ship *Volunteer*. In Monterey he had started his own small store, built the first "double-geared" flour mill on the Pacific Coast, invested in a sawmill at Santa Cruz, and in 1835 built the first two-story house in California.

Though he learned Spanish to do business on California, he remained an American citizen and a Protestant, renewing his visa annually. As a non-citizen he could not acquire land personally but did so in his children's names. His American citizenship did not prevent him from becoming involved in local politics, and he supported Alvarado's revolution of 1836. He became very wealthy as a Monterey shipper, trading with Mexico and Hawaii. In 1843 he was appointed United States consul at Monterey.

Isaac Graham was a mountain man from Kentucky who built a distillery and a lumber mill in the Pájaro Valley, near Santa Cruz. In 1836 he organized mountain men to support Alvarado's seizure of power, but in 1840 the governor arrested him with about 100 other foreigners to prevent them from overthrowing him. This became known as the "Graham Affair." He was exiled to Mazatlán, bound for prison in Tepic, but released due to official American and British efforts. Captain Thomas Farnam (1804-48) of the Oregon Dragoons went to Monterey from the Willamette Valley to petition for the release of the entire group and traveled on to San Blas and Tepic to meet the prisoners and secure their release. He was seconded in this action by the British consul and the vice consul at Tepic.[44] Graham returned to California a bitter enemy of Alvarado, though he supported him against Micheltorena in 1845. According to Bancroft, he was "a loud-mouthed, unprincipled, profligate and reckless man."

John Marsh was a Harvard University graduate who in 1836 fled from Missouri for illegally selling guns to Indians, abandoning his French métis mistress and their son. He joined a group of trappers on the Santa Fe and Old Spanish Trails and reached Southern California. He practiced medicine, though he had never studied it, using his Harvard diploma as a license, at Los Angeles. In the East Bay Area (the *contra costa*), he acquired Rancho Los Médanos ("dunes") near Mount Diablo, the site of current Brentwood, from José Noriega (1792-1870) in payment for medical care. He became a Mexican citizen and a Catholic. He ran cattle collected as medical fees.

On at least one occasion he got his comeuppance regarding these medical fees: He charged the rancheros cattle, fruit trees or grape cuttings he could plant on Los Médanos in exchange for his services. Once, when the patient thought the price too high for a house call, the latter charged Marsh for the room and board for the days he was in his home; to be fair, to see "patients" he sometimes had to ride as far as Sonoma and Salinas. He used Indian labor to build up his holdings, overcharged his "patients" and pioneers whom he aided, and cheated.

In 1851 he was introduced to Abigail Smith Tuck, a 33-year-old New England schoolteacher who had become the principal of a girls' school in San Jose; they married after a brief courtship and moved into his adobe. The next year they had a daughter, Alice, and he planned a great stone house with high English gables, but his wife died in 1855 before the house was completed. The following year he and their daughter moved into the Stone House. A few weeks afterward he was murdered by three of his disgruntled vaqueros in a dispute over wages. Reputed to be a "cantankerous soul," a mean, tight, disagreeable, and lonely man, he was also enterprising, well-educated, and thought by some to be very entertaining. Alice would later marry William Walker Camron, have two daughters and use her inheritance to buy what would become known as the Camron-Stanford House in Oakland; she died in

1927 in Santa Barbara. [45]

Edward Turner Bale (1811-49) was an English doctor shipwrecked off Monterey in 1837, who was appointed by General Vallejo to be surgeon of the California forces. He married María Ignacia Soberanes (1816-1901), a niece of the general, and was granted the Rancho Carne Humana in the Napa Valley (site of the towns of St. Helena and Calistoga).[46] In 1846 he built a mill on the grounds; for many years it ground the grains brought in by the local residents.

There was a definite advantage to having grain ground in such mills. The slow turning of the old stones and the dampness of the mill's site gave its meal an exceptional quality for making all kinds of breads. As the old timers put it, "When meal comes to you that way, like the heated underside of a settin' hen, it bakes bread that makes city bread taste like cardboard."[47]

An interesting story about Dr. Bale concerns his many personal quarrels. Bancroft tells us:

> [In 1844 Captain Salvador Vallejo, the general's hot-tempered brother and Carolina's uncle, paid a visit.] It seemed to Dr. Bale that the captain and the charming Señorita greeted each other too heartily. Their close family relationship and the fact that Salvador had just returned from dangerous Indian fighting did not seem sufficient reason for the warmth of those Latin embraces.
> The irate doctor quarreled with Vallejo and challenged him to a duel. Well might the soldier smile: he was the best swordsman in the land. The duel was a farce. Vallejo skillfully twisted his cumbersome opponent into ridiculous knots. Then sardonically, he beat the Englishman with his sword

as though it were a whip. In a rage, Bale drew a revolver and fired. Luckily, the attempted murder was a failure. The intention, however, was counted more important than the deed. The doctor found himself in jail [from which he was finally released].[48]

John A. Sutter had left his Swiss home in May 1834, fleeing large debts and a nagging wife (and mother-in-law). He traveled widely in the United States, New Mexico, Oregon, Alaska, and Hawaii, arriving in California in July 1839 with eight male and two female Kanakas (as Hawaiians were called), hoping to start a feudal colony. To checkmate his uncle Vallejo, Governor Alvarado gave Sutter a large grant, 48,827 acres (19,726 ha) he called Nueva Helvecia [later New Helvetia], on the Sacramento and American Rivers, using the Hawaiians and other foreigners for labor. Alvarado saw Sutter as a useful buttress against encroachment by Russians, British and Americans. He built a fort with outer walls three feet (91.4 cm) thick and fifteen feet (4.6 m) high, with bastions for cannon at two corners. He established friendly relations with the Maidu, and some of them helped with the building, although other Natives were sometimes enslaved, forced to work, and kept in deplorable conditions. They were confined to quarters at night and fed from troughs. The inner part of the quadrangle had quarters for the craftsmen who equipped his little empire. He bought Fort Ross for its cannon to keep the Indians peaceful and grew wealthy from wheat, whiskey, furs, and tanning. Noted for his hospitality and the assistance offered to overland travelers, Sutter allowed them short lodging and jobs at his fort, even sending relief parties as far east as the future site of Reno.[49]

The local girls whom many of these foreigners married have rarely been subjects of historical note. Of them, General Vallejo's daughter, discussing her own mother, told an interviewer, "I wish you not to forget that it was the faith and

love and brave strength of the pioneer mothers which helped
the founders of this great State to prepare our country, and my
mother was such a pioneer mother." Edwin Bryant (1805-69),
a Kentucky newspaperman who had come to California for
his health in 1846 and remained for several years, wrote:

> "There are no women in the world for whose manners
> nature has done so much, and for whom art and
> education, in this respect, have done so little, as these
> Hispano-American females on the coast of the
> Pacific. In their deportment towards strangers they
> are queens, when, in costume, they are peasants. None
> of them, according to our tastes, can be called
> beautiful, but what they want in complexion and
> regularity of features, is fully supplied by their
> kindliness, the soul and sympathy which beam from
> their dark eyes, and their grace and warmth of
> manners and expression."[50]

**

*"The Yankees are a wonderful people... If they were to
emigrate to Hell itself, they would somehow manage to
change the climate."*

-General Vallejo, 1862

**

The Migration of 1841

In the fall of 1840, some of Marsh's letters about
California were published in local Missouri newspapers.
Coincidentally, Antoine Robideaux (1796-1868), a retired
trapper from St. Louis, addressed a town meeting in Weston,
Platte County, Missouri. His topic: California, the perpetual
spring paradise. Most of the townspeople, enthusiastic about
such a place, banded together to form the Western Emigration

Society, but the town's businessmen, fearing loss of business, threw cold water on the idea, and zeal for migration evaporated by the following spring.

John Bidwell (1819-1900), the town's twenty-year-old teacher, did not lose interest in migrating, and in 1841 he helped put together a motley party of 89 to go west to California. They included temporarily cooperative Catholic (including Jesuit Father Pierre de Smet [1801-73]) and Methodist missionaries, as well as emigrants (intent on settling); trappers and adventurers; men and women; adults and children. Led by John Bartleson (1786-1848), an overbearing fellow who "knew little more about Plains traveling than the next man," but was chosen because of his mature years and his insistence on being chosen, [51]they left Sapling Grove, in neighboring Jackson County, Missouri, following their guide Thomas Fitzpatrick, since he was the only one among them familiar with the territory. Fitzpatrick had been hired to guide the Jesuits to the Flathead country (in present-day Montana), and the emigrants wisely chose to join them at least as far as the Rockies. They had 15 wagons and four solid wheel river carts. Their goal was Marsh's ranch. Bidwell's diary (published as "Gold Hunters of California. The First Emigrant Train to California" in *The Century* magazine in November 1890) recounts the whole adventure.[52]

In July, having reached Fort Bridger (in present day Wyoming), the party divided, 52 going to Oregon and the remaining 37 to California. They made it to Soda Springs (in present-day Idaho) in August. From there DeSmet and the other Catholic missionaries continued north with Fitzpatrick while Bartleson went to Fort Hall with three others to get information. Bidwell and the rest of the California-bound waited for Bartleson and his companions to catch up with them. Going north of the Great Salt Lake, they encountered misery: no food, no water, most of their provisions having been dumped to give the oxen a better chance of pulling the wagons, some of which were abandoned in Nevada's Pequop Range. With their surviving animals they eventually found Nevada's Humboldt River (then called the "Mary's River") and followed it to its sink, present-day Lovelock. From there they headed south to the Walker River and in October crossed the Sierra where Jed Smith had been the forerunner. They hunted fowl and coyotes in the Sacramento Valley - once having only one coyote to share among the three-dozen people (Bidwell getting a forepaw). In November they reached Marsh's ranch; true to form, he tried to cheat them into giving him free labor for the winter by telling them they hadn't yet crossed the Sierra and should stay at his ranch until spring. When they found out that Marsh had cheated them, they killed one of his prize oxen, roasted and enjoyed it, then left to go where they pleased, leaving him without paying. As to Marsh, Bidwell describes him as "the meanest man I ever met."[53] Numerous similar estimations, both from his contemporaries and posterity, have fixed his image in California history: a bitter, grasping, cheap misanthrope, brooding on his isolated rancho east of Mount Diablo. "Most historians contrast him with Sutter, praising the latter's geniality and dismissing Marsh as a neurotic hermit."[54]

Bidwell went on to work for Sutter, of whom he wrote "No pioneer ever did so much for the State as Sutter." [55]Bidwell managed Sutter's Hock Farm, the first large-scale agricultural settlement in Northern California, composed of grain, cattle, orchards, and vineyards on the Feather River for a few years, going on to fame and influence. Bartleson, for all his demanding to be made captain of the group, returned to Missouri as quickly as he could, having been permanently soured on California by starving in the Sierra. As in the case of the Hudson's Bay Company, had he waited a few more years he might have made some great profits from the gold discovery on Sutter's lands.

Many hundreds more Americans came via Iowa, Missouri, and Arkansas. Sometimes small parties combined into larger ones, while large parties at times broke up. Their letters home, published in local papers, increased California propaganda and the influx of settlers. In California they could count on Sutter's protection from the now hostile Mexican authorities.

The authorities could no longer jail all newly arriving Americans, as Echeandía had done to Smith and Pattie. There were too many of them; and they were a determined lot. Intent on settlement, they brought as much of their old home as they could carry. Unlike the Conestoga wagons, which were too heavy for the prairies, these were usually ordinary farm wagons with sides a mere 30 inches (76 cm) tall, fitted with canvas covers. Short of space, they had to decide what family heirlooms would remain behind. They worked together to pack the wagons for the best use of space, with weapons and medical supplies in easy reach. Bedding and tent supplies, cooking utensils, clothing, tools, and equipment, and a few luxuries (such as canned foods, plant cuttings, schoolbooks, musical instruments, dolls, jewelry, China, silverware, fine linens, iron stoves and furniture.) A rooster and hens in cages were hung inside from the bars. Cattle or sheep followed behind, kept in line by the family dog. There was no real room inside the wagon except for the old or sick, with nearly all except the driver walking the entire way. The wagons were supposed to carry 3,000 pounds (1.361 kg), but many pioneers had to unload things that had become unnecessary.[56]

Once they began to arrive as overland parties, the sheer numbers of Americans would add considerably to the population. Among the early pioneer groups to appear at Los Angeles in 1841 was the Workman-Rowland Party, largely

295

from Missouri. Driving along sheep as sustenance, they came into the pueblo by way of the Santa Fe Trail, Cajon Pass and Mission San Gabriel. Their leaders, William Workman (1800-76) and John Rowland (1791-1873), received a welcome of sorts, notwithstanding the previous general warning against mass American immigration into California. Both had been traders in Taos, English-born Workman becoming a Mexican citizen and marrying a Mexican woman and Maryland-born Rowland doing likewise. Political events in New Mexico had led to their expulsion; Taos had unsuccessfully revolted against the New Mexico government, and they had been coerced to swear allegiance to the rebels. In 1840 they had supported the Republic of Texas' claim to the land east of the Río Grande, and for a short time served as agents of the Texan president.

Among the other members of the party was Benjamin D. Wilson (1811-78), one of the founders of Pasadena, for whom Mount Wilson would be named. Big Bear Lake in the San Bernardino Mountains was named for one of his exploits: lassoing 22 grizzly bears with some *compadres* on a punitive expedition against Indian raiders); his companions in that adventure were William Gordon (1801-76) and William Knight (1800-49), pioneers of Yolo County. Gordon was a swine rancher who settled on Cache Creek, and Knight a trader who founded the town of Knight's Landing.[57] Others with him that day were Juan Manuel Vaca (1782-1856), a pioneer of Solano County for whom the town of Vacaville is named; and Workman's future son-in-law, Francis P.F. Temple (1822-80). In Los Angeles Workman was granted the 11,470-acres (4,642 ha) Rancho La Puente and built a large adobe as the headquarters for his ranching activities.

In 1845, Marsh estimated California's population at 7,000 persons of Spanish blood, 10,600 domesticated Indians, 700

Americans, and perhaps 100 of English, Scots and Irish, and another 100 of Germans, French and Italians.[58] Obviously, these figures are only rough approximations, but it is significant that Americans outnumbered all the other foreigners combined. Whether this is because they were comparatively energetic and aggressive or simply due to their superior numbers plus the advantage of proximity, is a subject that can be debated. The indisputable fact is that they had established an influential presence in California; the root had gone deep.

The Donner Tragedy

Most of these parties and their crossings were unremarkable, and their stories not very different one from the other. An exception was the Donner Party, which unwittingly drew national attention because of the stunning foolishness of its leadership.

In April 1846, a group of 87 left Springfield, Illinois under James Reed (1800-74) and the Donner brothers, George (1784-1847) and Jacob (1789-1846). It was a hodgepodge of types - rich farmers and poor, educated and illiterate, Americans and foreigners. Surprisingly, most of the group that set out that spring were elderly, and there were some small children.

Joseph Walker at Fort Bridger and James Clyman (1792-1881) at Fort Laramie (the latter an old friend of Reed's) warned them to stick to the standard route, but they listened to bad advice from Lansford Hastings (1819-70), a promoter who wanted to popularize a route below the Great Salt Lake he called "Hastings' Cut-off." Hastings, a lawyer, had dreams of being the leader of a California separated by American settlers from Mexican control as Texas had been. He made rousing speeches to emigrant groups and wrote an *Emigrant's*

Guide in 1845 to deflect migration from Oregon to California. His proposed "short-cut" was in fact only short as the crow flies, ignoring the contours of terrain. Hastings had never traveled the route he ballyhooed, which proposed traveling south of Great Salt Lake to Pilot Knob, then below the Ruby Mountains and thence to the Humboldt River near present Elko where the group would rejoin the California Trail. The party divided into the wiser heads who went north of Salt Lake and the foolish who went below it. In the desert this southern-route party met many hardships and delays. At one point they made only 36 miles (58 km) in 21 days. Their cattle were dying, wagons being jettisoned, their food and water running out, all as they faced perpendicular ridges in front of them. One man, John Snyder, tried to pass one of Reed's wagons and began beating Reed's oxen with his whip, which he turned on Reed when the latter protested. Reed killed him in self-defense, and Snyder's friends wanted to hang him in retaliation. Instead, he was banished from the group, one of his teamsters promising to watch over his family. It was fortunate he had not been executed, for his reappearance would be both fortuitous and fortunate. As to the shortcut Hastings proposed, those who went the regular way reached California 45 days ahead of those who took it.

By October, they had reached western Nevada. Despite signs of an early winter, they rested four days, and snows caused a wagon to tip over onto the Donner children, who were slightly injured. In the Sierra, at Truckee Lake, they paused for a snowstorm that left them snowbound with a pack 22 feet (6.7 m) deep. While paused, they had gathered no firewood, nor had they penned their animals. Their wandering animals became the prey of bears and mountain lions or were stolen by Indians, but at least they built three rude cabins for shelter.

By this time, there was a total breakdown of what little unity had ever existed, and it was every man for himself. The results were perhaps inevitable, but profoundly shocking to civilized and Christian sensibilities. Snowbound for four months, they turned to cannibalism. While nearly all participated, albeit unwillingly, Louis Keseberg (1814-95) was an enthusiastic practitioner; there is some evidence he may have murdered George Donner's wife for her money and then to eat her body. [59]

In February 1847 Reed took with him another of his teamsters with one-fifth rations to go ahead to Sutter's Fort, returning from Sutter with four relief parties of Indian trackers who managed to get 45 of the 87 out alive by April 1847. One died upon reaching Sacramento. All the Donner family adults died. One of the survivors of the group, Patrick Breen (1805-68), kept a diary by which we know most of what happened. His daughter Isabella, only a year old in 1846-47 was the last survivor of the tragedy, dying in 1936.

A month after the final rescue Virginia Reed, James' 13-year-old stepdaughter, wrote to her cousin Mary Keyes back in Illinois:

> I have not wrote of half the trouble we have had but I have
> wrote enough to let you know that you don't know what
> trouble is. But thank God we have all got through and the
> only family that did not eat human flesh. We have left everything but I don't care for that. We have got through
> with our lives but Don't let this letter dishearten anybody.
> Never take no cutoffs and hurry along as fast as you

can.[60]

Poor management, faulty judgment, and inexperience combined lethally to create a cautionary tale.

The site where the cabins stood became a tourist attraction as early as 1854, and fascination with the event grew. In 1927 the state of California created the Donner Memorial State Park. This was followed by its designation as a California Historical Landmark in 1934 and a National Historic Landmark in 1962. The state justifies this because the episode was "an isolated and tragic incident of American history that has been transformed into a major folk epic." Hundreds of thousands of tourists each year bear this out.[61]

The United States Looks Toward California

During the 1830s and 1840s, the United States began to take an active interest in California. The richness of the soil, the chance for trade with China, the increase of American residents, the weakness of Mexican control, and the fear that Britain, France, or Russia might seize it first and with it the strategic advantage of San Francisco Bay: All these features powerfully attracted the U.S. to take an interest.

The Democrats and Whigs divided the U.S. political scene between them at that time. The Whigs, devoid of principles or philosophy, chased one goal only: to keep the Democrats, detested heirs of Andrew Jackson, out of power. The Red River between Louisiana and Texas, the Arkansas River, and the Rockies formed the western border of the nation.

Slavery, practiced in all the original thirteen colonies, gradually receded in the northern colonies during and after the American Revolution, and when the nation was formed the Constitution effectively guaranteed its continuation by including the three-fifths clause, allowing many non-voting slaves to be counted as population for representation in the Congress. Not much could be done about regional differences in population growth, but since the Constitution guaranteed the equal representation of two senators each to the states, the first 40 years of the Republic insured an informal balance between the slave and free states: When a state was admitted on either side of the divide another would be admitted within the year on the opposite side. By 1819 there were twelve of each with free states able to expand into the Louisiana Purchase, but slave states were blocked by the border with Mexico. The Missouri Compromise of 1820 struck a precarious formal political balance between the slave and free states: When a free territory became a state, a slave territory would be admitted to the Union within a year, and vice versa. All land north of latitude 36o30'N (the Missouri-Arkansas border, which, extended west, passes near present-day Carmel and through Kingsburg, California) and west of Missouri was to be free soil, and all land south of it was to be open to slavery. It is important to note that in 1829 Mexico abolished slavery, and that much of the land below 36o30' was then Mexican, virtually eliminating the potential for expanding slavery and the power of the slave states, short of conquest. In foreign affairs, the default enemy was, as it had been from the beginnings of the Republic, Great Britain, and although no wars would be fought with that country after 1814, American politicians routinely twisted the British Lion's tail to please their constituents.

Four presidential administrations dealt with California as it journeyed steadily toward statehood.

Andrew Jackson (served 1829-37, Democrat) had appointed Anthony Butler (1787-1849) U. S. Minister to Mexico. Speaking no Spanish and being distinctly

301

undiplomatic in his manner he was unsuccessful in his post. Forbidden to meddle in Mexico's internal affairs, he attempted to bribe Santa Anna concerning Texas: In 1835 Butler offered half a million dollars ($172,950,756 in 2023) for San Francisco Bay and the north coast. His open contempt for the easily bribed Mexican officials led to the failure of his project and his recall. In 1836 Lieutenant William Slacum, U.S. Navy, (1799-1839) toured the Far West, and in his report urged American acquisition of the land from San Francisco Bay to Puget Sound. He served in a diplomatic post in Mexico and wrote a letter to Jackson praising California, whetting Old Hickory's interest in the province. In 1837 Santa Anna, having been sent as a prisoner to Washington, D.C. after his capture by Texan Sam Houston (1793-1863), managed to charm the anti-Hispanic Jackson and offered to sell California and New Mexico for $3.5 million ($113,345,351 in 2023). The deal fell through because the Northeastern states objected to adding territory which would be turned from free soil to slavery by the Missouri Compromise line.

The next president, Martin Van Buren (1782-1862, served 1837-41, Democrat), received Slacum's report. After Alvarado proclaimed independence and later arrested Isaac Graham, Van Buren considered a U.S. takeover of California. Instead, he only went so far as to double the Pacific Fleet to four ships to protect California's American residents and prevent another country from taking the province.

After Van Buren's presidency, William Henry Harrison died after a month in office. President John Tyler (1790-1862, served 1841-45, Whig) followed Harrison, naming South Carolina Congressman Waddy Thompson, Jr. (1798-1868) minister to Mexico. The Mexican government was deep in debt to foreign bankers and governments because of outrages against their citizens in Mexico, and obligations it had almost no chance of meeting. Thompson formulated a plan with the U.S. secretary of state, Daniel Webster (1782-1852), to add to American territory by offering Mexico a solution to its debt crisis. If Mexico gave up California and its claim to Texas, and if Britain would give up any claim to Oregon, the United States government would pay off Mexico's debt to American and British bankers and citizens. Lord Aberdeen, the British prime minister, declined to participate but said Britain had no objection to U.S. territorial acquisitions in Oregon.[62] Mexico rejected the offer, citing that it wanted new cash, not merely debt forgiveness. The real reason was the Jones affair.

Thomas ap Catesby Jones (1790-1859) was the commander of the U.S. Pacific fleet based in Callao, Peru. His primary assignment was to monitor British activity near California. While in Peru, he read a Panama newspaper report that war had broken out between the United States and Mexico. Deciding to seize Monterey before the British might do so (like the proverbial third dog who seizes the bone two other dogs are fighting over but have momentarily dropped), he rushed north. On October 19, 1842, Jones easily took the town because of its poor defenses, and installed Josiah Belden (1815-92), Larkin's agent at a store in Branciforte, as *alcalde*. Learning too late that the newspaper report of war between the U.S. and Mexico was in error, he withdrew the next day, greatly embarrassed and fearing for his career. He stopped at San Pedro where Governor Micheltorena received him with a fiesta and a large bill for damages. He also took Alfred Robinson back with him to the United States with 20 ounces (567 g) of Abel Stearns' Southern California gold (the first to reach the U.S. from California). The Californios treated the incident as a bad joke, but Mexico was outraged, and the Thompson proposal fell flat. Jones was briefly relieved of command by the navy, but he kept his rank and eventually was reinstated in his Pacific command.

James Knox Polk (1795-1849, served 1845-49, Democrat) had been elected on an aggressive platform to annex all of Oregon (up to latitude 54° 40'N, the southern border of Alaska), and all of Texas (everything east and north of the Rio Grande). Like his mentor Jackson he was an Anglophobe and had little use for Hispanics. Polk had two representatives in Mexico, the official minister, John Slidell (1793-1871), and an unofficial spy, William Parrott (1796-1863).

Parrott reported five British-centered activities that seemed to foreshadow a take-over of California: (1) the British Pacific fleet had been increased "to take possession of and hold Upper California, in case of war between the United States and Mexico"; (2) there were rumors that Father Eugene McNamara (1814-53), a missionary in British Guiana, had successfully proposed to Mexican President Joaquín Herrera his plan to bring 10,000 Irish Catholics to California as a bulwark against the U.S., "an irreligious and anti-Catholic nation," and Governor Pico had granted him 3,000 square leagues (20,235 sq mi or 52,410 sq km) in the San Joaquin Valley; (3) there were both British and French consuls at Monterey, but Parrott opined that there was insufficient trade to justify the appointment of a British consul; (4) the Hudson's Bay Company was operating in California; and (5) there was a rumor that Britain or British merchants in California would foot the bill for maintaining the Mexican army in California. Whether or not these rumors were exaggerated, Polk believed them and felt it was time to act. In addition to this fuel for paranoia, the *Times of London* had described San Francisco as "one of the finest ports in the world."[63]

A few years earlier Parrott might just as well have warned about French designs on California. In 1827-28 French merchant marine Captain Auguste Bernhard Duhaut-Cilly (1790-1849), in command of *Le Héros*, visited California and wrote extensively about it in his two-volume *Voyage autour du monde* (1834). Traveling from San Diego up to Fort Ross and Sonoma, he heaped scorn on Mission San Rafael Arcángel, noted the free-roaming mission cattle herds between Santa Cruz and San Francisco and – though he thought the greasy, cold dinner unpalatable – had nothing but praise for the architectural splendor of Mission San Luis Rey.[64] Then in 1837, Admiral Abel Aubert Dupetit-Thouars (1793-1864), who would annex Tahiti and the Marquesas to France in 1843 with his frigate *Venus*, was welcomed at Monterey. Also, in 1837 and 1839 naval Captain Cyrille Pierre Théodore Laplace (1793-1875), in command of *l'Artémise,* visited California ports on his scientific voyages around the world. He met with Alvarado, warned him of American, Russian, and British designs, and gave him a promise of "due consideration" if California should desire a French protectorate, giving the governor "a valuable sword" to commemorate their meeting.[65] Followed by Duflot de Mofrus' 1841 visit's visit suspicions of French interest stirred British interest in California. It is no surprise that Vallejo warned Alvarado in 1841: "There is little doubt that France is intriguing to become the mistress of California."[66] In 1843 France established a consulate in Monterey, the same year Britain and the U.S. established a diplomatic presence, to attend to the needs of French immigrants, mainly merchants and farmers.

In this atmosphere, Slidell was secretly authorized to offer $40 million (over $1.619 billion in 2023) for California. Word leaked out, perhaps from the British minister to Mexico. Mexican public opinion abhorred the idea of selling part of the nation, and President Herrera's political enemies made the most of the offer. Herrera needed the $40 million, but it would be worthless if he were overthrown. The offer was refused.

Polk then set about trying to repeat in California what had been done in Texas. Consul Thomas Larkin became his secret agent. U.S. Secretary of State James Buchanan secretly instructed him to welcome California should it again assert its independence. Larkin approached leading American and Californio residents with a view to liberating the province from Mexico. Initially Sutter, Stearns, Leese at Sonoma, and Warner at San Diego threw in their support, Vallejo was now enthusiastic, and José Castro gave conditional approval, foreseeing considerable increase in the American population. However, Larkin's plan failed when Castro withdrew after his encounter with John Frémont. His withdrawal was also influenced by his disputes with some of the other conspirators, as well as with Governor Pico. In short, he opposed what appeared to him to be a premature move.

Frémont's Adventures

After the last mountain men rendezvous (1842), the West was explored by U. S. Army surveying engineers, the most notable being John C. Frémont (1813-90). A lieutenant in the Corps of Topographical Engineers when he first came to California, he eventually reached the rank of general, in great part because of the five trips he made to the West.

General John C. Frémont (Courtesy of the California History Room, California State Library, Sacramento, California)

In 1843, Kit Carson guided him through Nevada and over the icy Sierra where he discovered Lake Tahoe. He arrived at Sutter's Fort in February 1844, proceeding down the Central Valley past the Kings River, crossing Tehachapi Pass, and finally turning east toward Utah and on to St. Louis.

In early 1845, tensions between the United States and Mexico increased over the question of Texas. In May 1845, Frémont, at the head of an exploring party (of which he was the only military man), again went west across the Great Basin and the Sierra, according to U.S. Secretary of State William L. Marcy (1786-1857), in search of "a new and shorter route from the western base of the Rocky Mountains to the mouth of the Columbia River." In December he reached Sutter's Fort.

Historians have speculated about Frémont's "real" motives for being in Upper California at this moment in history. Some contend he may have been under secret orders from none other than President Polk. Others maintain that Frémont, an ambitious man, acted of his own accord, or perhaps was encouraged by his expansionist father-in-law, Senator Thomas Hart Benton (1782-1858) of Missouri.

After resting, Frémont traveled south toward Monterey. Whatever his reasons for being there, in the early spring of 1846 he appeared in Monterey to seek permission of General Castro, head of Alta California's military forces, "to go to the valley of the San Joaquin, where there was game for his men and grass for his horses, and no inhabitants to be molested by his presence."

Permission was granted, but later, responding to rumors that Frémont was planning to incite the American settlers to revolt, Castro changed his mind and ordered Frémont out of California immediately. The explorer's response was to retreat to the top of Hawk's Peak (or Gabilán Peak), a mountain near Monterey, where he and his men built a fortified camp, declaring they would "fight to extremity...trusting to our country to avenge our death." After a few days, Frémont and his men decided instead to abandon their position and headed north for Oregon. Frémont then withdrew, claiming that he was leaving on his own rather than being evicted, and headed north toward Oregon, traveling six miles (9.6 km) per day to give the impression they were not retreating. Castro declared that in the event of a replay these "cowards" would be repelled by force in defense of Mexican honor and independence. Ferol Egan (1923-2015), Frémont's biographer, gives these protagonists a pass: "Both Frémont and Castro came away from this bloodless affair with heads held high and with all their pride intact."[67]

In the meantime, there arrived at Monterey, in the guise of a merchant, a messenger from Washington, U.S. Marine Lt. Archibald Gillespie (1812-73), bearing dispatches from Polk and Buchanan for both U.S. Consul Larkin and Frémont. When told that Frémont was in Oregon, Gillespie went there, finding the explorer and his men camped on the shores of Klamath Lake in south central Oregon. The nature of the messages to Frémont is unknown, giving rise to speculation from that day to this that the U.S. government, or certain individuals within it, were behind Frémont's subsequent actions. Having traveled through Mexico when Texas was annexed, Gillespie told Frémont that war was about to break out if it had not already done so.

How do historians interpret this early form of covert operations? According to Egan, the news that Gillespie delivered was "not expected."[68] Bernard DeVoto (1897-1955) calls Frémont a "liar" for stating in his public and private testimony that he received orders to go back to California and produce an incident, because when both Gillespie and Frémont were "brought to an unequivocal issue, each flatly declares that there were no such orders."[69] Allan Nevins (1890-1971), defending Frémont's reputation from Josiah Royce's 1886 history, *California from the Conquest in 1846 to the Second Vigilante Committee in San Francisco* and the 1911 edition of the *Encylcopedia Britannica* certain that Gillespie verbally transmitted orders to turn back because the State Department's written dispatches might have fallen into Mexican hands: "The very fact that Gillespie had been ordered without fail to find and talk with Frémont was full of significance."[70] Richard Dillon (1924-2016) noted that while neither Frémont nor Gillespie was later inclined to be specific about the verbal orders, the former "acted as if they gave him a free hand in California."[71] Caughey cites Frémont's actions as easily explainable, regardless of the existence of secret instructions. The "fact that Gillespie had traveled a dangerous 500 miles to overtake him was ample justification for [his] turning back to California."[72] David Lavender (1910-2003) takes it a step beyond Caughey's reasoning by acknowledging that, while "[t]here is no convincing documentary evidence of " an order to return to California, this "is an enigma which has troubled California historians for more than a century. Let us guess along with the rest."[73]

Returning to California, Frémont turned up at Sutter's Fort. Not long afterwards, the American settlers living nearby rose in revolt against the Mexican authorities. Two years later Frémont's actions would be the subject of a court-martial, and his hand in this revolt would be one of the accusations. Found guilty, he would be pardoned by President Polk.

The Bear Flag Revolt

In December 1845, the Republic of Texas, whose independence had never been recognized by Mexico, was annexed to the United States, diplomatic relations were broken, and American troops under General Zachary Taylor (1784-1850) were sent to the area the Texans claimed as theirs, the land between the Nueces and the Río Grande, about 150 miles (240 km) wide. On April 25, 1846, Mexican cavalry under General Mariano Arista (1802-55) fired on Taylor's dragoons, killing or wounding 16 Americans. The word reached Washington on May 9, and Polk determined from that moment to have his war of conquest: "Mexico," he declared, "has passed the boundary of the United States, has invaded our territory and shed American blood upon American soil."

There was a good deal of skepticism about the accuracy of Polk's report: Congressman Abraham Lincoln wanted to know the "spot" on which the blood had been shed, since Mexico claimed the land was Mexican, earning him the sobriquet "Spotty Lincoln". On May 13, 1846, the United States and Mexico went to war over Texas.

The news took nearly two months to reach California. Times were tense, and rumors were flying all over northern California. Fueling these was the Libbey-Spear affair, which arose out of an incident in October 1845 at Yerba Buena when eight Californios brutally attacked Elliott Libbey, an American sea captain, and a bystander took him to the home of (1802-49), an American merchant and long-time resident of the town. The attackers claimed that they were acting under orders from the California subprefect (like an American county sheriff).[74] Fearing a massacre, or at least a mass expulsion of American settlers, disgruntled Americans were encouraged by a returned Frémont to join in a rebellion under William B. Ide (1796-1852). On June 10, 1846, a band of horses was being taken by Francisco Arce (1819-78) from Vallejo to Castro in Monterey. When several settlers observed this movement of horses, it aroused their suspicions about their potential use by Mexican cavalry to attack them. Mountain man Ezekiel Merritt and his party stole the herd at Martin Murphy, Jr.'s (1806-84) ranch on the Cosumnes River and took them to Frémont's camp at the Sutter Buttes. Ide decided on a preemptive strike to prevent Vallejo from finding out about the theft: He and his followers marched on Sonoma and captured General Vallejo (and his home and headquarters), helping themselves to his brandy, on Sunday, June 14, 1846. Vallejo was sent as a prisoner to Sutter's Fort, a move that took Sutter by surprise. He reacted with anger that Frémont should have authorized such a warlike action while staying on his land by his courtesy. Sutter was also upset by

Frémont's rude behavior toward his host, his actions constituting an affront to the uniform of the Republic of Mexico which Sutter wore. Larkin was, for his part, disgusted at this action, for he had counted on Vallejo 's support in an American takeover. He later secured Vallejo's release, but to the dismay of both, the heretofore friendly Vallejo found his rancho stripped of its horses, cattle, and other commodities by Frémont and the Bear Flaggers.

News of the war had yet to arrive, so Frémont, remembering the Jones embarrassment, would not allow the American flag to be flown. Accordingly, Ide and his men designed the Bear Flag. The original consisted of a crudely drawn bear, a star drawn on unbleached cotton with blackberry juice, and the words "California Republic." A piece of red flannel was sewn onto the bottom of the approximately 3 feet by 5 feet flag to produce a red stripe. The star equated California's stance with Texas's willingness to go it alone as a large pioneer republic, the grizzly bear blazoning its independence and fierceness, and the legend "California Republic" showed bold confidence in California's future. On June18, Ide issued a proclamation in which he outlined the reasons for the "Bear Flag Revolt," declaring the rebels' intention to establish a republican form of government in Upper California: "A government to be prosperous and happifying [sic] in its tendency must originate with its people." The only battle fought by the Bears, as they were called, was engaged with American troops near San Rafael on June 24, with two young Californio casualties – both killed by Kit Carson.

CALIFORNIA REPUBLIC.

The Bear Flag of 1846

The Bear Flag Revolt came to an end after a few weeks when U. S. Navy Commodore John Sloat's (1781-1867) U.S.S. Savannah took Monterey without firing a shot on July 7. Sloat had become commander of the Pacific Squadron in 1844 and spent from November 1845 to June 1846 at Mazatlán, avoiding anything remotely bellicose but armed with instructions to move swiftly to forestall a British seizure of California in the event of war with Mexico. When he learned unofficially that war had begun in Texas, he sailed to Monterey, but without formal notice of war he remained outside the harbor for five days. On June 9 the American flag was raised at Yerba Buena and Sonoma by forces under the command of Captain John B. Montgomery (1794-1873) of the *U.S.S. Portsmouth*, and on the 11th, it was raised at Sutter's Fort. On June 14, Sloat, citing ill health, resigned, and was replaced by Commodore Robert Stockton (1795-1866), returning to the United States two weeks later. On August 13 the flag was raised at Los Angeles. All these actions on the part of the U.S. Navy had been carried out without firing a shot or spilling a drop of blood.

On August 4, Stockton had raised the flag at Santa Barbara. The Presidio commander's wife, Doña Cypriana

Llanos de Flores (1818-1921), was one of the few who did not take refuge in the mission or flee to the mountains. Instead, at the behest of her husband Gumersindo Flores (?-1860), who had originally come from Mexico with the Híjar-Padrés colony, she took down the Mexican flag so that it would not fall into enemy hands, and her husband chopped down the pole. That evening the Flores family dined with Stockton on the *U.S.S. Congress* as honored guests. Doña Cypriana kept the flag for many years, giving the red portion to a destitute neighbor for use as a petticoat.[75]

When the American flag was raised at Yerba Buena, its occasional *alcalde* Francisco Sánchez (1805-62) was a ranchero south of the village who had just completed building a home on what became Linda Mar Boulevard in Pacifica. He accepted the change of flags, but let it be known that his property was not part of the spoils of war. When a band of soldiers rode down the Peninsula to claim his cattle, he took one of the men hostage.

The two sides exchanged cannon fire, after which the hostage was released and the cattle returned. As one author put it, after "this incident, Sánchez returned to his role of model citizen, [and] when he died at the age of 57, he was one of the five wealthiest men in San Mateo County."[76]

Revolt and Reconquest

Sloat had been friendly and easy-going, while Stockton was inflammatory and threatening. Stockton promptly issued a proclamation threatening California leaders and created a California Battalion of Mounted Riflemen, making Frémont its leader and putting now-Captain Gilllespie under him. Still, Stockton could have kept the conquest peaceful had he but observed the standard rules of warfare by recognizing Governor Pico's authority in surrendering. Colonel (and former governor) José Castro was California's military commander headquartered at Monterey, while Pico used Los Angeles as his capital. Both were embroiled in a dispute over the funding of the military and civil branches of government and the location of the capital. Castro sent Captain José María Flores (1818-66) to negotiate with Stockton when Los Angeles was taken, but Stockton refused to trust either Castro or Pico and put Gillespie in command of Los Angeles. Gillespie immediately made himself unpopular by restricting activities: a curfew, no public gatherings of more than three people and no liquor sales on Sundays. On September 23 some drunks tried to attack Fort Hill, the American barracks behind the Plaza. Gillespie tried to arrest them, but a mob formed and stopped him.

The news spread quickly, and a few hours later some Americans were caught and disarmed by Californios at Chino Rancho. Castro appointed José Flores as commander of the Californio forces. The badly outnumbered Gillespie was besieged in Fort Hill by Flores, and he sent Juan "Flaco" ("Skinny") Brown (1800-59) to get help from Stockton at Monterey. The appeal for help, written on cigarette papers and concealed in his long hair, reached Monterey courtesy of Brown after a wild four-day ride, but Stockton had gone on to Yerba Buena. Brown covered that distance in another day. By that time Gillespie had surrendered. He had been allowed to retreat to San Pedro under a white flag, having first promised to leave by sea. The revolt spread throughout southern California with Flores in control of everything from San Luis Obispo to San Diego.

Gillespie set aside his agreement to leave when Stockton's forces arrived, 350 strong, under navy Captain William Mervine (1791-1868). On October 8 a one-hour fight was engaged, known in military annals as the Battle of Domínguez

Rancho, or more familiarly as "the Battle of the Old Woman's Gun." The Californios won the day because of the skill of their 50 mounted lancers and an old four-pounder (1.8 kg) cannon, an antique weapon that had been hidden by an old woman several years before. Dragged about by reatas [or lariats] attached to the saddles of the Californio partisans led by ranchero José Antonio Carrillo (1796-1862), this miniature cannon forced Gillespie's retreat to the ships. There would be no more Californio victories.

Colonel Stephen Kearny (1794-1848) came overland from Fort Leavenworth, capturing Santa Fe and with it all of New Mexico and Arizona. Along the way he learned from Kit Carson that Upper California was already in American hands. Regardless, Kearny continued his journey. After crossing the deserts in Arizona, he and his men arrived tired, dirty, and exhausted in early December. From Arizona he headed to San Diego and, six days after a Pyrrhic victory at San Pascual, took San Diego as well.[77]

Three forces then converged on Los Angeles: Kearny by land from the south, Stockton by sea from the west, and Fremont overland from the north with an army of 400 composed of regular soldiers, Bear Flaggers, and volunteers. On January 10, 1847 Kearny and Stockton retook Los Angeles after the battle of La Mesa (near present Montebello), Flores fled to Sonora, and on January 13 Governor Pico surrendered his authority to Frémont at Cahuenga, signing the document known as the Cahuenga Capitulation; Agustín Olvera, who would become Los Angeles County's first judge and for whom Los Angeles' Olvera Street is named (1820-1877), represented Pico, while Major Pierson B. Reading (1816-68) and Captain Louis McLane (1819-1905) represented Frémont. Pico chose to surrender to Frémont because the latter offered better, more conciliatory terms.[78] The feuding Pico and Castro

– whose enmity had made it easier for Frémont and Stockton to defeat them - fled to Sonora. Both would return as private citizens in 1848, Pico to his brother-in-law, John Forster's (1814-82) ranch at San Juan Capistrano, and then to Los Angeles; Castro to stay until the Mexican government appointed him military commander of Baja in 1853. When Los Angeles surrendered, Gillespie hoisted the flag he had been ignominiously compelled to haul down in September, and Stockton treated the citizens to a band concert, a gesture that helped to soothe hard feelings.

On March 7, Col. Jonathan D. Stevenson's (1800-94) New York Volunteers, ten battalions of 77 men each, arrived by sea at Yerba Buena and went on to join Kearny at Monterey. Stevenson was a New York Democratic politician, and his volunteers, led by only a few regular army men, were to remain in California and help to settle it. Many of the members of the regiment would be notable contributors to California, though some would not be remembered for positive accomplishments.

In July 1847 the occupiers of Los Angeles were joined by a volunteer Mormon Battalion under army Lieutenant Colonel Philip St. George Cook (1809-95), the vast majority of whom did not want to enlist, since Mormons as a group felt little loyalty to the United States at that time. To most of them the military campaign was but a means to much needed cash. Though theirs was the longest military march by American troops to that time, it occurred with them as with so many volunteer military groups in those days that they never experienced combat; indeed, the Mormon Battalion's only battle was against a herd of wild bulls. Upon their arrival in November 1846 at the San Pedro River in southern Arizona's present-day Cochise County, they encountered large herds of wild cattle who were curious about them. After the bulls of these herds caused destruction to some of the mules and wagons and resulted in two men being wounded, some of the troops loaded their rifles and killed about fifteen of the cattle. This event was dubbed "the Battle of the Bulls."[79]

With Alta California subdued, the navy's focus shifted to Baja California. In September 1846, Samuel F. DuPont (1803-65), commander of the *Cyane*, made a call at La Paz and received the pledge of Governor Colonel Francisco Palacios Miranda that Baja would be neutral. There, on April 14,1847, the port of La Paz was occupied, then Guaymas on October 19; and finally, Mazatlán, a major supplier for the Mexican army, on November 11. Numerous Mexican ships were captured by the Pacific Squadron, especially by the *U.S.S. Cyane*. Manuel Pineda (1804-91) tried to recapture the ports, and his attempts resulted in several small battles – the siege of La Paz and the siege of San José del Cabo. Lieutenant Colonel Henry Burton (1819-69) rescued captured Americans, captured Pineda, and dispersed the Mexican forces at the skirmish of Todos Santos. As at the end of the War of 1812, the two opposing forces were unaware that a peace treaty had already been signed. Similarly, when American forces finally left for Monterey, many Mexicans, believing that the U.S. would have conquered Baja as easily as they had Alta California, went with them. One of the refugees who left with Burton, María Amparo Ruiz (1832-95), married him and became the first female Mexican-American author to write in English.[80] Her two novels, *Who Would Have Thought It?* (Lippincott, 1872) and *The Squatter and the Don* (1885), were important in California literature because she addressed crucial issues of ethnicity, power, gender, class, and race in her writing.[81]

The End of the Old Regime

The main fighting was in Mexico, naturally, and two American armies pushed into areas that today remain Mexico, one under Taylor from Texas and the other under General Winfield Scott (1786-1866), who landed at Veracruz.

The ever-duplicitous Santa Anna, in exile in Havana, contacted the U.S. government with a proposal to send him back to Mexico with the promise that he would secure a peace and sell whatever contested territory the United States wanted at a reasonable price. At the same time, he requested of Mexican President Farías permission to return and help his country, swearing he had no more presidential aspirations. He kept his dealings with the Americans secret. Farías had no choice but to accept the proposal, and Santa Anna returned on an American ship. Back in Mexico he immediately announced he would be president and took command of a force of 15,000 to attack Taylor in the north and stop him at Buena Vista. "Santa Anna gave Taylor a respectable fight but had to withdraw, losing about 500 men, twice as many as the Americans" as Conrad Black (1944-) succinctly sums it up.[82] In September 1847 Scott entered Mexico City, Santa Anna fled after giving the order to stand and fight, and the war ended. Americans were in control of most of Mexico.

In February 1848 the two nations signed the Treaty of Guadalupe-Hidalgo. Mexico recognized the annexation of Texas and surrendered what are now the states of California, New Mexico, Utah, Nevada and parts of Colorado, Arizona, and Wyoming (everything below latitude 42°N and west of the Rockies). The United States left Baja California and the rest of Mexico, paid $15.5 million ($590,538,345 in 2023) outright, and repaid Mexico's American creditors an additional $7 million ($266,694,486 in 2023). Mexicans in the conquered territory were given a year to decide on citizenship; if they wished to become American citizens they merely had to stay, if they wanted to keep their Mexican citizenship they had to leave. Land grants were recognized, and the civil rights enjoyed by Americans were extended to the new area.

Meanwhile, in June 1846, the United States and Britain had peacefully divided Oregon along latitude 49oN. This peaceful division ensured that Britain would not become Mexico's ally in the war. Thus, in 1845-48 the United States got one third of its present territory, through annexation, peaceful settlement, or war.

According to Meyer and Sherman:

> "The war reinforced the worst stereotypes that each country held about the other, and these stereotypes in turn contributed to the development of deep-seated prejudices. United States historians rationalized, justified, and even commended the decision to wage the war as well as the prosecution of it. On grounds ranging from regenerating a backward people to fulfilling a preordained destiny, they went so far as to use this war of aggression for the purpose of instilling historical pride in generations of American children. Mexican historians, too, stereotyped and distorted. Not content with an understandably vigorous condemnation of the United States government, they pinned responsibility on the American people and the congenital defects of their Anglo-Saxon heritage.... But the war had at least one positive effect as well: it contributed to the development of a genuine nationalism in Mexico for the first time." [83]

The Mexican-American War was a pivotal moment for the United States in its relation to other nations, while it defined for the future many aspects of U.S. geo-political makeup and character. Mexico would forevermore harbor resentment against the United States, a visceral feeling that spread to Latin America in the form of an endemic suspiciousness of U.S. motives. Europe would suddenly find itself respecting the American army. In the U.S. itself a belief in Manifest Destiny was born, the conviction that the nation should, and would in time, own the entire continent: The evident and obviously foreordained future of the nation was not, however, to expand in an unlimited fashion from north to south, but most emphatically to stretch from east coast to west coast, "from sea to shining sea," as Katharine Lee Bates's patriotic phrase of 1893 would put it.

One could argue that "America" was not really born until Manifest Destiny was realized "from California to the New York Island," as Woody Guthrie's 1940 song celebrates. Until then it was simply the United States (of America), and to those in the western portions of the continent it was "the States." Now with the whole nation extended from coast to coast it made "the United States" and "America" synonymous throughout the non-Latin American world.

And who could have seen in the Mexican-American War the seeds of a great Civil War a dozen years later?

**

California, the poetic name of a fantasy land in a Medieval adventure tale, now belonged to a real land that nations fought over, one poised on the brink of becoming the world's center of attention. The ruthless Cortés, the explorers Coronado and Cabrillo, the pirate Drake, Vizcaíno, seeker of ports, and Kino, seeker of souls: These intrepid men had first made it known – but to an audience that showed little interest. Russian fur hunters and English seekers of Anián sparked an interest.

The organizer and taskmaster Gálvez sent Captain Portolá and Father Serra to checkmate these outsiders. The colony that was planted nearly died at birth, but it revived and thrived thanks to Captain Anza and Father Garcés. Soldiers, priests, and settlers came north from Mexico and established presidios, missions, and pueblos. The future looked bright. Then the Yuma Massacre severed its lifeline, leaving it to develop on its own. Slow, efficient, steady development under Spain was replaced after fifty years by an independent Mexico, whose internecine battles and inefficient government demoted California to stepchild status.

California, "stepchild" or not, possessed an indisputable attractiveness to outsiders, an allure that brought foreigners from the United States, Britain, and other nations to take advantage of its grazing land, its cattle, its furs. These foreigners, seeing Mexico's neglect of the land, were certain that California deserved better. As the United States, Britain, France, and Russia looked on the promising land, their appetites were whetted. As the United States expanded westward, Mexico tried too late to hold on to California but could not, and by its heedlessness lost it.

Chapter Six END NOTES

[1] Michael C. Meyer and William L. Sherman, *The Course of Mexican History*, 5th ed. (New York: Oxford University Press: 1995), p. 297.

[2] Meyer and Sherman, *The Course of Mexican History*, p. 294.

[3] William Spence Robertson, "The Recognition of the Spanish Colonies by the Motherland." Hispanic American Historical Review. 1, no. 1 (Feb. 1918), p. 90, http://www.jstor.org/stable/2506014.

[4] Hunt and Sánchez, *A Short History of California*, p. 188.

[5] He was president May 17- June 4, 1833, June 18 - July 5, 1833, October 27-December 15,1833, April 24, 1834 - January 27, 1835, March 20 - July 10,1839, October 10,1841- October 26, 1842, March 4 - November 8, 1843, June 4-September 12, 1844, March 21-April 2, 1847, May 20 - September 15, 1847, and April 20, 1853 -August 9, 1855

[6] John E. Fagg, *Latin America*, (New York: Macmillan, 1966), p. 534.

[7] Bancroft, *History of California*, vol. 3, p. 32; Caughey, California, 3rd ed., p. 107.

[8] James D. Hart, *A Companion to California*, (New York: Oxford University Press, 1978), p. 464.

[9] James Rawls, "Napa County Beginnings". Text of talk given to the California Historical Society Annual Meeting, March 25, 1977, pp. 4-6.

[10] C. Alan Hutchinson, *Frontier Settlement in Mexican California: Híjar-Padrés Colony and Its Origins, 1769-1835*, (New Haven: Yale University Press, 1969), cited in Caughey, California, 3rd ed., p. 111.

[11] Bancroft, *History of California*, vol. 3, pp. 421, 427.

[12] William Wilcox Robinson, *Land in California, the Story of Mission Land, Squatters, Mining Claims, Railroad Grants, Land Scrip, Homesteads. Chronicles of California.* (1948; repr., University of California Press, 1979), pp. 29-32

[13] Lynn Ludlow, "A land-grant rancho saved by Prop. 13," *San Francisco Examiner & Chronicle*, February 4, 1979, Section A, p. 4; John McKinney, "Happy Trails at Former Ranch in Pacheco State Park," *Los Angeles Times*, June 6, 1999, p. L-10.

[14] DaveManuel.com, Inflation Calculator, accessed September 16, 2023, http://www.davemanuel.com/inflation-calculator.php. This source is used throughout the work for prices prior to 1913. For prices since 1913 the optimal work is U.S. Inflation Calculator, accessed February 19, 2023, https://www.usinflationcalculator.com/

[15] F. W. Howay, *A List of Trading Vessels in the Maritime Fur Trade, 1785-1825*, ed. Richard A. Pierce (Kingston, Ontario: The Limestone Press, 1973), p. 82. John Suter is not to be confused with John Augustus Sutter.

[16] Timofei Osipovich Tarakanov, http://www.st-mike.org/medicine/docs/wreck_st_nicolas_tarakanov.pdf.

[17] Hunt and Sánchez, A Short History of California, p. 172.

[18] "Townsend, Charles Haskins" in *Who Was Who in America: Science and Technology. Marquis Who's Who* (Chicago: A.N. arquis, 1976), p. 610; NOAA Fisheries, Office of Protected Resources, Northern Fur Seal, http://www.nmfs.noaa.gov/pr/species/mammals/pinnipeds/northern furseal.htm; Ben Landis, "California sea otter numbers holding steady," University of California Santa Cruz News Center, http://news.ucsc.edu/2014/09/sea-otter-population.html.

[19] "A Plum Discovery," *Oakland Tribune*, editorial, August 8, 1922, p. 16.

[20] Nellie Van der Grift Sánchez, *Spanish Arcadia*, (Los Angeles: Powell, 1928), pp. 123-25.

[21] Daniel Brower, "Russian Romantics in America – Alexander and Helena Rotchev at Fort Ross" Fort Ross Conservancy Library, http://www.fortross.org/lib/51/russian-romantics-in-americaalexander-and-helena-rotchev-at-fort-ross.pdf. Courtesy of Fort Ross Conservancy, www.fortross.org.

[22] Jack Schreibman, "When Russians Were Californians", *Oakland Tribune*, April 3, 1977, p. 23.

[23] James Gibson, California Through Russian Eyes, 1806-1848. (Norman: University of Oklahoma Press, 2013), p. 459.

[24] Hunt and Sánchez, *A Short History of California*, p. 174.

[25] "William Gale Boston Trader", Goyodelarosa: 2008, https://goyodelarosa.wordpress.com/tag/william-gale-boston-trader/.

[26] Richard Somerset Mackie, *Trading Beyond the Mountains: The British Fur Trade on the Pacific, 1793-1843* (Vancouver: University of British Columbia Press, 1997), p. 66.

[27] Glyndwr Williams, "McLEOD, ALEXANDER RODERICK," in *Dictionary of Canadian Biography*, vol. 7, University of Toronto/Université Laval, 2003, http://www.biographi.ca/en/bio/mcleod_alexander_roderick_7E.html.

[28] Charles Wilkes, *Narrative of the United States Exploring Expedition: During the Years 1838, 1839, 1840, 1841, 1842*, Volume 4. (Philadelphia: Lea and Blanchard, 1845), p. 349.

[29] Alice Bay Maloney, "California Rendezvous," *The Beaver* (December 1944), p. 36. *The Beaver* was the official magazine of the Hudson's Bay Company 1920-2010.

[30] Maloney, "California Rendezvous," p. 34.

[31] Herman Leader, "HBC in California." *The Beaver*, (March 1949), pp. 3-7.

[32] Genini, "From Beaver House to the Golden Gate: The Hudson's Bay Company in California," *Pacific Historian* 22, no. 3 (Fall 1978), pp. 218-19.

[33] Jeffrey Nichols, "The Spanish Trail Cut a Roundabout Path Through Utah", *Blazer* (June 1995), Utah History to Go, http://www.historytogo.utah.gov/utah_chapters/trappers,_traders,_and_explorers/thespanishtrailcutapaththroughutah.html .

[34] Caughey, *California*, 3rd ed., p. 126.

[35] Hart, *A Companion to California*, p. 323

[36] "Jim Beckwourth," *PG&E Progress* 57, no.1 (January 1980)

[37] Quoted in Hunt and Sánchez, *A Short History of California*, p. 314.

[38] Caughey, *California*, 3rd ed., p. 139

[39] On the origin and evolution of the name see Sausalito Historical Society, "Sausalito or Saucelito?" (December 4, 2019), https://www.sausalitohistoricalsociety.com/2019-columns/2019/12/4/sausalito-or-saucelito

[40] Victor Walsh, "The Casa and the Don: Juan Bandini's Quest for Homeland in Early San Diego," https://www.sandiegohistory.org/journal/v57-1/v57-1walsh.pdf ;

Patricia Baker, "The Bandini Family", accessed October 16. 2015, http://www.sandiegohistory.org/journal/1969/january/part2/.

[41] Samuel Dickson, *Tales of San Francisco* (Stanford: Stanford University, 1960), pp. 405-14.

[42] The true meaning of "Putah" in Putah Creek has been the subject of discussion and speculation. Despite its name, the "Puta" form was rejected by the U.S. Board on Geographic Names, likely because of its resemblance to the Spanish word meaning "whore," and "puto" is a Spanish derogatory term meaning "homosexual." According to Erwin Gudde (1889-1969), the resemblance is "purely accidental;" the revised fourth edition of his California Place Names has the following entry: Putah Creek: From Lake Miwok *puṭa wuwwe* "grassy creek" (Callaghan; cf. Beeler 1974:141). The similarity to Spanish puta "prostitute" is purely accidental. In the records of Mission San Francisco Solano of 1824, the natives of the place are mentioned with various spellings from Putto to Puttato. In the baptismal records of Mission Dolores an adulto de Putü is mentioned in 1817, and the wife of Pedro Putay in 1821 (Arch. Mis. 1:94.81). In 1842 the stream was well known by its name: "I know that the Rio was called 'Putos.'...It is well-known by the name which has been given it" (J. J. Warner, land-grant case 232 ND). The name was probably fixed by William Wolfskill, who named his grant Rio de los Putos on May 24, 1842. In 1843 the name was used in the titles of three other land grants, in one of which the spelling Putas occurs. In the Statutes of the early 1850s, in the *Indian Reports*, and in the *Pacific R.R. Reports*, the spelling of the name is in complete confusion. The present version was applied to a town in 1853, was used in the Statutes of 1854, was made popular by the Bancroft maps, and finally was adopted by the USGS." Gudde, Erwin G.; Bright, William (2004). *California Place Names: The Origin and Etymology of Current Geographical Names* (4th rev. and enl. ed.). University of California Press. pp. 304–305.

[43] Cooper was married to one of General Vallejo's sisters, Encarnación (1809-1902).

[44] Charles B. Churchill, "Thomas Jefferson Farnam: An Exponent of American Empire in Mexican California," *Pacific Historical Review* 60, no. 4 (November 1991), pp. 517-537

[45] John Dengel, "John Marsh's House of Stone," Oakland Tribune, December 28, 1975, p. 8; John H. Henshell, "Diablo's

Hermit Pioneer," *Oakland Tribune Magazine*, July 29, 1923, p. 15; Wikipedia contributors, "Camron-Stanford House," *Wikipedia, The Free Encyclopedia,* https://en.wikipedia.org/w/index.php?title=Camron-Stanford_House&oldid=1162264918 (accessed February 20, 2024); "Old Resident Dies Following Long Illness," *Santa Barbara Daily News,* March 8, 1927, p. 10.

[46] The name means "human flesh" in Spanish. There is speculation as to why the name was chosen. The grant was originally known to the native residents as "Huilic Noma" and also "Colijolmanoc". One naming theory speculates that Bale, in a bit of black humor, twisted "Colijolmanoc" into the similar sounding Spanish "Carne Humana".

[47] California Department of Parks & Recreation, "Bale Grist Mill State Park," http://www.parks.ca.gov/?page_id=482.

[48] Mildred Brooke Hoover, *Historic Spots in California.* (Stanford University Press, 1990), p. 232.

[49] Richard Dillon, *Fool's Gold: The Decline and Fall of Captain John Sutter.* (New York: Coward McCann, 1967), pp 66-77; "John Sutter and California's Indians" *Wild West Magazine*, (June 2006), http://www.historynet.com/john-sutter-and-californias-indians.htm.

[50] Frances Montgomery, "Daughter Brings Back Memories of Gen. Vallejo", *Oakland Tribune*, April 14, 1923, p. 3. Edwin Bryant, *What I Saw in California,* p. 319, in Kevin Starr, *Americans and the California Dream 1850-1915,* (New York: Oxford University Press, 1973), pp. 24-25

[51] "Whatever Became of John Bartleson?" *Goldfields* (November 2013), https://nancyleek.wordpress.com/2013/11/09/what-ever-became-of-john-bartleson/; Harold Schindler, "The Ways West" in *Sketches of Utah History*, (Logan UT: Utah State University Press, 1998) , p. 11.

[52] John Bidwell, "Gold Hunters of California. The First Emigrant Train to California" *The Century* (November 1890), pp. 106-130, https://babel.hathitrust.org/cgi/pt?id=coo.31924080795341&view=1up&seq=988&q1=Bidwell

[53] Dave Weinstein, "Saving the House that Marsh built", *SF*

Gate, December 7, 2002, http://www.sfgate.com/bayarea/article/Saving-the-house-that-Marsh-built-1856-Contra-3308438.php#photo-2467944.

[54] John Calderwood, "The Sad Saga of a Misanthropic Pioneer", *San Francisco Sunday Examiner & Chronicle, California Living Magazine,* December 13, 1981, pp. 47-51.

[55] Hunt and Sánchez, *A Short History of California,* p. 329.

[56] Scott MacDonald, *Legacy: An Ancestral Journey Though American History,* (San Diego: Del Mar, 2022), p. 80.

[57] Nat B. Read, *Don Benito Wilson: From Mountain Man to Mayor of Los Angeles 1841-1878* (Santa Monica: Angel City Press, 2008); Tom Gregory, *History of Yolo County,* California. (Los Angeles: Historic Record Company, 1913), pp. 6, 46, 74, https://openlibrary.org/books/OL14013448M/History_of_Yolo_Co unty_California; "Covered Bridges of the Sierra Nevada", *Snowy Range Reflections* 2, no. 2 (Fall 2009), http://www.sierracollege.edu/eJournals/jsnhb/v2n2/CoveredBridge s-KF.html.

[58] Hunt and Sánchez, *A Short History of California,* p. 303. The domesticated Indian population had plummeted in the 75 years since the Spanish influx. It was estimated that there were 50,000 Indians in the future mission areas in 1770 and at secularization there were about 30,000 in the missions, and by 1900 there were less than 3,000. "Mission Indians of California: Vital Statistics," *Catholic Encyclopedia,* http://www.newadvent.org/cathen/10369a.htm.

[59] Bernard DeVoto, *The Year of Decision: 1846,* (Boston: Houghton-Mifflin, 1943), p. 444; Dana Goodyear, "Excavating the Donner Party," *New Yorker,* April 24, 2006, pp. 140-151 https://www.newyorker.com/magazine/2006/04/24/what-happened-at-alder-creek; Michelle Debczak, " How Lewis Keseberg was banded the killer cannibal of the Donner Party," Mental Floss (September 19, 2018), https://www.mentalfloss.com/article/542265/how-lewis-keseberg-was-branded-killer-cannibal-donner-party#:~:text=Lewis%20Keseberg%20never%20denied%20cannib alizing,she%20died%20of%20natural%20causes.

[60] George Stewart, *Ordeal by Hunger: The Story of the Donner*

Party. Supplement (1936; repr., Boston: Houghton-Mifflin, 1988), pp. 348-354

[61] State of California Park and Recreation Commission (2003). *Donner Memorial State Park General Plan and Environmental Report,* 1, pp. 39, 47, 59, https://web.archive.org/web/20100202175621/http://www.parks.ca .gov/pages/21299/files/donner%20gp%20vol%201%20final.pdf

[62] George L. Rives, *The United States and Mexico, 1821-1848: a history of the relations between the two countries between the independence of Mexico to the close of the war with the United States,* Vol 2 (New York: Scribner's, 1913), pp. 45-46.

[63] Caughey, *California*, 3rd, p. 159; Hunt and Sánchez, *A Short History of California,* p. 338-41; Brantz Mayer and Frederick Albion Ober, eds. *Mexico, Central America and West Indies*, vol. 22 of History of Nations, ed. by Henry Cabot Lodge (New York: Collier, 1928), p. 295; Patrick Lavin, "Father Eugene MacNamara and His Utopia Dream", *Toronto Irish News* (March 2008). California Missions Resource Center, "Three–Thousand Irishmen," http://www.missionscalifornia.com/stories/three-thousand-irishmen.html; A. P. Nassatir, "International Rivalry for California and the Establishment of the British Consulate," *California Historical Society Quarterly* 46, no 1 (March 1967), p. 60.

[64] His Italian naturalist, Paul Emile Botta (1802-70) described the Indians and fauna encountered in California and translated Voyage into Italian (1841). A variety of gopher he described was named Botta gopher.

[65] Rufus Kay Willys, "French Imperialists in California," *CHSQ* 8, no. 2 (June 1929), pp. 116-129.

[66] Hunt and Sánchez, *A Short History of California*, p. 338.

[67] Egan, *Frémont, Explorer for a Restless Nation*, (Reno: University of Nevada, 1977), p. 322

[68] Egan, *Frémont*, p. 330.

[69] DeVoto, *1846*, p. 198.

[70] Allan Nevins, *Frémont: The West's Greatest Adventurer, Being a Biography from Certain Hitherto Unpublished Sources…* (New York: Harper, 1928, I, 273-322) in Leonard Pitt, California

Controversies, p. 51

[71] Richard Dillon, *Humbugs and Heroes: A Gallery of California Pioneers,* (Garden City: Doubleday, 1970), p. 98.

[72] Caughey, *California,* 3rd ed., p. 164.

[73] David Lavender, *California: Land of New Beginnings,* (Lincoln NE: University of Nebraska, 1987), p. 131.

[74] Onlive Archives of California (OAC). Captain Elliott Libbey Depositions. The Society of California Pioneers, http://www.oac.cdlib.org/findaid/ark:/13030/c8jq135k/admin/#ref5 . For an explanation of the position of subprefect see Theodore Hittell, *History of California,* Vol. 2. (San Francisco: Pacific Press and Occidental Publishing, 1885), p. 368.

[75] OAC. Flores Family Papers, MS-03, Presidio Research Center, Santa Barbara Trust for Historic Preservation, http://www.oac.cdlib.org/findaid/ark:/13030/c8ms3tgc/entire_text/.

[76] JDB, "Sánchez Adobe," *CSAA Motorland,* September-October 1977, p. 48.

[77] Richard Griswold del Castillo, "The U.S.-Mexican War in San Diego, 1846-1847: Loyalty and Resistance," *Journal of San Diego History* 49, no. 1 (Winter 2003). Of Kearny's 150 men 18 were killed and 13 wounded, while Pico's 75 men suffered 12 wounded and one captured. Everything Explained Today, "Battle of San Pasqual explained," (2016), http://everything.explained.today/Battle_of_San_Pasqual/

[78] Peter Conmy, "Augustín Olvera: LA County's First Judge," *The Native Son* 19, no. 1 (January-February 1980), p. 1.

[79] B.H. Roberts, *The Mormon Battallion: Its History and Achievements.* (Salt Lake City: Deseret News, 1919).

[80] Michael Hall, "Baja California," *The Encyclopedia of the Mexican-American War: A Political, Social, and Military History,* Volume 2. ABC-Clio, 2013, pp. 43-44. "The Mexican-American War in Baja California Sur," Baja Insider (2009), accessed May 8, 2016, bajainsider.com/article/mexican-american-war-baja-california-sur/.

[81] Rosaura Sánchez and Beatrice Pita, "Maria Amparo Ruiz de Burton and the Power of Her Pen," *Latina Legacies: Identity, Biography, and Community,* (New York: Oxford University Press, 2005), pp.72-83.

[82] Conrad Black, *Flight of the Eagle: The Grand Strategies That Brought America from Colonial Dependence to World Leadership.* (New York: Encounter Books, 2013), pp. 187-88.

[83] Meyer and Sherman, *The Course of Mexican History*, p. 352.

Chapter Six FURTHER READING

(BOOKS LISTED WITH AN "*" ARE FICTIONAL)

1. Beard, Franklin. *Charles Hopper and the Pilgrims of the Pacific.* La Grange: Southern Mines, 1981.

2. Bemis, Samuel Flagg. *A Diplomatic History of the United States.* 5th ed. New York: Holt, Rinehart and Winston, 1965.

3. Bruemmer, Fred. "My Life Among Wild Pinipeds", *International Wildlife,* July-August 1996.

4. Chisholm, Hugh ed. "Dana, Francis". *Encyclopaedia Britannica.* 11th edition. (1911). Includes material on his descendants.

5. Dana, Richard Henry. *Two Years Before the Mast* 1840. Reprint, New York: Bantam, 1963.

6. Descendants of Mexican War Veterans. "The Conquest of California." http://www.dmwv.org/mexwar/history/calcon.htm.

7. DeVoto, Bernard. *Across the Wide Missouri.* New York: Houghton-Mifflin, 1947.

8. Dillon, Richard. *Siskiyou Trail.* New York: McGraw-Hill, 1975.

9. Hill, Joseph J. *Ewing Young and the Fur Trade of the Far Southwest, 1822-1834.* Eugene OR: Koke-Tiffany Co, 1923.

10. Joy, Robin. "How the Sea Otter Hunt Began." http://www.fortrossstatepark.org/seaotter.htm.

11. Kownslar, Allan. *Manifest Destiny.* Lexington, MA: Heath, 1964.

12. Lightfoot, Kent, Thomas Wake and Ann Schiff. *The Archaeology and Ethnohistory of Fort Ross, California.* Number 49 of Contributions of the University of California Archaeological Research Facility, Berkeley.

http://digitalassets.lib.berkeley.edu/anthpubs/ucb/text/arf049-001.pdf.

13. Nautilus Explorer, "Elephant Seals of Guadalupe Island" (September 19, 2010). http://nautilusatsea.com/2010/09/20/elephant-seals-of-guadalupe-island-one-of-the-most-amazing-comebacks-in-the-world-divemaster-images-19-september-2010/.

14. Nevin, David. *Dream West*, New York: Signet, 1983. *

15. Payne, Stanley G. *History of Spain and Portugal* (1973). 2:248 (Fernando VII). The Library of Iberian Resources Online. http://libro.uca.edu/payne2/payne16.pdf.

16. Robinson, Alfred. *Life in California*. 1846. Reprint, Santa Barbara: Peregrine, 1970.

17. Shumway, Burgess. *California Ranchos: Patented Private Land Grants listed by County.*

18. San Bernardino: Borgo Press, 1988.

19. Wilcox, Desmond. *Ten Who Dared*. Boston: Little, Brown, 1977.

Part 3: Gold Changes Everything (1848-70)

Chapter 7: Gold Begets a New State

**

"Boys, by God I believe I have found a gold mine."

-Marshall, Sutter's Mill, January 24, 1848

**

The Discovery

Despite the Spaniards' great reputation as gold miners in Mexico and Bolivia, they never discovered California's *veta madre*, the Mother Lode, the deeply buried main vein of gold, some outcroppings of which reach the surface. Some gold was found in San Feliciano Canyon in 1841, near where Six Flags Magic Mountain (Valencia) is located today. Francisco López (1820-1900), the majordomo of the Rancho San Fernando, hunting about two dozen stray cattle with a companion, paused to pluck some wild onions for his lunch and found some shiny flakes on the roots.[1] López had been trained in mining techniques at the Colegio de Minería in Mexico City, and had often searched for placer gold. His chance discovery caused a small, localized excitement that died down after a month, but it was from this little rush that Alfred Robinson acquired the 20 ounces (567 g) of gold he brought to the United States.[2]

Gold has been valuable from the beginnings of recorded history in nearly every culture because it is rare, beautiful, and malleable. The Spaniards had come to California looking for gold, but apparently never found it. There were stories - Indian buried treasure, missionary treasure, Russian treasure -

according to which fabled wealth had been so well hidden than no one ever came upon it. The occasional serendipitous find caused little excitement.

The real discovery of gold, when it came, would also be by chance and would, for a while, cause barely a ripple of excitement.

On January 24, 1848, James Marshall (1810-85), a carpenter and contractor working for Sutter, was cutting a tailrace for a lumber mill at Coloma on the American River. Spying a few shiny objects in the water he took them to Sutter, excited enough at the glittering possibilities to ride all night in the rain. Sutter, referring to the *Encyclopedia Americana* (1836), performed several tests on the dime-sized flakes (sinking them, smashing them, and touching them with nitric acid). He found them to be the real thing – gold. Sutter then told Marshall to keep quiet, as he had no intention of losing his workers or his empire before he could file ownership papers on the area.[3] He had figured out in an instant that all economic structures in the region were about to change forever.

Curiously, however, Sutter did not keep quiet. He sent a sample to Military Governor Richard Mason (1797-1850), bragged to Vallejo, and allowed Marshall's workers to prospect on Sundays. He also permitted his teamsters to use it for cash at Sam Brannan's (1819-89) store - where Brannan kept it in a jar.

Brannan, a newspaper man by training, had been ordered by Mormon leader Brigham Young (1801-77) to bring 238 Latter-Day Saints, better known as Mormons, to a place outside the United States. The American public despised polygamy and the Mormons' unorthodox and seemingly treasonous notions, as they were reputed to hold. This ill will had resulted in the killing of their Prophet, Joseph Smith (1805-44) after he smashed an opposing Mormon group's printing press and instituted dictatorial laws in that group's Nauvoo, Illinois, colony. Brannan's chartered ship, the *Brooklyn*, took them and their equipment, including a printing press, to Yerba Buena (as San Francisco was then known), only to find, to their disappointment, that the United States had seized California three weeks earlier. Brannan's first words upon seeing the American flag flying over Yerba Buena were "There's that damned rag, again!" A dynamic opportunist, Brannan established a flour mill and California's second newspaper, *The California Star* (the first was *The Californian* in Monterey in late 1846). He had collected tithes from the Mormon colonists, and when Brigham Young demanded the money, Brannan refused. Young sent his enforcer, Porter Rockwell (1813-78), but Brannan stared him down and kept the money. The Mormons who had sailed with him charged Brannan with embezzlement; American California's first jury heard the case, but it was unable to come to a decision. Whether it was Brannan's "sparkling courtroom oratory [or] the insupportable premise of the complaints," he was acquitted. Brannan was excommunicated from the Mormon church, but he kept the money and prospered for a time with a store a few miles (4 km) from Sutter's fort on the Sacramento River. Despite the excommunication, he would continue to be known as "the gay Saint," due to his jovial personality.[4]

Public reaction in California had been quite indifferent to tales popping up here and there over the years about gold finds. The *Star's* correspondent, writing from the northern Sierra, described that region as: "great country. . . see it now. . .full-flowing streams, mighty timber. . . fragrant flowers, gold and silver." Little attention was paid to such effusive statements; to many "All that glitters is not gold" seemed true enough. Stories of gold had not really panned out over the years, so why bother?

This yawning attitude – the *Star* gave practically the same amount of space to a local horse race - changed to rapt interest in June 1848, when Brannan, having collected a jar-full of gold dust, rode with it through the streets of San Francisco shouting, "Gold! Gold from the American River!" An astute businessman, he had invested in mining equipment and supplies miners would need. (The city's name had just been changed in January 1847 from "Yerba Buena" by its *alcalde*, navy Lieutenant Washington Allon Bartlett [1816-65], the new name, at least in retrospect, portending a new style of life.)

All it took was one day's hard work crying it in the streets. By the end of the day San Francisco was virtually deserted. Within a week Monterey and San Jose were deserted. One more week saw Los Angeles remarkably depopulated. Ships were abandoned by captains and crews, labor was nonexistent at any wage, and nearly every shop closed (unless it sold mining items.) Creditors forgot to collect - in short, all that was not gold withered or vanished. Many abandoned ships were later beached, buried, and paved over to become part of the waterfront. Some of them were turned into stores or warehouses, and excavations continued to find their remains into the 1980s.[5]Prices for equipment and transportation skyrocketed as everyone scrambled for his piece of the action.

The Season of 1848

Throughout 1848 the mining frontier spread out from Coloma, first to other parts of the American River and then to other rivers. Downstream at Mormon Bar, Henry Bigler (1815-1900), one of Sutter's workers, who recorded the date of Marshall's "goald" [sic] discovery in his diary, found gold.

Upstream, Marshall did the same at Live Oak Bar. Isaac Humphrey (?-1867), who had mined in Georgia in the 1830s and was very familiar with gold mining techniques, began mining at Coloma with his newly invented rocker or cradle, his experience confirming Marshall's discovery. Bidwell struck it rich at Chico on the Feather River, and P.B. Reading on the Trinity River, while to the south German-born San Jose miller and store-keeper Charles Weber (1814-81) found his gold on the Stanislaus River.[6]

The greatest concentration of gold, however, was on the American River, and the best place on the American was Dry Diggings, soon to be known as Hangtown, and finally Placerville. Most of the men mining in this area used Indian labor, and daily took out anywhere from three ounces (85 g) to five pounds (2.27kg) per man (gold was then worth $16 per ounce [28.3 g]). In the northern mines, on the American and Feather, most of the miners were Americans, generally army deserters from the Mexican-American War, or ranchers. In the southern mines, on the Stanislaus and Merced, most of the miners were Mexicans.

At first only *placer*, or surface mining, was practiced. Gold could literally be plucked from a pan of gravel or out of cracks in rocks and even the laziest man could get an ounce a day. With so much new wealth floating around, merchants were quick to raise prices, true to the classic definition of inflation: more money chasing the same amount of goods. Money bought a lot more in those days (a dollar [$38.74 in 2023 dollars] a day being a good wage) but gold rush prices should dissuade anyone from complaining about the cost of living today. Typical prices were $800 ($31,402 in 2023) for a barrel of flour, $100 ($3925 in 2023) for a gallon of whiskey, $1.50 ($58 in 2023) for an egg or 25 cents ($9.82 in 2023) for a nail; even a shovel cost $50 ($1962 in 2023)!

Through 1848 the mines were relatively crime free because they were uncrowded, most of the miners were still friends, and there was a general feeling that there was plenty for everyone. Crime, when it did occur, was dealt with swiftly and severely, as at Dry Diggings (soon to be known as Hangtown), where five men were whipped for robbing a Mexican gambler. Three of them (a Frenchman and two Mexicans) were subsequently hanged when recognized as wanted murderers. Since racism was common in the camps, some have pointed to these executions as examples of racist behavior, but while two of the executed were Mexicans, so was the victim: The racist charge, at least in this case, seems unfounded.

The Trek of the Forty-Niners

As in California, the initial reaction to Marshall's discovery of gold was indifference in the United States and in Europe. The mood changed to feverish interest after Archibald Gillespie managed to bring some samples to President Polk. The president was known to be an honest man, so when he announced the discovery to Congress in December 1848, the human stampede known as the Gold Rush was on.

From every state and territory of the United States, from Canada, from Mexico and the Pacific countries of South America, from nearly every country in Europe, from Hawaii and China and Australia, thousands of men poured into California. Few planned to remain.

For the Americans there were three main ways to get to California: by sea, around Cape Horn, by sea and land via Panama, and across the continent.

**

"Witnessed a funeral at sea today. A child dropped into the fathomless deep."

-Dr. Isaac Reed, 1851

**

The Cape Horn route was the longest - up to five months - but the easiest, and except for the Antarctic storms at the Cape, was fairly safe, if boring. The Cape route was popular in New England because there were so many ships and experienced sailors there. Some of these formed joint-stock companies to purchase a ship, then sell it at great profit in San Francisco, something that would not materialize. The New Englanders, more than others, saw this as a chance to improve on California's lifestyle. One cleric advised them to "Go there with the Bible in one hand and your New England civilization in the other and make your mark." Not all the voyagers enjoyed their sea-going experience; Enos Christman (1828-1912), later editor of the *Sonora Herald* (and other newspapers), recounted that when the ship's food supply ran low, the captain had promised to purchase additional food when they would arrive at Valparaiso. However,

> "these promises he has forgotten or at least not fulfilled.
> Although he has made considerable addition to the number of
> mouths, as we now have about 100 persons aboard, he has only
> about 800 pounds (363.87 kg) of flour to feed these for a period
> of sixty to ninety days, and other
> supplies are rated in the same meagre proportion. Much
> feeling exists on the subject and should our

340

grievances go
unredressed, disturbances may be expected before
we reach our destination." [7]

The trip through Panama was short but rotten. One
could, with the right connections, make the journey in three
months. Sailing from New Orleans to Colón and then trekking
through the jungle to Panama City, the traveler would wait for
a ship to San Francisco. Pacific Mail Steamship Company
started an incomplete, desultory service between Panama and
California, cynically ignoring its own timetable because of its
monopoly. The voyage from Panama cost about $1,000
($49,480 in 2023) for steerage, and there were many left
behind. This route was favored by those who wanted to get to
California quickly "to mine the miners": gamblers,
prostitutes, merchants, saloon-keepers, and recently defeated
politicians.

Typical of the time delays and transportation expenses on
the Panama route were those reported in the diary of New
Yorker Hiram Pierce (1810-81):

> Left Troy, New York, for New York City on 7 March
> 1849, cost $4 ($162 in 2023)
> Left New York for Chagres on 9 March, cost: $45
> ($1,821 in 2023)
> Arrived at Chagres on 28 March
> Left Chagres for Panama City on 29 March, cost $10
> ($404.80 in 2023)
> Arrived at Panama City on 4 April
> Left Panama City for San Francisco on 9 May, cost
> $2925 ($119,215 in 2023, which he called "a
> bargain")
> Arrived at San Francisco on 30 July1849

Total days from Troy to San Francisco, 145; travel cost $2984.[8]
($121,602.80 in 2023)

Some of the Americans who took this route started to reap riches by catering to the needs of those traveling with them. Among these were two who would become famous in California, Collis P. Huntington (1821-1900) and Asbury Harpending (1839-1923); Harpending had started out at age seventeen from Kentucky with five dollars ($202 in 2023) and a pistol and had made his first million by the age of twenty!

How did he do this? Eschewing more comfortable transportation, he held on to his original five dollars and walked from Kentucky to New Orleans, using his money on the way to buy fruit and vegetables when he observed that his fellow-travelers had not provided for themselves. The produce had cost a few cents apiece; in Panama he was able to sell it for a dollar ($40.48 in 2023) apiece. He walked across the isthmus, sailed to San Francisco with $400 ($16,192 in 2023) and the pistol, and headed to the mines. Soon tiring of profitless mining, he went back to San Francisco, speculating that there would be other disappointed miners who would need places to stay or do business in the city. He bought property at slashed prices, and several months later sold or leased it for thousands of times what it had cost him.[9]

**

"Any man who makes a trip by land to California deserves to find a fortune."

-Alonzo Delano, 1849

**

There were two basic routes across the continent - South

Pass (near the site of present-day Casper, Wyoming) or the Gila. It took four or five months, and the scenery was often bleak. This was the way most pioneers had been coming since 1841 - up the Missouri and Platte Rivers, then down to Salt Lake City where Brigham's people were ready to sell needed supplies. The Gila route started at Fort Smith, Arkansas, took the travelers to Tallequah, in the Indian Territory, where they helped enrich the Cherokees with their purchases, then across Texas to the Gila, and on to California. On both branches people found that previous travelers had sometimes burned the grass or poisoned water to cut down on competition. The Indians were not often a threat, since the gold seekers were just passing through and presented no perceptible threat to them, although some Pawnees and Mojaves could be occasional problems for the "forty-niners," so nicknamed for the fateful year of California gold discovery, who might stray from the trail. Accounts of trading between Indians and the forty-niners filled many pioneer diaries. There were regional diseases to contend with, such as cholera on the Plains and tick fever in the Rockies. A few even walked the entire way. Donner-type tragedies were avoided because a relief system had been established.

After the Donner tragedy the emigrants were looking for safer routes over the Sierra, and they came up with three: Donner Pass (now Interstate 80) which they would use earlier in the year, the Lassen route (now U.S. 395 from Goose Lake), also known as Nobles' Emigrant Trail, and Carson Pass (now Highway 88), also known as Emigrant Road. A group of Mormons returning from the Sacramento Valley to Salt Lake City were first to travel via Carson Pass. Almost as direct a route over the Sierra to Sutter's Fort as Donner Pass, it became the preferred trail from Utah.

James A. Wilkins (1808-88), an artist who traveled over

Carson Pass in late September 1849, described the trail:

> "He must have a bold heart and a daring spirit, that first conceived the idea of the possibility of wagons traveling thro' this mountain pass. Imagine a mountain 6 miles (7.2 km) thro' at its base/cleft in twain, like an immense crack and all the loose rocks and debris thrown together at the bottom. . . and sometimes up steep hills loaded wagons had to pass in places where loose cattle could hardly keep their feet. The great difficulty was in steep places and short turns, where only one or two yoke could pull at a time, every man had to put his shoulder to the wheel. . . the way all along was strewn with broken wagons -. . . but we got through safely, and congratulated ourselves so much that we took a 'horn' on the strength of it."[10]

The overland trip to the West was one of the most documented events in American history. Nearly all who made it, regardless of wealth, education, age, or sex, realized its importance, but few waxed philosophical. Most of the diaries they kept concentrated on the weather, the availability of grass for their animals, encounters with Indians, and descriptions of the terrain. Few reported on the people they met on the trek, and fewer expressed their private thoughts except for the desire to get rich. Since for most their days passed in relentless physical labor, most of the diaries are simply short and factual accounts. The diary of Hamden Aubrey Cagwin (1810-95), who came from Wisconsin with his brother Orville, does give brief insights into his thoughts. In one of his writings, which he titled "21 Wayside Incidents", he describes, for example, men he meets on the trail, discusses the comparative advantages of travel by horse, ox, or mule train, and comments on how each traveler judges the other man's trip is easier than his own. He argues for the need of army protection through Indian land. Once safely arrived at their California destination, the Cagwin brothers, whose trip had been financed by other brothers at home, were able to profit from mining, and after 18 months send the agreed upon one-third of their profits ($2,659.85 [$107,678 in 2023]) back to Wisconsin.[11]

While the overland trail could be dismal, boring, and tedious, marked by the graves of emigrants from newborns to elderly who had succumbed on the way, the gold seekers tried to lighten their burden in time-honored fashion. David Leeper (1832-1900), who left Indiana in February 1849, recalled that, "we were able to muster several musical instruments -- violin, banjo, tambourine, and castanets. We were all virtuosos from the backwoods conservatories, and our repertoire was amply equipped with the popular plantation melodies of the day..." [12]

Leeper spent five years in California, mining at Redding's Diggings, Hangtown, and on the Trinity River, before going on to lumbering at Eureka. He showed a great deal of interest in the "Digger" Indians and included illustrations of their tribal garb.

The very large foreign element made Americans more conscious of other cultures, more cosmopolitan, though this awareness sparked hostility as often as appreciation. Most Americans in the States and in California were white of English or Celtic origin, Protestants whose parents and grandparents were native born. What they knew of other nations and cultures was minimal, and few had formerly traveled more than 100 miles (160 km) from their birthplace. Now they were mingling with Americans from other sections of the country, as well as French, Italians, Germans, Chinese, Australians, Mexicans, Peruvians, and Chileans -- to name but a few. Many of these were Catholics, Jews, or worshippers of Asian deities;[13] many were darker complexioned; all those of different backgrounds from most Americans were to some degree difficult to understand. Even the English-speaking Australians spoke an unfamiliar dialect. All had customs and diets that were markedly different from those known to Americans.

The French had become so numerous that Bastille Day was a publicly recognized holiday in San Francisco and the mining camps. A good number of French people often traveled back and forth between France and California. The Italians, who would one day become a significant ethnic group in the state, were few during the Gold Rush: only a few adventurous people who had not been demoralized by Italy's poverty and high illiteracy rate, its wars and their accompanying despoliation. Like the French, many of them often commuted between their homeland and California, while many others did return permanently to their native land. The Germans, on the other hand, generally meant to stay in California, maintaining a love for Germany but developing a loyalty to their new land. Germans soon numbered about half of San Francisco's merchant community, providing most of its professional musicians and operating most of the beer parlors and cigar stands. Their May Day celebrations, with parades and contests, became a publicly observed holiday, much as Bastille Day had done. The Chinese, Australians, Mexicans, Chileans, and Peruvians would all encounter persecution, although they were ignored at first. Welcome or not, immigrants from diverse peoples continued to come, bringing with them elements of cultures that were making California's character as one of the most heterogeneous of the American states.

This diverse atmosphere often encouraged the breaking

down of old prejudices and the abandonment of old ways. One Forty-Niner's long diary entries recount how he came from Connecticut, mined at Nevada City, and met a pretty French woman, a card dealer, to whom he lost $70 ($2,834 in 2023) ("four days of work for nothing"). Smitten, he determined to break his engagement to Hetty (sometimes Hettie), a woman back home. Marie, the French woman, went back to France for eleven months, during which time they exchanged some letters, his French and her English improving. When she returned to California, a year and eight months after they first met, they were married. This vivid entry indicates the change California had wrought in his attitudes:

> "what will the old folks say: a foreigner and a Catholic, and I brought up a strict Presbyterian. . . [anyway] she would make me a truer and more agreeable companion than some little, sniffling narrow-minded Puritan brought up on Calvinist doctrine and mince pie, predestined to dyspepsia and doctrinal doubting."[14]

The Gold Rush, as it quickly became known, was truly a spectacular, unique event where thousands of men, women, and children swarmed California seeking instant wealth. Where else has the discovery of a flake of one of earth's elements caused so many human beings to reorient their life's compass, pack belongings, and traverse thousands of miles into an unknown future?

**

"We feel puzzled to know our locality. We are here but do not know where here is."

–John Banks, 1849

**

In the Diggings

In the Diggings, as the mining country was called, the newcomers had to learn the arts of primitive living. There was no medicine. Homes were uncomfortable tents and shanties while clothing was nondescript and inadequate. Slow-cooking methods familiar to crock pot users today were used to prepare such food as there was.

The buildings in the camps sprang up without any thought to form or plan. Rough planks or canvas walls were the rule, and when fires burned them down, they simply sprang forth anew. A vacant spring valley might take on the appearance of a mushrooming metropolis by summer, then of a ghost town by fall when the last ounce of gold was mined. Or a bustling town might be washed into a gulch by the hoses of the later technology of hydraulic mining when gold was found under its foundations.

Wherever miners moved to rebuild, a retinue followed. Saloonkeepers came, often opening with nothing more elaborate than a plank spanning two barrels with hastily rigged canvas walls. One bartender reported a profit of $7,000 ($283,363 in 2023) on every barrel of whiskey sold. Prostitutes came next, filling the dance halls, gambling dives and brothels with the smell of perfume and cigars. Then came the merchants with their exorbitant prices.

Pimps in San Francisco waited for ships to arrive from Mexico with a load of women. They would go out on a small boat or launch, go aboard, and buy the women, who were then forced to prostitute themselves for a year, the pimp taking nearly all the cash. Some came fully knowing and willing, but the majority were duped. Patrice Dillon (c. 1812-57), first French consul in San Francisco, commented on those who sent indentured women to brothels in California: "Weeks never pass that some Chilean or American brig loaded by speculators does not discharge here a cargo of women. This sort of traffic is, they assure me, that which produces at the time the most prompt profits." [15]

The demand for prostitutes was insatiable. There were few other women in San Francisco in 1849-51. In 1849 only 300 women arrived, and many left for the mining camps. At the same time there were 8,000 men living San Francisco. In 1850 several thousand women came to San Francisco, but there were 20,000 to 25,000 men by then. Bayard Taylor (1825-78), sent by Horace Greeley (1811-72) to cover the Gold Rush for the *New York Daily Tribune*, painted the scene:

> "Think of a city of thirty thousand inhabitants peopled by men alone! The like of this was never seen before. Every man was his own housekeeper, doing in many instances, his own sweeping, cooking, washing, and mending. Many home arts, learned rather by observation than experience, come conveniently into play. He who cannot make a bed, cook a beefsteak, or sew up his own rips and rents is unfit to be a citizen of California." [16]

Another newspaperman, Benjamin E. Lloyd, added to the picture:

> "[When a young woman walked down the street the men] would gather around them, gaze earnestly upon them, and give utterance to some joyous exclamations, so pleasant were the recollections the sight awakened." [17]

To complete the picture so that even the most sheltered and naïve reader understood, as a young Frenchman, Albert Bernard de Russailh (1819-52), wryly recalled: "There are also some honest women in San Francisco, but not very many."[18] Being more direct in his observation he concluded, no doubt shaking his head, "If the poor fellows had known what these women had been in Paris, how one could pick them up on the boulevards and have them for almost nothing, they might not have been so free with their offers of $500 and 600 a night ($20,240-$24,288 in 2023)."[19]

This practice was once known as "white slavery," later "trafficking in women and children," and today is called "human trafficking," defined in federal law as "the threat or use of force, fraud, or coercion to obtain commercial sex acts, labor, or other services" (22 U.S.C. §7102[11]). There was no concerted international effort to suppress it prior to the 20th century; though condemned and warned against, it had been tolerated for millennia throughout the world. In 1902 a treaty between 17 nations (including the United States) was signed to adjust domestic laws to prosecute trafficking in girls under the age of 20, even if the victim gave consent, and criminalizing the act if committed across national borders; to take effect in 1910. In 1921 the newly formed League of Nations took up the issue with a Convention for the Suppression of the Traffic in Women and Children. This was adopted by the United Nations in 1947. Nevertheless, human trafficking remains a problem in California involving girls and women from Latin America, Russia, and Asia. It has grown exponentially with the growing control of the U.S. southern border from Texas to California by Mexican cartels.[20]

**

"There is no easy work about mining... it makes a man feel old in the morning."

-letter from Long Bar, 1856

**

Mining was hard work. But the miners did not typically complain about the hardships they found in the camp. It was often necessary to stand for hours in mud or icy streams, but the miners were conditioned to accept the rigors they found at their settlements. It was said that "the cowards never started; the weaklings died on the way."

Several anecdotes illustrate why miners were not much given to complaining: One man found a three-ounce (85 g) nugget while making a hole for a tent stake; another found a half-pound (227 g) nugget by rolling aside a rock he had been using for a seat; still another brought wealth back to town when he made a rich gold strike one moonlit night while he searched for his lost cow near what was thought to be a mined-out area. Who could believe that there would be an end to it all when a 141-pound (63kg) nugget was found in Sierra City, a 75-pound (34 kg) nugget in Woods Creek, and a 214-pound (97 kg) nugget in Calaveras County near Carson Hill?

Still the rewards of mining were uncertain. In 1848, men had easily taken a pound (454 g) a day, but by 1850 the average take was only a few grams, amounting to about two dollars ($77.48 in 2023) a day. Gold Rush prices made wealth elusive anyway.

Who ended up with the miner's gains? Given that the census of 1850 found that in Mariposa County, then California's largest, embracing most of the San Joaquin Valley and southern Sierra, men outnumbered women 22-1, and that the average age was twenty-four, the answer should not be hard to discern.

The favorite amusements in the camps were drinking, gambling, whoring, and dancing. Regarding gambling, one forty-niner wrote to his parents that "almost every public

House is a place for Gambling, this appears to be the greatest evil that prevails here. Men make *[sic]* lose thousands in a night, frequently small boys will go up bet $5 or 10-- ($202.40-$404.80 in 2023) if they lose all, go the next day dig more."[21]

There was an old ditty popular for many years after the Gold Rush to describe the origins of some of California's most influential families:

> The miners came in '49,
> The whores in '51,
> And when they got together
> They made the native son.[22]

The camps were not, in fact, as dissipated as pictured in legends and movies. Sundays in many camps were religious days, whether to hear the sermon of a traveling preacher, get over Saturday's hangover or do the week's wash. It could be a quiet day. The theater, the only form of entertainment the men knew from home, came to the camps, and such famed performers as Lotta Crabtree (1847-1924), Lola Montez (1818-61) and Edwin Booth (1833-93, brother of John Wilkes Booth, President Lincoln's assassin) played to enthusiastic audiences; in fact, there was a theater circuit between Mariposa and Rabbit Creek, in Butte County.

In the camps life was fast and cheap. Loans were made based on a month's calculated interest rather than on a years. A man who ran afoul of another might get himself shot; the shooter might be lynched, but that did nothing to help his victim.

Franklin Buck (1826-1909), a 23-year-old native of Maine, who came to California around the Horn in August 1849, left a description of miners' personal appearance in one of the many letters he wrote to his parents:

> "I am getting to be perfectly savage and at the same time quite domestic, for until within a week we cooked on board and I washed up the dishes. Have washed my own clothes ever since I left N.Y. I don't use much starch. White shirts I have discarded. They get dirty too quickly and don't wash half as easily as red flannel or calico. Shaving is all humbug. Nobody shaves here and you can't find a better looking set of men. I am going to have my daguerreotype taken and sent home to show you how I have improved. Full dress here is a pair of buckskin pants, fringed, with a red silk sash, fancy shirt and frock of buckskin trimmed with bell buttons and broad brimmed felt hat and revolver slung on one side and a Bowie knife on the other, with a pair of skins about a foot long. The horses are fine looking animals. The saddle I can't describe and here you have a picture of most of the miners. Although most everyone goes around with a revolver I have never seen one used but once."[23]

Holidays such as Christmas were not forgotten. *The Recollections of Joseph McCloskey* describes the Christmas of 1849 as it was experienced in the mining district:

> In the untrodden wilderness, 100 miles (161 km) as we supposed from any living soul..., seven of us built a gorgeous fire and sat around and swapped yarns. Every man had some tale of Christmas. Filled with the glow of
> good food and kindly company, we all sang the old Christmas songs again and again, the eyes of each man seeking and finding in the flames familiar scenes of home life far back in the East. Then when the blaze

had fallen to embers and the shadows began to steal in upon us from the forest, we shook hands all around with the clasp of friends, wished each other once more a Merry Christmas - and so to our blankets.[24]

On the Fourth of July,1851, Alfred Johnson, a possibly fictional character created by Chauncey Canfield (1843-1909), wrote "Everybody in the neighborhood [of Nevada City] went over to Selby Flat for the Fourth. Kellogg read the Declaration of Independence and Pard made one of the best speeches I ever listened to. The crowd went wild over it and I was mighty proud of him."[25]

**

"I really hope that no one will be deterred from coming here. The more fools the better -- the fewer to laugh when we get back home."

-Letter from the mines, 1850

**

"Now one word in relation to emigrating here: Say to all my friends: Stay at home, Tell my enemies to come."

-Jerome Dutton, 1850

**

A woman and three men panning for gold in 1850. (via Wikimedia Commons)

Many disillusioned miners ("the fools of '49' ") eventually left the pursuit of elemental gold. Some took up ranching in the Sacramento Valley, some returned home, and others - too proud to admit defeat or too poor to afford the passage - ended up in the cities. Many departed to follow gold discoveries elsewhere – to Oregon's Klamath Mountains (1850) and Willamette Valley (1861), to Australia's New South Wales and Victoria (1851), to Washington's Yakima Valley (1853), Colorado's Pike's Peak and British Columbia's Fraser River (1858), New Zealand's Otago province (1861), Idaho's Boise Basin and Montana's Bannack (1862), Arizona's La Paz and Maricopa (1863), and South Dakota's Black Hills (1874).[26] A little over a century ago, University of Wisconsin historian William Trimble noted the prevalence of those who had experienced the California mines in the new digs as they were opened: "But whatever elements of population prevailed in one or the other place, there was one everywhere present,

355

everywhere respected, everywhere vital – the Californian. To (many gold mining regions]. . . went the adopted sons of California – the youngest begetter of colonies – carrying with them the methods, the customs, and the ideas of the mother region."[27]

San Francisco, Sacramento and Stockton owe their growth to the Gold Rush, mainly because of men who put away their pans, picks and shovels; San Francisco's population went from 812 in January 1848 to nearly zero in June 1848, only to burgeon to 40,000 in December 1849, while rents skyrocketed as the El Dorado gambling saloon, at Washington and Kearny (across from Portsmouth Square) had to pay a rent of $40,000 ($1.6 million in 2023) a year.

Other places, the big cities of the Gold Rush - Grass Valley, Auburn, Sonora, and Placerville - rose and fell, becoming quasi-ghost towns for many years until the 1970s when urban pressures pushed many urbanites to mountain suburbs.

Stockton, named for the conqueror of Los Angeles and unique as one of the first planned communities in California, was founded by Charles Weber (1814-81), a German immigrant who had come west with Bidwell. In 1847 he created what became the city of Stockton, and in 1848 organized the first mining company in California, the Stockton Mining Company, as a general merchandising business. He soon decided that it was more profitable to outfit the miners than to prospect for gold. He sold the company and used the money to develop his new town, deciding to supply the thousands of wealth seekers going to the Stanislaus mines. He built a new commercial house and chartered ships to bring lumber and other material from San Francisco and Santa Cruz.[28] Like Sacramento, Stockton prospered because of its location on the rivers draining into San Francisco Bay; both cities were halfway between San Francisco (the investment center) and the mines (the investment), and all three were connected by stately riverboats that made overnight runs between San Francisco and the other two for many years - even after the railroad was built.[29]

In Los Angeles, wealth came from the huge cattle herds densely grazing on the nearby hills. The miners' demand for beef brought a new prosperity to the rancheros, who could build larger adobe homes, furnish them with expensive furniture and wear fancy clothes.

San Francisco would become a city of great restaurants, but it was not always so. In 1849 and 1850 restaurant meals were badly cooked, limited in choice and frightfully expensive. Most of the forty-niners had no alternative to eating out since they lived in rooming houses and hotels, several men to a room, without any cooking facilities.

At one of the better hotel dining rooms, a reasonably well-prepared but hardly lavish dinner cost five to twelve dollars ($197-$472 in 2023), without beer or wine, according to *The Annals of San Francisco*. Roast duck usually was to be had for five dollars; broiled quail for two dollars ($102 in 2023); a dozen canned oysters, one dollar ($39.25 in 2023); a small piece of roast pork or mutton seventy-five cents ($29.44 in 2023); and a piece of beef, the cheapest meat at the time, fifty cents ($19.62 in 2023). A helping of cabbage or squash was added for another fifty or seventy-five cents, and boiled potatoes - the size of walnuts - were twenty-five cents ($9.82 in 2023) each.

Only the most successful forty-niners could afford to eat so well. Most went to noisy, crowded restaurants in shacks or large tents and paid two dollars for a piece of greasy beefsteak, a weak cup of coffee and a slice of starchy pie. Cleanliness was virtually unknown in these establishments. Wrote Englishman William Ryan (1791-1855) in a letter back East: "There was dust on the counter, on the shelves, on the seats, on the decanters, and in them, on the tables, in the salt, on my beefsteak, and in my coffee." [30]

Under these trying circumstances, running a good restaurant or hotel dining room took hard work, imagination, and more than a little luck. "I found it difficult to keep up the boarding department," recalled John Henry Brown (1810-1905), manager of the City Hotel on Portsmouth Square, "and would have failed entirely had it not been for the fact that I was acquainted with captains of vessels, and consequently had an opportunity of procuring from them a portion of what they had for the use of their ships." Every time one of these ships sailed to Oregon, Brown ordered butter, ham, bacon, and eggs.

An old man named Herman delivered fresh cabbages, lettuce, carrots, and turnips to the City Hotel every day - at twenty-five dollars a bushel ($982 in 2023). "Another item of considerable expense to me," wrote Brown, "was the hiring of two hunters and a whale boat to go off up the creeks after game; they would make two trips per week and were usually very successful." [31]

Some men supported themselves by hunting, filling the city's markets with "delectable fresh game: deer, elks, rabbits, geese, ducks, quails, squirrels, even grizzly bears." To avoid the dollar-a-piece price for fresh eggs, some collected sea bird eggs by the hundreds at the Farallon Islands. "Climbing around the barren, windswept islands was hard work, as birds frantically circled overhead, but it was better than the job of sorting rotten eggs from the good ones on the mainland." [32] The removal of 14 million sea bird eggs certainly caused the near extinction of several bird species, but the hunters' introduction of invasive species such as dogs, cats, goats, and rabbits caused more harm. Today the main culprits are house mice, who have destroyed at least 54% of the island fauna by consuming their eggs.[33]

Even though Brown, like everyone else, charged inflated Gold Rush prices for his meals, the City Hotel dining room lost $100 ($3,925 in 2023) a day on food. Brown nevertheless made up his losses and turned an overall profit on the dining room from enormous sales of wine and liquor with the meals.

One major change in dining habits that added a sophisticated air to San Francisco restaurants was the introduction of snails - *Helix aspera* or escargots - from France. Antoine Delmas (1818-88) came to San Jose from France in 1849, and two years later imported the first French vines (labeled Cabrunet, Merleau and Black Meunier) to California. In 1861 he brought with him something less appreciated at first, a sack of European brown snails. Thus began the California gardener's problem with the mollusk, previously unknown anywhere within its borders.[34]

Another culinary innovation utilized something that had been there all along but had gone unnoticed by all but the Indians – the abalone. Coastal Indians had been harvesting, boiling, or smoking abalone for untold centuries. Chinese fishermen, who knew abalone from the coast of China, began to fish for it in the 1850s, collecting most of it from the shallow intertidal zones. Abalone was also known in England, the west coast of France and the Mediterranean, but it had not caught on with Americans because it was not found on the East or Gulf coasts. A new market opened for this suddenly new food, and San Francisco restaurants were quick to adopt it.[35]

Not all of those who returned home after giving up on mining were losers. Deaf and mostly blind, Edmund Booth

(1810-1905), an Iowan who spent five years in the camps (1849-54), was called home by his wife and eventually went into the newspaper business. He described a California scene that was anything but one of poverty:

"In January or February [1854] a letter came from wife urging me to return home. It was very urgent and I concluded to return and no further delay. I was then working a good place at Camp Seco. "The ground we were working was paying well. That is, we would spend a day in stripping off the top of say four feet (1.22 m) wide, six feet (1.83 m) long and three (91.5 cm) or five feet (1.5 m) deep. Next day turn the water from the ditch into our long tom and dig and throw in the lower dirt till we reached rock, perhaps two feet (61 cm). Took out $10 to $30 ($392.50- to $1,177.50 in 2023) each day we washed the dirt....

"But, being anxious to return home, I proceeded to San Francisco by stage and steamer. I waited, with friends, a few days till the steamer sailed.

We were twelve days at sea and reached port in due time. Crossed over to Virgin Bay in Lake Nicaragua on mule back. We were in all 500 passengers.

Took two steamers to foot of lake and there changed to two stern-wheelers and entered the San Juan River and thence to its mouth on

the Atlantic. Saw tropical vegetation and many curiosities on the way.

"We reached the fort on the Atlantic side of the continent without any accident. Waited some hours. A large boat took us to a vessel for New Orleans, and another did the same for those bound

for New York."[36]

The Rush was over for Mr. Booth; in a few years it would

be over for everyone else.

The Gold Rush would have five major effects: (1) a change in worldwide price structure by flooding the market with o gold while significant amounts of labor and goods were diverted to gold-seeking, (2) new arguments for developing American transportation, (3) increased population diversity in California, (4) the development of San Francisco as a major world port, and (5) the beginning of a persistent belief in California as a place to start over.

**

Bancroft gives a short list of mining camps' names derived from natural features, discoverers, nationalities, experiences, and lifestyle. Some of these were renamed after the Gold Rush, some remained, and others disappeared as towns themselves disappeared. Among the names listed: Whiskey, Brandy and Drunkard's Bars, Keno, Euchre, and Poker Flats, Fiddletown, Jim Crow, You Bet, Red Dog, Ranty Doodler, Greenhorn, Loafer Hill, Chicken Thief Flat, Yankee Jim's, Dutch Flat, Hoosier, Buckeye, Nigger Bar, Greaser Flat, Chinese Flat, Horseshoe Bar, Last Chance, Lousy Level, Liar's Flat, Pinch-em-tight, Bogus Thunder, Humbug, and Poverty Flats, Murderer's Bar, Gouge Eye, Dead Man's Gulch, Otter, Grizzly, Jackass, Wildcat, Green Mountain, Deadwood, Blizzardville. There were, as one might expect, some respectable and patriotic new California place names dating from the mining era, such as Washington, Jackson, Carson, and Boston.[37]

Military Government Protested

During the Mexican-American War, both Sloat and Stockton had promised a territorial government as soon as practical. Every American state except the original thirteen colonies, Vermont, Kentucky, Maine and Texas had been territories before becoming states so this was not an unusual step. Territories differed from states in several respects: states elected their governors while territorial governors were appointed by the president; states made their own laws without congressional review while territories could not; states had voting members of Congress while territorial delegates could only speak, but not vote. When a territory acquired a sufficient population it could apply to Congress for statehood, and if Congress passed an enabling act, it could set up a state government, the form of which Congress and the president had to approve.

While the war went on the new American territories were ruled by the army, the revolt in southern California seeming to justify the lack of a civilian government. Between July 1846 and December 1849, there were seven military governors with the title of Governor General; the only civilian officials in California were the *alcaldes*. When the hostilities ceased with the Cahuenga Capitulation, the only conflict in Upper California during the remainder of the Mexican War involved Stockton, Frémont, and Kearney, who could not agree on who was to be the supreme authority in this newly conquered land. In this volatile dispute Stockton and Frémont took sides against Kearney. The problem was resolved only after Colonel Richard Mason (1797-1850) was sent from Missouri to be interim governor, and Kearney, Frémont, and Stockton had departed. On the journey home, Kearney had Frémont arrested. A court-martial followed, which led to the Frémont's resignation from the army, something his powerful father-in-law, Senator Thomas Hart Benton, could not prevent. However, President Polk pardoned him.

The Californios accepted military rule, having nothing better to compare it to, but Americans in California despised it. The Americans believed in the principle dating from the beginning of the Republic that "the Constitution follows the flag." According to this principle, people in any place ruled by the United States had the rights and duties of any person within the borders of the United States; nowhere were American civilians ruled by the army. (This principle was rejected by the Supreme Court in the Insular Cases in 1901). The alcaldes functioned in some places as combination mayor, sheriff, judge, and tax collector, while in other, larger places there were several *alcaldes*. Brannan's *California Star* contrasted the Americans' governmental convictions with the Californios' quite different attitude: "the alcaldes exercise authority far greater than any officer in our republic - the president excepted.... The grand autocrat of the Russians [sic]. . . is the only man in Christendom I know of who equals him."[38]

This was the "no-government period" of the state's history. Governor General Mason realized that the system of military government could not be changed until after the Treaty of Guadalupe Hidalgo was ratified, so he composed a temporary code keeping such Mexican laws as were practical for the current situation. The treaty had been ratified on May 20, 1848, three months after it was signed, and the news reached Mason on August 6, about the time his code was printed and set to be distributed. He might have saved his energy, for it would not be distributed after all. It would have been ignored in any case, since most people did not respect military authority. The public demanded a legal system – a civilian legal system, the sooner the better.

These demands became more intense after news of the peace reached California. The end of the war seemed to intensify demands for civilian government, as the exigencies of warfare were now removed. However insistent, these demands were generally ignored. Thus began a 28-month period of no legitimate government, a desperate situation as hard to comprehend now as it was then, a plight associated today with regions of the world racked by government breakdown due to tribal warfare, for example, in parts of the Middle East, areas often branded "failed states." In the words of Josiah Royce (1855-1916), although with short-sighted exaggeration, "[California was] to be morally and socially tried as no other American community ever had been tried."[39]

Congress saw the need to do something about California and the Southwest, but it procrastinated. In August 1848 Congress created the Oregon Territory, separating it from California because Oregon had a large white population while California was popularly but incorrectly characterized as composed of a "half-Indian population." Since California was being ignored by Congress, President Polk justified the existence of a de facto government there by what he termed the "great law of necessity" under the President's War Powers.[40] The prevailing opinion was that Oregon was a land of boundless fertility, but few politicians on the East Coast viewed California as likewise promising. South Carolina Senator George McDuffie (1790-1851) expressed a typical doubt as to the value of the entire western third of the continent: "Of what use will it be for agriculture? I would not for that purpose give one pinch of snuff for the whole of it."[41] Massachusetts Senator Daniel Webster reputedly argued against a bill to extend mail service to California by saying that he "would not vote one cent from the public treasury to bring the Pacific Coast one inch (2.54 cm) closer to Boston. What do we want with that desolate land?"[42] To add insult to injury, in March 1849 Congress created the Minnesota Territory, and further complicating matters, in May 1848 Wisconsin became a state, temporarily tipping the balance in favor of the free states; the next admitted state would have to be a slave state to restore the balance demanded by the Missouri Compromise. Oregon and Wisconsin were free soil territories while California would be questionable. President Taylor, a hero of the Mexican-American War, elected in 1848, chose political caution and decided not to deal with the matter; an older man (now 64), he wanted a quiet, non-controversial administration. Despite his preference for avoiding conflict, when the issue came to a head, he would deal with it forthrightly.

The Gold Rush briefly took peoples' minds off politics, but in the winter of 1848-49, when the Sierra snows kept men from mining, interest was renewed. Senator Benton had written a public letter to the people of California contending that with the end of the war they had the right to be rid of military authority and to govern themselves. A public meeting in San Jose on December 11, 1848, demanded self-government. There followed another such meeting on February 12, 1849, in San Francisco's Portsmouth Square (named for John Montgomery's U.S.S. *Portsmouth*, his vessel when he raised the flag at Yerba Buena.) The crowd gathered there formed the Legislative Assembly for the District of San Francisco. There were additional mass meetings in Sacramento, Monterey, and Santa Cruz, also demanding a constitutional convention to form a civilian territorial government. The petitions were presented to Mason's replacement, Governor General Persifer Smith (1798-1858), who, in part because of his racist sentiments regarding Mexicans and Indians, absolutely rejected them and the authority of the San Francisco Assembly; his attitude was best summed up by his proclamation that all non-U.S. citizens in the gold mines were trespassers. It would be in Congress' authority to call for the convention, but Smith refused to accept the petitions for forwarding.

Two theories framed the arguments during this "no-government period": The *"Settlers Theory,"* so named by Hunt and Sánchez; and the *"Administration Theory."*[43] The Settlers Theory expresses the philosophy espoused by the vast majority of Americans residing in California, and expounded by Benton in his letter to the people. It held that with the end of military necessity it was time for self-rule. The Administration Theory, stoutly upheld by Mason and Smith, was the belief that until Congress authorizes a change for the Mexican Cession, the laws on the books at the end of the war remain in force. On the one hand, the Administration Theory had, and would have to this day, support in international law; furthermore, the office of civil governor being then vacant, the military governor would be the ex-officio civil governor as well, making bodies such as the Legislative Assembly of San Francisco unnecessary and illegal. On the other hand, with the Mexican civil law in fact superseded, it was Congress' duty to create a territorial government. Since it had not done so, the people were within their Constitutional rights to create some sort of civil government, making bodies such as the Legislative Assembly practical, necessary and legal.

Something had to be done. Fortunately, a solution was at hand.

**

"California entered the union on a bet. The bet was that the country would eventually be called California and not America."

-Will Rogers

**

Organizing a State

In the election of 1848, war hero Zachary Taylor, a Whig, defeated the Democrat Lewis Cass (1782-1866). He was a Southern slave owner who did not favor expanding slavery into the West because he knew that cotton and sugar would not easily be grown on profitable plantations as they were in the South. To avoid the inevitable sectional problems over slavery he encouraged both California and New Mexico to apply for statehood as soon as possible.

In April 1849 General Bennett Riley (1787-1853) became California's military governor. When Congress adjourned in June without acting on California or the Southwest, Riley took matters into his own hands.

Riley was particularly irritated by the politicians because they did not appreciate his situation. He had been given the task of maintaining law and order in California, but without the necessary tools. The army hardly existed as soldier after soldier deserted to mine: Gold at $16 per ounce was far more intriguing than army pay of seven dollars per month ($648 and $284 in 2023). Riley was often heard to declare that he didn't have enough men to stop a dogfight, let alone maintain real order.

The politicians did not realize what was happening in California. There, "for the first time in human history, gold belonged exclusively to the man who found it. No god demanded a tithe, no king expected a fifth, nor did any landowner keep a percentage."[44] There were no laws to prescribe who could dig for gold, or where or in what manner. The laws of Mexico no longer applied, and the United States had no legislation covering this type of situation. The military officers in charge of this newly acquired land had no orders. California had no government, so miners made and enforced their own laws, many of which remain as working rules within the mining industry. Gold had made California, but the United States government did not know what to do with this new creation. Some sagely realized that if the situation persisted, California might look elsewhere for national identity. Forty-niner Sheldon Shufelt (1839-1901), who had come from New York via Panama, wrote to his cousin in the East that "if something is not done soon by the government, we shall make our own laws execute them too, for we have the cash plenty of *grit* enterprise to carry them out."[45]

Though he had no legal authority to do so Riley ordered elections for delegates to a convention to meet at Colton Hall, home of Monterey *Alcalde* and newspaper publisher Walter Colton (1797-1851), to organize a civilian government. It was his intention to present the United States government with a *fait accompli*, and legal formalities be damned!

Almost coincidentally Georgia Congressman Thomas Butler King (1800-64) was sent as a secret agent by President Taylor to San Francisco to find out as much as possible about the desire for self-government, and to promote the idea of a state constitution and eventual admission to the Union.

There were ten election districts, and 48 men were elected to attend the convention. Most of these delegates were from the northern districts, most had lived in California before the Gold Rush, and most were under the age of fifty. They were a strangely assorted gathering of men: politicians in silk and beaver top hats, serious-minded scholars, and opportunistic miners in high boots and fur caps. Men of learning convened with men who could neither read nor write. Riley opened the motley convention in September, and the delegates elected seven-foot (2.1 m) tall Robert Semple (1806-54) of Kentucky as chairman. Semple had been a trailblazer, dentist, doctor, backwoodsman, preacher, editor of the *Philadelphia North*

American, and, with Walter Colton, founder of California's first newspaper, *The Californian*.

The first act of the delegates was to reject any notion of a territorial government and choose a state government instead. Though unprecedented for a place that was not independent (Vermont and Texas) or part of another state (Kentucky), California did have the population and the relative wealth to qualify.

The major problem the delegates confronted was the location of an eastern boundary. The northern and southern boundaries had been established by the Adams-Onís Treaty and the Treaty of Guadalupe-Hidalgo, and the southeastern boundary had been in effect since the province of Sonora was created. What criteria would be used to define California's eastern boundary?

Some wanted a large state, with the boundary at the Rockies. Others wanted a small state with the boundary at the crest of the Sierra. There were three proposals for lines in between, for example at 116o W (today Battle Mountain, Nevada). The westernmost of these other three was finally settled on, although it would not become official for another decade. The selected one did not include the Mormons at Salt Lake since they were not represented at the convention. It did not include most of the Great Basin because there was a general desire to let the army be responsible for the expense of protecting travelers, but it did include the entire mining district.

There were heated debates on whether dueling should be allowed (it was not); and on whether women should be allowed to continue to control property in their possession before marriage (they were). When it was proposed that all persons charged with criminal offenses be tried by a jury of their peers, one delegate reportedly shouted: "What the hell do we want with peers? This ain't no monarchy!"

There were no other controversies at the convention. It was agreed (even by those from the slave states) that California would be a free state, there would be a bicameral legislature modeled on Congress, laws would be in English and Spanish, and judges would be elected.[46]

Although most delegates had no political training or experience, they crafted a fine document, and when it was submitted to the voters during the stormy December of 1849 it was accepted almost unanimously (12,900 for, 800 against). As 1849 was ending, superior court Judge Peter Burnett (1807-95) of Oregon was elected governor, a legislature was elected, and William M. Gwin (1805-85) of Tennessee, a medical doctor and a lawyer, and Frémont were chosen as U. S. senators. They left for Washington to apply for statehood, presenting their petition to Congress on February 13, 1850.

A striking tribute to the excellence of the document is that it inspired the constitution Argentina adopted in 1853. The father of that constitution, Juan Bautista Alberdi (1810-84), said of the California document:

"Without universities, without academies or law colleges, the newly-organized people of California have drawn up a constitution full of foresight, of common sense and of opportunity."[47]

Congress was less than thrilled that the Californians had constituted a government without an enabling act, and Southern congressmen were outraged that California would be a free state. Though a Southerner, Gwin could not talk them out of their anger about it. The Southern states feared that if California came in as a free state the balance would be forever tipped against them. At the same time Southerners were incensed that the spoils of the war with Mexico would not fall to them, especially since they had been loudest in support of the war and had done much of the fighting. After all, James Russell Lowell had predicted in a poem:

> They just want this Californy
> So's to lug new slave states in
> To abuse ye, an' to scorn ye,
> An' to plunder ye like sin.[48]

On August 8, 1846, three months after war had been declared and two days before Congress was to adjourn, Polk submitted a bill to authorize $2,000,000 ($80.9 million in 2023) to facilitate negotiations with Mexico over the final settlement of the war. Congressman David Wilmot (1814-68) of Pennsylvania, who had not cast a vote on the issue of declaring war, introduced a rider to the appropriations bill that any new territory that might be won from Mexico be closed to slavery. The Wilmot Proviso, as it became known, was passed by a House vote of 83-64. In the Senate it was not voted on because the session ended. When the next session opened in December, Polk asked for an additional $3,000,000 ($121.4 million in 2023), and the House re-attached the Proviso to this request. The entire bill passed 115-106, while in the Senate the appropriation bill passed, but without the Proviso, and the Senate version prevailed. The Wilmot Proviso, considered insulting by moderates, might have gone nowhere, but the numbers were in its favor, and its chance of prevailing in a Congress where the representatives of the free states outnumbered the slave states 60% to 40% infuriated the South.

To protect themselves nine of the fifteen Southern states held a convention in Nashville in June 1850 to consider secession. 176 attended, mostly from South Carolina, Tennessee, and Mississippi (Louisiana and North Carolina did not). The South Carolinians were hot for secession, but cooler heads prevailed, and the convention took a watchful, waiting stance. Its presiding officer, Mississippi Judge William Sharkey (1798-1873), declared that it had not been "called to prevent but to perpetuate the Union," and his influence carried the day with an endorsement of the idea that the Missouri Compromise line be extended to the Pacific Coast.[49]

**

"California became a full-grown state while one-half of the world still doubted its existence."

-J. D. Borthwick, 1857

**

Senator Henry Clay (1777-1852) a Kentucky Whig, had served in the Congress since 1806 as an appointee, since 1811 by election, and had been secretary of state in 1825-29. His career bore fruit in two nation-saving compromises: the Missouri Compromise of 1820 and the Tariff of 1833, which rolled back the Tariff of 1828 that had hurt Southern planters to benefit Northern factories. Both were in response to the South's fear of what it perceived as creeping Northern dominance and a threat to slavery.

Two other Senators stood with Clay on the pillars of American history in the first half of the 19th century: Massachusetts Whig Daniel Webster and South Carolina Democrat John C. Calhoun (1782-1850). The three were known as the "Great Triumvirate", sometimes allied, at other times opposed to one another, but each patriotic, upright, and gifted with great oratorical skills.

Now, with California applying for a *fait accompli* statehood as a free state and the Southern states again talking secession, another compromise was worked out by Henry

Clay, the Compromise of 1850. It provided several points for each side: that California would become a free state; that the rest of the Mexican Cession would be divided between two territories, Utah and New Mexico, with no mention of slavery; the slave trade – but not slavery – would be abolished in Washington, DC; Texas would be compensated for the land given to New Mexico Territory; and a stronger, federally-enforced Fugitive Slave Law would be enacted. Webster backed it; Taylor and Calhoun opposed it. President Taylor felt the South deserved nothing, and Calhoun because he felt the South was being hurt, perhaps mortally. Great debates were held, a somewhat free-for-all scene of Southern Whigs versus Southern Democrats versus Northern Democrats versus Northern Whigs.[50] Clay, a Southern Whig, was supported by Northern Democrats and initially opposed by Northern Whigs, while Calhoun, a Southern Democrat, was supported by Southern Democrats but opposed by Southern Whigs.[51]

The Compromise of 1850 was ultimately adopted, although in the Senate voting on each provision, sectionalism reared its head. Ironically, neither Calhoun nor Webster nor Clay voted on the finished product as Calhoun had died on March 31, Webster had become secretary of state on July 23, and Clay was absent. Taylor had died of intestinal illness on July 9, a disappointment to the Southern Whigs, who had looked on him as one of theirs. He was succeeded by his vice president, Millard Fillmore (1800-74, served 1850-53), a conservative and practical New Yorker. California was the first issue to be taken up by the new administration, and on August 13 the Compromise passed 34 to 18, with eight (including Clay, its author) not voting. None of those present from the free states voted against it, six of the 23 present from the slave states voted for it, three of the slave states were split (Missouri, Tennessee and Texas), and neither of North

Carolina's senators voted. Had the absentees in fact voted with their section, it would not have changed the outcome.[52]

In the House the vote to admit California was even more decisive. On September 7 the measure finally passed by 150 to 56, with 23 not voting. Again, all of those from the free states voted in favor of admission, as did all of those from slave states Delaware and Maryland, while four split also on party lines (Kentucky, 6 Whigs and 1 Democrat in favor, 2 Democrats against; Missouri, 4 in favor, 1 against, all Democrats; North Carolina 2 Whigs in favor, 4 Whigs and 3 Democrats against; and Tennessee 4 Whigs and 3 Democrats in favor, 4 Democrats against.) [53]

In the House Virginia Democratic Congressman James Seddon (1815-80), replying to Georgia Whig Robert Toombs (1810-85), who had voted "no," assessed the prospect of "compensating" the South for the "loss" of California and the "truncating" of Texas by "offering" it Utah and New Mexico:

> "The only chance remaining to the South is in the isolated desert portion of the Great Basin, which has been abandoned, from its worthlessness, to the Mormons, and even in regard to that I wish now to test whether there is really to be, on the part of the South, due privileges of participation in its enjoyment.... "I ask him in all sincerity... if he does not consider the sanctions which have been taken this day given by Congress to the unauthorized usurpations by the hordes who occupied California, of the vast domains embraced by their constitution, and to the exclusion by a proviso in the form of organic law, of the citizens of slaveholding States with their property, from all participation in the enjoyment of this modern El Dorado,
> an aggression and a wrong?"[54]

374

On Monday, September 9, 1850, President Fillmore admitted California as the 31st state. Four Southern senators led by Mississippi Democrat Jefferson Davis (1808-89) objected to the seating of Senators Frémont and Gwin when they presented themselves on the 11th but, in Bancroft's words, "it was the last kick at their dead lion, and ineffectual."[55] When the news reached San Francisco six weeks later, on October 18, by the clipper ship Oregon, there was "a day of great rejoicing." The ship entered "the Golden Gate at noon on a beautiful day – with flags and banners flying at every pennant, firing a salute of minute guns. We had already heard the reports," Henry Lee Dodge (1825-1902) wrote to his brother in Vermont, "and suspected their true meaning. She made the shortest trip on record for a mail steamer, eager to give us the earliest information.... We now look for a dawn of better days....[F]lags were raised, guns fired – and any quantity of champagne spilled...."[56]On a political note the state government created by the voters in December could now function legitimately, able to enact and enforce laws and collect taxes.

The first two legislatures were very poor examples of democracy in action. The first (1849-51) was known as the "Legislature of a thousand drinks" because Senator Thomas Green (1802-63) always moved for adjournment to a nearby saloon before taking a vote; on a more staid note, he also sponsored the bill that created the University of California. The second legislature (1851-53) was called "ignorant, infamous and rowdy."

The capital moved around a bit. The military governors had been stationed at Monterey, but the importance of the gold district led to a movement to locate a seat nearer to the wealth. San Francisco, San Jose, San Luis Obispo, Stockton, and Santa Barbara all put in bids. San Jose became capital in 1849-

51, but the legislators were not happy with the location because there were no buildings suitable for a state government. Then General Vallejo offered the state land at Benicia on the Carquínez Straits, so the capital was there in 1852-53. Tired of the post, Governor Burnett resigned in January 1851 to resume his legal practice in San Francisco. His successor, John McDougal (1818-66), moved the government archives from San Jose to Benicia in June 1851, and still no suitable place for state business had been found. The windiness at Benicia, from the climate, not from politicians, added to the legislators' displeasure, and they sought a better place. San Jose put in a bid, as did San Francisco and Sacramento. Finally, Sacramento was chosen in March 1854 for its location halfway between San Francisco, the investment center, and the mines, the wealth source. Budget problems delayed completion of the present capitol building until 1874.

**

The last official description of the Great Seal of the State of California, written in 1937, was encapsulated by James Hart: "This seal, adopted (October 2, 1849) by the Constitutional Convention, was designed by Major Robert S. Garnett [1819-61], a Virginia-born army officer stationed in Monterey. It depicts Minerva ([Roman] goddess of wisdom, sprung full-grown from Jupiter's brow, just as California was conceived as being born a full-fledged state, without infancy as a territorial government) seated on a mountain side, a small grizzly bear, wheat, and grapes at her feet. San Francisco Bay with ships and the Sierra Nevada in the background, (a Spanish mission on the upper left side of the waterway,] a miner at work, the motto 'Eureka,' ['I have found it' in Greek] and 31 stars (representing the number of U.S. states upon the admission of California) above Minerva's helmet and spear.

The whole circular picture is framed by the words "The Great Seal of the State of California."[57]

**

The First Counties Organized

In February 1850 the first legislature imported the system used in most of the United States and their organized counties. They were to be the immediate tier of government between the statewide and the local government, each county to have a superior court and to be governed by an elected board of supervisors who would operate in a county seat. They would then be divided into *townships* of 36 square mile (93.24 sq km) units, a square mile (2.6 sq km) to be a *section* for surveying and platting property lines. At the beginning there were 27. Since 1907 there have been 58. As a county's population increased in different areas, one area might seek to become its own county. Owen C. Coy's (1884-1952) 1923 compilation of the development of county boundaries remains the standard.

Prior to the American conquest there were five districts in California: San Diego, Los Angeles, Santa Barbara, Monterey, and San Francisco. When General Riley called for election of delegates to the Constitutional Convention of 1849, he designated ten districts: San Diego, Los Angeles, Santa Barbara, San Luís Obispo, Monterey, San José, Sonoma, San Francisco, San Joaquín, and Sacramento. When the first state legislature divided the state into counties, it created a special committee under General Vallejo to achieve this goal. The committee presented its report in January 1850 and proposed 18 counties. Finally, on February 18, Governor McDougal signed the act creating the first 27.

They were San Diego, Los Angeles, Santa Barbara, San

Luis Obispo, Monterey, Branciforte (changed to Santa Cruz), San Francisco, Santa Clara, Contra Costa, Marin, Sonoma, Solano, Yola (changed to Yolo), Napa, Mendocino, Sacramento, El Dorado, Sutter, Yuba, Butte, Colusi (changed to Colusa), Shasta, Trinity, Calaveras, San Joaquin, Tuolumne, and Mariposa. With the exceptions of Sutter and Butte (named for a Hudson's Bay Company trapper), the first counties' names were of Spanish or Indian origin.

Beginning in 1851, the first counties were subdivided. In 1851-57 Nevada (from Yuba), Placer (from Yuba and Sutter), Alameda (from Contra Costa), Humboldt (from Trinity), San Bernardino (from Los Angeles and San Diego), Sierra (from Yuba), Siskiyou (from Shasta), Tulare (from Mariposa and Los Angeles), Amador (from Calaveras and El Dorado), Plumas (from Butte), Stanislaus (from Tuolumne), Merced (from Mariposa), Fresno (from Mariposa, Merced and Tulare), San Mateo (from San Francisco), Tehama (from Shasta, Butte and Colusa), and Del Norte (from Klamath) were formed. In 1861-66 Lake, Mono (from Calaveras and Fresno), Alpine (from Amador, Calaveras, El Dorado and Tuolumne), Lassen (from Plumas and Shasta), Inyo (originally to be called "Coso," from Mono and Tulare), and Kern (from Los Angeles and Tulare) were formed. In 1872-74 Ventura (from Santa Barbara), Modoc (from Siskiyou) and San Benito (from Monterey) were formed. In 1889-93 Orange (from Los Angeles), Glenn (from Colusa), Kings (from Tulare), Madera (from Fresno) and Riverside (from San Bernardino and San Diego) were created. In 1907 Imperial (from San Diego) was the latest county brought into existence by these amoeba-like splits.

There were four other counties in the state's early history: Klamath, Pautah, Buena Vista and Nataqua. Klamath had been created from Trinity in 1851 on the northwest coast at the Oregon border, but it lost most of its territory when Del Norte was created in 1857. A small population and low assessed values made county government for Klamath too burdensome; in 1874 the people voted to disestablish it, the only county to be disestablished, and to petition the legislature to divide it between Siskiyou and Humboldt, an act finally completed in 1876. Pautah was a former county (1852-59) created by the legislature out of land that it believed was to be ceded by Congress. Congress never did so, and the county that never really existed was abolished by the legislature and officially ceded to then-Utah Territory; it now consists roughly of several Nevada counties: Douglas, Esmeralda, Lyon, Mineral, Storey, Washoe (southern half), and Carson City. Buena Vista never really existed either. It was created by the legislature in 1855 out of the southern portion of Tulare, but was never organized, and became part of Kern when it was created in 1866.

Nataqua Territory, at Honey Lake Valley in northeastern California, was proclaimed independent of the state in 1855 by Peter Lassen (1800-59) and Isaac Roop (1822-69). It was short-lived as a maverick political entity because it was never recognized by Congress. When Congress created the Nevada Territory out of Utah Territory in 1861, the region was conditionally included if California would cede it. A boundary dispute ensued in February 1863, known as the Sagebrush War. When California reasserted jurisdiction over the claimed separate entity, Roop continued to claim independence, even naming his cabin in the "capital" of Susanville "Fort Defiance." Hunkered down in his "fort" he defied the sheriff of Plumas County in a gun battle that was the only actual shooting campaign of the so-called war. When he accepted an armistice, the California-Nevada boundary was redrawn by the legislature to include Roop's territory in Lassen County. Susanville (named for Roop's daughter) became the county seat.

Chapter Seven END NOTES

[1] *Los Angeles Times*, January 21, 1900: "DEATH OF A PIONEER Francisco Lopez Succumbs to Infirmities of Old Age / Francisco Lopez, one of the oldest residents of Los Angeles, died . . .in his eightieth year. The deceased was born in what is now San Diego county in 1820 and was a family of early settlers..." Santa Clarita Valley History, http://www.scvhistory.com/scvhistory/obituary_franciscolopez.htm.

[2] David McLaughlin,"The Padre's Gold," California Missions Resource Center, https://www.missionscalifornia.com/wp-content/uploads/2022/01/The-Padres-Gold-Final.pdf Michael Warren, "California's First Gold Rush," *The New 49'ers,* http://www.goldgold.com/californias-first-gold-rush.html; Leon Worden, "California's REAL First Gold" , *COINage Magazine* (October 2005), http://www.scvhistory.com/scvhistory/signal/coins/worden-coinage1005.htm.

[3] Theodore H. Hittell, "The Gold Discovery" in *History of California*, vol 2. San Francisco: N.J. Stone, 1897, http://www.sfmuseum.org/hist6/impact.html.

[4] Bill Bagley, "Latter-Day Scoundrel Sam Brannan" History Net; originally published by *Wild West Magazine* (August 14, 2008), http://www.historynet.com/latter-day-scoundrel-sam-brannan.htm; Dickson, *San Francisco*, pp. 10-18; Richard Dillon, *Humbugs and Heroes: A Gallery of California Pioneers.* (Garden City NJ: Doubleday, 1970), pp. 56-59; Paul Bailey, "Sam Brannan and the Mormons in Early California," Part 3, The Improvement Era 45, no. 1 (December 1942), p. 793, http://files.lib.byu.edu/mormonmigration/articles/SamBrannanAnd TheMormonsInEarlyCalifornia.PDF. "Mormon Role in California is Outlined," *Fresno Bee*, March 21, 1954, p. 32-D.

[5] There was even a lawsuit (*James Eldredge v. John Cowell*) filed in May 1852 and decided by the state Supreme Court in January 1854 over claims to three of the ships by one man who wanted to extend a pier and another who wanted them for a

warehouse; Cowell got his warehouse. Eldredge vs Cowell (1854), 4 Cal Sup Ct 80. Reports of Cases Determined in the Supreme Court of the State of California. H. P. Hepburn, Reporter. Volume 4 with Notes on Cal. Reports. San Francisco: Bancroft-Whitney, 1906. 80-88, https://books.google.com/books?id=C8hGAQAAIAAJ&dq=James +Eldredge+vs+John+Cowell&source=gbs_navlinks_s; Judith Robinson, "Ships Beneath the City," *San Francisco Sunday Examiner & Chronicle: California Living*, December 7, 1980, pp. 54-61.

[6] M. Guy Bishop, "After Sutter's Mill: The Life of Henry Bigler, 1848-1900," wchsutah.org/people/henry-william-bigler3.pdf; Albert S. Bowles, "Gold Mining in America" (1879), in *Old West Legends,* http://www.legendsofamerica.com/we-mininggold.html.

[7] *California As I Saw It: First-Person Narratives of California's Early Years, 1849-1900*: Enos Christman to Ellen Apple, December 14, 1849, in the Sea Journal 2, p. 62, in Florence Morrow Christman, *One man's gold: the letters and journal of a forty-niner, Enos Christman.* (New York: McGraw-Hill, 1930), https://catalog.loc.gov/vwebv/search?searchArg=christman%2C+e nos&searchCode=GKEY%5E*&searchType=0&recCount=25

[8] *California As I Saw It*: Hiram Dwight Pierce. *A forty-niner speaks; a chronological record of a New Yorker and his adventures in various mining localities in California, his return trip across Nicaragua, including several descriptions of the changes in San Francisco and other mining centers from March 1849 to January 1851.* With illustrations by the author. Introduction signed by Sarah Wiswall Meyer. (Oakland: Keystone-Inglett, 1930), https://catalog.loc.gov/vwebv/holdingsInfo?searchId=20598&recC ount=25&recPointer=0&bibId=9216846

[9] Dickson, *San Francisco*, pp. 359-64.

[10] "Highway 88: the historic trail of Kit Carson and the Mormons," *Motorland*, September-October 1978, pp. 40-43. *Motorland* is the official magazine of AAA. This is taken from Thomas Hunt, *Ghost Trails to California,* (Reno: Nevada Publications: 1987).

[11] Lynn Bonfield Donovan, "Cagwins Give Overland Diary to

CHS", *CHSC*, April 1977, p. 3.

[12] *California As I Saw It*: David Rohrer Leeper. *The argonauts of 'forty-nine, some recollections of the plains and the diggings.* Illustrated by O. Marion Elbel. (South Bend IN: J.B. Stoll, 1894), https://catalog.loc.gov/vwebv/holdingsInfo?searchId=20504&recCount=25&recPointer=2&bibId=9595450

[13] For a guide to the top 10 Chinese deities see "Chinese mythology: Your Guide to the Gods of the Middle Kingdom," (2012), www.godchecker.com/pantheon/chinese-mythology.php

[14] *California As I Saw It*: Chauncey Canfield, editor. *The Diary of a forty-niner.* (Boston: Houghton-Mifflin, 1920). Purports to be the diary of Alfred T. Jackson probably a fictitious name, https://catalog.loc.gov/vwebv/holdingsInfo?searchId=20250&recCount=25&recPointer=0&bibId=9146433

[15] Charles Lockwood, "All That Glitters is Not Gold," *San Francisco Sunday Examiner & Chronicle: California Living*, February 26, 1978, pp. 36-38.

[16] Bayard Taylor, *Eldorado, Or, Adventures in the Path of the Empire.* (New York: G.P. Putnam, 1859), p. 305.

[17] Benjamin E. Lloyd, *Lights and Shades in San Francisco.* (San Francisco: A.L.Bancroft, 1876), p. 511.

[18] Jacqueline Baker Barnhart, *The Fair but Frail: Prostitution in San Francisco, 1849-1900.* (Reno: University of Nevada: 1986), p. 82.

[19] Julia Cooley Altrocchi, *The Spectacular San Franciscans.* (New York: E.P.Dutton, 1949), p. 44.

[20] David Rosen, "The New White Slave Trade," *Counterpunch*, (August 24, 2012), http://www.counterpunch.org/2012/08/24/the-new-white-slave-trade/.

[21] *The California Gold Rush, 1849"* EyeWitness to History (2003), accessehttp://www.eyewitnesstohistory.com/californiagoldrush.htm.

[22] Herbert Asbury, *The Barbary Coast.* (1933; repr., New York: Capricorn, 1968), p. 35n.

[23] *California As I Saw It*: Franklin Buck, *A Yankee trader in the gold rush; the letters of Franklin A. Buck.* Compiled by Katherine A. White. (Boston: Houghton-Mifflin, 1930), https://catalog.loc.gov/vwebv/holdingsInfo?searchId=20108&recCount=25&recPointer=3&bibId=9685041

[24] California Digital Newspaper Collection. "Two Christmases In The Days of Old, The Days of Gold, The Days of '49," *San Francisco Call*, December 19, 1909, http://cdnc.ucr.edu/cgi-bin/cdnc?a=d&d=SFC19091219.2.235.3.

[25] *California As I Saw It*: Canfield, p. 90.

[26] On the Australia and New Zealand connections to California see Patricia Bowie, "The Shifting Gold Rush Scenario: California to Australia to New Zealand," *The Californians* 6, no. 1, (January-February 1988), pp. 12-23, 26-30; Jules Archer, "Eureka Stockade," *The Californians*, ibid., pp. 23-25.

[27] William J. Trimble, "The Mining Advance Into the Inland Empire," *Bulletin of the University of Wisconsin, History Series*, Vol 3 (Madison, 1914) cited in Genini, "The Fraser-Cariboo Gold Rushes: Comparisons and Contrasts with the California Gold Rush," *Journal of the West*, 11:3 (July 1972), p. 487.

[28] Helen Kennedy Cahill, "Stockton Salutes its Founder, Captain Chas. M. Weber", *The Native Son* (February-March 1977), Supplement. Official publication of the Native Sons and Native Daughters of the Golden West after 1971.

[29] Lucius Beebe and Charles Clegg, *San Francisco's Golden Era.* (Berkeley: Howell-North, 1960), pp. 39-41.

[30] California As I Saw It: William Redmond Ryan. *Personal Adventures in Upper and Lower California, in 1848-9; with the author's experience at the mines.* Illustrated by 23 drawings. (London: W. Shoberl, 1850), p. 270, https://catalog.loc.gov/vwebv/holdingsInfo?searchId=4449&recCount=25&recPointer=4&bibId=8658671

[31] *California As I Saw It*: John H. Brown, *Reminiscences and incidents of the "early days" of San Francisco; actual experience of an eye-witness, from 1845 to 1850.* (San Francisco: Mission Journal, 1886), p. 75, https://catalog.loc.gov/vwebv/holdingsInfo?searchId=20069&recC

ount=25&recPointer=2&bibId=6785294

[32] Lockwood, "A Look at Gold Rush Cuisine," *San Francisco Sunday Examiner & Chronicle: California Living*, March 1, 1981, pp. 18-20.

[33] Brandon Wang, Farallon Islands National Wildlife Reserve, https://prezi.com/uihnblqb7pve/farallon-islands-national-wildlife-reserve/.

[34] Antoine Delmas, *If the Legends Are True.*, http://www.palmspringsbum.org/genealogy/getperson.php?personI D=I54585 ; Charles Hillinger, "One Man's Dish One Big Pest," *Los Angeles Times*, August 21, 1975, p. II-1.

[35] George Blasiola, Jr. "From Rock to Plate," *San Francisco Sunday Examiner & Chronicle: California Living*, April 6, 1980, p. 22.

[36] *California As I Saw It*: Edmund Booth, *Edmund Booth forty-niner; the life story of a deaf pioneer, including portions of his autobiographical notes and gold rush diary, and selections from family letters and reminiscences.* (Stockton: San Joaquin Pioneer and Historical Society, 1953), chapter 5, https://catalog.loc.gov/vwebv/holdingsInfo?searchId=19978&recC ount=25&recPointer=6&bibId=8380838

[37] Bancroft, History of California. San Francisco: History Company, 1888. Vol. 6, pp. 438-39.

[38] Caughey, *California*, 3rd ed., p. 212.

[39] Josiah Royce, *California From the Conquest in 1846 to the Second Vigilance Committee in San Francisco: A Study of American Character.* (New York: Houghton, Mifflin, 1886), p. 222, https://archive.org/stream/californiafromroyce/californiafromroyce _djvu.txt.

[40] *Message from the President of the United States to the Two Houses of Congress, at the Commencement of the Second Session of the Thirtieth Congress.* Wendell and Van Benthuysen, 1848, p. 49.

[41] *Congressional Globe*, 27th Congress, 3rd Session, pp 198-201

[42] *Utah Genealogical and Historical Magazine* 7, p. 12, (Salt Lake City: Deseret News Press, January 1916), http://books.google.com/books?id=Kmrz_lC_x4EC&pg=PA11&source=gbs_toc_r&cad=3#v=onepage&q&f=false.

[43] Hunt and Sánchez, *A Short History of California*, pp. 407-10.

[44] Howard Kern, "No Rules in Gold Rush Days" *The Native Son* (February-March 1977), p. 1.

[45] *Gold Rush Stories – factual and fictional.* Document 1: Letter, S. Shufelt to "Cousin," describing his trip to California's Gold Fields in 1849 and his subsequent adventures there, http://web.csulb.edu/~quamwick/goldrush.html.

[46] *Reports of the Debates of the Convention of California, on the formation of the state constitution, In September and October, 1849*, https://digitalcommons.csumb.edu/hornbeck_usa_3_d/18/ The Constitution of 1879 made English the sole official language. Due to the increased pressure to restore Spanish as one of the official languages in the 1970s and 1980s, the voters in 1986 passed Proposition 63 by 3-to-1 to make English the official language of the state of California. A federal lawsuit, Gutierrez v Municipal Court, was filed against Proposition 63 after it was enacted. As a result of the lawsuit, the Ninth Circuit ruled in 1988 that the proposition was "largely symbolic." A year later, the U.S. Supreme Court reversed the Ninth Circuit's ruling, allowing Proposition 63 to stand (as of February 2024 it is still in force). Following up on that Proposition 227, the "English in Public Schools" initiative, was passed by the voters in 1998 by 6-to-4, effectively eliminating "bilingual" classes in most cases. As a result, a 2009 analysis found that "Hispanic test scores on a range of subjects" rose significantly. In November 2016 Proposition 58, repealing most of Proposition 227 and restoring bilingual education, passed. Election materials are printed in English and Spanish under the Federal Voting Rights Act of 1975, renewed in 2006. The return of bilingual education has resulted in greater emphasis on dual-immersion programs for native- and non-native-English speakers, and a de-emphasis on providing instruction in the student's native language as was typical prior to 1998. http://ballotpedia.org/California_Proposition_63,_English_is_the_Official_Language_Amendment_(1986); http://ballotpedia.org/California_Proposition_227,_the_%22Englis

h_in_Public_Schools%22_Initiative_(1998);
http://blogs.edweek.org/edweek/learning-the-
language/2014/09/california_voters_to_get_chanc.html   ;
http://www.washingtonpost.com/wp-
dyn/content/article/2006/07/09/AR2006070900553.html.
https://ballotpedia.org/California_Proposition_58,_Non-
English_Languages_Allowed_in_Public_Education_(2016)

[47] Caughey, *California*, 3rd ed., p. 215.

[48] James Russell Lowell, "A Letter from Mr. Ezekiel Biglow,"
http://www.bartleby.com/380/poem/80.html.

[49] William W. Freehling, *Road to Disunion: Secessionists at Bay, 1776-1854.* (New York: Oxford University Press, 1990), pp. 458-62, 475-86; William J. Cooper, Jr., *The South and the Politics of Slavery, 1828-1856.* (Baton Rouge: Louisiana State University Press, 1978), pp. 287-99.

[50] Cooper, *The South and the Politics of Slavery, 1828-1856*, pp. 285-91.

[51] Michael Fitzgibbon Holt, *Forging a Majority: The Formation of the Republican Party in Pittsburgh, 1848-60.* (New Haven: Yale University Press, 1969), p. 86.

[52] *Congressional Globe.* 31st Congress, 1st Session, December 12, 1849-September 30, 1850, p. 1573

[53] *Congressional Globe.* 31st Congress, 1st Session, p. 1772

[54] *Congressional Globe.* 31st Congress, 1st Session, pp. 1772, 1774

[55] Bancroft, *History of California*, Vol. 6, p. 345.

[56] "A Day of Great Rejoicing," *CHSQ*, October 1974, p. 7.

[57] Hart, *Companion to California*, p. 426.

Chapter Seven FURTHER READING

1. "California History: Education: Smart Resources for Students and Parents," *Los Angeles Times*, August 4, 1997. http://articles.latimes.com/1997/aug/04/local/me-24045.

2. Christensen, D. T. "Cholera: The Scythe of Death on the Emigrant Trails." *Oldwest*. February 16, 2024, oldwest.org.

3. Congressional Globe: The Oregon Question: Speech of Augustus Dodge. February 7, 1846.

4. Gardiner, Howard C. *In Pursuit of the Golden Dream: Reminisces of San Francisco and the Northern and Southern Mines, 1849-1857*. Ed. by Dale L Morgan. Stoughton MA: Western Hemisphere, 1970.

5. Holliday, J. S. *The World Rushed In: The California Gold Rush Experience*. 1981. Reprint, Norman: University of Oklahoma Press, 2015.

6. Lewis, Oscar. *Sea Routes to the Gold Fields*. New York: Ballantine, 1971.

7. Lockwood, Charles. *Suddenly San Francisco. San Francisco* Examiner, 1978.

8. MacMullen, Jerry. *They Came By Sea*. San Diego: Ritchie, 1969.

9. Museum of the City of San Francisco. "1849 California Gold Rush." Accessed July 17, 1998. http://www.sfmuseum.org/hist1/index0.1.html#gold.

10. Nash, Gerald D. "A Veritable Revolution: The Global Economic Significance of the California Gold Rush." *California History* 77, no. 4 (1998): 276–92. https://doi.org/10.2307/25462518.

11. Paul, Rodman. *California Gold*. Lincoln: University of Nebraska Press, 1965.

12. Ring, Eugene. "Sketch of a three years travel in South America, California and

13. Mexico."   OAC. http://www.oac.cdlib.org/search?query=Eugene;group=Items;idT= AEQ-1362.

14. Roske, Ralph J. "The World Impact of the California Gold Rush 1849-1857." *Arizona and the West*. 5, no. 3 (1963): 187-232. http://www.jstor.org/stable/40167071.

15. Rozwenc, Edwin. *The Compromise of 1850*. Lexington, MA: Heath, 1957.

16. Santos, Robert. *"The Gold Rush of California: A bibliography of periodical articles*. Denair, CA: Alley-Cass, 1998.

17. Sargent, Shirley. *Seeking the Elephant*, 1849. Glendale: Clark, 1980.

Chapter 8: New Political and Economic Systems

**

"With the law or without the law, whichever is most convenient."

-Los Angeles vigilantes, 1854

**

Law and Justice in the Diggings

The miners, whose numbers quickly made up the majority population in California, found themselves operating under a legal system both foreign to them as (predominantly) Americans and inadequate to address the realities of a rapidly evolving society. In response they devised their own mining codes and improvised courts based on the legal ideas then current in the United States, which inflicted quick punishment on the guilty. (Whether or not "Let's give 'em a fair trial and then hang 'em" was a current phrase from those times, its counsel seemed to prevail in most cases.)

The unwritten rule of personal behavior was that each man was free to act as he chose as long as his actions were socially harmless. As soon as they became harmful the culprit would be removed by exile or death. Criminal law enforcement began at Dry Diggings in January 1849, and other mining camps soon followed its example.

There was no state prison. In 1851 the *Waban*, one of the hundreds of ships abandoned by passengers and crews to go to the mines, anchored in San Francisco Bay, became a prison to handle 30 inmates. Those inmates were then set to work building San Quentin, and when it opened in July 1852 it had 68 inmates.[1]

Generally, the courts and sentences were just. Exceptions, however, stood out as in the lynching of Josefa Loazia (1825?-51), better known as "Juanita" at Angel's Camp on July 5, 1851; she was a Mexican, perceived, perhaps incorrectly, to be a whore, who stabbed a man for breaking into her cabin to rape her. She was hanged despite being pregnant. (The lynch mob, when they realized too late her condition, was remorseful). [2] In Bancroft's generally pro-American-settler opinion, "It mattered not so much to them who or what she was; she might be chaste and fair or as wicked as Jezebel." While her being Mexican and the victim an American justified her hanging in the eyes of most of the white population, such bias was far from universal. The *Sacramento Times and Transcript* editorialized on the shame brought upon themselves by the mob:

> "The act for which the victim suffered was entirely justifiable under the provocation. She had stabbed a man who had persisted in making a disturbance in her house and had greatly outraged her rights. The violent proceedings of an indignant and excited mob, led on by the enemies of the unfortunate woman, were a blot upon
> the history of the state. Had she committed a crime of really heinous character, a real American woman would have revolted at such a course as was pursued toward this friendless and unprotected foreigner. We had hoped that the story was fabricated. As it is, the perpetrators have shown themselves and their race." [3]

There were cases of hangings being carried out before a verdict was reached, and of persons hanged who were later found to be innocent. Such an event, in August 1851, was described by Alfred Johnson (through Canfield): "Only three weeks ago the mob hung a Chilean at Rose's Bar for horse stealing and then next day the horse he was accused of stealing was found in the hills above French Corral."

California's last lynching occurred at San Jose in November 1931 when two men who had kidnapped and murdered a young man for ransom were taken from the county jail by a mob and hanged in a local park. Instances of "lynch law" decreased as sheriffs and regular courts appeared in the new counties. Exceptions to the increase of law and order by this presence still troubled the peace, with 62 men lynched between 1875 and 1920. Most of these lynching's were carried out by small groups wreaking private revenge rather than the results of mob violence.[4] Egregious examples of lynching in the face of an adequate in-place legal system were in Sutter County where a man who should have been tried at the county courthouse in Marysville was "tried" and lynched in Grass Valley, which happened to be a rival for the county seat, and in Napa County where a man was captured and hanged by a self-organized posse before his friends could bring the sheriff.

The San Francisco Committees of Vigilance

Nearly every Western community had a vigilante committee at one time or another, "vigilante" meaning "watchman" in Spanish, and in nearly every case they were modeled on San Francisco's two committees of 1851 and 1856.

On June 13, 1851 the *Daily Alta California* printed this statement:

"WHEREAS it has become apparent to the citizens of San Francisco, that there is no security for life and property, either under the regulations of society as it present exists, or under the law as now administered: Therefore the citizens, whose names are hereunto attached, do unit[e]

themselves into an association for the maintenance of the peace and good order of society, and the preservation of the lives and property of the citizens of San Francisco, and to bind ourselves, each unto the other, to do and perform every lawful act for the maintenance of law and order, and to sustain the laws when faithfully and properly administered; but we are determined that no thief, burglar, incendiary or assassin, shall escape punishment, either by the quibbles of the law, the insecurity of prisons, the carelessness or corruption of the police, or a laxity of those who pretend to administer justice."

This interesting study in self-contradiction – "binding" themselves "to do and perform every lawful act for the maintenance of law and order, and to sustain the laws when faithfully and properly administered" while declaring themselves free to act outside "the quibbles of the law" – apparently was not unnoticed as the Alta printed an unfavorable comment by one who signed himself "Baltimorean" three days later.

There were several criminal gangs operating openly in San Francisco, the two worst known as the Hounds and the Sydney Ducks. The Hounds were usually discharged soldiers from Colonel Jonathan D. Stevenson's regiment of New York Volunteers; unlike most of their fellows, honest and law-abiding, there were men who had had a few brushes with law back home in the States. Led by Lt. Sam Roberts, they called themselves the "Regulators," and like many Americans of that time they were xenophobic racists who wanted to "hound" (or drive) foreigners - especially the Spanish-speaking - out of California. The Ducks were escaped convicts from the British penal colonies in Australia.

On a Sunday in June 1851 the Hounds attacked Chile Town, at the base of Telegraph Hill, burning, beating, raping, and looting. The *chilenos* were an inoffensive group, most of their men being poor miners and their women prostitutes, as were most women from Mexico and South America. They were almost all brought to San Francisco under false pretenses, in conditions that would today be classified as human trafficking.

The middle class in San Francisco had little use for the chilenos, but even less use for the Hounds. Sam Brannan, the merchant who had launched the Gold Rush, called a town meeting in Portsmouth Square to denounce the Hounds and what they had done, a collection was taken up for the *chilenos* and an ultimatum was issued to the Hounds: Leave town within 24 hours or dance on the end of a rope. 230 men joined Brannan and were sworn in as special deputies. The Hounds took the hint and began to flee, but several were caught and returned to San Francisco for trial. Duly convicted, Roberts was sentenced to ten years at hard labor and eight other thugs got lighter sentences. Their politician friends got them freed within a few days, but an independent non-partisan slate of candidates replaced those venal politicians in the next election. Seeing how things had changed against them, they wisely fled to the mining camps, bringing their criminal activity with them, where they would again be dealt with by impromptu or formal justice.[5]

In the previous 18 months San Francisco had been burned down six times. A tent and wooden shack city, it was easy to burn, but the cost had reached $12 million ($485.7 million in 2023 dollars). The Ducks were blamed for starting the fires as a cover for their burglaries and other criminal activities. One of these, "English Jim" Stewart, known popularly as "the Lightkeeper" was a major suspect.[6] At about the same time the Hounds were expelled, a Duck, John Jenkins, was caught stealing a safe in broad daylight. Indifferent to his arrest because he believed his criminal friends would break him out, he waited for freedom. Since the police and courts had little power, Brannan also believed Jenkins would soon be sprung by friends. The police were afraid to go into the criminal haunts, and the courts were frequently and easily bribed. To prevent Jenkins from getting off easily or being broken out by other Ducks, Brannan called another town meeting in Portsmouth Square and stirred up the crowd, which proceeded to the city jail, took Jenkins out and lynched him. There is a story, perhaps apocryphal, that ever the smart businessman, Brannan charged people a dollar ($40.48 in 2023) a tug to pull on the rope long after the Australian was dead. The Reverend Timothy Dwight Hunt (1821-95) of the First Congregational Church was moved to reflect on the event, preaching a rousing sermon in support of the Committee, printed as a pamphlet by Marvin & Hitchcock, "Sermon Suggested by the execution of Jenkins, on the plaza, by 'The People' of San Francisco during the night of the 10th of June, 1851." Within a few days other Ducks were lynched: "English Jim" Stewart, Samuel Whittaker, and Robert McKenzie. Another was whipped, fourteen were deported to Australia, another fourteen were told to leave California, and fifteen were handed over to the authorities (who took note of how the public would react if they did not do their job). This quick, decisive, and often lethal action, albeit illegal, struck terror into the hearts of the criminal underworld. They soon fled, leaving San Francisco a relatively safe place for its good citizens.

By 1856 San Francisco was again plagued by criminal activity, this time by a corrupt city government. Elections were rigged; ballot box stuffing was routine, the courts were corrupt and weak, and there were city contract scandals along with rising municipal expenses. James King of William (1822-56), anti-Catholic owner of *The San Francisco Daily Evening Bulletin*, began a campaign against Supervisor James Casey (c. 1827-56), accusing him of having served time in Sing Sing, the New York State Prison (then reputed the toughest place in the country), and of ballot box stuffing.

Casey had been involved in a fight with a "Mr. Bagley" over some matter lost to history, which led to his being charged with criminal assault. Bagley took his story to King of William but was unable to convince the editor of his innocence. King of William, though known to be an opponent of Casey's, weighed in editorially on the side of fairness:

> "Our impression at the time was, that in the Casey fight Bagley was the aggressor. It does not matter how bad a man Casey had been, nor how much benefit it might be to the public to have him out of the way, we cannot accord to any one citizen the right to kill, or even beat him, without personal provocation. The fact that Casey has been an inmate of Sing Sing prison in New York, is no offence against the laws of this State; nor is the fact of his having stuffed himself through the ballot box as elected to the Board of Supervisors from a district where it is said he was not even a candidate, any justification for Mr. Bagley to shoot Casey, however richly the latter may deserve to have his neck stretched for such fraud on the people. These are acts against the public good, not against Mr. Bagley in particular, and however much we may detest Casey's former character, or to be convinced of

the shallowness of his promised reformation, we cannot justify the assumption by Mr. Bagley to take upon himself the redressing of these wrongs."[7]

The Bulletin under King of William was a scandal sheet like today's cheaper tabloids, yet it was a respectable paper for its time: The Bulletin was the first in California to publish Sunday school announcements and Sunday sermon topics in the Saturday edition.[8]

King of William was not the editor's real last name; his name was James King, but the commonplace combination of his given name and surname inspired him to add his father's first name to his surname to distinguish it from the rest.

Casey challenged King of William to a duel, which King of William refused. Not happy about missing the opportunity to get King of William in this more socially acceptable manner, Casey shot him on sight, mortally wounding him as he left the newspaper office, after which Casey turned himself in to the police to be put in protective custody. He was astonished to see that his cellmate was his friend, Charles Cora (1816?-56), an Italian gambler who had shot the town marshal, William Richardson (1795-1856), because the man had publicly insulted Cora's fiancée, Belle Ryan (1827?-62), and the next day had drawn a gun on Cora. Belle was the town's leading madam.[9] Cora had been acquitted of the murder, but had sought police protection, since The Bulletin had speculated that he had gotten off because of political connections.

Four days after King of William was shot, Dr. Strother Griffin (1816-98), who had come from New Mexico with Kearny as an army doctor and settled in Los Angeles, "the second pioneer educated physician to arrive" there, was summoned to San Francisco for consultation.[10] Doctors who first treated King of William had inserted a sponge into the bullet wound to stanch the bleeding and were debating whether to remove it. Griffin advised against the removal, fearing hemorrhage from a severed subclavian artery that supplied blood to his left arm. The patient died two days later. Though leaving the sponge in place sealed King of William's fate due to probable rampant infection, Griffin and the doctors he sided with (including Hugh Hughes Toland [1806-80], later founder of what would eventually become the University of California's Department of Medicine) were sued for malpractice by King of William's friend, Dr. Richard Beverly Cole (1829-1901), who had argued for removing the sponge. In what became known as the Sponge Case of 1856, the coroner's jury returned a verdict of "no medical malpractice," stating that the editor would have died of the bullet wound regardless of the sponge.[11]

Though not a very admirable character, King of William was raised to martyr status simply by having been gunned down. Richardson, having been killed by Casey's good friend and sometime cellmate, Charles Cora, was also popularly accorded the status of martyr, though every bit as deficient in admirable qualities as King of William.

William T. Coleman (1824-93), a businessman, called for a reorganization of the original Vigilante Committee and was met by 6,000 volunteers. This Second Committee, as it was known, then went to the city jail, removed Casey and Cora, tried them for murder, and, as King of William's funeral was in progress, hanged them. The Committee would go on to hang petty thieves as well as personal enemies, who were often accused on trumped-up charges.

Unlike the very popular 1851 Committee, this one faced some opposition from a group calling itself the Law-and-Order Committee. Its leaders were state Supreme Court

Justice David Terry (1823-90), army Lieutenant William T. Sherman (1820-91; later famous for his Civil War march through Georgia), attorney Edward Baker (1811-61; Cora's defense lawyer) and Governor John Neely Johnson (1828-72, served 1856-58). Its platform was simple: if the voters were that concerned about corruption and crime, they could turn out the scoundrels at the next election without resorting to vigilantism, lynching or anarchy.

In this conflict between the two groups, the Vigilantes attempted to arrest Terry for questioning. Terry, a brilliant jurist but a hothead, drew his Bowie knife and stabbed Sterling A. Hopkins, a Vigilante - not a helpful boost for the Law-and-Order position. [12] The Vigilantes arrested Terry and went through the motions of a seven- weeks-long trial; but since he was no ordinary prisoner, they were probably glad to let him go when the stabbing victim survived. The Vigilantes, their work finished, paraded in front of Fort Gunnybags, their headquarters on Sacramento Street, and disbanded.

Opinions of the Second Committee vary. Lucius Beebe (1902-66) and Charles Clegg (1916-79) praised it in 1960: "[It] was composed of San Francisco's most reputable and substantial citizens and its administration of justice was the most salutary in the record of California crime." Walton Bean's (1914-71) assessment, in 1968, condemned the Second Committee: "As for vigilante jurisprudence, its record of violations of due process was appalling. The leaders of the vigilance committees would have served California far better if they had confined their activities to legal methods and to genuine reforms. It is doubtful they accomplished anything whatever of real value, and they left a vicious, dangerous, and persistent tradition of contempt for the normal processes of government." In 1978 John B. McGloin's history stated much "of the indiscriminate praise [of the 1856 Committee] is undeserved, some of it stemming from that pietism which comes largely from genealogical or familial considerations." [13]

Though it is generally accepted that the state of affairs in San Francisco needed reform, vigilantism was not the answer. Those who joined the Second Committee were themselves as much to blame as those they fought in city government. Had they not been preoccupied with other matters they would have kept a watchful eye on their government and prevented abuses from occurring. Because they did not act promptly, they allowed a situation to develop for which they overcompensated by vigilantism. They learned their lesson, and future changes were made at the ballot box and in the jury rooms.

The only intervention the state government made to remedy the problem was when the legislature in early 1856 imposed a new charter on San Francisco, which, among other things, did not take effect until November, five months after the preceding administration's term expired. To fill the interim, the legislature, "representing the statewide country-bumpkin electorate," told the San Francisco voters that they would be ruled for the time being by a temporary Board of Supervisors made up of four justices of the peace who would name their own "mayor," then called the "board president." George J. Whelan, of whom virtually nothing is known except that he was a lawyer, was chosen, to which the Alta California sniffed – without giving a reason – that he "is exactly the kind of man who should never have been selected." [14]

Rustic Vigilance

Inspired by San Francisco, communities all over the West resorted to vigilantism when it was deemed necessary. Their committees lacked the drama and organization of the San

Francisco Committees, but they were much bloodier. In 1855, for example, there were 47 vigilante hangings in California, none of them in San Francisco. (Imagine 6,200 lynching's in a year among California's present population, and you will sense the impact of the 47 which occurred in 1855). Sacramento, Weaverville, Los Angeles, and Visalia were among the cities with active vigilante committees.

Not all episodes of vigilante justice ended with fatalities. In Visalia in 1858, vigilantes forced a man to return property swindled from his nephew. They took him to a tree and hoisted him several times by a rope around his neck until he agreed to return the property. He spent the night in jail until a lawyer and notary handled the transfer in the morning.

One of many Los Angeles lynching's of that decade occurred in January, 1855, when Mayor Stephen C. Foster (1820-98) resigned his office to personally direct the lynching of a man named Dave Brown. The hanging done; Foster was immediately re-elected mayor. Interestingly, the incident was reported in the *Southern Californian*, printed several hours before the event so that it could be sent to San Francisco on the morning steamer.

In San Diego, at Whaley State Historic Park, there was an occurrence which added the Whaley house to the list of America's haunted houses. A French Canadian known as Yankee Jim Robinson had stolen a rowboat for a drunken paddle around the bay but returned the leaky craft. He was caught, tried for grand theft by an anti-foreign vigilante jury and a drunken judge, and hanged on the site where the Whaley house would be built a few years later. The hanging was carried out so badly that it took him 45 minutes to die. It is claimed that his footsteps are heard frequently pacing the area near where the gallows stood – or so tourists are told.

William Hubert Burgess (1825-93), an artist and writer from London, came to California in 1849, tried prospecting but found more money by using his artistic talents to make jewelry for the miners. In a letter to his mother in 1855, he told of the violence that surrounded him in West Point, Calaveras County:

> "California is a thousand times worse than the penal settlements in Van Dieman's lands [Tasmania]. The uncaught villains from all countries are here. Their skill is as consummate that they rise (of course being unknown) to the most responsible positions and are not found out
> ntil too late.... For two or three thousand pounds a man can cut another's throat and be sure to get off."[15]

The same letter also described how the local vigilante committees hounded thieves and murderers.

Bandits

Numerous bandits, primarily Mexicans (or "Greasers" as they were disparagingly known because of wartime bad feelings), plagued California in the 1850s. The most famous was Joaquín Murrieta (c 1832-53), originally from the Mexican state of Sonora. Having endured the rape of his wife by American miners, being driven from his mining claim, being flogged for the alleged theft of a horse, and seeing his brother hanged for the same theft, he swore revenge on the Americans. Murrieta turned criminal, and for two years led a gang of desperadoes who spread robbery and murder throughout the diggings.

He thought nothing of "lassoing a victim, dragging him on the end of a rope until unconscious and then cutting off his ears before finally killing him. Yet many a miner escaped such

401

a death because of some forgotten kindness shown the bandit many years before." His most famous lieutenant was Three-Fingered Jack Garcia, whose delight was to tie "six or seven Chinamen together by their queues and then slitting their throats."[16]

In 1852, in Mariposa County, he narrowly escaped capture by Captain Harry Love (1810-68), deputy sheriff of Los Angeles County, who on his own initiative had tracked the bandit to one of his hiding places. A fresh series of robberies and murders in the spring of 1853 led the legislature to create the mounted California Rangers under Love. The company took to the field, and on a morning in late July surprised Murrieta's band at a point in the hills near Coalinga. In a running fight the bandit chief and three of his men were killed, two were captured, and two escaped. For purposes of identification Murrieta's head was cut off and preserved in alcohol, to be exhibited in various parts of the state. The jar was kept behind the bar in the San Francisco's Golden Nugget Saloon until destroyed, perhaps mercifully, by the 1906 earthquake and fire.

There is some question as to whether there really was a Joaquín Murrieta. At the time the legislature created the Rangers, there were five Joaquíns' accused of committing the same crimes. However, since there were no other depredations by a Joaquín (of any last name) after 1853, there probably was a Joaquín Murrieta, and he probably had been killed by Love. His legend grew into a strange mixture of cruelty, hate, genius, love, kindness, and daring that would assure him a premier ranking in the history of crimes.[17]

There were other bandits, of course, but the most famous among them was no doubt Tiburcio Vásquez (1835-75). In the 1850s the Vásquez gang had robbed stagecoaches and stolen horses and cattle, activities that sent them to San Quentin.

During the 1860s the Vásquez gang had been released from prison, regrouped, and again spread terror; one of its new members was Murrieta's nephew Procopio (c 1841-c 1890), known as "Red-Handed Dick." Having served in San Quentin for cattle rustling, he "returned to his practices like a dog to its vomit."[18]: In August 1873 the gang raided a town in San Benito County. Three men were killed by the bandits: a deaf man who did not hear Vásquez's orders; a Portuguese, who did not understand them; and the hotelkeeper across the street who refused to open his door and was felled by a bullet through it. This deed so incensed the locals that Vásquez had to flee south. Staying ahead of the law, the gang made a raid on a Kings River town around Christmas of 1873, binding 39 men and robbing two stores. Various sheriffs trailed Vásquez, and when Los Angeles Police Chief Emil Harris (1839-1921) caught him five months later, he demanded to be tried in San Jose rather than in Los Angeles. Harris obliged. Tried at San Jose, he was hanged in March 1875.[19] Procopio and others continued their lives of crime.

Two others of note were Salomon Pico (1821-60), a man of a great and honorable family who became a highwayman, supposedly in protest against American rule, and Jack Powers (1827-1860), a Mexican-American War veteran, gambler and expert horseman who turned to a life of crime. Of Pico, the first mayor of San Luis Obispo, Charles Johnson, recalled him "once [riding] through Monterey Street, with the ears of victims tied like scalps to his saddle-bow."[20] Pico was later executed in Baja California, presumably for other crimes. With his San Luis Obispo native lieutenant, Pio Linares (1831-58), Powers' gang terrorized the Central Coast region for years, operating by the pirate maxim "Dead Men Tell No Tales" to eliminate witnesses to their depredations. At last, about two dozen vigilantes cornered Linares and a couple of companions, shots rang out, and the criminals were caught and hanged the next day. Powers reportedly fled to Mexico and died there in a gunfight.

Southward and Outward the Course of Empire

During the 1840s and 1850s there were several attempts by American citizens to invade lands in Central America and the Caribbean, in the South Pacific, or wherever the opportunity presented itself to conquer these areas on a private enterprise basis. Manifest Destiny and what it had achieved encouraged the wish to extend national influence or even to imitate the old conquistadores by personal conquest. The American public enjoyed newspaper accounts of their exploits, but these men were usually charged by the U.S. government for violating the Neutrality Act of 1794 which made it illegal for an American to wage war from the United States against a foreign power with whom the U.S. was at peace.

There was a group of angry Irishmen who sought to invade British Canada to hold it for ransom to secure Ireland's freedom from Britain. And there were Southerners who wanted to turn Spanish Cuba into five new slave states. These adventurers, called filibusterers[21], came from every part of the country, motivated by the conviction that they were a law unto themselves. Those who came from California looked to Hawaii, northern Mexico, and Central America as potential conquests. Of these, there were seven major filibusterers.

The first to emerge from California was Los Angeles businessman Alexander Bell (1801-71), who planned to reinstate the deposed president of Ecuador, Diego Noboa (1789-1870), who had been overthrown by José María Urvina (1808-91) in 1851. The dispute involved Ecuador's claims to Amazon lands against Peru. Before Bell reached Quito,

404

however, the rival factions composed their differences, uniting in a desire to rid the country of the Americans. Bell was sent back to Panama, where his party was stranded. The expedition was a fiasco, but fortunately bloodless, unlike some other ventures.[22]

Joseph C. Morehead (1832-63), a Kentuckian who had come with Stevenson's New York Volunteers, attempted to conquer the Mexican state of Sonora in April-October 1851 by offering to suppress Yaqui Indian attacks. He had been employed by the state of California to fight the Yumas, and was successful, but felt that his skills could be put to better use in Sonora and Baja California. He raised the money to finance his expeditions of about 200 men, some of the money probably stolen, and sent three groups to Sonora before navy authorities could stop him. He and most of his men managed to escape when the Mazatlán authorities found out about his plans.[23]

In November 1851 French Marquis Charles de Pindray (1816-52), who had settled in the United States after the 1848 French Revolution, was invited by the Mexican government to bring 140 Frenchmen to Sonora to settle and keep the Apaches away from the gold mines, in return for which he would receive a large tract of land to settle these Frenchmen. His buffer colony would lie between Tubac and the Gila River, still a part of Sonora. Welcomed at first and joined by some natives, de Pindray headed to Arispe, and then began the march to the mines. Difficulties such as internal dissentions, hostile Indians whom the French did not know how to fight because they were used to European warfare, growing ill-feeling on the part of both the French invitees and Mexican locals, as well as an attack of a painful and debilitating fever, resulted in de Pindray committing suicide in front of his people in 1852. Most of his men then joined another

California Frenchman, Gaston de Raousset-Boulbon, who had just arrived from California.

A French count, Gaston de Raousset-Boulbon (1817-54), having failed in his attempts to become a great colonizer in Africa, and sorely craving the respect he thought due him as a noble after the French Revolution of 1848, sailed to Colombia in third class because of a lack of money, eventually finding his way to San Francisco. Not appreciating the general sense of equality that was part of the Gold Rush culture, he was most disillusioned when he did not receive the treatment he thought he deserved as a count. He tried mining, but not succeeding in that either, he looked south for fulfillment. He was invited to Sonora to start a mining colony known as La Compenia Restauradora de la Mina de la Arizona in 1852. He soon got into a tax dispute with the local authorities, retaliating by taking the town of Hermosillo hostage to his demands. The Mexican army routed him, and he escaped to San Francisco where the Mexican and French consuls encouraged him to try again, in violation of U.S. laws against filibustering. He immediately began planning to bring 5,000 Frenchmen from California, ostensibly to settle Sonora as a buffer against the United States and to keep the Yaquis and Apaches from attacking, but really to create an empire for himself. Two years later he was back in Sonora with 400 men but failed to get popular support and was defeated at Guaymas by a Mexican army in July 1854. The next month he faced a firing squad in Guaymas, refusing to wear a blindfold. Twelve years later, while Mexico was under the rule of Emperor Maximilian (1832-67, reign 1864-67), his remains were exhumed and taken to France for reburial. Thus ended the last attempt of California-based French adventurers to detach Sonora from Mexico and turn it into a realm of their own.

In 1855 Henry Crabb (c. 1823-57) a Tennessean who had

settled in Stockton, became interested in gaining new slave territory in Central America (where it had been abolished in 1824). He left Stockton to head for New Orleans, where he took ship for Nicaragua. His interest in the project was short-lived, and in 1856 he formed the Arizona Colonization Company with Sonora as his objective. He had married into a prominent Sonora family. "Colonel" Crabb departed for Sonora, taking with him about 75 people, including families, to shore up his in-laws' land claims. He outfitted his expedition in Los Angeles and El Monte, traveling over San Gorgonio Pass to Yuma. He set up a base at what became known as "Filibusters Camp," near modern Welton (Yuma County), Arizona. Besides the land claims, he had been invited by a local revolutionary, Ignacio Pesqueira (1820-86), to help him seize the Sonora state government while Mexico was hurtling towards a civil war known as the War of the Reform (1858-61). The War of Reform was the culmination of the liberal versus conservative strife since Independence. Things changed when Pesqueira gained shortly before Crabb and his party arrived. Since Pesqueira was now governor he sent his troops and Tohono O'odham Indians to attack Crabb. In eight days of fighting in April 1857, about 25 Americans and 200 Mexicans and Indians were killed in battle. Henry Crabb and all but a few of his party were executed for interfering in Mexican affairs.[24] As Hunt and Sánchez wrote, "It was the old story – leaders of rival factions got together and turned against the foreigner."[25]

Sam Brannan tried to conquer Hawaii. By 1851 King Kamehameha III (1813-54) had ruled the Islands for 26 years. Once considered wise, he had descended into "intemperance and loose morals," and Hawaii's naturalized Americans were restless under their domination by "a set of ignorant, indolent savages or their bigoted quondam-missionary rulers."[26] In this atmosphere Brannan took 24 of his most trusted associates aboard the Game Cock from San Francisco to Honolulu with a plan to bribe the king to abdicate and make him governor-general. In what took on the air of an international comic-opera, the king was away on vacation, a Hawaiian military force was assembled, and a group of American whalers were needlessly antagonized (their mail from home had been destroyed by Brannan's men who were looking for letters warning the Hawaiian government of his plans). A month later they sailed back to California and ridicule.

The most important, and certainly the most famous of the solo conquistadores that sprang up in those years, was William Walker (1824-60). Trained in Philadelphia and Europe as a medical doctor and admitted to the bar in New Orleans, he tried his hand at journalism when he moved to California in 1850, first at San Francisco and then Marysville. He then cast his lot into politics, but his ambitions reached farther: In 1854-60 Walker conquered Baja California but was forced to evacuate it by the Mexican army. He went on to Central America, becoming President of Nicaragua with only 60 followers. The takeover embarrassed the United States government, but he was finally brought down by Vanderbilt interests. The Vanderbilt family-owned transportation operations in many countries, among them a ferry system on Lake Nicaragua. Walker had the temerity to expropriate the Vanderbilt ferry line. The United States government might be embarrassed by a fly-by-night filibusterer, but Cornelius Vanderbilt (1794-1877) was not about to let the insult pass without notice. Fleeing to the United States where he was greeted as a hero, Walker snuck back into Honduras to reclaim the country he believed still his. The other Central American republics were paid by Vanderbilt to declare war on Nicaragua, and Walker put up a fight. Moving around Central America, he avoided the British Navy sent to protect their British Honduras (today Belize) and Mosquito Coast. He was finally captured by the British, turned over to the Hondurans, and executed by firing squad in Honduras.[27]

Walker presented the U.S. another problem, the purchase from Mexico of the Mesilla Valley, the area below the Gila River, was cancelled. Southern railroad men sought an opportunity of connecting the South with the Pacific Coast and saw this area as perfect for a part of the route since the land taken in 1848 was too mountainous for speedy construction. The U.S. offered to buy the strip. However, Santa Anna balked until the price was to his taste ($10 million [$370 million in 2023]), selling it then to the United States after the American minister, James Gadsden (1788-1858), hinted that the Americans would just take it if Santa Anna, feeling threatened by Walker in Baja California, refused to sell. Thus, in 1854 the United States achieved its final piece of land to round out the "Lower 48 states," the Gadsden Purchase. For his part, Santa Anna then declared himself dictator-for-life and was promptly overthrown, ending his 11th and final presidency in August 1855.

Some Californians might have intended to annex British Columbia when they rushed north to the Fraser River area for its gold in 1858, but such dreams were put to rest by the Royal Navy, which maintained a vessel at Victoria after the settlement of the boundary conflict in 1846. From time to time, Americans showed a desire for U.S. annexation of that portion of Canada, but never went beyond talking and writing.[28]

The Contest Between Gwin and Broderick

In the 1848 national elections the Whigs had taken the White House and the Congress, putting many Democratic politicians out of work. The Gold Rush served as their safety net, many Democrats hurrying to California to take advantage of a new state government. History has given us numerous examples of the sometimes-bitter divisions that occur when one group completely triumphs over its rivals only to find that by removing the common enemy the victors divide and become opponents. This was the case in California. Through the 1850s the Democrats were California's majority party, but there was a sharp split among them over the national slavery question. Senator Gwin, hailing from Tennessee and Mississippi, was the leader of the "Chivs," or Chivalry Democrats, the Southern wing of the party. A well-educated physician-lawyer-politician and leader at the Colton Hall convention, he had achieved congressional authorization of the Mare Island Navy Yard and the San Francisco Mint for California. David Broderick (1820-59) from New York, was the leader of the "Short Hairs," the Northern wing of the party. A popular saloonkeeper and Tammany Hall politician, he had gotten rich in San Francisco by private coining of slugs with stated face values far above their gold content and by dealing in waterfront real estate; for example, his $10 gold coins contained $8 in gold ($370 and $297 in 2023). He had also gotten a good reputation as the head of a private fire engine company, and he gathered a group of political henchmen such as James Casey and Edward ("Ned, the ballot box stuffer") McGowan (1807-93) around him.

Broderick had been elected to the state senate in 1850, and in 1851 became its president as the state's second lieutenant governor, a position he held for a year. This brought him nearly absolute control of San Francisco as it degenerated into that state of boundless municipal corruption that brought out the Second Vigilante Committee. Six decades later, when the state was again fighting a corrupt government, his method was described by Jeremiah Lynch (1849-1917):

In San Francisco he became the dictator of the

410

municipality. His political lessons and observations in New York were priceless. He introduced a modification of the same organization in San Francisco with which Tammany has controlled New York for lo! These many years. It was briefly this. At a forthcoming election

a number of offices were to be filled; those of sheriff, district attorney, alderman, and places in the legislature. Several of these positions were very lucrative, notably that of the sheriff, tax-collector, and assessor. The incumbents received no specified salaries, but were entitled to all or a certain proportion of the fees. These fees occasionally exceeded $50,000 ($1.85 million in 2023) per annum. Broderick would say to the most popular or the most desirable aspirant: 'This office is worth $50,000 a year. Keep half and give me the other half, which I require to keep up our organization in the state. Without intelligent, systematic discipline, neither you nor I can win, and our opponents will conquer, unless

I have money   enough to pay the men whom I may find necessary. If you agree to that arrangement, I will have you nominated when the convention assembles, and then we will all pull together until after the election.' Possibly this candidate dissented, but then someone else consented, and as the town was hugely Democratic, his selections were usually victorious.[29]

Broderick, able to hand out state jobs and contracts, controlled the state's patronage and contracts, and so became a powerful factor in the state legislature. In those days before the Seventeenth Amendment state legislatures elected United States senators, and Broderick wanted to be one. He ran against John B. Weller (1812-75), Gwin's choice in 1852, and was defeated despite his prodigious political clout. Such bitter division ensued between the two Democratic wings that in

1856 the American party, informally known as the "Know-Nothings," more anti-foreign than anti-Catholic, managed to elect the governor, John Neely Johnson, although most legislators were still Democrats of one type or another.

The Democrats' split became more complicated when California's Governor John Bigler (1805-71, served 1852-56) defected from the Broderick camp to the Gwin camp when Broderick failed to get him appointed Minister to Chile, but Gwin did. The split led to a duel between Broderick and one-term Congressman Joseph McCorkle (1819-84) with rifles at 30 yards (27.4 m). Reminiscent of the battles usually fought between political factions when California was Mexican, the skirmish ended with an ass being killed, but no human casualties when bullets were fired.

So began a scene of political turmoil in California, with bribery, physical intimidation and non-stop political maneuvering being the rule of the day. By 1854 the Whig party was dying as the slavery controversy proved stronger than partisan loyalty, and the party split, many northern Whigs becoming Republicans and many southern Whigs joining the American ("Know-Nothing") party. For the first time in twenty years the Whigs did not nominate anyone for president in 1856. The national Democratic party was also moving toward a similar split, but it would maintain unity for a few more years.

In 1853 Governor Bigler became an ally of Broderick and his Free-Soil Democrats, the former "Short Hairs", while the Chivs in Southern California began agitating for a state division to create a slave state. As governor, Bigler aligned with the new anti-Chinese movement that began to grow when hard times hit the mining district after gold was discovered in Australia. Blame was heaped on these people who, it was believed, would never assimilate into American society.

Governor Bigler approved legislation ("An Act to protect free white labor against Competition with Chinese coolie labor, and to Discourage the Immigration of Chinese into California") imposing a $2.50 per month head tax on Chinese miners as well as a $50 head ("Capitation") tax ($100 and $2,000 in 2023) on all Chinese arriving in California ports; these were later overturned by the state Supreme Court in *People v Downer* (7 Cal. 169 [1857]) and *Lin Sing v Washburn* (20 Cal. 532 [1862]) because they interfered with the exclusive federal jurisdiction over immigration.[30]

To heal this Chiv-Short Hair division and to prevent a common political enemy from again taking advantage of the situation, Broderick and Gwin agreed to a compromise of sorts: Gwin would support Broderick for the Senate in 1857, and not hinder his acquisition of the federal patronage for California. For his part of the bargain, Broderick would support Gwin's reelection to the Senate in 1860.

Gwin tried to keep his part of the deal, but President James Buchanan (1791-1868, served 1857-61) and most of the Democratic Senators disliked Broderick, considering him tactless, and refused him the patronage, keeping it with Gwin. The president had no use for Broderick because the senator had opposed his Kansas policy of allowing a territory's settlers to choose whether their state should be Free or Slave, the policy known as "Popular Sovereignty." Those who supported Buchanan's policy were known as "Lecomptonite Democrats" as opposed to the "Anti-Lecomptonites;" Free Soil Kansans supported a government at Topeka and the Pro-Slavery Kansans supported the government at Lecompton while a mini-civil war, a dress-rehearsal for the one soon to follow, erupted. True, he had been praised by Senator William Seward (1801-72) of New York as "the brave young senator," but Seward was a Whig-turned-Republican.

413

Embittered and criticized by his own legislature for disobedience to instructions, Broderick left the Senate and blamed Gwin for these slights. Back in San Francisco he began an editorial campaign against Gwin and the Chivs. Justice Terry and Broderick had once been great friends, but this turn of events would have unfortunate consequences. Broderick's campaign attacked Terry for his pro-slavery position when the Justice ran for re-election and Terry lost, thereupon blaming Broderick. The Chivs returned the mud which Broderick had begun flinging. Broderick then retaliated by declaring that

> "Terry [is a] 'damned miserable wretch [who was as corrupt as Buchanan and Gwin]. I have hitherto spoken of him as an honest man--as the only honest man on the bench of a miserable, corrupt Supreme Court--but now I find I was mistaken. I take it all back. He is just as bad as the others.'"[31]

This led to a duel in September 1859 between Broderick and Justice Terry in San Mateo County, just over the line from San Francisco, where gunshots were prohibited. Broderick was killed when his hair-trigger gun accidentally discharged first, and Terry took careful aim.

Public opinion denounced Terry and the Chivs as murderers, many of Broderick's followers joined the newly formed antislavery Republican party, and the state outlawed dueling. The penalty would be lifetime deprivation of the right to vote, a most effective deterrent, since most of the duelists were politicians and being a registered voter was the first requirement for anyone seeking office. Dueling was now all but a thing of the past.

It is hard to imagine the level of political violence common at that time. In 1859 Charles S. Fairfax (1829-69), clerk of the state Supreme Court, was nearly killed in a fight when Assemblyman Harvey Lee (1819-66) stabbed him in the chest with a sword. He drew his pistol, and with Lee begging for his life, spared the "miserable coward" for his family's sake. Later Fairfax hosted a duel between two assemblymen at his Marin County estate, that ended with one dead and the other in flight. In 1860, Assemblyman John C. Bell (ca 1831-60) of El Dorado County was shot and stabbed during a recess in the session inside of the Capitol Building by Dr. W. H. Stone (1816-82), dying four days later; the reason for their argument has been forgotten.

Movements for State Division and for a Pacific Republic

Throughout the 1850s there was strong sentiment in southern California to divide the state below Monterey. With only three percent of the state population paying 66% of the state taxes, the southern counties naturally felt put upon. Mining property was virtually untaxed while landholdings were tax liabilities, and landholdings abounded in the south. Los Angeles complained, rightly, of paralyzed commerce. The southeast complained of no protection from Indian depredations. In 1852 Governor McDougal admitted as much. Legislation in a legislature controlled by California's northern counties usually benefited only the north; the south was not to have equitable legislative representation for another 80 years.

In 1851 a Convention to Divide the State of California met in Los Angeles and voted to divide the state into the state of California and the Colorado Territory. (Named for the river that today forms California's border with Arizona, the latter bore no relation to what would become the state of Colorado other than its reference to the great Southwestern river that gives its name to today's state of Colorado.) The six counties of Southern California – Los Angeles, San Bernardino, San Diego, San Luis Obispo, Santa Barbara, and Tulare - lumped together as "the cow counties" would form this new territory. "Separation, friendly and peaceful but still complete" they demanded.[32] This idea was heavily pushed by Andrés Pico (1810-76), lately a state senator after having been a military leader and governor in the last year of Mexican rule. In 1859 he introduced it to the legislature, and it was approved. There was no question that the six counties would overwhelmingly vote for it, but Congress, with civil war approaching, gave it scant attention.

At every real or imagined slight, Californians contemplated secession. Had the Bear Flaggers not incorporated with Frémont's army, had the Congress prolonged military rule, had the federal authorities intervened against the Second Vigilante Committee – which appeared very likely, then secession, whether spoken of openly or secretly, would have seemed to be a feasible solution. As it was, if some politician or newspaper editor suggested that the state's needs were being ignored, many leapt to the secession solution. With the approach of civil war clouds, Governor John Weller (1812-75, served 1858-60) proposed the Pacific Republic, a combination of California, Oregon and the territories of Washington, Nevada, Utah, and New Mexico, anticipated as a neutral region in case war broke out. Neutral status would prevent Westerners from fighting against their Northern or Southern brethren.

Sober second thoughts discouraged such a radical move. The population of the proposed nation was too small, Oregon and Utah could not carry their fair share of the financial burden, most of California's trade was with the Northern states, and the federal government had spent millions on California's development, which would then stop.

The Civil War

Throughout the 1850s significant numbers of blacks had come to California despite the tougher Fugitive Slave Act (part of the Compromise of 1850) and the intense discrimination they faced there. Though generally unwelcome in California, they came because California sheriffs were generally indifferent to the Fugitive act, the remuneration for enforcement simply not enticing to most. Some free blacks mined, as at Nigger Bar (a place destined to undergo name changes in 1855 to Granite City and in 1856 to Folsom), and many southern slave-owners brought their slaves to work for them in the mines or elsewhere, causing a great deal of opposition, sometimes violent, by whites. A few successful black miners bought their freedom in California, and so did others who prospered elsewhere than in the mines, like Biddy Mason (1818-91). Her owner had become a Mormon who went to Salt Lake City, where Brigham Young counseled him to free her, but he refused and headed to San Bernardino, a Mormon colony. Her owner planned to leave for Texas when California was admitted as a Free state, and she escaped with some other slaves. In 1856 she petitioned the court in Los Angeles for her freedom, and Judge Benjamin Ignatius Hayes (1815-77) granted her petition. She went to work as a midwife and nurse for Dr. Griffin (of the "Sponge Case") and saved her money to invest in Los Angeles real estate, amassing a fortune of $300,000 ($10,226,600 in 2023).[33]

Despite Mason's success, blacks who arrived before statehood were subject to the Fugitive Slave Act, and, like Archy Lee (1840-73), had to be constantly cautious about being returned to their home states despite the lackadaisical attitude of most sheriffs. Lee had come to Sacramento with his Mississippi owner, Charles Stovall, and was rented out for wages. A few months later Stovall, having become ill, decided to return to Mississippi but Lee escaped and was given shelter by two politically active blacks who owned a hotel in Sacramento. Stovall had him arrested, but an abolitionist attorney, Edwin B. Crocker (1818-75), defended him.[34] The court in Sacramento ruled that Lee was free because though Mississippi was a slave state, California was Free and Stovall had become a permanent resident, who therefore could not own slaves. Stovall appealed and the California Supreme Court, with Justice Terry sitting on it, overturned the verdict. Stovall prepared to leave the state. However, California abolitionists were outraged by this reversal, prevented Stovall from removing Lee, and had him arrested for kidnapping, in defiance of the court's ruling. An appeal to the U.S. District Court in San Francisco upheld the original decision, adding that Lee had not crossed state lines to escape slavery, hence Stovall did not come under the protection of the Fugitive Slave Act. Lee was declared a free man.[35] About this time California's own Fugitive Slave Law, enacted in 1852, was allowed to lapse.

The black population in California grew from about 1,000 to 2,200 in 1850-52. They established churches, two newspapers, and formed civic and literary clubs. Some were able to rise from menial positions to help themselves and other blacks to also rise to better positions. Among these were poet James Madison Bell (1826-1902), journalist Philip Bell (1808-89), Rev. Barney Fletcher (1824-?), lawyer Mifflin Gibbs (1823-1915), stage driver George Monroe (1844-86), caterer Mary Ellen "Mammy" Pleasant (1814?-1904), teacher Jeremiah Sanderson (1821-75), and Rev. Darius Stokes (1815?-?).[36]

Despite any contributions or their efforts, blacks were subjected to prejudice and hostility. Unable to own land or give testimony in court, and having to attend segregated schools, some of northern California's blacks began to look elsewhere for a home. Many of them went north to British Columbia in 1858, led by the Reverend J.J. Moore of the African Methodist Episcopal Church in San Francisco's North Beach district,[37] Mifflin Gibbs, and John W. Townsend when gold was discovered on the Fraser River.[38]

In 1860 one fourth of California's population came from the Southern states, but the split in the Democratic party that year helped Republican Abraham Lincoln (1809-65, served 1861-65) to carry the state's four electoral votes despite winning only 32.3% of the popular vote. Democrat Stephen Douglas had 734 votes less than Lincoln and chalked up 31.7%, Southern Democrat John Breckinridge garnered 28.4%, and the Constitutional Union party's John Bell took 7.6%.[39] California's two at-large congressmen were Republicans, each with a little over 15% of the popular vote out of a field of nine candidates representing Independents, Republicans, Breckenridge, and Union Democrats.

Upon Lincoln's election the Southern states began to secede and to form their own Confederate government. In 1861 Sacramento businessman Leland Stanford (1824-93) was elected the state's first Republican governor.

In April 1861 the Confederates attacked Fort Sumter, in Charleston, South Carolina, igniting the Civil War. When the news reached California Union sympathy exploded, fomented by the Rev. Thomas Starr King (1824-64), a Unitarian minister whom Lincoln dubbed without any exaggeration "the man who saved California for the Union." King's greatest contribution to the Union war effort was helping the Sanitary Commission (a forerunner of the Red Cross) to collect a great deal of money from California. Though California had less than two percent of the national population it contributed one-fourth of the money the commission collected. Two other

419

leading Unionists in California were Edward Baker, the anti-Vigilante lawyer who had moved to Oregon, joined the army and died fighting in Virginia; and a Methodist minister, Rev. Martin Briggs (1820-1903), who made many patriotic speeches and penned many editorials in the *California Christian Advocate*, a newspaper he had helped found in 1851.[40] The *San Francisco Bulletin* had been a Democratic newspaper when King of William founded it but with the start of the war it switched to the Union-Republican party.

California provided 17,000 soldiers to the Union Army, but few saw real battle. Some, like Baker, were attached with other Westerners to, the California Hundred led by Captain J. Sewall Reed (1832-64) and attached to the Second Massachusetts Cavalry under the command of Boston Brahmin Colonel Robert Lowell (1835-64), and spent several months in the summer of 1863 battling John Singleton Mosby's (1833-1916) Rangers in Virginia's Shenandoah Valley; Reed would be killed at Dranesville after a chance encounter with the Rangers routed the Union troops. Of that encounter Mosby wrote "[that although the other Union troops retreated the] Californians, especially notoriously good fighters, were standing up to the rack like men, dealing out to us the best they had. They rallied at every call on them and went down with banners flying." [41]

Most of the California troops were confined to garrison duty in the West. The Union government did not want to risk exposing the West to Confederate attack. The army that had garrisoned the Western forts had disappeared, with Northerners gone to fight for the Union and Southerners to desert to the South, leaving the West exposed to Indian uprisings or Confederate invasion. The largest unit from the state was the California Column. Aided by mountain men from Colorado, it drove Texas Confederates out of Arizona and New Mexico Territories in 1862. Tucson was a hotbed of Confederate sympathy, and the arrival of the Column caused the town to become a ghost town for a short time. Other California troops were sent to Nevada to protect the Comstock silver mines from the territory's one-third Southern-born population. Still others went to Utah to keep an eye on the Mormons, whose loyalty was questionable after the army had been involved in the "Mormon War," a result of the Mormon church's involvement in the Mountain Meadows Massacre of September 1857.[42] Mormons would not likely have joined the Confederacy, but might well have used the war as an opportunity to assert their independence. Lincoln had promised to "let Brigham Young alone if he will let me alone,"[43] a pledge that in all probability forestalled Mormon alliance with the Confederacy.

Though a minority, the pro-Confederate "Secesh" were loud. From pulpit and press, they agitated against the Union. In some papers, there was subtle reference to "President Davis" and "Mr. Lincoln," in others, direct attacks on Lincoln as "an unprincipled demagogue," an "illiterate backwoodsman," and a "narrow minded bigot." Their papers were banned from the mail, off-duty soldiers smashing their presses, as in the case of the *Visalia Equal Rights Expositor*, when its Thanksgiving Day, 1862, edition "prayed":

> "O Lord we thank thee for letting the rebels wallop us at
> the battle of Pittsburg Landing – for letting them smite us
> hip and thigh, even unto the destruction of 9,600 of our
> good loyal soldiers, and 463 of our officers; and for giving
> speed to their legs through the awful swamps of

Chicahominy; and, O Lord, most especially do we thank thee for the licking they gave us at Bull Run the second, and assisting our flight from the field...."

Loyal congregations expelled - and sometimes threatened the lives of - disloyal ministers such as the Southern-born Reverend Mr. William A. Scott (1813-85) of San Francisco, who had the temerity to insist "before presbytery" (a church leadership board) that Jefferson Davis was no more a traitor than George Washington had been.[44] *The Monitor*, San Francisco's Catholic newspaper, was suspected of disloyalty, and a mob smashed its office, throwing its press into the Bay. While the City's Protestant churches flew American flags from their steeples on July 4, 1861, Archbishop Joseph Alemany did not permit the "flagging" of Catholic churches because, even though he supported the Union, he did not feel that a nation's flag should be raised over a building dedicated to the worship of God.[45]

Fort Miller, in Fresno County, was reopened to keep the largely Southern-born population of the San Joaquin Valley under control. The biggest Secesh activity was scotched by the federals when Asbury Harpending tried to outfit a munitions ship for the Confederates under pretext of going to Mexico on a trading venture. Spies exposed the plot, and Harpending was arrested, fined a million dollars ($40,480,482 in 2023), and confined to Alcatraz for the duration (about 35 other men were to come in and share his accommodations as the island became a civilian federal prison, specifically to hold Confederate sympathizers, even those who had merely been heard making a toast to Jefferson Davis). As popular San Francisco historian Samuel Dickson relates, after the war Harpending's loyalty to the Union was never challenged.[46]

Other Southern attempts were equally unsuccessful.

Stagecoach robberies near Placerville or Santa Cruz, perhaps temporarily successful, were thwarted before any of the purloined gold reached the Confederacy, either being recovered or never leaving the robbers' possession.

Despite some entrenched feelings on both sides, the popular mood was perhaps better described as neutral or "a plague on both your houses," if the letters of Franklin Buck are an indication:

> "I read *Harpers* and sometimes see the *Atlantic Monthly,* but not regularly. It is getting to be full of abolition articles, Sumner's doctrines and Theodore Parker. I don't subscribe to it. They are just as much enemies of the Constitution and the Union as Jeff Davis and the rest and should all be hung together and if ever this difficulty is settled at the South I hope the people will settle their hash effectually at home. I have always regarded `Charles Sumner' as one of the greatest humbugs in New England..."[47]

San Francisco was protected from a possible Confederate sea attack by Fort Point, built on the site of the original Castillo de San Joaquín that Anza had built to protect the Presidio. The old fort and the hillside on which it stood had been razed and in 1853-61 Fort Point was constructed by the army engineers with the assistance of Col. Robert E. Lee (1807-70) (later a Confederate general), who designed it to be "the Gibraltar of the West." Because of Lee's skill it became one of the best examples of masonry in the nation and the largest masonry fort west of the Mississippi River. With a garrison of 600 soldiers and armed with 126 cannon spread over three levels, capable of shooting balls ranging from 24 pounds (10.9 kg) to 128 pounds (50.1 kg) up to two miles (3.2 km), as well as the gun emplacements on Alcatraz and Fort

Lime Point (now Fort Baker) on the Marin County side of the Golden Gate, the port was well guarded.[48]

Nevertheless, the threat of an attack by the iron-clad *CSS Shenandoah* under Lt. James Waddell (1824-86), who ranged from Australia to the Arctic, was very real until he learned that the war had ended four months earlier. In fact, after devastating the American whaling fleet he was on his way to capture San Francisco, which he believed lightly protected, when he heard the news and saw proof of it from a British whaler he encountered in the North Pacific.[49]

The greatest social event of the war years was the 1863 visit of the Russian Pacific fleet of four corvettes (one, its flagship *Bogatyr*) and two clippers to San Francisco. It was widely believed for many years in the North that Czar Alexander II (1818-81, ruled 1855-81) was friendly to the Union - indeed he was the only European monarch to show sympathy for the Northern cause. He wished to prevent his fleet from being bottled up in case of a war with Britain or France, a reprise of the Crimean War a decade earlier. Nevertheless, the visit was the occasion of many parties, toasts and celebrations, including the magnificent Russian Ball hosted by Governor Frederick Low (1828-94, served 1863-67), attended by 2,500 people ("all presumably loyal to the Union") and covered by the *Daily Alta California* for two days in a long story headlined "A Magnificent Festivity."[50] Portraits of Lincoln and the czar adorned the walls, supper was served at eleven o'clock in the evening and went on until five in the morning. There was the added excitement of a rumor that evening that two Confederate raiders might sail into the Bay that very night and begin bombarding the city. Admiral Andrey Alexandrovich Popov (1821-98), deeply flattered by his reception, issued orders to his men to repel any such attack, which never came. When his superiors in St.

Petersburg were apprised of this offer, they immediately countermanded it. They had not come to fight the South.[51]

San Franciscans had a special reason for appreciating the squadron's presence. On the night of October 23, 1863, a disastrous fire broke out and destroyed most of a block near downtown. Popov had sent 200 of his sailors to reinforce the fire companies. Several were severely hurt and six were killed. The citizens were touched by this kindness, and a public collection was taken up, with Barry and Patten's Saloon in the financial district as the repository for contributions to underwrite gold medals for the injured men. In return Popov offered to help defend the city should Confederate raiders attack, a move that the Russian ambassador Edouard de Stoeckl (1804-1892) applauded while cautioning Popov not to aggravate the situation. The Confederates never attacked, and many residents credited the Russian presence for dissuading it.[52]

The war caused not a few inconveniences for Californians. The cost of maritime insurance rose due to rumors of Confederate raiders off the coast, letters from the East might be delayed or lost because of Indian attacks on the Pony Express or the Overland stages, and any men arriving from the East had to have passports to prevent Confederate volunteers' leaving through Southern California or sailing to Europe to return to the South.

The war ended in April 1865, a week later Lincoln was assassinated, and these events altered the destiny of two San Francisco newspapers. Throughout the war *The Democratic Press* had hurled its vitriol against the president. Hearing of his assassination, an angry crowd destroyed its office, putting it out of business; it would be reborn two months later as *The Daily Examiner*. A new paper, The Daily Dramatic Chronicle, had been started on January16, 1865 by two brothers, Charles

(1845-80) and Michael H. de Young (1849-1925), to report theatrical news. The Chronicle scooped the other San Francisco newspapers by publishing the news of Lincoln's assassination on April 16,1865, following this report with an engraving of the Lincoln assassination scene, published on April 25 and again the next day. This was one of the earliest illustrations to appear in the American press. The response was so tremendous, that it announced on the following day that the engraving could be procured "on satin-surface cards at all the stationers and news dealers, at one bit (121/2 cents [$2.38 in 2023]) per copy." The brothers spread their newspaper into the state's interior in an ingenious way: copies left on theater floors were retrieved, ironed smooth on an ironing board, and brought to the docks to be taken up to the mining camps. Within three months it would lead the others in subscriptions. The "failing" *Daily Examiner* would be bought by U.S. Senator George Hearst (1820-91) "as partial payment of a poker debt" and turned over to his son, William Randolph Hearst (1863-1951), in 1887.[53] The *Dramatic Chronicle* would become the *Daily Morning Chronicle*, a general newspaper, in 1868. Both would be used to further their owners' political careers.

The end of the war brought the end of the political struggles, rooted in the slavery question, that had plagued California since statehood. For the nation and for California it was new chapter to be filled with new adventures.

Mining Techniques

Most of the Argonauts, as the miners were called by a generation steeped in classical literature regardless of grade level attained, often arrived in California with no intention of staying, but for various reasons many did remain in the Far West. After 1855, California gold mining changed: It was now beyond the "rush" era. By 1865 miners had taken out over $750 million (over $14 billion in 2023) in gold, necessarily an estimate because plenty of gold was hidden to avoid freight costs. The miners practiced three types of mining techniques: placer, hydraulic and quartz.

Placer mining was the simplest, requiring only a pan. However, most placer miners fitted boxes together to make a sluice box. The interior bottom of the sluice box was concave with riffles along the edge to catch any gold particles being carried in the two-inch-wide (5cm) stream that rinsed the shovelful of dirt tossed in. To make it easier to catch the gold, mercury was often used, since mercury amalgamates with gold. The mercury came from the New Almaden Mine near San Jose, and its use later led to pollution of some streams and even coastal waters.

When the easy placer pickings gave out in 1850, the red-shirted miners started exploring the hillsides and using mules to pack the gold-bearing gravel to streams to sluice the gold from the gravel. In Nevada County two small ditches were dug from Mosquito and Deer creeks, and the water was sold repeatedly until the last miner down the line got it, full of mud, for a dollar a day ($39.25 in 2023).

A man named Moore (first name unknown) got the idea of building a large-scale ditch. In August 1850 he started to dig one from Deer Creek, above Nevada City, to Rough and Ready. The miners thought he was crazy, but he continued digging for a mile (1.6 km) before he quit. Others later completed it, but four other men built a ditch from Rock Creek to Coyote Hill - a distance of nine miles (14.5 km) at a cost of $10,000 ($392,499 in 2023). The investment was recovered in less than six weeks by the sale of water to the miners who had claims lying along the ditch.

Ditch and water companies sprang up all over the Diggings as miners moved farther back into the hills. Within twenty years there more than 6,000 miles (9,656 km) of canals, ranging from short laterals to the $1.5 million ($60,720,724 in 2023) South Yuba canal with its 3,100-foot (949.9 m) tunnel through a granite peak and its cliff-hanging flume - engineering marvels of the day.

Hydraulic mining at Nevada City. The card from the Western Card Company in Reedley is dated 1912. After the ruling in the Sawyer Decision, hydraulic mining could only be practiced if none of the debris left the miner's property. (Courtesy of the California History Room, California State Library, Sacramento, California)

Hydraulic mining was the most efficient but the most polluting and damaging to the environment. A water cannon shot a high-pressure stream against a mountainside to coax the gold out. The displaced soil would eventually clog rivers and land on private property, doing considerable damage. No one particularly stopped to think of injury being inflicted on ecosystems, since such considerations come from a thought category not yet invented. In 1884 the state Supreme Court outlawed hydraulic mining with the "Sawyer Decision."

Justice Lorenzo Sawyer (1820-91) handed down a decision in *Woodruff v North Bloomfield Mining and Gravel Company*, an anti-debris lawsuit alleging that the company's tailings had destroyed Edwards Woodruff's farmland in Marysville.[54] The complainant prevailed against the company.

Quartz mining involved digging inside mountain caves to find veins of gold to tap into. The first quartz gold was discovered by George Knight (sometimes McKnight) in October 1850 on a hillside at Grass Valley. He saw a large outcropping of white rock laced with yellow and began pounding it with a cast iron skillet and hammer. Then he had only to wash the gold. Looking for more gold, he dug down into the outcropping and found a gold vein about four inches (10 cm) long. Grass Valley and Nevada City took off with over 150 buildings put up in the next year to accommodate the thousands of people who moved there. He and some friends then built a crude stamp mill from pine logs and metal boots, powering it with Wolf Creek's rushing water. This was the Gold Hill Mine, and by the time it was done in 1864 it had produced over $4,000,000 ($79.6 million in 2023). Several other large companies operated quartz mines, and although the individual miners despised quartz mining - because they couldn't compete with it - it did produce a third of California's gold. In the long run this method caused the least long-term damage to the environment. In 1883, inventor Lester Pelton (1829-1908) discovered a new method for powering stamp mills, using a water wheel with rotating cups on the inner edge to accelerate it and extract more gold from the ore.[55]

Mercury is not biodegradable. In sufficient quantities it can cause blindness, insanity, or death. (Lewis Carroll's Mad Hatter, from his *Alice's Adventures in Wonderland* [1865], was understood to be "mad" because hat makers inhaled mercury vapors and used their fingers and brushes to rub mercury on the fur hats they manufactured to preserve them and enhance their appearance.) The mercury poured into streams by mining eventually found its way into the Pacific Ocean via the Sacramento or San Joaquin River systems and San Francisco Bay. The damage continues today. Every ten to twenty years there are seasonal prohibitions on the catching and selling of certain ocean fish species which are found to be too high in mercury content. The scars left on hillsides by hydraulic miners can still be seen in the Sierra, and the flooding which routinely threatened Central Valley towns until the 1960s was in great part due to the mud that washed down and stayed in the stream and riverbeds, raising the normal water flow above the crest line.

Trade and Freighting

A tremendous increase in consumers and their purchasing power caused stores to spring up all over the Diggings. Their inventories started with basics such as salt pork, flour, and whiskey, plus a few tools. Eventually they sold other commodities as the supply system improved. Although minimally efficient, the supply system was handicapped because there was no regular way for merchants to order goods from Eastern or foreign suppliers. Surplus goods from the East or other countries might be shipped to California. This caused some goods to be overstocked and some to be scarce - only to result in a reversal in which items were surplus and which ones scarce a month or two later.

Freighters coming out of Stockton and Sacramento used wagons and pack trains to haul goods to the remotest districts, and often performed mail, freight, and banking services for the miners.

Typical of merchandising strategy was that of New York medical doctor Daniel Knower (1817-97), who arrived in San

Francisco in 1849 with a dozen prefabricated wooden houses.

As a class, storekeepers, necessary as they were, were not well thought of because of the high prices they charged.

Many of the merchants were Jews, primarily from Germany, while a few were from Russian Poland. Two of these were brothers Michael (1821-1903) and Joseph Goldwasser (1833-89); they migrated from London (where Michael had married a Jewish lady, Sarah Nathan [1828-1905]) to New York, then to California via Panama, to search for gold. Coming into California late in 1852, Joseph headed for the mining camp of Sonora, arriving in 1853. There were already many other Jewish merchants there, but the Goldwassers found they did not have the resources to start a merchandising operation. The least expensive venture would be in a saloon. When Michael's English wife Sarah and their two children came to Sonora, she was not pleased with the business her husband had chosen, and even less so when she learned that upstairs from the bar someone else was running a brothel.

The Goldwasser brothers did poorly in Sonora and fared no better when they moved to Los Angeles, where the brothers had a billiard parlor, bar, and tobacco shop in the Bella Union Hotel. Renamed Goldwater, Michael had brought with him from the Sonora failure more than $3,000 ($111,032 in 2023) in debts, and he filed for a bankruptcy plan in which he could pay off his creditors (like a Chapter 11 bankruptcy today.) A friendship with a Los Angeles doctor, Wilson W. Jones (1826-96), transformed the Goldwaters' fortunes. Dr. Jones had been to the Arizona mining camp at Gila City and convinced Michael of the business possibilities there. Brother Joe advanced funds for Michael to purchase a wagon, merchandise to be peddled to the miners, and four mules to pull all of it on the hard desert ride to the Colorado River. Gila

City was some twenty miles (32 km) north of the present site of Yuma, Arizona, and home to a thousand miners.

Sarah apparently never enjoyed life in the American West. San Francisco, compared to London, was crude; Sonora, even rougher. Naturally she believed the Arizona Territory was no place for a cultured Jewish woman, and it is thought that she spurned coming to the area where her husband was establishing what was to become the Goldwater empire; it is possible that she came to Arizona only once. Most of her life was spent in Los Angeles and San Francisco, where her husband visited often enough to expand the Goldwater family to eight children; one of these, Baron (1866-1929), became the father of Arizona Republican Senator (and 1964 presidential candidate) Barry Goldwater (1909-98).

Michael was very active in Jewish affairs on the western frontier. In California he had been a member and officer in three Jewish congregations. When he completed his Arizona adventures and returned to San Francisco to be with his wife, he once again became a leader in Jewish affairs. He was chairman of the committee that founded Hills of Eternity Cemetery at Colma (where Marshall Wyatt Earp [1848-1929] is buried in the Marcus family plot, his third wife being Josephine Sarah Marcus [1861-1944].) Michael headed the first Hebrew Benevolent Society in San Francisco and chaired the first Zionist meeting in that city March 1, 1898, a year after the world Zionist movement was organized in Basel. Michael's role in the movement made him an anomaly, since the richer, better educated Jews typically despised Zionism.

Another enterprising Jewish merchant was Levi Strauss (1829-1902), who immigrated from Bavaria in 1850. When he got to San Francisco he unpacked yards of heavy drill, needles, thread, and scissors. At first thinking them destined to make tents, but he used them instead to sew up durable clothing for the miners. He made a succession of quick sales. From the mines he wrote to his two brothers still in New York to bring a supply of brown canvas, duck, and denim pants. When Strauss' sister married David Stern (1820-75), he joined the business, a tradition that has been followed by the in-laws in all the succeeding generations. In the 1860s he heard a Virginia City tailor recount jokingly how he had repaired a miner's pants with rivets that he got from a harness shop. To Strauss the "joke" was a business idea, and he had his lawyer obtain a patent for copper-riveted pants pockets. The use of riveting distinguished Strauss' work clothes, making them durable and popular, establishing the founder's first name, Levi, as a household word in the U.S. and abroad.

The original product was slightly modified after several businessmen went on a fishing expedition, and one wore these riveted pants. When he sat too close to the campfire the rivets at the crotch heated up, and he had to remove the pants in a hurry; when he got back to San Francisco he complained to the store, and from then on rivets were removed from the pants' crotch area.

After his death in 1902, bachelor Levi's four nephews succeeded him in the business.

Anti-Semitism was as present in California as elsewhere in the Western World. Santa Cruz lemon grower and lawyer William Stow (1824-95), Whig and Know-Nothing speaker of the state assembly (January-May 1855), sponsored a Sunday closing bill intended to attack Jews as undesirables who had come to the state for gain; since most people had come for this very purpose, the accusation was not only bigoted but inane.

Speaker Stow proposed an expensive head tax on Jews to force them to leave the community. The *Los Angeles Daily Star*, which frequently encouraged lynchings to solve criminal cases, responded: "Such bigoted views show an intolerance entirely adverse to the spirit and character of our institutions.... Our just tribute to our Jewish fellow citizens will be read with admiration by every person possessing the enlarging ideas, the generous impulses that constitute a true American."[56] After he left office another Sunday closing law, aimed at Jewish businesses, was passed in 1858. That same year a Jewish man sued for the right to work on Sunday and the state Supreme Court ruled in his favor, declaring the particular law unconstitutional because it was a discrimination in favor of one religious profession.[57] In 1882 the same court declared a Sunday-closing law constitutional if it was not meant to promote or denigrate any particular faith, but merely "as a day of rest... imposed on the people of the state as members of the body politic, without reference to the religious faith and worship of any."[58]

Not all of California's successful merchants were European Jews. Stephen C. Davis (1833-56), a young Yankee Protestant from New Hampshire, and his brother came to California via Panama in 1850, as agents for local merchants. He went into business, crossing the Isthmus three more times by1854. After his second crossing and return to California the brothers, reunited in San Francisco, and took boats to Marysville. They began a quest for gold on the Yuba River near Rose's Bar, but with only $1.40 ($82.58 in 2023) to show for three days of backbreaking labor Stephen decided to try his luck at some other kind of "prospecting." After several abortive business ventures, Stephen and brother Josiah (ca.1830-54) set up a store and boardinghouse for miners at Long Bar on the Yuba. On their trips to San Francisco and Sacramento for supplies they carried the miners' mail.

They enjoyed a good deal of success during the next six months. When Stephen returned to New Hampshire, the New

434

England winter convinced him that California was the place to be.

When a ship arrived at Long Wharf in San Francisco April 1, 1852, he boarded it. Purchasing "pickles, cheese, segars," potatoes, and other provisions, Stephen boarded a sloop for Stockton, intending to set up a store in the area south of the Mokelumne River. Setting out from Stockton for Sonora, Stephen passed through Knight's Ferry, Chinese Camp, and Shaw's Flat, then trudged around for more than a month searching for work, visiting Coulterville, Agua Fria, and Mariposa. He had met a man from his native New England, and during the latter part of May arranged to go into business with him at Coulterville. For two years Stephen kept a store at Coulterville on Maxwell's Creek, writing during this period about his expeditions to Stockton and San Francisco for supplies. Business was brisk, causing gaps in his journal entries of more than a month. Josiah moved to Oregon, but news of his death soon reached Stephen, in April 1854. This loss intensified Stephen's desire to be once more with his family and friends.

After settling affairs with his business partner, Stephen left Coulterville on April 24. He carried with him more than $3,000 ($121,441 in 2023) in gold dust, the fruit of his two years of storekeeping, as well as part ownership in two quartz veins. He later received from J.A. Hilliard (c1830-?), his partner, a check for $769 ($31,129 in 2023) for his remaining share in the store on Maxwell's Creek.[59]

**

"All the Sacramento Valley is good for in my opinion, is to raise mosquitoes and fever ague."

-Visitor from Vermont, 1864

435

Agriculture and Industry

At first California was heavily dependent on other areas for goods and services. Oregon supplied eggs and grain, Chile sent jerky and Hawaii did California's laundry! (While some are skeptical about this claim, several others assert it was the case).[60] Soon, however, local producers came to the rescue. Many would-be wealthy men who had been disappointed by mining turned to the land for wealth.

In 1847 Iowa Quaker Henderson Luelling (1809-79) loaded several wagons with seven hundred trees, vines, and shrubs, including such varieties as apple, cherry, pear, plum, black walnut, and quince, and set out on the Oregon Trail. His imports helped launch a multimillion-dollar orchard business in California and Oregon.

Los Angeles shipped crops to San Francisco to satisfy a growing demand, but shipments were inefficient and irregular. Many Easterners who went south had innovative ideas about capital improvements in the harbor area. The Sepulvedas' landing at what became San Pedro, made known to Americans by Richard Henry Dana, was improved by A. W. Timms (1825-88) and J. J. Tomlinson (?-1904). At the same time, Delaware native Phineas Banning (1830-95) and David W. Alexander (1812-86), the collector at San Pedro, upgraded inland transportation by applying Eastern commercial techniques. Banning built railroads and stage lines 21 miles (34 km) from the new town of Wilmington to San Pedro. Seeing that the area would become agriculturally productive, he foresaw that the San Pedro Bay harbor would be the natural exporting base, serving not only Los Angeles but the San Fernando and San Gabriel valleys as well. By 1853 a regular shipping service was operating between San

Pedro harbor and San Francisco.

Those four Easterners – Timms, Tomlinson, Banning and Alexander –had observed railroads from ports inland since their childhoods, and when they became landowners in Southern California, eager to develop their lands, they began drilling and building canals and flumes to irrigate. In 1854 they purchased Manuel Domínguez's 2,400 acres (971 ha) for about a dollar ($37.01 in 2023) an acre (0.4 ha). Ridiculed as "Banning's goose pond" in the winter weather when thousands of ducks and geese gathered, it would make a better harbor closer to Los Angeles, and its flat ground would make an easy railroad route. When the federal government in 1855 agreed to improve the Los Angeles-Salt Lake City Road for $50,000 ($1.799 million in 2023), Salt Lake City could use San Pedro harbor for imports and exports. The Pacific Mail Steamship Company and the Butterfield Stage Route (more about them later), received federal subsidies to operate and improve communication between the "States" (the distant "rest of the U.S." beyond those endless territories) and San Francisco. Southern California was ignored in this, the mail just being dropped off sometimes on the beach by a shore boat. Banning would go to the seashore when he knew a boat would be coming in and bring the mail sacks back to town.

Several disasters plagued Los Angeles during these early American decades. A smallpox epidemic in 1861-62, storms that brought over 50 inches (1.27 m) of rain that swelled streams and washed away adobes, drought that wiped out the cattle industry, the wreck of the *Ada Hancock* with the death of over 50 passengers: Such catastrophes seemed to point to a non-existent future. In fact, southern California was about a decade away from exploding with agricultural prosperity.[61]

Cattle and sheep production soared. In 1848 there had been 300,000 head. In the 1850s cattle from Texas and sheep from

New Mexico were driven in until a blooded stock was available in California, and by 1860 there were three million head. Then a severe drought followed by floods and accompanied by ruinous interest rates destroyed the old cattle empires. In 1870 only 630,000 head were counted. In response to heavy demand for leather, several tanneries opened in Sacramento and other northern towns. Beginning in 1858, the Miller and Lux Ranch (owned by German immigrants Henry Miller, originally Heinrich Alfred Kreiser [1827-1916] and Charles Lux [1823-87]), with headquarters at Los Banos, became the largest spread in California. Miller and Lux held additional land in Oregon and Nevada, 1.4 million acres (5,666,000 ha) directly owned, and they controlled nearly 20,000 square miles (57,000 sq km) of cattle ranchland. It was once estimated that they owned one-seventh of California, and it was said, perhaps with some exaggeration, that they could start their cattle as the southern limit of Arizona and drive them to Oregon without ever leaving their property.[62] Raising Durham, Hereford and Devon cattle, stronger breeds than those raised by Californio rancheros, allowed Miller and Lux to survive the droughts and floods that plagued California in 1855-56, 1863-64, and 1898-99.[63] Miller was a major player in the development of the San Joaquin Valley during the 19th and early 20th centuries, maintaining and micromanaging his corporate farming empire in the style that became common with the industrial barons of the Gilded Age. In part he acquired large tracts of the normally arid land by using the federal Swamp Act of 1850, originally enacted for use in Arkansas, which was intended to help people to lay claim to any swamp land that one could row a boat across. Miller waited until flooded San Joaquin land dried and then hoisted a rowboat onto a wagon chassis and drove for miles over the area, thus claiming it as reclaimed swamp land and earning for some the soubriquet "Swampy Miller." He corresponded with his employees in great detail, insisting that the cattle he sold met his high standards, and kept track of weather and water availability for his ranchland.[64]

The Central Valley became the wheat-growing center of California, existing mainly to feed the miners. California's mildew-resistant wheat soon became the preferred one to grow in the tropics. From 17,000 bushels (600 cu m) in 1850 to 5.9 million (207,900 cu m) in 1860, California became a leading wheat producer and exporter, selling to the nation and the world.[65] All vegetables were found to have long growing seasons in California, and several areas became specialty districts for certain fruits - strawberries in the Santa Clara Valley, oranges in southern California and apples in Sonoma County.

Wine production, growing steadily since early mission days, became a major industry when Hungarian Count Agoston Harazthy (1812-69) brought zinfandel and tokay cuttings from Europe to the Napa Valley in 1858. In 1861 the legislature sent him to Europe as Grape Commissioner to discover the best means of cultivating vineyards in California and published a report in *Grape Culture, Wines and Wine-Making; with Notes upon Agriculture and Horticulture* (1862). In 1866 business reverses cost him his own 300 acres (121.4 ha) of vines and 5,000 acres (2, 023 ha) of farmland just east of Sonoma. Two of his sons, Attila (1835-86) and Arpad (1840-1900), married daughters of General Vallejo but he left for Nicaragua where he planned to cultivate sugar. He died when he was attacked and eaten by an alligator after falling into a Nicaraguan river. In 1852, Frenchman Charles Lefranc (1825-87) brought grape cuttings from France to southern California to plant in the soil where Almaden's home winery in San Jose had stood for many years (the company moved to Madera). Paul Masson (1859-1940) came from

France in 1878 to work for Lefranc, soon became a partner, married Lefanc's daughter and became head of the firm, planting new vineyards in the Saratoga foothills. Up in Napa, German Jacob Schram (1826-1904) founded his Schramsberg Vineyards north of St. Helena in 1862 with the largest underground wine storing tunnels of any United States vineyard. These had been dug by Chinese laborers. In *The Silverado Squatters* (1883) Robert Louis Stevenson (1850-94) celebrated Schram's wines. By 1870, with 28 million vines, California's two million gallons (7,570,824 L) of wine annually made it the leading producer in North America. Then in the 1880s came the root-destroying *phylloxera* and other pests, driving out the enthusiastic beginners and speculators and leaving the industry in the hands of the more experienced. Ironically, American grapes are more resistant to phylloxera than are European varieties, but it was the importation of infected vines that spread the disease in California. Grafting and hybridization finally made the problem manageable, saving the industry.

At first California wines were stronger and less delicate than European wines, but gradually, by experimentation, soil analysis, and the use of more scientific methods to extract and ferment the juice, the market for California varieties was increased.

German Claus Spreckels (1828-1908) came to San Francisco penniless in 1848 and worked as a grocery boy until he opened his own store and became interested in sugar refining, acquiring a small plant of his own in 1863. He studied European ways of production on a trip to Germany, tried to grow sugar cane in southern California, but failed, so he had to rely on Hawaiian cane for his sugar refinery at Crockett. Financing the Hawaiian kingdom by making personal loans to the king he was able to control most of the

Islands' production and shipping to San Francisco.[66] He used his wealth to create independent gas, light, and power companies, as well as a streetcar line to rival the established utilities. His four sons, John (1853-1926), Adolph (1857-1924), Claus (1858-1946) and Rudolph (1872-1958) would exert great influence in civic and business matters for many years to come.

James Folger (1835-89) from Massachusetts came with his brothers via Panama for gold when he was fourteen but soon got a job as a clerk and bookkeeper in the Pioneer Steam Coffee and Spice Mill founded in 1850 by William Bovee (1824-94) in San Francisco. Commercially roasted coffee was a luxury on the East Coast, and was unknown to the population at large, while ground coffee was unheard of at the wholesale level. Bovee, learning that Folger was a carpenter, hired him to build his first mill. The next year he went looking for gold but took along samples of coffee and spices to take orders from grocery stores in the Diggings until he arrived at Yankee Jim's, where he had a mining claim. In 1865 he returned to San Francisco, became a full partner in Pioneer Steam Coffee, and in 1872 bought out Bovee and the other partners, including August Schilling (1854-1934), who would go on to found his own spice company nine years later. He renamed the company J. A. Folger & Company and controlled most of the coffee market on the West Coast.[67] Bovee moved to the East Bay and became the eighth mayor of Oakland (1863-64).

Domenico Ghirardelli (1817-94) from Genoa learned chocolate making in Italy, moved to Uruguay and Peru, and was encouraged to go to California in 1849 by James Lick, who had brought 600 pounds (273 kg) of chocolate to San Francisco the previous year. Caught up in the Gold Rush, Ghirardelli, who had changed his first name to Domingo when living in South America, went to the mines and eventually settled as a merchant in Hornitos. In 1852 he moved to San Francisco, where he eventually became the City's most successful chocolatier. In 1865 one of his workers noticed that by hanging a bag of ground cacao beans in a warm room, the cocoa butter would drip off, and the residue could then be converted into ground chocolate. This became known as the Broma Process, and soon became the commonest method for producing chocolate. An interesting note about his name: The family spent a lot of money trying to get people to pronounce it correctly, with wall-sized ads showing a parrot instructing the public to say "GEAR-ar-delly" rather than the natural-to-English-speakers "Jeer-ar-delly".[68]

During the 1860s the state encouraged silkworm cultivation with various bounties. Frenchman Louis Prévost (1806-69) planted mulberry trees all around Riverside, but when the cost of eggs went to ten dollars ($220 in 2023) per ounce the bounties stopped, so Prévost stopped production. About the time of Prévost's death, a group of 26 Japanese, known as the Wakamatsu Colony, arrived in Gold Hill, near Coloma. This group of settlers was composed of people who had backed the losing Shogunate side in Japan's brief (1867-68) civil war between the Emperor Meiji (1852-1912, reigned 1867-1912) and Tokugawa Yoshinobu (1837-1913), the last Shogun, and led by John Henry Schell, a Dutchman who had married the daughter of a samurai of the Wakamatsu clan. They planted mulberry trees, grape cuttings, and other plants, hoping to establish silk and tea plantations, but failed due to drought and the lack of promised financial aid from Japan,[69] They abandoned the project after two years. English-born Taos trader and naturalized Mexican William Workman tried planting cotton in Kern County but failed because of a labor shortage. With failed unsuccessful projects abounding until mid-20th century, San Francisco's textile mills were limited to producing wool and jute, the latter needed for grain sacks.

Lumber and explosives were required for the mines and lumber for the many homes and other buildings going up. Most of the lumber was redwood from Humboldt County or pine and redwood from the Sierra, and Contra Costa County had explosives plants. Once on the ground the logs were sawed into twenty-foot (6 m) lengths and then moved to the mill fastened with steel cables down "log chutes" pulled by donkeys or mules, by horses pulling them on wheels, or by flumes such as the one built in 1876 with an approximately 2,500-foot (762 m) elevation drop from the headwaters of the Fresno River 52 miles (83.7 km) to Madera.[70]

The wagon industry was as common in the 19th century as car dealerships and automotive repair shops are today. One of its leaders was John Studebaker (1833-1917) from Pennsylvania, who settled in Placerville, starting as a wheelbarrow maker for miners (he was known as "Wheelbarrow Johnny"), and whose wagon making business founded in 1852 would eventually (1902) move to Indiana and evolve into the automobile manufacturing business. Much of the iron needed for mining and the railroads came from ship's scrap iron ballast turned into steel in San Francisco foundries.

Not all entrepreneurs were successful. Daniel Knower recounted how a friend, a poor credit risk, wanted to borrow money to start California's first brewery. Knower had loaned him a modest amount but balked at larger loans. The friend secured the money elsewhere, but "When most completed, a barrel of alcohol that was in the building bursted, [sic] and it ran down to the furnace and set it on fire, and burnt it up. That was the fate of the first brewery started in California. Since then, there have been millions made in that business there." [71]

Banking and the Comstock

Gold Rush banking began with saloon and storekeepers who held deposits and charged 5% per month storage fee, while making loans at 36% annual interest. Having been hurt by bank failures in the late 1830s and again in 1855, most Americans in California distrusted banks. Anyone could start one with minimal regulations. Most of California's denizens despised paper money, preferring gold or silver coin, and money from all over the world circulated in San Francisco for many years, as well as coins struck off by private companies. Despite the quantity of gold pouring into San Francisco, there was a scarcity of coin and currency.

About a dozen private coin issuers operated in San Francisco between 1849 and 1855, some for only a year. The federal government did not recognize coins struck outside of the U.S. Mint, but prior to 1864 they were legal because while states were forbidden to coin money, private individuals were free to produce coinage as long as theirs did not resemble those of the United States. The first privately minted coins were $5 ($202.40 in 2023) pieces struck by Norris, Grieg, and Norris in Benicia, although bearing the imprint of San Francisco. John Little Moffat (1788-1865) and three other New Yorkers formed Moffat & Company in early 1849, and when Congress authorized the Treasury Department to establish an official Assay Office in San Francisco soon after statehood, Moffat & Co. obtained the right to operate it. Augustus Humbert, (1817- c 1905) a German-born New York watchmaker was appointed official assayer and began stamping $50 ingots in January 1851. Early in 1852 Moffat withdrew from the company to start a diving bell business, and his erstwhile partners reorganized the business as the United States Assay Office of Gold, issuing $50, $20, and $10 ($2,024, $810, and $404.80 in 2023) coins in 1853. In

December 1853 the business closed to make way for the official U.S. Mint. Since the Mint could not begin operations immediately because of a lack of refining acids, a former employee of Moffat & Co. and a former assayer from the Assay Office, formed Kellogg & Co. to supply businessmen with urgently needed coinage; they began minting private $20 coins. Following several changes in ownership, Kellogg & Co. closed its doors in 1860. [72]

William Ralston (1826-75) and his very sound Bank of California ended the general distrust of banks. As will be seen, what allowed Ralston and his bank to achieve stability was the discovery of silver in Nevada in 1859.

The Grosh brothers, Ethan Allen (1825-57) and Hosea Ballou (?-1857), two Pennsylvanians who were veterans of the California Gold Rush, had found some samples of silver in 1857, in what became the Comstock. They tried to go to California to raise money for mining, but both died on the way. Before leaving they had given a map of the find and access to their cabin to Henry Comstock (1820-70), a Nevada assayer known as the "sanctimonious gaffer."[73] An uneducated man, he thought nothing of the scientific papers the Grosh brothers had left behind, but then Comstock discovered that the bluish rock miners were throwing away as a waste product while searching for gold at nearby Gold Hill actually had silver of sufficient grade to produce $4,800 ($172,716 in 2023) per ton (907 kg) of rock.

Peter O'Reilly and Patrick McLaughlin are also credited as the discoverers of the silver lode. They had started working at the head of Six-Mile Canyon but were about to abandon it when they discovered "a layer of rich black sand" that turned out to be the top of the hidden Ophir Bonanza. Comstock claimed that they had made their discovery on land originally belonging to the Grosh brothers, but that he, Comstock, had claimed. There was some doubt as to the accuracy of this assertion. Unhappy with what he was finding at Gold Hill, he forced himself into the O'Reilly-McLoughlin partnership, others joined, adding improvements such as arrastras (water-powered rock grinders) and rockers. What they found was sand that they thought was a rich sulfide of silver, but which was, in fact, about 75% silver and 25% gold. With the discovery of this amazingly rich lode on June 27, 1859, silver mining in the United States began.

There is a great deal of muddled lore about the discovery, who really did it, where it was precisely, but that seemed to matter little as a boom started: 10,000 Californians headed east over new roads to begin mining. The Comstock never made its discoverer rich, nor for that matter did Marshall and Sutter ever get wealthy from the gold they discovered at Coloma. The vein was only about two miles (3.2 km) long and only a few hundred feet wide at most. The Ophir Mine, in which Comstock was a partner, was washing $50 to $75 ($1,851-$2,776 in 2023) a day from a single tub of crushed ore, but Comstock received very little of it; in fact, disgusted that he never made his fortune from anything he attempted, he committed suicide in Montana. Thanks to Banker Ralston's willingness to invest in silver mining, Mount Davidson was soon honeycombed with 750 miles (1,207 km) of crisscrossing tunnels and shafts, and Virginia City became a boom town on the slope of the mountain. The town was named by a drunken but skillful miner known as "Old Virginny" (rather than by his real name of James Fennimore), an enemy of Comstock. One night in 1859, Old Virginny, "who," according to Comstock historians Warren Hinckle (1938-2016) and Frederic Hobbs (1931-2018),

"had not suffered the debilitating effects of sobriety

during this period, stumbled and dropped the last bottle of his stash on the rocky crust of the mountainside. He fell to his knees and swilled the last drops of tarantula juice from the remaining cup-shaped bottom of the bottle. Staying put on his knees, he made of the horrifying incident a baptismal party by shouting to the sky, 'I christen this place Virginia Town.'"[74]

The miners who went down into the hard ground with pick, shovel and candle were the best paid in the world. At the same time, conditions in the mines were among the worst - thermal activity heating the tunnels up to 140 degrees Fahrenheit (60o Celsius). The miners often wore ice-pack hats, yet more died from underground heat than from any other single cause.[75] In 1868 a railroad was built between Virginia City and Carson City, the Virginia & Truckee Railroad, to carry silver ore and miners between the mines and the mint.

There were six major bonanzas during the first five years of the Comstock. The Ophir was prosperous until 1864, producing 70,000 tons (63,503 metric tons). Though rich and having a length of 500 (152.4 m) feet at the surface, the ore body wedged out at a depth of 500 feet (152.4 m). The Gold & Curry bonanza included 500 feet (152.4 m) of the El Dorado outcrop but dipped southward into the Savage at 500 feet (152.4 m). The ore gave out by 1866. The Savage bonanza included this ore body and a second bonanza, an ore body shared with Hale & Norcross to the south, at the 600-foot (182.9 m) level. This ore body played out by 1869. The Chollar-Potosi bonanza was consolidated in 1865. The 1875 Combination Shaft was a joint effort by Chollar-Potosi and Hale & Norcross. The Original Gold Hill bonanza consisted of the Old Red Ledge, 1,000 feet (304.8 m) long, 500 feet (152.4 m) wide, and 500 feet (152.4 m) deep. The associated

Gold Hill mines were merged into the Consolidated Imperial by 1876. The Yellow Jacket shared the Gold Hill bonanza on its north, and shared a second bonanza with Crown Point and Kentuck [sic] to the south, these last two discovered in 1864.

The Crown Point-Belcher bonanza's ore body, discovered in 1870, extended from the 900 (274.3 m) to the 1,500-foot (457.2 m) level, had a length of 775 feet (236.2 m) and a width of 120 feet (36.57 m). The ore, 54% gold and 46% silver, lasted only four years. The Consolidated Virginia bonanza was discovered at the 1,200-foot (365.76 m) level in March 1873. The ore body was 900 feet (274.32 m) long and 200 feet (60.96 m) wide, and terminated at the 1,650-foot level (502.92 m).[76]

The wealth of the Comstock - estimated at over one billion dollars ($19 billion in 2023]) - helped the Union finance the Civil War and built much of San Francisco. Virginia City was for a time the biggest city between St. Louis and San Francisco, with 25,000 people, and one of the most fashionable. As Beebe and Clegg summarized it: "Con-Virginia, Best & Belcher, Yellow Jacket, Hale & Norcross and Ophir became household names throughout the entire world….[and] in its years of teem Virginia City was a dateline in the news as familiar to millions as that of Paris, London or Boston."[77] During the Civil War modern fund raising is said to have had its genesis when a 50 pound (22.7 kg) sack of flour was auctioned off for the Sanitary Commission and eventually garnered $5,000 ($122,206 in 2023) from Virginia City; each winning bidder would put it up again and again. Julia Bulette (1832-67), the town's most famous and popular prostitute, had addressed a town meeting to support the Commission and was one of those who started the bidding.[78]

Scores of millionaires and multimillionaires had been made by the Comstock, and they had the money to lavish upon their mansions, their town, their mistresses, and their liquor. In fact, the Comstock became famous for both its development of mining techniques and the amount of wealth it generated.

Recalling those days in Roughing It (1872), Mark Twain (1835-1910) wrote:

> "Virginia has grown to be the 'livest' town, for its age and
> population, that America had ever produced. The sidewalks swarmed with people. . .
> it was generally no easy matter to stem the human tide. The streets themselves were just as crowded with quartz wagons, freight teams, and other
> vehicles. The procession was endless. . . buggies frequently had to wait half an hour for the opportunity to cross the principal street. Joy sat on every
> countenance, and there was a glad, almost fierce, intensity in every eye, that told of the money-getting schemes that were seething in every brain
> and the high hope that held sway in every heart. Money was as plenty as dust.... The 'flush times' were in magnificent flower!"

Two Irish saloonkeepers in San Francisco, James Flood (1826-89) and William O'Brien (1825-78), had harkened to their customers' advice and invested wisely. Flood's and O'Brien's saloon, the Auction Lunch, was located next to the city's most important produce market, where many gentlemen shopped, stepping into the bar afterward for a drink. Then the San Francisco Mining Exchange opened a few doors down from the saloon, and the Exchange's patrons became the saloon's patrons. The two Irishmen soon moved up to forming their own mining brokerage. Two other Irishmen would encounter them, "genial and urbane" John Mackay (1831-

1902) and James Fair (1831-94), "well and unfavorably known to his associates as Slippery Jim."[79] McKay and Fair, practical miners, formed a partnership with Flood and O'Brien. In 1875 the four, known as the "Silver Kings," founded their own San Francisco bank, the Nevada Bank, with a capitalization of $5,000,000 ($140,801,677 in 2023); the next year the capitalization was doubled, making it the largest of any bank on the Pacific Coast. When Ralston had tried to keep these competitors from growing, they engaged in an economic war from which they emerged successful.

On October 31, 1864, the Nevada Territory was admitted as the state of Nevada, the 36th state. Its first senators were Republicans William Stewart (1827-1909) and James W. Nye (1815-76), the territorial governor appointed by Lincoln when the Nevada Territory was organized. Stewart had gone from New York to California for gold and then moved to Virginia City, where he participated in the mining litigation which helped design the Comstock.

The Comstock's peak came in 1863 when the richest ore pockets were hit. Unfortunately, they were inaccessible at first due to some caverns' emitting scalding water as soon as a pick hit the rock wall containing it. Adolph Sutro (1830-98), a German engineer, built a tunnel to drain off the waters, and workers gained better access.

It had not been easy. Ralston and his partners Darius Ogden Mills (1825-1910) (about whom, according to Beebe and Clegg, "there was no democratic nonsense [nor] folksiness...in the frosty old moneybags"[80]) and future U.S. Senator from Nevada (1875-81) William Sharon (1821-86) had appeared to support Sutro, but really did not want his competition. They applied pressure on the California and Nevada legislatures to withdraw official support for the Sutro Tunnel Company and applied enough financial pressure in those states to dry up funding for it. Former Sutro Librarian Richard H. Dillon's *Humbugs and Heroes* says that Sutro "found the hard rock of Nevada's Washoe country to be like butter in comparison to the obstacle of the Bank of California."[81] He fought back against these great odds but seemed to be going nowhere until the Yellow Jacket Mine caught fire in April 1869, killing 45 men. The anger of the miners, directed at first against the financiers, was turned to support for the lone man fighting them. At a meeting in Piper's Opera House in Virginia City, Sutro addressed the men: "Miners and laboring men, what is the price of your health, your liberty, your independence? Who is there among you so avaricious as to refuse to give or donate outright a few paltry dollars per month to a cause which will make you the power of this land, make powerless your oppressors, and break up your arch enemy, the California Bank?" The Miners Union responded with a $50,000 ($1,136,294 in 2023) donation; Congress heard the cry, authorized two million dollars ($61.6 million in 2023), and a British investment company put its money behind the cause. The tunnel was finally completed in 1879, but the peak days were over, and the ore reached now was low-grade. The Carson City Mint, created in 1863, was not put into operation until 1870 and ran 15 years, then went on hiatus but resumed operations in 1889 until it permanently closed in 1893. Its purpose was the minting of silver coins from the Comstock's production, as well as gold coins in greater numbers.

At this point Asbury Harpending re-entered the picture. Having speculated in produce for the '49ers in Panama, he never lost his zeal for chance and profit. After he was released from prison for his pro-Confederate activities, he made another fortune in gold and, with Ralston's help, in real estate. In 1871 two miners named Philip Arnold (1829-78) and John Slack (1820-96) had gone into Ralston's bank and showed

451

him a sack of uncut precious jewels, diamonds, emeralds, and rubies. These were shown to a reputable local jeweler, who judged that if Arnold's and Slack's boasts were true, their mine could be worth at least $50 million (over $1.269 billion in 2023). Leading jeweler Charles Tiffany (1812-1902) in New York corroborated the claim. Ralston jumped at the chance to form a partnership with the two and sent Harpending to investigate the mine. Arnold and Slack were vague as to its exact location, but it turned out to be in a remote part of the Wyoming Territory. The field appeared to be exquisitely rich, but unknown to everyone else, Arnold and Slack had salted it with cheap cast-off South African diamonds, the refuse of gem cutting, bought in London and Amsterdam. As cautious and experienced as these investors were, it is inexplicable how they could have been so unsuspecting. Based on Harpending's enthusiastic reports and the corroboration of the jeweler who first examined them and mining expert Henry Janin (1838-1911), Ralston formed a company whose officers included Janin, David Colton (1832-78), Tifffany, Baron [Nathan] von Rothschild (1840-1915), Horace Greeley, and Civil War Union Generals George McClellan (1826-85) and George Dodge (1833-81). Ralston convinced Arnold and Slack to sell their interests in the mine for $660,000 ($15.5 million in 2023). The firm collapsed in 1873 when geologist Clarence King (1842-1901) proved the fraud. The affair soon came to be known as the Great Diamond Hoax, the title later used by Harpending in his book of reminiscences published in 1913. As for Arnold and Slack, Arnold became a successful banker in Kentucky but was killed in a duel with a rival banker, and Slack became a coffin maker and undertaker in New Mexico; both were sued, and each settled with the duped investors.[82]

In 1869 the federal government offered bonds at whopping interest rates, and many investors withdrew money from savings accounts to buy the bonds. Banks, including Ralston's, began to feel the pinch. A year earlier there had been an earthquake in San Francisco. A buildup of strain on the Hayward Fault produced a 6.8 magnitude earthquake that violently shook the San Francisco Bay Area. Thirty were killed in San Francisco and property damage amounted to $300,000 ($6,5866,654 in 2023).[83] It would be nearly 40 years before another earthquake of nearly the same significance would be felt in the region.

These events combined to inspire doubts about the stability of life, a lack of confidence that threatened a run on the Bank of California. President Ulysses S. Grant refused Ralston's pleas for gold coin to prevent a ruinous run. Facing ruin, Ralston somehow managed to get two men into the Subtreasury office in San Francisco one night, who surreptitiously proceeded to removed five tons (4.53 metric tons) of gold coin, exchanging it on the spot for five tons of gold bullion from the bank. This was technically illegal, but since no value had been changed, it was no more than a clever slight-of-hand. The trickery went off without a hitch, thanks to Ralston's friendships with Henry R. Linderman (1825-79), the director of the Philadelphia Mint (who happened to be in San Francisco for business) and Louis Garnett of the San Francisco Assaying and Mining Company. The books were doctored, but there was no loss to the government; hence no indictable offense resulted. The next morning worried depositors were relieved to see stacks of gold coins in the tellers' cages. Was a financial disaster averted, as these three men believed? Probably not. Within a few days the money had been spent in day-to-day business, and perhaps a run on the bank had been averted, but no real problems had been solved.[84]

The national Panic of 1873 caused many bankruptcies,

bank failures, and high unemployment. There were several contributing factors. The new German Empire stopped minting silver thaler coins (1/14 of a mark) in 1871, dropping a huge market for the metal; the U.S. reacted with the Coinage Act of 1873 (called "the Crime of '73" by the silver miners), which stopped minting silver coins except for silver dollars and put the nation on the gold standard. Then came the Chicago fire of 1871, an equine influenza outbreak in 1872, weakening or killing 10% of the nation's horses and mules, and the crash of Jay Cooke's bank in New York over his inability to market long-term bonds for his Northern Pacific Railroad. All these elements converged to launch a major depression with worldwide impact. This time Ralston was unable to pull any stunt as dramatic as his daring coin for bullion caper, and the catastrophic economic collapse did not spare Ralston himself, who went bankrupt and may have committed suicide in August 1875.[85] By 1890, the Comstock was finished as a producer of lavish wealth; there is scientifically based speculation, however, that silver still lies hidden deep in the Comstock.

William Sharon, whom Ralston had raised from nothing to millionaire status, led the attack to destroy his benefactor, and would do worse. Unaware of Sharon's manipulations and betrayals, Ralston deeded his assets to Sharon in trust for his wife. When Ralston died, Sharon cheated his widow out of most of her just due. Sharon's own wife died in 1875 and he, in pursuit of female companionship, began to hire young women by the month to be exclusively at his beck and call, in consideration of $1,000 (about $35,900 in 2023). In September 1880, he met lovely, 27-year-old Sarah Althea Hill, who refused his money but said she would marry him. Whether or not they married is unknown, but they did live together for at least a year, and he was known to address her as his "dear wife." Sharon then tired of her, but she refused to give up her station, and he sued for divorce so that he might find someone more intriguing. She hired Justice David Terry as her attorney and won. Sharon appealed, based on his Nevada citizenship, and that any written agreement with Sarah was spurious and should be thrown out of court because she was suing in California. During the appeal he died, as did Terry's wife. Sarah and Terry, who had struck up a close relationship during the litigation of the lawsuit, married. Sharon's attorneys pursued the case and, as a lawsuit in the federal courts, it happened to come before Associate U. S. Supreme Court Justice Stephen Field (1816-99), an old enemy of Terry's. The judgment went against Sarah, a physical altercation ensued, and Terry was ordered to jail for six months. Terry, always a hothead, was only angrier when released, and in August 1889, chancing to be at the same train station in Lathrop as Field, he impulsively attacked Field. Field's bodyguard, U.S. Marshall David Neagle (1848-?), shot and killed Terry. Neagle was charged in state court for Terry's murder, since – for probably the first time in his public life – Terry was unarmed. The U.S. Supreme Court ruled that as a federal officer cannot be prosecuted in state court for acts committed in his capacity as a federal officer.[86]

Wells Fargo, founded in 1852 by Henry Wells (1805-78) and William Fargo (1818-81) in San Francisco as a bank and express company, was another financial institution that encouraged confidence in hard times. Its headquarters have always been on Montgomery Street between California and Sacramento Streets.

Wells, who had been in the express business since 1836, in 1850 formed Wells, Butterfield & Company with John Butterfield (1801-69). Fargo had also been in the freight business since 1841 and in 1844 he organized, with Wells and Daniel Dunning, the first express company (Wells &

Company; after 1845 Livingston & Fargo) to operate west of Buffalo, New York. Within five years Livingston & Fargo extended to Cleveland, Detroit, Chicago, and St. Louis. In March 1850 American Express was founded through the consolidation of competing lines with Wells as its first president and Fargo as secretary. Wells and Fargo wanted to extend the service to California, but Butterfield and other American Express directors objected to the plan, so in 1851 Wells, Fargo and others organized Wells Fargo & Company to conduct an express business between New York and San Francisco via Panama.

Settlement of the Land Titles

Mexican land grants in California, extensive as they were, never had precise boundaries. A rock, a tree, a place where someone watched the sunset each day, might be a boundary angle mark. Fences were unknown. In an uncrowded land of huge holdings this posed few, if any, problems. The Treaty of Guadalupe-Hidalgo had guaranteed the integrity of the land titles, but its negotiators had not foreseen the Gold Rush. To the average American from the Ohio Valley and the border states, the size of these holdings was shocking because they did not understand cattle raising in a semi-arid land. The men who streamed in searching for gold moved onto the land grants as squatters, their sheer numbers preventing landowners from dealing with trespassers in the usual fashion, that is, by legal eviction or at gunpoint.

Some of these squatters were honest men who felt that such large estates should be broken up in favor of small farmers, but many were scoundrels, some of whom were hired by an individual with designs on the land to squat on the land "for him." The objective was to force the owner into court, so that litigation costs would ultimately cost him his land.

Occasionally the owner's attorney was the secret employer of the squatters. The founders of the city of Oakland, for example, employed this stratagem against the Peralta family.[87]

Part of the problem lay in the unavailability of public lands prior to 1862. All public lands belonged to the state, and they were not for sale.

Henry W. Halleck (1816-72), an army officer who had been in California since the conquest and served under military Governors Mason and Riley, had compiled the California Archives,[88] and in 1850 composed a *Report on Land Titles in California*, in which he contended that most Mexican claims were imprecise and so encouraged American squatters.

On the other side was William Carey Jones (1814-67), Frémont's brother-in-law, who had been sent to California by the third secretary of the interior, Alexander H. H. Stuart (1807-91) as an attorney to investigate the legitimacy of the land grants. He upheld most of them, including Frémont's. Congress ignored Jones' recommendations but now had a new problem to solve.

To deal with this problem Senator Gwin proposed and Congress enacted the Land Act of 1851 establishing the Federal Land Commission, which met in San Francisco in 1853-56. Its chairman, appointed by President Fillmore, ex-Congressman and future Vermont Governor Hiland Hall (1795-85), was accompanied by his son-in-law, Trenor Park (1823-82), who would later help establish the *San Francisco Bulletin* and, most notably, be one of the founders of the Republican party in California. The owners of California's vast landholdings were required to appear before the commission to prove their ownership and show why the squatters should be evicted.

Halleck, as a civilian lawyer, formed a partnership with Frederick Billings (1823-90) and Archibald Peachy (1820-83) to establish Halleck, Peachy & Billings, the state's largest legal firm in San Francisco. Trenor Park, whose father-in-law sat on the Commission, became a partner in the firm after the Commission adjourned. [89] It would handle at least half of the cases brought to the Commission.[90] Even though Halleck had written the report that encouraged squatting, he did not approve the Commission, and the firm generally defended land titles. It was said that Halleck handled the preparation, writing the briefs; Peachy handled the oratory; and Billings brought in the business.

The commission's mood was generally pro-squatter, but it reluctantly approved 553 of the 750 cases brought before it. The landowners had won - or had they? In many cases the owners had no cash to pay their lawyers (some of whom, as previously noted, had encouraged squatters to generate business, if not encouraging the outright seizure of land.) Owners were often obliged to give their land in payment or sell it to pay other bills.

From the wealth accrued to him by money-generating land disputes, Halleck was able to buy the Montgomery Block in San Francisco to house the firm in the largest office building on the West Coast. When the Civil War began, Halleck was appointed a major general and became Lincoln's Chief of Staff. Since Halleck had left California, the firm dissolved in 1861. Peachy became a member of the state senate in 1860. Billings was credited by some for helping to keep California in the Union, and after the war he returned to his native Vermont, becoming president of the troubled Northern Pacific Railroad, which he reorganized.

Development and settlement were hindered, since no one would invest in property, agricultural or otherwise, that could be taken away so easily. Even squatters would be unwilling to invest in property that other squatters might as easily take from them. Finally, in 1872, the state legislature adopted the Field Civil Code (named for David Dudley Field, 1805-94 of New York), which at last provided legal guarantee of property rights. Field, an attorney, was devoted to codification to unify laws and simplify procedure, for example, having to file only a single action instead of several in a lawsuit, whether or not the plaintiff sought monetary damages. He originally devised four codes: penal, criminal procedure, political and civil. The Civil Code was divided into four sections: personal, property, obligations, and lawsuits. Thanks to Field's brother Stephen – Justice Terry's old enemy, who it will be recalled was an Associate Justice of the U.S. Supreme Court (1863-97) – California took a stand for reliable property rights in the Field Code, surpassing in this aspect of law all other states at the time, although it later was adopted in most of the nation. Nevertheless, squatters can claim and win "adverse possession" in California by such acts as openly improving the property, paying the real estate taxes, remaining on the property for five years, or openly occupying the property and not sharing it with another squatter. While law still favors the owner, evicting squatters requires a legal process, and owners who have accepted rent from the squatter or who have ignored the squatter can lose their ownership. [91]

Chapter Eight END NOTES

[1] Carla Leshne, "San Quentin Prison: The Origins of the California 'Corrections' System." Shaping San Francisco's Digital Archive,
http://foundsf.org/index.php?title=San_Quentin_Prison:_The_Orig

ins_of_the_California_%22Corrections%22_System; Dan Reed, "Killer Location May Doom San Quentin Prison," *San Jose Mercury News,* August 20, 2001.

2   "Hanging   in   Downieville,"   (cf http://yerbabuenal.com/history/hanging.htm)

3 Hubert Bancroft, *Popular Tribunals.* (San Francisco: History Company, 1887), Vol 1, pp. 578, 587.

4 "Bay Area Mob Lynched Kidnappers 75 Years Ago," *SF Gate,* November 23, 2008, http://www.sfgate.com/crime/article/Bay-Area-mob-lynched-kidnappers-75-years-ago-3183800.php; California   Lynchings, http://www.irwinator.com/126/wdoc119.htm. Cf Ken Gonzalez-Day, *Lynching in the West* (Durham NC: Duke University Press, 2008) states that there were 350 lynchings in California between 1850 and 1935, most of the victims being Latinos, Native Americans and Chinese.

5 Frank Soulé, John H. Gihon, M.D., and James Nisbet, *The Annals   of   San   Francisco,   1855,* http://www.sfgenealogy.com/sf/history/hbann3-1.htm.

6 Roger Graysmith, Black Fire. (New York: Crown, 2011), passim.

7 *San Francisco Bulletin*, May 14, 1856.

8 It had been started with help from other leading reform-minded citizens such as Trenor Park [1823-82], a Vermont attorney who became a partner in the largest law firm in California and whose father-in-law would preside over the Federal Land Commission handling the Mexican land grants. Find A Grave: Trenor William Park,   http://www.findagrave.com/cgi-bin/fg.cgi?page=gr&GRid=41314974.

9 "The Gambler and the Madam," Bite-Size History, http://www.bitesizehistory.net/the-gambler-and-the-madam/.

10 H.D. Barrows, "Memorial Sketch of Dr. John S. Griffin," *Annual Publication of the Historical Society of Southern California and Pioneer Register,* Los Angeles. Vol 4, No. 2, 1898.

11 Ira M. Rutkow, "A Surgical Sponge and Medical Malpractice in 1856," *Archives of Surgery*, October 1999; *CHSC,* "UCSF Toland

Hall Frescoes", November-December 1977.

[12] "Exciting Events of Saturday, June 21st, 1856: Archives of the City of San Francisco, sfmuseum.org/hist10/shopkins.html

[13] Beebe and Clegg, *San Francisco's Golden Era*, p. 27; Walton Bean, *California: An Interpretive History*. (New York: McGraw-Hill, 1968), cited in Caughey, *California*, 3rd ed., pp. 234-35. Cf John B. McGloin, SJ, *San Francisco: The Story of a City*, (San Rafael CA: Presidio Press, 1979), p. 66

[14] "Historian Finds One in the Files," *San Francisco Chronicle*, October 3, 1974, p. 3.

[15] Gary Kurutz, "Eyewitness Letters, Sketches Tell Gold Rush Violence", *CHSC*, November-December 1976.

[16] Stanford Calderwood, "Joaquin Murrieta: Bandit Extraordinary" *Pacific Pathways* 2, no. 2 (March 1947), pp. 4ff.

[17] Chandler Vaughn, "Joaquin Murrieta: California's Injustice" True Crime California, http://www.truecrimecalifornia.com/joaquin-murrieta-californias-injustice/.

[18] *San Francisco Bulletin*, originally in *Alameda Gazette*, August 28, 1871. The expression is a reference to Proverbs 26:11 (KJV), that is, a fool always goes right back and does the same foolish thing again.

[19] Kurutz, "Outlaws and Bandits", *CHSC*, October 1977; Robert Eschman, "The 'Macher' Who Tamed L.A.", *Los Angeles Magazine,* (November 1991), pp. 76-88.

[20] Myron Angel, *History of San Luis Obispo County*, (1883; repr., Berkeley: Howell-North, 1966), quoted in Genini and Richard Hitchman, *Romualdo Pacheco: A Californio in Two Eras*. (San Francisco: Book Club of California, 1985), p. 42.

[21] The term filibusterer has no connection to practitioners of the filibuster in the U.S. Congress. See "The Difference Between: Filibuster vs Filibusterer...," http://wikidiff.com/filibusterer/filibuster .

[22] Hunt and Sánchez, *A Short History of California*, p. 484.

[23] Joseph Allen Stout, *Schemers & Dreamers: Fillibustering in*

Mexico, 1848-1921. (Fort Worth: TCU Press, 2002), p. 16.

[24] Books of the Southwest: *Chapter 20: The Crabb Massacre.* University of Arizona Library, http://southwest.library.arizona.edu/hav1/body.1_div.20.html.

[25] Hunt and Sánchez, A Short History of California, p. 491

[26] Jean Ingram Brookes, *International Rivalry in the Pacific Islands, 1800-1875.* (Berkeley: University of California Press, 1941), p. 195.

[27] "The biography of William Walker: The Ultimate Yankee Imperialist,"http://latinamericanhistory.about.com/od/historyofcentralamerica/a/wwalker.htm.

[28] Genini, "The Fraser-Cariboo Gold Rushes: Comparisons and Contrasts with the California Gold Rush," passim.

[29] Jeremiah Lynch, *A Senator of the Fifties: David C. Broderick of California.* (San Francisco: A.M. Robertson, 1911), pp. 68-69.

[30] UC Hastings College of Law, Anti-Chinese Laws: 1855 Cal.Stat. 194; 1862 Cal. Stat. 462, http://librarysource.uchastings.edu/library/research/special-collections/wong-kim-ark/laws3.htm .

[31] Leonard Richards, *The California Gold Rush and the Coming of the Civil War*, First Vintage Books (New York: Knopf Doubleday, 2008), prologue p. 2.

[32] Caughey, *California*, 3rd ed., p. 220.

[33] "From Slavery to Entrepreneur, Biddy Mason," African American Registry, http://www.aaregistry.org/historic_events/view/slavery-entrepreneur-biddy-mason .

[34] Brother of Charles Crocker (ch. 9-10), later a member of the California Supreme Court and founder of the Crocker Art Museum in Sacramento.

[35] *In re Archy*, 9 Cal. 147 (1858).

[36] Hart, *Companion to California*, p. 43; "George Frazier Monroe," http://www.blackpast.org/aaw/monroe-george-frazier-c-1844-1886; "Jeremiah Sanderson,"

http://www.blackpast.org/aaw/sanderson-jeremiah-1821-1875.

[37] Delilah L Beasley, *The Negro Trail Blazers of California: A Compilation of Records from the California archives in the Bancroft Library at the University of California, in Berkeley; and from the diaries, old papers, and conversations of old pioneers in the State of California* ... (Los Angeles: Times Mirror, 1919), p. 160.

[38] Sometimes confused with Jonas H. Townsend, died 1872. Guy Washington, "Guide to Pioneers of African Descent." (Oakland, 2010), http://mwphglcal.org/images/forms/California-Pioneers-of-African-Descent.pdf.

[39] The total vote was 119,827. David Leip, *U.S. Election Atlas* (2012): 1860 Presidential General Election Results – California, http://uselectionatlas.org/RESULTS/state.php?year=1860&fips=6&f=1&off=0&elect=0&minper=0.

[40] Rev. A. C. Hirst, "Methodism in California." (San Francisco, 1892), http://freepages.genealogy.rootsweb.ancestry.com/~npmelton/METHODISM.htm. Earlier, Rev. Briggs "did more than any other man to prevent California from becoming a slave state." C. V. Anthony, *Fifty Years of Methodism: A History of the Methodist Episcopal Church Within the Bounds of the California Annual Conference from 1847 to 1897* (San Francisco: Methodist Book Concern, 1901), p. 34.

[41] John Munson, *Reminiscences of a Mosby Guerrilla* (New York: Moffat, Yard & Co, 1906), p. 86.

[42] Tom Generous, "Over the River Jordan: California Volunteers in Utah During the Civil War," *California History* 63, no. 3 (Summer 1984), pp. 200-211.

[43] William Nester, *The Age of Lincoln and the Art of American Power, 1848-1876,* (University of Nebraska: Potomac Books, 2014), p. 154.

[44] George H. Tinkham, "California During the Civil War." (California State Military Museum. San Francisco, 1913), http://californiamilitaryhistory.org/CAandCW2.html. "William A. Scott, Missionary to California." (Presbyterians of the Past, Sept 11, 2022), https://www.presbyteriansofthepast.com/2022/09/12/william-a-

scott-missionary-to-california/

[45] John B. McGloin, S.J., *San Francisco's First Archbishop: The Life and Times of Joseph Sadoc Alemany, O.P., 1814-1888* (New York: Herder & Herder, 1966), pp. 181-182.

[46] Samuel Dickson, *Tales of San Francisco*, pp. 362-64, 367.

[47] *California As I Saw It: First-Person Narratives of California's Early Years, 1849-1900: Franklin Buck, A Yankee Trader in the Gold Rush.* Op cit., p. 191, https://catalog.loc.gov/vwebv/holdingsInfo?searchId=20108&recCount=25&recPointer=3&bibId=9685041

[48] Jeff Dwyer, *Ghost Hunter's Guide to the San Francisco Bay Area:* Revised. (Pineville LA: Pelican, 2011). However, in the postscript to *Two Years Before the Mast*, Dana records that the fort was then being built under the direction of Lee's son, Lt. George Washington Custis Lee (1832-1913). In any case, whether father or son, it is ironic that the fort should have been so well built that it would withstand attack from the Confederate forces that both Lees joined two years later.

[49] "Rebel ship that kept fighting gets its due," *Washington Times,* March 25, 2005, http://www.washingtontimes.com/news/2005/mar/25/20050325-082539-5981r/?page=all.

[50] "The Russian Ball," *Daily Alta California*, November 18, 1863, p. 1; "More of the Russian Ball," *Daily Alta California*, November 19, 1863, p. 1. Lowell Clucas, "The Time San Francisco Embraced Russia's Fleet", *San Francisco Chronicle*, November 9, 1980, Sunday Punch, p. 1.

[51] Thomas Bailey, *America Faces Russia: Russian-American Relations from Early Times to Our Day.* (Ithaca: Cornell University Press, 1950), pp. 85-86.

[52] Norman Saul, *Russian-American Dialogue on Cultural Relations, 1776-1914.* (Lincoln: University of Nebraska, 1997), pp. 104-06.

[53] *New York Times*, May 15, 1993.

[54] California Historical Landmark No. 852; Mark Robertson, *Gilded Empire: San Francisco's Early Keys to Regional*

Dominance. (January 2012), https://gildedempire.wordpress.com/tag/woodruff-v-bloomfield/.; 18 F. 753, 1884 U.S. app. LEXIS 1893, 9 Sawy. 441

[55] "Lester Pelton: Discoverer of 'white gold'," *PG&E Progress,* Vol. 57, No. 3, March 1980.

[56] *Los Angeles Star,* April 7, 1855, http://mountainviewpeople.blogspot.com/2009/07/william-stow-1824-1895-attorney.html.

[57] *Ex parte Newman,* 9 Cal. 502

[58] *Ex parte Koser,* 60 Cal. 177

[59] *California As I Saw It: First-Person Narratives of California's Early Years, 1849-1900: Stephen C. Davis, California Gold Rush Merchant; the Journal of Stephen Chapin Davis.* Edited by Benjamin B. Richards. (San Marino CA: Huntington Library, 1956), https://catalog.loc.gov/vwebv/search?searchArg=Davis%2C+Steph en&searchCode=GKEY%5E*&searchType=1&yearOption=define d&limitTo=DATE%3D1956-1956&fromYear=1956&toYear=1956&limitTo=LOCA%3Dall&li mitTo=PLAC%3Dcau&limitTo=TYPE%3Dam&limitTo=LANG %3DENG&recCount=25&filter=Y

[60] Nina Wu, *Inside Oakland: A Retellling of Gold rush History: The Lives of Chinese Miners,* (2011), journalism.berkeley.edu/projects/Oakland/culture/ninagr.html. Others who discount the idea generally offer no support.

[61] Christine Shirley, "Entrepreneurs & Economics of the Los Angeles Shipping Industry, Part I (1850-Civil War): Development of a Dream." *CHSC,* nd.. p. 3.

[62] Michael Colbruno, *Lives of the Dead: Mountain View Cemetery in Oakland: Charles Lux,* http://mountainviewpeople.blogspot.com/2008/03/charles-lux-once-owned-17-of-california.html.

[63] Joy Berry and Natalie Cowan, "Weather and Water in California", *CHSQ,* March 1977, p. 3.

[64] David Igler, *Industrial Cowboys: Miller & Lux and the Transformation of the Far West, 1850-1920.* Berkeley: University of California, 2001; "Anecdotes about Henry Miller for final 'Ask

Us' of 2013, *Modesto Bee*, May 30, 2013; Henry Miller Papers Collection, "Correspondence to Superintendent Turner," July 18, 1912, Special Collections, Fresno State Library, California State University, Fresno.

[65] James Gerber, "The Gold Rush Origins of California's Wheat Economy," *Scielo*, July-December 2010, https://www.scielo.org.mx/scielo.php?script=sci_arttext&pid=S14 05-22532010000200002

[66] Jeanne Moore, Hawaii-LL Archives, http://archiver.rootsweb.ancestry.com/th/read/HAWAII/2005-06/1119398040.

[67] Michael Colbruno, *Lives of the Dead: Mountain View Cemetery in Oakland:James A. Folger,* http://mountainviewpeople.blogspot.com/search?q=James+Folger.

[68] Sidney Lawrence, "The Ghirardelli Story" *California History*: vol 90. (March 2002)

[69] "Relative to the Wakamatsu Tea and Silk Colony Day. 30 April 2007". SCR 44. California Senate Concurrent Resolution 44, http://www.leginfo.ca.gov/pub/07-08/bill/sen/sb_0001-0050/scr_44_bill_20070430_introduced.html.

[70] Occasionally, lumber men in a hurry to get down to the valley to spend their money in town would ride the flumes at about fifty miles an hour (80 kph) on a log instead of the slow, bumpy trip by wagon.

[71] Knower, *Adventures of a Forty-Niner*, p.85

[72] *Standard Catalog of World Coins, 1801-1900*. 5th official edition. Iola WI: Krause, 2006, pp. 1127-28; Society of Private and Pioneer Numismatics. *Augustus Humbert and the United States Assay Office,* https://pioneergold.wordpress.com/2011/11/02/augustus-humbert/.

[73] Beebe and Clegg, *Legends of the Comstock*, (Stanford University Press, 1956), p. 12. Hal V. Hall, "The Grosh Brothers Story," https://historyexp.org/the-grosh-brothers-story/\

[74] Warren Hinckle and Frederic Hobbs, *The Richest Place on Earth*. Boston: Houghton- Mifflin, 1978, p. 34.

[75] For an explanation of the thermal activity in the area see "Steamboat Springs Geothermal Field," http://www.onlinenevada.org/articles/steamboat-springs-geothermal-field.

[76] Grant H. Smith, *The History of the Comstock Lode, 1850-1920.* (Reno: University of Nevada, 1943).

[77] Beebe and Clegg, *Golden Era*, p. 43.

[78] Genini, "Red Light Lady With a Heart of Gold: Will the Real Julia Bulette Please Come Into the Parlor?," *The Californians* 4, no. 4 (July-August 1986), p.26.

[79] Beebe and Clegg, *Golden Era*, p. 45. Along this line is a story recounted by journalist Irvin S. Cobb (1876-1944): "The Differences That Money Made. In the old boom days at Virginia City James Fair, the famous silver magnate, was sitting one day in a barroom. It will be recalled that Mr. Fair, despite his lack of book-learning, amassed a great many millions of dollars and became a leader in several different lines of endeavor.

"As he sat there the barkeeper, who was writing a letter, called out to him, asking him how to spell the word 'bird.'

"'B-U-R-D,' answered Mr. Fair.

"'That's the way I thought it was,' said the letter-writer.

"An educated gambler who had overheard this conversation, bided his time. On the following day, finding Mr. Fair in company of a group of mining men, the gambler offered to bet him a hundred dollars that he could not correctly spell the word bird.

"'B-I-R-D,' said Mr. Fair, reaching for the stakes.

"'My Lord!' exclaimed the loser, 'You didn't spell it that way yesterday.'

" 'Son,' answered Mr. Fair softly, 'there wasn't any money up on it yesterday.'"

Irvin S. Cobb, "My Favorite Stories," *Oakland Tribune*, January 17, 1923, p. 20.

[80] Beebe and Clegg, Golden Era, p. 53

[81] Dillon, *Humbugs and Heroes*, p. 309.

[82] Henry Ferguson, "The Double Deal at Diamond Mesa," *The Elks Magazine* (December 1975), pp. 15-17.

[83] *San Francisco Call*, October 22, 1868; United States Geological Survey. "A virtural tour of the 1868 Hayward Earthquake in Google Earth," http://earthquake.usgs.gov/regional/nca/1868virtualtour/ ; USGS, "Historic Earthquakes," http://earthquake.usgs.gov/earthquakes/states/events/1868_10_21.php .

[84] David Lavender, *Nothing Seemed Impossible: William C. Ralston and Early San Francisco*. (Palo Alto CA: American West, 1975), p. 285.

[85] An expert swimmer, he went for his daily swim at North Beach and drowned.

[86] Robert Wash, "David S. Terry: A Biography" part 2, *Fresno Past & Present* 17, no. 3 (September 1975); *In re Neagle*, 135 U.S. 1 (1890), https://supreme.justia.com/cases/federal/us/135/1/

[87] Beth Bagwell, "The drama of Mayor Horace Carpentier and the waterfront." *The [Oakland] Montclarion*, July 16, 1980, p. 9.

[88] The California State Archives, located in a building in Sacramento, houses records that document the broad scope of state government and its impact on the people of the state. The collection consists of millions of textual records and thousands of graphic records (such as maps, architectural drawings, and photographs).

[89] *New York Times*, December 21, 1882

[90] OAC, Guide to the Halleck, Peachy & Billings Records.

[91] Genini, "The Codification of California Statutory Law." In *Revue Hellénique de Droit International*. (Athens: L'Institut Hellénique de Droit International et Étranger, 1972), pp. 372-74. Even with the guarantees in the Field Civil Code there continued to be challenges to secure property ownership through exceptions such as "notorious trespass," as used by the plaintiff in a 2022 Monterey County case, *Cederquist v Lode*, case number 19CV004596. PropertyClub Team, "Squatters Rights in California ," (July 5,

2023), https://propertyclub.nyc/article/squatters-rights-in-california

Chapter Eight FURTHER READING

(BOOKS LISTED WITH AN "*" ARE FICTIONAL)

1. Beilharz, Edwin, and Carlos López. *We Were 49ers!* Pasadena: Ritchie, 1976.

2. Bowen, John. *The History and Battlefields of the Civil War.* Edison, NJ: Quarto, 1991.

3. Considine, John L. "Californian Filibusters." *Oakland Tribune*, Sunday Tribune Magazine, January 20, 1924, p. 11,

4. Coy, Owen. *California County Boundaries.* 1923. Reprint, Fresno: Valley, 1973.

5. Hurley, Richard. *California and the Civil War.* Charleston SC: History Press, 2017.

6. Lewis, Oscar. *Silver Kings.* New York: Ballantine, 1971.

7. Pitt, Leonard. *Decline of the Californios.* Berkeley: University of California Press, 1970.

8. Stewart, George. *Committee of Vigilance.* New York: Ballantine, 1971.

9. Thompson, Wallace. *The Sacrilegious Shore.* 1960. Reprint, New York: Ballantine, 1972.*

Chapter 9: A New Culture, the Indians, a Natural Wonderland, and the End of Isolation

Churches and Schools

The Gold Rush Americanized California's culture, quickly erasing all but small vestiges of its Spanish and Mexican days. Most of the Americans who came to California were Protestants whose faith was generally not merely cultural but sincerely held and dynamic. "New England ministers cherished the idea of remaking California in the image of their homeland...a great Puritan city on a hill, toward which all the world would look for an example of a perfect civilization."[1] Their goal was to limit or eradicate Catholicism.[2]

The first Protestant church in California was organized by Presbyterians in Benicia in April 1849, and a month later the First Presbyterian Church of San Francisco was established. William Roberts (1812-88) was appointed by the Methodists to preside over the mission conference embracing California and Oregon.[3] By 1855, San Francisco had 32 Protestant churches. The most socially prominent clergyman was Episcopal Bishop William Kip (1811-93), who presided over the founding of the mother church, Grace Cathedral, in San Francisco and oversaw the entire state and Nevada as his diocese. When he was appointed in 1853, he decided to tour his see frequently, and at Fort Miller in 1855 performed the first Protestant baptism in California – of a soldier's newborn daughter. Methodist Reverend William Taylor (1821-1902, nicknamed "Father Taylor") was the most active Protestant clergyman in the state, working as a street preacher and

470

circuit-rider in the Methodist style and building the state's first hospital, San Francisco General, in 1857. The Mexican government objected to having parishes in Baja subject to a bishop in US Alta California and so the Vatican divided the see of Alta and Baja California into American and Mexican sections in November 1849. Catholic Archbishop Joseph Alemany (1814-88) completely separated the Catholic church in California from its former Mexican control and made it in effect an Americanized diocese in 1850, serving as the first bishop of Monterey until he became archbishop of San Francisco in 1853.

Born in Spain and ordained in Rome, Alemany, a multilingual priest, went to the United States in 1840 and worked as a missionary in the Ohio Valley, becoming a naturalized American citizen within a few years. In 1850 he travelled to Rome, where Pope Pius IX (1792-1878, reigned 1846-78) told him that he was assigned to Monterey: "Where others go for gold, you must carry the cross." He took up his duties, though the cultural shift he represented was less than welcome in his new territory, especially among members of his own Dominican Order. As bishop, and later archbishop, he promoted Catholic education and invited members of teaching orders, the Jesuits and Christian Brothers, as well as his own Dominicans, the Sisters of Notre Dame and Holy Names to open school; their institutions have endured to the present day.[4]

A Catholic nun, Sister (later Mother) Mary Baptist Russell (1829-98) from Ireland had arrived in San Francisco nine months before a cholera outbreak in September 1855. Half of the Bay Area's residents were stricken, and no one except Sister Mary knew what to do. Having seen cholera in Ireland she sprang into action with the seven Sisters of Mercy, nuns of her order who had accompanied her to California. First,

471

they went to the filthy building at the corner of Stockton and Vallejo Streets known as the Marine State Hospital, finding it staffed by brutal, ignorant, and lazy men who knocked the patients senseless and called it "care." She and the sisters pushed these louts aside, and for six weeks Sister Mary and her crew ministered to the sick and indigent. When the legislature made counties responsible for the care of their indigent sick, the city supervisors asked her to organize and manage the hospital at her expense, with a monthly reimbursement. To get the money to start the program she hit up any moneyed citizen she could find, especially Catholics. Since the supervisors reneged on their promise of reimbursement, and ignored her dunning, she ended the city contract after two years and opened St. Mary's Hospital in 1857. By 1861 it had grown and moved to larger quarters, leaving Sister Mary free to concentrate on schools, which she founded in San Francisco and Sacramento for children while setting up night school classes for the illiterate and immigrants.[5]

Black congregations, primarily of the African Methodist Episcopal Church but some Baptist, were organized in Sacramento (1850), San Francisco by Rev. J. J. Moore (1852), Grass Valley and Marysville (1854), and Oakland (1858). Rev. Darius Stokes by 1856 founded 14 AME churches in California before leaving for British Columbia.

There was considerable competition among churches, as indicated by the memoirs of a New England Congregationalist missionary, the Reverend William Pond (1830-1925), which recounted the founding of the Greenwich Street church in San Francisco. He wrote: "The great majority of residents in that part of the city were Romanists [Catholics]. I remembered, however, that I cheered myself with the thought that Christ had sent me there and would certainly stand by me."[6] An instance of cooperation among denominations was the Pacific Theological Seminary (now the Pacific School of Religion), founded in 1866 by Methodists, Congregationalists, and Disciples of Christ to train ministers; Presbyterians, however, were disinclined to join until many years later.

Brigham Young had sent Mormon colonists from Salt Lake throughout the west and claimed territory for a projected state of Deseret reaching from Idaho to Arizona and the Pacific coast. When in 1848 Sam Brannan (still in good standing as a Mormon) had arrived in Yerba Buena, he preached the first non-Catholic sermon and performed the first non-Catholic wedding in the settlement. However, in 1857, the federal government sent troops into Utah to overthrow the Mormon theocracy and replace Young with a non-Mormon territorial governor appointed by President Buchanan, partly in response to the Mountain Meadows Massacre, a horrifying incident in which a wagon train from Arkansas was attacked and its party massacred except for some children taken and adopted by members of a party of Mormons from Cedar Creek, Utah, under John D. Lee (1812-77.) Local Utes joined in the massacre, and the victims' cattle and other possessions were looted. That the massacre was carried out without Young's approval is unlikely, given the Mormon hierarchy that held sway in Utah at the time.[7] To counter the threat of federal intervention Young called all the dispersed Mormon colonists back to Salt Lake. One of the sites they abandoned was San Bernardino, founded on 35,000 acres (14,160 ha) purchased from the Lugo brothers in 1851. It was a successful agricultural colony of 450 industrious people operated by Bishop Nathan Tenney (1817-83), who had operated the Lugo family's farms in the area. A sawmill, dams and ditches were built, and grape vines, fruit trees, wheat, and cattle were introduced. With the recall of the Mormon settlers and the abandonment of San Bernardino, the

Mormons lost their chance to gain an important foothold in California.

For all their religious activity the future success of the churches was doubtful. Though remaining a culturally religious people, many of the Argonauts fell away from religion and religious practices during the Gold Rush, while those that remained active in churches tried to transplant Eastern, Southern, and European styles of architecture and worship. Reverend Pond reported that in 1867, 55 Baptist churches "were extinct" as were 13 Presbyterian churches. He blamed this on "young men, sometimes more eager than wise... and... circumstances in which we wrought were unprecedented."[8]

In December 1846, a school was operated in a former stable attached to Mission Santa Clara by Olive Mann Isabell (1824-99), a teacher who had come overland to California with her physician husband, arriving at Sutter's Fort in October. During the conquest Frémont told Americans to assemble at the Mission for safety, and Mrs. Isabell kept school without paper, slates, pencils or proper readers. In March 1847 the couple was at Monterey, and Walter Colton, hearing of her teaching at Santa Clara, asked her to do the same service there. She was given a refurbished adobe for a schoolroom and supplied by naval and whaling vessels in the bay, while Thomas Larkin donated paper and pencils, which replaced the stop-gap method she had recurred to at the Mission, writing the letters of the alphabet on the backs of the children's hands so that they could learn the basics of literacy. She was even given a salary. The young couple moved to the Sierra foothills in 1848 when gold was discovered.[9] She continued to teach wherever their moves took them.

In April and May of 1848, there was a public school in San Francisco, but the Gold Rush closed it: The teacher, Yale-educated Thomas Douglas, the trustees, and the parents of the half dozen pupils headed for the hills. In 1851 the legislature provided for a public school system, and in 1866 state school superintendent John Swett (1830-1913) announced that there was at least one grammar school in each county with high schools in the larger towns. In 1853 the state's first free public school in a dedicated building for white children had opened, and in 1854, the first school for black children was founded by Jeremiah Sanderson in Stockton. The first for Chinese children followed in 1859, the law specifically forbidding racial integration. In 1851, the Jesuits established California's first college, the College (later University) of Santa Clara, the Sisters of Notre Dame de Namur established the College of Notre Dame in Belmont, and Methodists established the California Wesleyan College (now University of the Pacific) in Santa Clara. The next year Mills College for women was organized in Oakland, in 1855 the Jesuits organized the College of St. Ignatius (now the University of San Francisco), and the Methodists opened the College of California in Oakland. This Methodist institution, taken over by the state in 1868 because of financial problems, moved to Berkeley and became the University of California. Under David Gilman (1831-1908), who became president in 1872, the University chose to become a learning center for liberal arts and science in 1874. After three years at Berkeley, when the state legislature gave Gilman more problems that he cared to deal with, he accepted an appointment to found Johns Hopkins University in Baltimore. In 1857 San Jose State College was organized, the first of the state universities, initially as Minns' Evening Normal School in San Francisco. It moved to San Jose in 1871, where it was given its present location at Washington Square Park. In 1861 Chapman College was organized in Orange by the Disciples of Christ. In 1863 the Christian Brothers established St. Mary's College in San

Francisco. Heald's Business College, a vocational school, was established in San Francisco in 1868.[10] In the same year the Sisters of the Holy Names established Holy Names College in Oakland for teacher training.

Such promising statistics had not been easily achieved. In 1863, Superintendent Swett visited a crowded and dingy Santa Clara classroom. His identity unknown to the teacher, he was told to sit at the back of the room. After a few minutes, he asked to speak to the children, complimenting them on their behavior and their teacher on her skills. He concluded with a startling announcement:

> You and your teacher are too good for this miserable little shanty...I want you to pack up your books, carry them home, and say to your parents that the state superintendent of public instruction, Mr. Swett, visited you today and directed you to tell them that you have struck work and are not going to school any more until you are provided with a better schoolhouse.[11]

As the children left, the superintendent, all of 33 years old, told the flabbergasted teacher, "That should wake up the people around here." The school kids' strike was just one of the highlights of Swett's first year in office. Years later the Santa Clara teacher told him, "You did wake them up. The trustees immediately secured a larger room, and in the course of the year we had a new schoolhouse."

Swett served as the state superintendent until 1867, during which term he organized teacher' institutes, established teacher certification, helped form what became the California Teachers Association, pushed for increased teacher salaries and building maintenance, won legislative support for school taxes, wrote a revised school law, organized the schools into grades, established school libraries, lengthened the school year, provided for uniform textbooks throughout the state's public school system, and abolished tuition, making the schools absolutely free in all districts for at least five months in the year. Defeated for re-election, he went on to become principal of the Denman girls' school in San Francisco and eventually superintendent of the San Francisco public schools, retiring in 1896.[12]

At the university level, things did not progress much more smoothly. As noted, the Jesuits established St. Ignatius College in 1855. Two Italian Jesuits, Fathers John Nobili (1812-56) and Michael Accolti (1807-78), had been sent down from the Oregon Territory to establish the college while continuing with their other, mandatory, priestly functions. Accolti had requested the assignment but upon reaching Gold Rush San Francisco, he was shocked, unprepared for what he found. "Whether it should be called a villa, a brothel or a Babylon," he lamented, "I am at a loss to determine."[13] Another Italian Jesuit, Father Anthony Maraschi (1820-97), secured a favorable real estate loan and built a one-room schoolhouse where the San Francisco Shopping Centre (formerly the Emporium department store) stands in downtown San Francisco. The college moved twice after that, locating at its present site in 1906.

Theater

California's first theater was Swan's in Monterey, a store, saloon, and boarding house for sailors that British sailor Jack Swan (1817-96) built when he arrived in 1843. During and immediately after the Mexican-American War, the boarders were members of Stevenson's Regiment who put on their own entertainments as a money-making venture. Swan put up a small stage, provided benches, whale-oil lamps, candles for footlights, and blankets for curtains. Swan charged $5 ($203 in 2023 dollars) for a ticket and when the first night was over had taken in $500 ($20,240 in 2023 dollars).[14] Since 1937 Swan's has featured old-time melodrama.[15]

California's first professional actor was an Englishman, Stephen Massett (1820-98), who had gone to New York City when he was 17 to begin his career as an actor and singer. In June 1849 he arrived in San Francisco with his one-man show: He sang his own songs, mimicked an opera and a town meeting, portrayed Shakespearean characters, and did Yankee monologues. Following him on stage were numerous minstrels, always popular. His *Drifting About, or What "Jeems Pipes of Pipesville" Saw-and-Did* (1863) is an autobiographical account of early California theater.[16]

California's first professional theater was the Bella Union in San Francisco, noted for its vaudeville and minstrel shows and for the odd characters that haunted it. Sam Tetlow (c. 1822-98), its proprietor, put on burlesque shows one night and legitimate drama the next. A handbill for one night advertised: "Full-grown People Are Invited to Visit the Bella Union if You Want to 'Make a Night of It.' The Show Is Not of the Kindergarten Class, but Just Your Size, if You Are Inclined to Be Frisky and Sporty." On another was the dramatization of a new best-selling Dickens novel called *Dombey and Son*; it was reported that "the full-bearded miners drank their libations and sobbed great tears into their cups as they listened to the trials and heart-rending tribulations of Paul Dombey."

Other San Francisco theaters were Tom Maguire's (c.1824-96) Jenny Lind Theater (1851) and his Opera House (1856), Ralston's California Theater (1869), the New American Theater (1872), and the Baldwin Theater (1876). In what appeared to be a scandalous deal in 1852, Maguire sold the Jenny Lind to the city for a new city hall and used the profit to build his Opera House, featuring the most modern appointments, such as gas lights. Aware that controversy would stimulate sales, he ever "pushed the envelope." For example, in 1863 he featured the famously risqué Adah Isaacs Menken (1835-68) in a then-shocking performance of *Mazeppa*, where the heroine rode a horse on the stage in a beige-colored body stocking.

The miners, even the unlettered ones, liked Shakespeare, and the louder the lines were read, the better they liked it. The first Falstaff to come to the city was James Hackett (1800-71), who gave great performances from which hundreds were turned away. On October 14, 1863 the *Daily Alta California* published a letter he had received from President Lincoln, who wrote that he wanted to see him as Falstaff again, and that he preferred Hamlet's "O my offense is rank" soliloquy over "To be or not to be." The president requested that he read from *Richard III* when he should again visit Washington. [17]

The best actress of the Gold Rush was eight-year-old Lotta Crabtree (1847-1924), who made her debut at entertainment-hungry Rabbit Creek (in Mariposa County) where she started by dancing an Irish jig while waving a miniature shillelagh. Her red hair, her bright eyes, and her constant laughter while dancing got the miner crowd laughing back. They loved her, showering her with gold dust, gold nuggets, and silver Mexican dollars. Lotta learned banjo, soft shoe, and flamenco from other noted personalities such as Lola Montez, traveling with her mother from San Francisco into the hills and up and down California, adding drama and broad comedy to her dancing and singing. Soon she was California's most popular and beloved star.

Irish-born Lola Montez, neé Eliza Rosanna Gilbert (1821-61), had been the mistress of poets, composers and kings, including Ludwig I of Bavaria (1786-1868, reigned 1825-48), who made her Countess of Lansfeld and was overthrown for his trouble.[18] She was popular, and famous for her Spider Dance, a whirlwind of scandal wherever she went. When she came to San Francisco by steamer to play at the Bella Union, men unhitched the horses from her carriage and pulled the carriage to the theater where they demanded she dance and sing, neither of which she could do very well. Nevertheless, the miners threw bags of gold on the stage, nearly concealing her -- as the story goes.

Edwin Booth, son of Junius Booth (1796-1852), played in San Francisco, Sacramento, and the mining camps. He became popular in California because of his ability to deliver his lines in a natural manner rather than in the declamatory fashion of the day, although this novelty was not highly regarded at first. Later, fulfilling a long-held desire, he played Hamlet in Sacramento, to uproarious applause[19]. Four years earlier, in 1852, Junius, Edwin and Junius Brutus, Jr. (1821-83) had toured California, performing in San Francisco and Sacramento. Torrential rains closed the theaters in Sacramento, the tour made no profit, and the Jenny Lind, the theater they played in, was sold by the owner to the city for a city hall. Food supplies were depleted, leading to an inflation that forced the Booths to return to San Francisco. They split up to seek new acting opportunities. [20] President Lincoln's assassin, John Wilkes Booth (1836-65), another actor son of Junius, never performed in California and played only once opposite his brothers, in a single engagement in *Julius Caesar* at New York's Winter Garden in 1864; to prevent confusion with his family, early in his career he preferred to be listed as "J. B. Wilkes" although later he was listed as "J. Wilkes Booth."

Graphic Art

California's contributions to the graphic arts were not particularly spectacular as the American period began. As in the rest of the European and American art worlds, there was competition between romanticism and realism for the patron's gold, the former being subjective and imaginative and the latter striving for an accurate or literal portrayal of life. Realism eventually dominated the market. There were several noted California artists: Charles Nahl (1818-78) was known for his street and crowd scenes, J. W. Audubon (1812-62) for his travel sketches, William Jewett (1792-1874) for his nature paintings (especially of Yosemite), Grafton T. Brown (1841-1918) for his cartography and lithography, and Edward Vischer (1808-78) for lithography.[21]

Vischer was a German merchant in South America and Mexico who came to California in 1842 and created accurate, beautifully executed, and lively sketches of scenes depicting the state's early days. In the late 1850s he visited Captain J. Warren Osborn at his Oak Knoll ranch in the Napa Valley. Impressed by the charts Vischer had drawn on various voyages all over the world, the captain asked him to make a drawing of his house and grounds. The results were so striking that soon the merchant was sketching everywhere he went, often making rough, rapid drafts that he filled in with greater detail later. He set himself the task of picturing the missions, which were then falling into decay, stage line stops, cock and bull fights, covered wagons with emigrants from the East and South to California, and camels that had been brought to the state to work in the deserts. He and his family had a home on Nob Hill in San Francisco, for which he created three terraces connected by a broad flight of stairs, planting a marvelous garden watered with an artesian well.[22]

481

Englishman W. Hubert Burgess, whose letters home described the crime and vigilantism in the mines, was first and foremost an artist. When the mines played out, he taught drawing and lithography in San Francisco's public schools for 25 years. While living and working in the Mother Lode, he depicted scenes of violence and hardship in minutely detailed pencil drawings.[23]

Parody was provided by numerous Eastern publishers, notably Currier & Ives in New York. A widely circulated lithograph by Nathaniel Currier (1813-88) and James Ives (1824-95) called *The Way They Go to California* (1849) typified the comic exaggeration popular at the time. A ship has left the dock in New York filled with passengers while others, left behind, angrily brandish their picks, shovels and pans; one-man shouts, "Hold 'em there I've paid my passage and I ain't aboard!" Another laments, "Bill, I'm afraid we can't get aboard," to one who has jumped into the water; the latter replies "I'm bound to go anyhow." Another fellow rides a rocket while the wind blows his hat off, while several cruise in the gondola of a not-yet-invented airship.

Several European publishers, notably the French artist Cham (1818-79), pseudonym of Charles Henri Amédée, Comte de Noé, were inspired by the Gold Rush. In his *Arrivée D'une Famille En Californie* (1849), a French servant couple abandon their employers upon arrival in San Francisco, tossing aside baggage and small children. "My God," their mistress cries, "already our servants are leaving us to run off to the mines... maybe it is necessary to promise them an increase in their wages!" [24]

Music was also part of the half-serious, half-humorous mood of those smitten by Gold fever, and of those observing them. "Ho! For California," was a popular New England song typical of those expressing dreams of California wealth, sung to a company setting out from Salem harbor on their ship *La Grange* in March 1849:

> We've formed our band and we're all well mann'd
> To journey afar to the promised land,
> Where the golden ore is rich in store,
> On the banks of the Sacramento shore.
> Then, ho! Brothers ho!
> To California go.
> There's plenty of gold in the world we're told,
> On the banks of the Sacramento.
> Heigh O, and away we go,
> Digging up the gold in Francisco
> Heigh O, and away we go,
> Digging up the gold in Francisco....[25]

Journalism

Americans pouring into California were so information-hungry that they were willing to pay a dollar for penny New York, Boston and New Orleans newspapers that were four months old when ships brought them in. Daniel Knower recounted how "The New York papers at first sold for $1 each ($40.48 in 2023). Then they got down to fifty cents. I sold the *New York Herald*, that was more than a month old, that contained the latest news there from the states in the interior, for $5, and the man coaxed it out of me at that, for I wanted to give it to a party of friends I was going to see in the mining districts. I knew it would be a great treat to them."[26] Most likely the man who got the *Herald* from Knower took it to his own camp, mounted a stump and read it aloud and then passed it on to another camp, where this process would be repeated until the paper was "literally worn thumb-bare by frequent readings and handling, for the greatest luxury in a mining camp was a late newspaper."[27]

The first Monterey paper was *The Californian*, first brought out by Colton and Semple on August 15,1846, using an ancient press with rusty type that had to be scoured so that the letters could show their face. To provide rules and leads (the lines on the page), several sheets of tin were cut with a jack-knife. Ink there was, but no paper until they bought paper sent to wrap cigars, making the pages of the first issues about the size of a legal pad sheet. Half of the newspaper was in English, half in Spanish. It sold for 121/2 cents ($4.75 in 2023) and was considered a bargain. Its first issue reported on the declaration of war between the United States and Mexico. Although it had met its expenses and began to turn a profit, it had to move from Monterey to Yerba Buena in May 1847, where Semple became the sole owner. Meanwhile in January 1847, another paper, Brannan's *California Star* appeared in Yerba Buena. It was printed better than Semple's paper, and even though its press had been brought to California by the Mormons, Brannan announced that it "would eschew sectarian discussions and confine itself strictly to the news."[28] The Gold Rush took away both newspapers' writers and readers, so they suspended publication until they merged and were reborn in San Francisco as the *Alta California* in January 1849. Primarily a business newspaper - though not skipping other news stories - it was a respectably journalistic paper that lasted until 1891. The *Placer Times*, published in Sacramento in April 1849, was the first paper in the interior. To serve the many non-English-speakers in the Gold Rush, there were several foreign language papers published in San Francisco: French (*Californien* and *Gazette Republicaine*, 1850; *Le Courrier du Pacifique*, 1852), German (*California Demokrat*, 1852), Chinese (*Gold Hill News*, 1854) and Italian (*Voce del Popolo*, 1859), among the first. The first newspaper in Los Angeles was half in Spanish and half in English, *La Estrella de Los Angeles* or *The Los Angeles Star* (1851); in June 1855 the all-Spanish *El Clamor Público* began competing with the *Estrella/Star*.[29] Two black newspapers were established in San Francisco, Mifflin Gibbs' and James Townsend's weekly *Mirror of the Times* (1856-58) and Peter Anderson's (1822-79) *Pacific Appeal* (1862-80), which Philip Bell joined as associate editor. They soon clashed, and in 1865 he formed his own weekly newspaper, *The Elevator*, to demand that the California legislature ratify the three Reconstruction Amendments (the Thirteenth, Fourteenth, and Fifteenth) recognizing black citizenship and voting rights [30]Sanderson worked with Anderson and Bell to end desegregation of schools for black children, which was achieved by1875.[31]

New York City was the nation's newspaper capital, but California papers far exceeded the New York papers in numbers sold per capita. Their quality was somewhat lower than that of New York newspapers. California newspapers used cheap materials, overused space fillers, and covered the news haphazardly.

Most of the better California papers were in San Francisco, the metropolis, but there were fine newspapers elsewhere in the state as well. The *Sacramento Union* was founded by four disgruntled printers in 1851 who had left their work at the *Sacramento Transcript* when it cut their wages after a cutthroat advertising war with the *Placer Times* forced it to cut costs. It changed hands twice until James Anthony (1823-76) and two partners bought it and announced that their editorial policy was to champion the common man and support the Union in the Civil War. Fellow pro-Union James McClatchy's (1824-83) *The Sacramento Bee* was founded as a competitor in 1857. Anthony's support for the Northern cause was praised as more effective for it than an army corps, though this might have been somewhat of an exaggeration since California was far removed from the conflict. The *Bee* was able to scoop the *Union* on many stories because its office was closer to the capitol building and the Western Union telegraph office. The *Union* declined when Anthony and his partners refused to relocate to San Francisco, thus sapping its effectiveness. It merged with the *Sacramento Record* in 1875.

The growth of newspapers in California in the first 20 years of statehood is impressive: in 1850 there were only four dailies and three weeklies; by 1860 the number had risen to 22 dailies, two tri-weeklies, three semi-weeklies, and 89 weeklies; and by 1870 the number had shot up to 33 dailies, four tri-weeklies and semi-weeklies, and 140 weeklies – a testimony to increased population, civic development, literacy and money.[32]

Joseph Goodwin's (1838-1917) *Virginia City Territorial Enterprise* was Nevada's first printed newspaper.[33] It gave Mark Twain his literary start by publishing his story The *Celebrated Jumping Frog of Calaveras County*. Goodwin and Denis McCarthy bought the paper in 1861 and moved it from Carson City. Not the most responsible journalist, but quite the amusing character, Goodwin allowed his writers to employ any hyperbole they desired. For his part Goodwin enjoyed perpetrating hoaxes and printing whenever he felt like it.

Goodwin left Virginia City after a feud with William Sharon, who bought the Enterprise in 1874. He took a seat on the Pacific Coast Stock Exchange, became the managing editor of the *San Francisco Post*, grew grapes, founded a literary magazine, and wrote his memoirs. His interests ranged to creditably deciphering the Mayan calendar; he published a book on the subject in 1897. Archaeologists still use the Goodman-Martinez-Thompson method to date Mayan sites.[34]

The *Enterprise* became the mouthpiece for mines, its

fortunes necessarily linked to the Comstock's prosperity. It merged with The *Virginia City Chronicle* in 1916. Many of the stories reported in the *Enterprise* were reprinted by the San Francisco dailies, whose editors kept an eye open for what was and was not hyperbolic, discarding the former. The *Enterprise* remains a good source for the spirit of the times, but much like today's *The Onion* or *The Babylon Bee*, it is too tongue-in-cheek to be a reliable historical source.

From the *Golden Era* to the *Overland Monthly*

Most of the newspapers in those days, in California and elsewhere, carried literary pieces. Poetry almost crowded out other matter in letters to the editor, leading newspaper editors to ban poetry submissions, a standard journalistic practice to this day. Some purely literary magazines sprang up almost immediately. *The Golden Era* (1852-1900) gained immediate popularity, which it sustained by catering to miners' tastes and not "putting on airs."

The Golden Era had several competitors, most of which failed after a short time. Ferdinand Ewer's (1826-83) *Pioneer* (1854-56) had good writers, but he changed "-isms" with what appeared to be wild abandon, switching religious affiliation often. He sequentially espoused Unitarianism, Episcopalianism, atheism, Trinitarianism, spiritualism, and back to Episcopalianism, always trying to push his current beliefs in his magazine. Actor Stephen Massett also put his talents to writing on becoming editor of the *Marysville Herald*, printing the first of the letters of "Dame Shirley," which he got for the *Pioneer*, contributing both to it and to the *Golden Era*.

The "Letters of 'Dame Shirley'" nom de plume of Louise Clappe (1819-1906), were written to her sister Molly back in

Amherst, Massachusetts, from September 1851 to November 1852. She and her medical doctor husband, Fayette Clapp (1824-64,) had moved to California in 1849 and lived in rough mining camps (Rich Bar and Indian Bar) on the fork of the Feather River where he had his practice. What she saw provided subject matter for the twenty-three lengthy letters she penned. Describing herself as a "frail, home-loving little thistle," "Dame Shirley" probably intended these for publication as she carefully and self-consciously commented with wit and sentimentality upon a man's world. *The Letters* display a compassion for the Mexicans she encountered in the mining areas, realistic observations about the coarse and barbarous lifestyle of the camps, and an appreciation for the beautiful natural setting. Ewer was delighted to publish them when Massett sent them on. As for Clappe, she became a San Francisco public school teacher in 1854, divorced her husband in 1857 (adding the "e" to her last name in an independence-asserting flourish at the time of the divorce), and in 1878 returned to Massachusetts.[35]

Hutchings California Magazine's (1856-61) publisher James Hutchings (1820-1902) loved nature and did whatever he could to promote love of the wilderness. He was famous for his "The Miner's Ten Commandments" the first of which ordained "Thou shalt have no other claim save one."[36] First printed in the *Placerville Herald* the humorous Decalogue was soon reprinted as a letter and sold 100,000 copies, being snapped up by miners and prospectors. Hutchings steered away from controversies involving politics and religion, with one exception: He thoroughly hated the Mormons and Brigham Young, mocking him for his twenty-seven wives, "Goddesses..[who] vary from joyous sixteen to wrinkled sixty. Beauty and education are sadly wanting in his collection." He fulminated against Young for the Mountain Meadows Massacre.[37]

The Californian (1864-67) was founded by *New York Times* correspondent Charles Henry Webb (1834-1905), who came to San Francisco in 1863 and worked as the *Evening Bulletin's* literary editor and as a columnist and staff member of The Golden Era. Known for his humorous social criticism written under the pseudonyms Inigo and John Paul, he tried to produce his own magazine. He attracted writers such as Mark Twain, Bret Harte (1836-1902), Charles Warren Stoddard (1843-1909), Ina Coolbrith (1841-1928), Ambrose Bierce (1842-c1914), and Henry George (1839-97.) Including reprints of ordinary English and French fiction, it failed because it was "too high-toned" for its audience. Webb was also attacked for his satirical view of California's history and leaders. Discouraged by such a cold reception and by losses in mining investments, he returned to New York for good.

A competitor to the *Golden Era* that managed to survive for some time was the *Overland Monthly*. Taking a cue from the *Atlantic Monthly's* style, it was launched by Anton Roman (c1828-1903) for the West, especially California, with local interest stories and articles on history, science, travel, politics, and literature. It was published in two editorial phases, July 1868-75 in San Francisco, reopening, after a hiatus, in 1880, as *The Californian*; becoming The Californian and Overland Monthly in October 1882; reverting to *The Overland Monthly* (1883-1921), and finally merging with *Out West* as *The Overland Monthly and Out West Magazine*. It ended its run in 1935. Its first editor, Bret Harte, made it a respectable journal, publishing many fine pieces, promoting the West's potential, and forcing young writers to improve.

Nine months after Roman started the magazine, he became ill and sold it to John H. Carmany. For a few years it did well: In its first two years it published work by J. Ross Browne, Ina Coolbrith (who was also an associate editor), Ambrose

Bierce, Henry George, Josephine Clifford McCracken (1839-1921), Prentice Mulford (1834-91), E.R. Still, C.W. Stoddard and Stephen Powers (1840-1904). In 1871 Harte left California for better literary prospects in New England. One of his co-editors, William C. Bartlett (1818-1907), succeeded him, and two other editors followed in turn. In 1875 the magazine collapsed because nobody could match Harte as editor, as evidenced by Carmany's bitter complaint that he had "spent thirty thousand dollars to make Bret Harte famous." [38]

A Galaxy of Writers

The Gold Rush era was also an era of many fine California writers. Mark Twain got his start with his silly story *The Celebrated Jumping Frog of Calaveras County*, which catapulted him to world fame. Bret Harte was himself a prolific writer of Western fiction, usually with heartrending plots, such as *The Luck of Roaring Camp* (1868), inspired by reading "Dame Shirley's Letters" in *Pioneer*. Others were Alonzo Delano (1806-74), known as "Old Block," George Derby (1823-61), and Joaquin Miller (1837-1913), nom de plume of Cincinnatus Heine.

Delano's popularity centered on his personal magnetism and long nose, reputedly the longest in California. (One of his friends wrote: "Indeed, he seems rather to belong to the nose than the nose to him," while another suggested that if he were buried in a shallow grave, Block's nose could be used as a tombstone). He wrote *Pen Knife Sketches* (1853) and *Live Woman in the Mines*.

George Derby, a Massachusetts native, graduated from West Point in 1846 and served in the Army Topographical Engineers in Mexico before being sent to California. He remained there for seven years, leading three exploring expeditions and winning a place as one of the state's first

490

humorists, with pieces published in the *San Diego Herald* and republished around the nation, poking fun at such topics as military surveyors and explorers, contemporary travel accounts by visitors to Mission Dolores, Benicia, Sonoma, San Francisco, and San Diego; and at literary societies, women's clubs, astrology, and army life. Notorious for practical jokes, he evoked laughter without making fun of the way people spoke, a favored comic technique of the time; instead, he created funny situations. His humorous short stories were collected in a book, *Phoenixiana* (1856).

Joaquin Miller, known as the "Poet of the Sierras", was an old fraud, according to Kevin Starr, [39]who, Starr asserts, invented his life story as well as his name and was not above inventing the stories he reported to the press. On the positive side, Miller demonstrated his love of California through poetry.

**

"When Red Cane comes we Wintu forgot our songs."

-On The Coming Of The White Man

**

Indian "Wars" and Massacres

During the first generation of American California, three-quarters of California's Indians – approximately 16,000 people - were killed in a state-supported or encouraged genocide for which the state officially apologized in 2019. Americans called most of these operations "wars," but they were little more than massacres. The term "war" presupposes that there is a fight between relative equals. In these conflicts there was no equality of combatants. The common policy, permitted until the Penal Code was adopted in 1872, was to consider killing an Indian no crime; theoretically, one could use an Indian for target practice and suffer no legal consequences. Usually, the miners began the conflict, despising the state's Indians as similar to the Nevada "Diggers," people who scratched the earth with sticks for edible roots and insects, people they thought no more of killing them than flies.[40] **(Chapter 2)**

On occasion the Indians started trouble at the sight of the first whites in an area. Nevertheless, quickly outnumbered by whites, the Indians did not have a chance to mount a resistance such as that of Sitting Bull (c1831-90) and Crazy Horse (c1840-77) in the Dakotas and Montana, or Geronimo (1829-1909) in Arizona and Sonora.

During the early American period the former mission Indians had become demoralized. In Los Angeles they were reduced to starvation, begging, drunkenness, and petty crimes, there and elsewhere in the state having been set free from the missions with inadequate training for survival in the white man's world. The missionaries, their former keepers and protectors, usually unable to help them, could only watch them sink into a state of homeless despair as they approached extinction.[41] On Monday mornings their labor would be auctioned off by the courts in a quasi-slavery to pay their fines for being drunk and disorderly on Saturday night.

During the first two decades after the gold discovery there was a litany of massacres and other outrages:

Spring 1848. Coloma. Thirty Indians killed at one village to keep them from competing with the miners.

1849. Yuba and Kings Rivers. The natives flayed the first whites they saw in the area. At Clear Lake, 175 Pomo Indians were killed by locals and the US Cavalry for killing two settlers who had been cheating them. One of the few survivors was a six-year-old girl named Ni'ka, who stayed alive by hiding in the lake and breathing through a reed.

1850. The Yubas were temporarily suppressed, but revolted and put up a good fight, while a posse only destroyed their huts and storehouses. In southern California a company of men was drafted to punish the Yumas for killing eleven thieving American ferrymen. The Indians were forced to fight. About twenty were killed.

1851. The Yumas and Luiseños were finally crushed when their chiefs were captured and executed, making southern California peaceful at last. The major Indian-related event of the year was the Mariposa Battalion of James Savage (1817-52) rediscovering Yosemite while crushing Chief Tenaya (?-1853) after the Awahneechee had attacked several mining camps.[42]

1852. The Shastas went on the warpath because of an Indian war in southern Oregon. The Modocs slaughtered a wagon train, and during peace negotiations the whites retaliated by slaughtering forty Modocs in an operation called "Ben Wright's Massacre."

1854. The Klamaths were suppressed and forced onto a reservation.

1858. Following trouble in the San Joaquin Valley, whites killed 100 Indians from a Coast Range tribe. Compounding the tragedy, the attackers mistakenly attacked a tribe whose members had nothing to do with the provocation.

1859. On the Mad and Eel Rivers 200 Indians were killed for rustling. When Bret Harte condemned the killings in the local paper he was driven out of Eureka by vigilantes.

1860. At Gunther's Island in Humboldt Bay opposite

Eureka, a small number of whites attacked during the night and wantonly killed Indians while they slept. That same evening various other Indian villages surrounding the bay were attacked and many Indians killed. No action was taken against those responsible for these massacres, and in retaliation attacks by Indians increased to alarming proportions in the entire Humboldt area. The American soldiers at Fort Humboldt, who often went months without pay or mail, bored by the tedium of their service, and depressed by the weather, were blamed for failure to control the natives. The state militia was sent in to fight until the arrival of four infantry companies. In August 1864 a treaty was signed with the Hoopa Indians setting aside the Hoopa Valley exclusively for their use, an accommodation that led to a gradual decline in the conflict between the Indians and the whites. In 1866 the fort was abandoned.[43]

1865. In the Owens Valley 100 Indians were forced into Owens Lake to drown for stealing cattle. Their forage lands had been taken over by ranchers, preventing them from making a living as they had done in the past.

1867. Indian attacks in the Pit River area were answered by punitive expeditions that led to mass killings on both sides.

The Rediscovery of Yosemite and the Modoc War

Two incidents resulted from the forced removal of tribes from their ancestral lands. In both cases, the whites showed no immediate interest in the lands in question. The first of these incidents was the re-discovery of Yosemite.

The Modoc War, as seen, began with misunderstandings and retaliatory murders on both sides. Because of the importance of Yosemite to California, and because of the

494

nature of the Modoc War, these events are important beyond their place in the litany of killings just recited.

In the Southern Mines some of the Indians were working for the miners, providing low-cost labor, but Tenaya's band kept its distance, with some young braves participating in occasional raids that chiefly targeted the miners' horses and mules for food.

Mariposa was headquarters for mining activity in the area, and when raids became more frequent, whites living there demanded action. There was enough at stake to guarantee full support for an expedition to quell the Indians, and white gold seekers made no distinction among different villages and tribes. Yosemite Valley was not an objective for the whites: Its existence was virtually unknown to them, the 1833 Joseph Walker expedition being long forgotten and the scant gold there offering little attraction.

A year earlier, in 1849, an itinerant millwright, William Abrams (1820-76), along with a companion, had become lost while hunting grizzly bears in the Sierra. They reached a summit affording a look into the valley, and Abrams later (October 8, 1849) wrote a description of Bridalveil Fall and Half Dome:

[We walked] over an Indian trail that led past a valley enclosed by stupendous cliffs rising perhaps 3,000 feet (914 m) from their base and which gave us cause for wonder. Not far off a waterfall dropped from a cliff below three jagged peaks into the valley while farther beyond a rounded mountain stood, the valley wide of which looked as though it had been sliced with a knife as one would slice a loaf of bread and which Reamer and I called the Rock of Ages. [44]

Among the settlers near Mariposa was James D. Savage, a trader and gold miner who in 1849-50 operated in the mountains at the South Fork of the Merced River. The South Fork runs near Wawona and empties into the Merced's main fork about fifteen miles (24 km) downstream from the Yosemite Valley.

Early in 1850, Savage's camp was attacked by a band of Indians who claimed the territory as home and saw the white men as trespassers. Savage and his men repelled the attack, but, under Savages's direction, pulled back to a site on Mariposa Creek. He soon established another trading post on the Fresno River. Savage prospered through hard-nosed business tactics, charging high prices for traded goods and paying low wages to Indians he hired to mine gold. He also took five Indian wives, representing various factions active in the area, thus establishing an intelligence network to warn him of impending attacks.[45]

Later in 1850, one of his five Indian wives warned Savage that a new attack was being planned. Indian workers in his mining operation confirmed that tribal leaders meant to strike again. He did not withdraw but warned his fellow whites that trouble could be expected. Settlers in the Mariposa area scoffed, but attacks soon came, and twelve whites were killed in three raids. Reports of these incursions, and rumors of others, finally aroused the settlers. A posse of about 100 whites set out to find the raiders.

On January 11, 1851, the whites caught up with the Indian force at a point on the Fresno River. A skirmish followed, in which one lieutenant was killed and several other whites were wounded. A counterattack struck the Indians at dawn of the next day. Twenty-three Indians were killed, but no whites died in the second skirmish. Eight bands of Indians, including some from Tenaya's Yosemites, participated in the raids. About 500 warriors were involved and some 100 whites opposed them, according to white accounts.

The fighting, plus additional Indian raids, spurred state authorities to action. Governor John McDougal called for a volunteer force, and 200 men quickly responded. The unit, which included most of those involved in the earlier skirmishes, was called the Mariposa Battalion. Its members were mustered into service on January 24, 1851.

The first expedition by white men into Yosemite Valley occurred in 1851, when the Mariposa Battalion set out to deal with the "Indian problem."

Savage was made commanding officer and given the rank of major. Among his recruits was Dr. Lafayette Houghton Bunnell (1824-1903), a frontiersman and physician who had served in the Mexican-American War and who had left his home in Minnesota to seek golden fortune and adventure in California. He would chronicle the battalion's activities.

The Mariposa Battalion's assignment was to subjugate the Indian tribes on the east side of the San Joaquin Valley from the Tuolumne River all the way to Tejon Pass. Most of the action, however, was limited to the Mariposa area. Protecting the gold camps in the Southern Mother Lode was the real priority. Federal officials, who had the responsibility of supervising Indian affairs, arrived on the scene and attempted to make peace between the tribes and settlers. Russio, a Miwok chief from the Tuolumne River area, warned that "the Indians in the deep rocky valley on the Merced River do not wish for peace and will not come in to see the chiefs sent by the great father [the U.S. president] to make treaties. They think the white men cannot find their hiding places and that therefore they cannot be driven out." Scattered groups of mountain Indians continued stealing from the miners' camps and taking horses and mules from area ranches.

At this point the Mariposa Battalion was placed under the

direction of the U.S. commissioners sent by the federal government, who were still trying to make peace with the Indians by establishing reservations while ever prepared to act against any holdouts. Major Savage was ordered to move against holdouts in the San Joaquin and Merced valleys. Any captured Indians were to be moved to the commissioners' camp on the Fresno River. The battalion, according to Bunnell, was a body of hardy, resolute men. Many of them had seen military service and fought Indians while crossing the plains. Few were inclined to be touched by the spectacular Yosemite scenery.

The force traversed difficult terrain to a point on the South Fork of the Merced about a mile (1.6 km) south of what is now known as Wawona. Scouts reported an Indian village a short distance away. The whites surprised the Indians at daybreak, and Savage informed Ponwatchee, a chief of the friendly Noot-chu band (and an old enemy of Tenaya's), of the alternatives: capitulate or fight. They surrendered.

The Yosemite Valley Indians, holed up in their approximately 7.5-mile-long glacial valley bounded by 3,000-3,500-foot (914 m-1 km) cliffs, were the next target. They had refused to respond to peace offerings, but now a special envoy went to the tribe and demanded a response. The next day Chief Tenaya appeared at the battalion's camp. Fearing that Major Savage would seek personal revenge for raids upon his operations, he was cautious about delivering his people into white control. "My people do not want anything from the Great Father you tell me about," Tenaya said. "The Great Spirit is our father, and he has always supplied us with all we need. We do not want anything from white men. Our women are able to do our work. Go, then; let us remain in the mountains where we were born; where the ashes of our fathers have been given to the winds. I have said enough."

Tenaya admitted raiding, but adamantly resisted moving his people to the plains where they would be forced to live among hostile tribes. When Major Savage ordered the Yosemites to report to the white commissioners or take the consequences, Tenaya promised to bring his people in promptly. However, when his tribesmen didn't appear as demanded, soldiers were sent into the valley after them.

The troops headed north to the Merced River, encountering heavy snow as they approached. Before reaching the valley, they again met Chief Tenaya, this time accompanied by 72 men, women, and children. "This is all of my people who are willing to go with me to the plains," he announced. Others who had been with them previously he claimed to have been from other bands. These others he referred to had reportedly taken their families and moved in with the Tuolumne and Mono Indians. Major Savage had been told the Yosemites numbered about 200, so he decided to move into the valley and see for himself if others remained.

On March 21,1851, the battalion descended toward the main branch of the Merced. There they were exposed to a full view of El Capitan and a portion of the valley beyond. It was the first time, as far as is known, that non-Indians had ever seen the spectacle from the valley floor. Four decades later Bunnell described the effect:

> "It has been said that it is not easy to describe in words the precise impressions which great objects make upon us.' I cannot describe how completely I realized this truth. None but those who have visited this most wonderful valley can even imagine the feelings with which I looked upon the view that was there presented. The grandeur of the scene was but softened by the haze which hung over the valley -- light as gossamer and by the clouds which partially dimmed

the higher cliffs and mountains. This obscurity of vision but increased the awe with which I beheld it, and as I looked, a peculiar exalted sensation seemed to fill my whole being, and I found my eyes in tears with emotion."[46]

The mood was broken when Major Savage ordered him to stop dreaming and join the troops or "he might lose his hair."

That first night in the valley, Bunnell insisted that a name should be chosen. His companions agreed, and after long discussion, he proposed "that we give the valley the name of Yo-sem-i-ty, as it was . . . euphonious and certainly American; that by so doing, the name of the tribe of Indians which are leaving their homes in this valley, perhaps never to return, would be perpetuated."[47] Some opposed a name honoring a group they considered their enemy. But after a discussion, a vote was taken and *Yosemity* was chosen. Major Savage concurred. Later, an army lieutenant altered the spelling to Yosemite and that became the accepted form.

When informed that Yosemite was the valley's new name, Chief Tenaya objected. Bunnell understood from his sign language that the name belonged to his band and meant grizzly bear. Tenaya was in fact objecting that his people called the valley Ah-wah-nee. (Later historians say Bunnell misunderstood the sign language, and that the name "Yosemite" in fact meant something related to the Yosemite Valley Miwoks' being known as a fierce people.)

The battalion continued its search for the rest of Tenaya's band, and the chief was allowed to return to the valley to try to talk other holdouts into surrendering. Searchers soon found a just-abandoned Indian village, confirming the suspicions of Savage and his men. Scouts found more trails and villages farther up the valley, but no Indians were sighted, except for

500

an elderly woman. All dwelling places and food supplies were destroyed to try to starve the Indians from their hiding places. Bunnell reported with unintended irony: "We were not a party of tourists seeking recreation, nor philosophers investigating the operations of nature. Our business there was to find Indians who were endeavoring to escape from our charitable intentions toward them."[48]

With supplies depleted, Major Savage ordered the party to pull back to a base on the South Fork to avoid being trapped by another heavy snowstorm. From there, the battalion marched the Indians who had surrendered out of the mountains to be placed with others rounded up earlier. They were relocated to lands in the Fresno area, but later drifted back into the mountains. On May 9 another force under Captain John Boling (1825-64) returned to search for the remaining Indians, but the natives spotted them and fled up into the mountains. Bunnell saw five warriors across the river, keeping a safe distance but making no effort to flee. Reinforcements were ordered up and eventually the five were captured. One of the five, a son of Chief Tenaya, was killed while supposedly trying to escape.

Tenaya also was captured, and Boling tried to persuade him to call in his people. He pretended to do so but later, enraged by the death of his son, he vented his feelings: "You may kill me, sir captain, but you shall not live-in peace. I will follow in your footsteps, I will not leave my home, but be with the spirits among the rocks, the waterfalls, in the rivers and in the winds; wheresoever you go I will be with you. You will not see me but you will fear the spirit of the old chief and grow cold. The great spirits have spoken! I am done."[49]

With the help of Indian scouts from another tribe, the expedition chased after another thirty-five members of Tenaya's band in the high country near what is now Tenaya

501

Lake. Tenaya's granddaughter, Totuya, then twelve years old, recalled years later the sight of soldiers in red flannel underwear running through the snow after the exhausted remnants of the Indian tribe. She also remembered Indians being shot, and women being raped. The captured Indians were marched out of the valley to Fresno River rancheria and turned over to federal officials. The Mariposa Battalion had completed its task.

In 1852 a small party of miners went back into the valley searching for gold, ignoring warnings not to trespass on Indian territory. Details are not clear, but an Indian boy was killed, and the miners were attacked by Indians. Two of the miners were killed and another seriously injured. An army force, under the command of Lieutenant Treadwell Moore (1824-76), who had first built Fort Miller, went into the valley after them. Indians were rounded up and five suspects identified by articles of white men's clothing they were wearing. On that evidence, Moore pronounced the Indians guilty and ordered them shot. Other Yosemite Indians were marched back out of the valley or ran away to the east.[50]

This occurrence ended the presence of the Yosemites in the valley, until later years when they drifted back and quietly resettled in small groups.

Chief Tenaya and remnants of his tribe fled to live with Indians near Mono Lake, where he had been raised and where his people had lived years earlier. Tenaya died there during a fracas with Mono Indians stemming from a dispute over a native gambling game, according to his granddaughter.

In 1864 the Modocs had agreed to go to an Oregon reservation. They were unaware that they would be sharing the reservation with their traditional enemies, the Klamaths. The Klamaths, superior in numbers and very haughty, immediately started picking on the Modocs, so Chief Kientipoos (c 1837-73), known to the Americans as "Captain Jack," took his people back to Lost River.

The Modocs were persuaded to return to the reservation in 1869, but this time the Klamaths were even less civil in their treatment of the Modocs, taunting them for having left and edging them out of available supplies, so they departed once again. This time the army was told to round up Captain Jack and his 200 people. The Modocs hid in the Tule Lake lava beds, caves, and outcroppings, which they knew intimately and in which they could hide indefinitely.

In January 1873 the soldiers, who outnumbered the Indians by several hundred, attacked and were driven back. The Indians managed to capture rifles from dead soldiers, improving their situation somewhat. Embarrassed, the army in response sent in reinforcements to double the number of soldiers. Armed as the American soldiers were with repeater rifles and Gatling guns against the Indians with their bows-and-arrows and a few guns, their sense of humiliation in defeat must have been sharp indeed.

In March 1873 General E. R. S. Canby (1817-73) came up from San Francisco to take charge of the war. He called for talks with Captain Jack, during which Canby demanded that the Modocs surrender. They were not losing, so this seemed to them a bad idea, but since Captain Jack had merely deigned to speak to the Americans, some of his people began to call him a coward and an old woman, threatening to overthrow him. To keep his position, he determined to kill Canby at their next meeting in April. Not knowing the American military, his advisers told him that the soldiers would be sure to leave if their leader was killed. Canby was warned by the Indian wife of a trader not to meet with Captain Jack or at least not to go unarmed to the meeting, but, ignoring this advice, he

503

went to the meeting unarmed and met his death.

The public, while not sympathetic to the Indians, ridiculed the army for being unable to bring a few savages to heel.

Canby's killing and the public's mockery infuriated the army, motivating many more army assaults on the lava beds. The soldiers couldn't enter the rough terrain, but the Indians couldn't get out, and when their food and water ran low, that would permit their capture. Finally, facing starvation, some Modocs deserted. Captured, they led the soldiers to Captain Jack's hideout in return for food (some of these deserters were the same warriors who had insulted and threatened their chief the previous spring).

Captain Jack and several other Modoc chiefs were tried for murder and hanged. The tribe was removed to Indian Territory, now Oklahoma.

Captain Jack's execution was probably unwarranted. True, he had murdered Canby. However, Crazy Horse and Sitting Bull's warriors had killed General George Armstrong Custer (1839-76) and the entire Seventh Cavalry while Geronimo's Apaches spread death and terror in Arizona and Sonora for twenty years. When these two chiefs were caught, they were put on reservations and even made some money performing for American audiences in shows. Captain Jack was executed not so much for General Canby's murder as for embarrassing the army.

Introducing the Reservation System

It must have been with a certain feeling of *déjà vu* that California's Indians began to be confined to reservations. After all, Indians of various tribes had been confined within mission properties. When the United States took California, the first two Indian agents appointed by the new authorities were Vallejo and Sutter. U. S. Indian policy since 1830 had been based on the reservation system, that is, restricting the Indians' movements and dwellings to certain areas where whites were never supposed to go. For their part, Indians would be free to roam as they pleased within their reserved lands, hunting, fighting each other, planting, or doing whatever the tribe or group wanted to do. In January 1851 three federal commissioners arrived at San Francisco and negotiated eighteen treaties with the tribes, giving them much of the San Joaquin Valley in return for keeping the peace. Colonel Edward Beale (1822-93), the superintendent of California Indians, supported this plan but the U. S. Senate rejected it overwhelmingly. The commissioners had inflated their expense accounts, some of the Indians who marked the treaties were not chiefs but persons with no tribal authority, and Governor Burnett objected that the land was thought too good to give to Indians. That "a war of extermination," the governor declared, "will continue to be waged between the races until the Indian race becomes extinct must be expected."[51]

Beale devised a new reservation plan. This would be styled on the old Spanish missions - congregating the Indians, teaching them the English language, a trade, and American customs. It would not be religious, but missionaries would be welcome to work among the natives. His first reservation was at Fort Tejon at the top of the Grapevine (Tejon Pass over the Tehachapis), one of five with about 2,500 Indians each. Opened in 1853 it was an immediate success. Beale also made surveys for a railway between Missouri and California and for a wagon road between New Mexico and California. For this project he imported single-humped dromedaries and a few two-humped Bactrian camels, some from a herd used in Texas and others imported directly from Tunis for transport over the 1,200-mile (1,930 km) route from Ft. Defiance, New Mexico, to the Colorado River border of California.

Although Beale's reservations were successful, political enemies had him removed and replaced by Thomas Henley (1808-65), former Democratic congressman from Indiana (1843-49).

Henley opened new reservations near Fresno, Tehama, and Cape Mendocino. Ironically, Beale had been falsely accused of using his office for political gain, but it was Henley who did so and under whom the Natives suffered. He was replaced after an investigation in 1859.[52] He became postmaster of San Francisco, serving 1860-64.

During Henley's term there occurred the largest earthquake to strike California in historical times. It rocked southern and central California on January 9, 1857, uprooting trees in the San Bernardino Mountains and causing the Kern River to flow backwards for a time. Because of the state's small population in 1857 (perhaps 350,000 people), there were only two fatalities, one of them near Fort Tejon, where many buildings were destroyed. Strong shaking from the earthquake was said to have lasted from one to three minutes. The best estimate of the earthquake's magnitude is 8.3, stronger than the Mexico City earthquake of 1985, which killed over 10,000, or the Nepal earthquake of April 2015, which killed over 9,000.

In 1863 Tejon was abandoned because of Henley's administrative abuse. Although within a few years the Beale system appeared to be collapsing, the definitive wresting of the Plains, Rockies, and Southwest from the Indians in the 1870s led to the system's reinstatement. Beale's system became, in fact, the basis for reservations in the United States for a century.

Stages and Steamers

From the start of the Gold Rush there were stages and steamers carrying passengers, freight, gold, and mail inside and outside the borders of California. Of all these companies only two remain in business, neither one in transportation, Wells Fargo and American Express. By 1854 most of the smaller stage lines had been taken over by the California Stage Company, with Wells Fargo its main rival for territory. Most of these used the Concord stages, made by Abbot-Downing Company of Concord, New Hampshire. These were the coaches Phineas Banning imported to San Pedro to improve the efficiency of road travel while he was developing the port. The coach had a great capacity for its size, carrying nine passengers inside and six more perched on the roof, with room for luggage on top and in the leather boot behind. These coaches were *works* of art, egg-shaped coaches suspended on leather by braces, nicely painted on the outside but hell to ride in. The leather suspension system kept road shock in the coach rather than let it telegraph to the driver, reins, and horses, thereby sparing the driver, and even the horses, – but not the passengers. Several of these passengers reportedly went insane because of the ride, and on one occasion Horace Greeley (1811-72), owner of the New *York Tribune,* is said to have endured such a rough ride that his head was forced through the roof of the stagecoach.[53]

The man who held the reins and cracked the whip over a six-horse team was, in the 1850s and '60s, often more highly esteemed than the millionaire or statesman who rode behind him. An equally popular figure was the appropriately named "shotgun rider" who accompanied the driver and protected the company's shipments. He was armed by the company with a double-barreled shotgun, and often carried in addition a "Wells Fargo Colt," a pocket pistol designed in 1849 for use by express guards and police.

Naturally, the treasure shipments of Wells Fargo drew the attention of many a highwayman, and when the messenger met his match and the coach was robbed, hastily printed reward posters went up in key locations all over the area. The one man responsible for the greatest number of reward posters was mild-mannered Black Bart (1829-1888+), a white man whose real name was Charles Bolton, English-born Union Army veteran. In his flour-sack disguise with two cut-out eyeholes, he politely robbed at least 28 stages single-handedly. On his first robbery, in July 1875, he stopped a stage between Sonora and Milton, about 100 miles (160 km) east of San Francisco. "Please throw down the box," he requested, and when the driver saw what he thought were the six gun barrels of the robber's accomplices poking out of the rocks, he complied. A woman on the stage asked if he wanted her watch, to which he gallantly responded, "I don't need your money. I only want Wells Fargo's." When he disappeared, the driver saw that the six "guns" were only sticks. To add insult to injury, he usually left these or similarly mocking verses at the scene of each crime:

> I've labored long and hard for bread,
> For honor and for riches.
> But on my corns too long you've tread
> You fine-haired sons-of-bitches.
> (signed) Black Bart the Po8

After almost a decade of robbing, this cunning and intelligent robber was caught by detective James Hume (1827-1904) and Alameda County Sheriff Harry Morse (1835-1912), thanks to Hume's keen observation of a laundry mark on his handkerchief. He always used an unloaded gun, and never drank or used tobacco. Sentenced to serve five years in San Quentin, upon release he disappeared from history.[54]

Black Bart never encountered Charlie Parkhurst (1812-79) of Jim Burch's (1827-57) fledging California Stage Lines in the Santa Cruz Mountains or the Mother Lode, or his initial success would have ended differently. Parkhurst's first encounter with highwaymen ended with the highwaymen successfully taking the box. The second time, Charlie fired his shotgun before the command "Throw down the box" could be shouted, killed the leader of the bandits, and drove his coach into the other six, so that they scattered. One night in the Sierra the author J. Ross Browne (1821-75), delighted that he could ride beside the famous whip, asked him how he could see his way. Parkhurst replied, "Smell it. Fact is, I've traveled over these mountains so often I can tell where the road is by the sount [sic] of the wheels. When they rattle, I'm on hard ground. When they don't rattle, I genr'ly [sic] look over the side to see where she's going." For twenty years he drove stagecoaches until a horse kicked him in the eye, blinding that one and forcing his retirement as a saloon and wagon station owner in Watsonville. There is evidence he voted in 1868, which would not be exceptional except that when he died in 1879, Charlie Parkhurst was discovered to have been a woman – and women did not have the vote in California until 1912! [55]

The Concord coach driver's seat was over the treasure box, which carried placer washings, gold dust and ore. Countless millions in gold were carried all over the West by Wells Fargo stages. In handling the miners' gold from the Mother Lode, Wells Fargo's principal services were two-fold: transporting it from the mines to San Francisco (express) and keeping it safe and exchanging it for money (banking). In those days express and banking services went hand in hand.

To messengers or officers of the law who successfully

fought off or captured bandits, Wells Fargo was generous. Rewards were usually fine examples of the engravers and jeweler's art. When James Wales Miller, who started the Sacramento-Auburn line, saved a $30,000 ($588,806 in 2023) payroll shipment from attempted holdup in the 1860s, he was awarded a fine watch encased in two pounds (907 g) of Nevada silver! Stephen Venard (c1823-91), for killing three bandits who held up and robbed the North San Juan coach in the Yuba River's Myer's Ravine in May1866, was awarded $3,000 ($58,881 in 2023) and a handsome Henry Rifle engraved with a drawing of the exploit and the inscription "... for his gallant conduct May 16, 1866...." [56]

To provide the growing population with the express and banking services it needed, Wells Fargo established a network of offices throughout the West. In 1880 there were 573 Wells Fargo offices, agents, and correspondents - over 100 of them located in the Mother Lode area.

Besides its overland routes, Wells Fargo used fleet Clipper Ships and Pacific Mail steamships to carry gold, bullion, express and mail. Like other express and banking companies of that day, Wells Fargo issued Firsts, Seconds and Thirds of Exchange to transfer money East. One document went around the Horn by sea; another to Panama by ship, across the Isthmus by rail and then by ship to the East Coast; and a third by overland stagecoach. When the first document to be presented was paid, the others became worthless. The point of this was to try all three routes at once so that at any rate one would get to its destination the fastest, but all three would make the attempt because it was quite unpredictable which one would get there first.

A big banking day in San Francisco was Steamer Day, a twice a month event when the Eastern mail left by steamship for Panama. Because of this schedule, all bills were called due according to the sailing schedule. All San Francisco settled accounts before the twice-monthly sailings, a custom observed up to the turn of the century.

The California Steam Navigation Company operated riverboats connecting Sacramento, Stockton, and San Francisco, veritable floating palaces. On the coast, connections to the outside world were provided by Pacific Mail.

Probably the most famous of California Steam Navigation's ships, without seeking fame, was the *Brother Jonathan*, built in Brooklyn in 1851 for use in the California and Fraser River gold rushes and for a short time owned by Cornelius Vanderbilt. In 1862 it had unwittingly set off a smallpox epidemic in the Pacific Northwest when an infected passenger from San Francisco landed at Victoria.

By this time the ship had an enviable reputation of being one of the finest steamers on the Pacific Coast and the fastest steamer to make the run in 69 hours each way. The owners began to neglect proper caution, adding more passengers and goods to make more money – even if the ship dipped below the water line. On July 30, 1865, this devil-may-care attitude caused the worst ocean disaster in the history of the mainland Pacific Coast of the US. A gale near the California-Oregon border forced the captain to try to turn the ship around, to go back to Crescent City. About 4.5 miles (7.2 km) southwest of Point St. George and close to port, the ship hit an uncharted rock (in the area known as the Dragon Rocks) and within half an hour it sank. Most of the lifeboats could not be deployed, with the result that only 19 survived while over 200 perished. The amount of gold it carried, worth over $64.7 million in today's money, began to be recovered in the 1930s and the ship's location was found by a two-man submersible (a mini-submarine) in October 1993, leading to recovery of the treasure.[57]

In 1891 a Fresnel lens was installed in the St. George Reef Lighthouse to warn mariners away from the Dragon Rocks.

To connect to the East two stage lines appeared, the Butterfield Overland and the Central California Overland and Pike's Peak Express. John Butterfield (1801-69) received a contract to carry the mail from San Francisco to St. Louis via Los Angeles and Texas in 1858. The semiweekly run was made in 28 days or less. Butterfield was not popular with his passengers because of poor accommodations that had to be paid for in advance. It lost the mail contract in April 1860 to the Pony Express, the creation of Russell, Majors & Waddell. At the same time, Northern congressmen began objecting to subsidizing a line through Confederate states (Texas and Arkansas), so Butterfield sold out to Ben Holladay (1819-87).

The Pony Express ran for just eighteen months from Sacramento to St. Joseph, Missouri, via the California Trail, now part of Interstate 80. Founded by Russell, Majors & Waddell, it charged by the ounce and used skinny teenaged orphan boys as its riders to get the mail through. A typical letter carried a $5 ($185 in 2023) price tag for 1/2 ounce (14 g), then $4 ($148 in 2023) and finally a 25c ($9.25 in 2023) stamp issued by Wells Fargo. (Until 1895, when the federal government took over all mail services, some 400 express companies also carried the mail and issued their own stamps). The Pony Express was put out of business by Western Union, founded in 1856 by Ezra Cornell (1807-74), which had established a telegraph line from New York to San Francisco via Chicago in 1860. Western Union charged per word, but the message would flash across the continent in under an hour.

Holladay's Central California received a mail contract and could carry passengers and freight on its coaches in 1862, using the California Trail to St. Joseph to avoid confrontations with Indians. His friendship with Brigham Young smoothed the way to a contract to handle staging in Utah, and he started building a railroad from the Willamette Valley to California, and then a line of Oregon steamships. In 1866 he was able to sell his holdings to Wells Fargo for $1.5 million ($29,440,351 in 2023). The financial crisis of 1873 destroyed most of his holdings. Like so many of the original builders of California's financial and transportation infrastructure, such as William Ralston, E. J. "Lucky" Baldwin (1828-1909), James Lick, Sam Brannan, Charles Crocker, and Collis Huntington, he was something of a mystery, and a seemingly larger than life phenomenon. Journalist and financier Henry Villard (1835-1900), to whom he sold out, wrote of him after his death: "[he was] illiterate, coarse, boastful, false and cunning," Holladay's attorney said of him, "[he possessed] many of the characteristics of Napoleon, the bearing of one born to command, being clever, shrewd, cunning, illiterate, coarse, and completely unscrupulous" and a railroad competitor summed him up as "wholly destitute of fixed principles of honesty, morality, or common decency."[58]

In an age when coach travel was still the most common and fastest, these delivery times were acceptable. But with greater distances to cover and with a greater demand for news and goods, something would have to replace it. That something was chugging along slowly but surely in the innovation known as the Iron Horse.

From Asa Whitney to Theodore Judah

The railroad was an English invention of the 1820s copied by Americans in the 1830s. In 1845 Asa Whitney (1791-1874), having ridden the newly opened Liverpool and Manchester Railway on a trip to England and taken a business trip to China, enthusiastically proposed the first transcontinental railroad line, stretching to Oregon on the Pacific, to help the United States take advantage of newly opening trade with China. He did not stint on spending money to interest Congress in the project and in 1849 published *A Project for a Railroad to the Pacific*. The idea was, however, premature: There was not yet a standard gauge for rail tracks. There was no one rich enough to finance it, the government did not compete with business, and most of the territory, being unsettled, could not support a railroad. Within the decade the idea would not seem so premature.

In 1854 Theodore Judah (1826-63), a young New York engineer, was hired to build the first railroad west of New Orleans. It would be a short line from Sacramento to Folsom called the Sacramento River Railroad. When he completed it, he was commissioned to chart a wagon route across the Sierra. He chose Dutch Flat Pass and made his report a plea for a railroad rather than a wagon route.

The reaction was predictable. He was called "Crazy Judah." He was, in fact, not even mildly insane. Rather, he was a fervent railroad buff and supporter, having studied everything he could get his hands on regarding railroads. His ardor did not blind him to the realities of railroad construction, but though the Comstock had not yet been discovered, he was somewhat inexplicably sure of the potential economic base for a trans-Sierra railroad.

Others were less certain. To most Easterners the 19,000 mile (30,577 km) trip from Sandy Hook, Connecticut around the Horn to San Francisco Bay was nothing very objectionable. Abolitionist, social reformer and a powerful speaker, the Rev. Henry Ward Beecher (1813-87) had made the rugged journey across the plains by covered wagon and averred that the West could never grow until a railway was built; most people felt that a preacher could not be expected to know about such things, and nothing would come of his advocacy. There was no future in the west, as the gold rush would soon be over, white Americans would leave California, and San Francisco would fade away as all mining towns eventually did. Such a railroad could never be built.

In 1857 Beecher memorialized Congress to appropriate money for a railroad survey and to allow capitalists rather than politicians to decide the route. He was well aware that the slavery controversy would be reflected in the choice of an eastern terminal. Despite the soundness of the suggestion, Congress rejected it. To the frock-coated gentlemen in Washington, the dream of a railroad was impractical; all steel and building materials would have to travel 19,000 miles (30,577 km) over treacherous seas.

Western congressmen, few as they were, supported him, and as a result of the Pacific Railroad Convention in San Francisco in 1859, secured him a lobbying office in Washington. However, because he was not inclined to play the political game of "wining and dining" congressmen, he was unsuccessful in getting Congress to re-examine his suggestions.

Organizing the Central Pacific

The Civil War and the Union's need for Western gold and silver finally got the railroad started. Because so many railroads had gone bankrupt in the late 1830s and early 1840s federal law required that new railroads deposit a security bond of $1,000 ($42,136 in 2023) per mile (1.6 km) for the first 50 miles (80.4 km). This was a considerable amount of money in those days, beyond the reach of even the wealthiest Americans. Judah went to San Francisco bankers, but they were cold to the idea; how could any train climb the Sierra, to

515

say nothing of the Rockies? In only three states did railroads ascend mountains: Georgia, Pennsylvania, and Vermont; and in none of these were the mountains higher than 6,600 feet (2 km); the Sierra and Rockies rose from 6,000 (1.82 km) to 13,000 feet (3.96 km)!

He next approached Sacramento merchants, who warmed to the idea of a railroad when Judah pointed out that Sacramento would become the western terminus and would reap the benefits of trade and transportation. So it was that in Sacramento Judah organized the Central Pacific Railroad. Four Sacramento businessmen, Mark Hopkins (1813-78), Collis Huntington, Leland Stanford, and Charles Crocker (1822-88) bought less than one percent of the new company's stock, but by certain manipulations now illegal they managed to take over the company. These men became known as "the Big Four."

Back to Washington Judah went. There he visited another dreamer, another man able to see that the nation's future greatness hinged on the railroads' binding it together. Judah and this "dreamer" talked long about the project, which the latter agreed to support. "He" was none other than Abraham Lincoln.

Because of the Union's needs and the removal of Southern congressmen in 1862, Congress passed - and Lincoln signed - the Pacific Railroad Bill authorizing the construction of a railroad from Sacramento to Omaha, Nebraska. The required deposits would have to be made but the government would pay the new railroad $5,000 ($154,212 in 2023) and substantial land grants for every mile (1.6 km) after the first fifty (80.4 km). In other words, the railroad received 12,800 acres (5,180 ha) (or twenty sections) of land from the public domain for every mile (1.6 km) of track laid. The land granted was to be strips in checkerboard pattern (to keep the railroad from obtaining exclusive control) extending twenty miles (32 km) on either side of the tracks. As a first step, the federal government would advance, on 30-year six percent bonds for each mile (1.6 km) of track laid, $16,000 ($505,134 in 2023) to the mountains, $48,000 ($1,480,429 in 2023) in the Rockies and the Sierra, and $32,000 ($986,953 in 2023) on the intermountain section.

The Big Four wanted to make money. Judah wanted to make a railroad. Since their goals were at cross purposes, they tried to buy him out, finally forcing him out for a relatively paltry $100,000 ($3,084,227 in 2023). Judah, aged 37, was not finished. He determined to go to New York to interest the House of Morgan, the nation's largest bank, in the project. However, in Panama he caught yellow fever and died. His former partners, holding no regard for his memory, failed to name so much as a whistle-stop for the man who had dreamed their railroad up. Not until 1930 would the railroad honor its founder with a plaque in Sacramento's Old Town, just east of 2nd and J Streets; in 1940, a 8,245 foot (2.5 km) peak in Placer County adjacent to Mount Lincoln and Donner Peak was named Mount Judah by the U.S. Board of Geographic Names.

The Big Four at Work

As soon as Judah was removed from the company the Big Four were off like a shot toward their goal of making money regardless of the means. Unscrupulous, they falsified maps to show that they had already reached the Sierra when they were still in the Valley, so that they could start collecting government bounties. In this they secured the assistance of the state geologist and later Harvard professor, Josiah Dwight Whitney (1819-96), and received $640,000 ($19,739,054 in 2023).

As individuals the Big Four had many things in common.

All had had a rigorous, poor boyhood in the East, each had come to California to mine but soon – Huntington and Hopkins after a half-day in the mines - turned to trade as more profitable. One was a grocery clerk, one a dry goods merchant, and two were dealers in hardware. Thanks to historian Oscar Lewis' magnificent book, *The Big Four* (1938), we can understand what made them the monumental characters they were.

Huntington was indifferent to popularity, and despised politics, newspapers, formal education, and charities. By age fourteen this son of a frugal tinkerer had earned $100 ($3,810 in 2023) from doing odd jobs for neighbors. At that moment his single motivation in life was wealth, and in its acquisition, whatever worked for him was right for him. He cared nothing for what other people, including his partners, did or thought as long as they did not cross him. It was not until his seventies that he began to live extravagantly like the other multimillionaires of the day.

Stanford was the most extroverted, and at 220 pounds (100 kg) was only the third heaviest of the group.[59] He was ultimately to be the most generous of the Big Four. Although he never graduated with a degree, he started a law practice in Wisconsin, which soon burned down and spurred him to California. Unlike Huntington, he enjoyed politics while others enjoyed the genial personality that helped to elect him governor after two electoral defeats. While the railroad was being built, he was its greatest promoter in the West, and served as its president. His attitude towards wealth, unlike Huntington's obsession, was expressed in a comment he made to David Starr Jordan, later president of Stanford University: "I learn every year more and more to love the landscape, and this the poorest man in California can enjoy as well as the richest."

518

Crocker had been an enterprising boy, having a newspaper subscription agency before he was twelve, and working for farmers, millwrights, and blacksmiths to earn money for his family. Going to California for gold he quit after two years and joined his brothers in a Sacramento store. When he felt financially able to marry, he returned to his home and married the daughter of a farmer who had employed him. Summing up his character Crocker recalled that during the construction of the railroad, "[e]veryone was afraid of me. I was just looking for someone to find fault with all the time. My faculty of leadership grew more and more." The largest of the Big Four, at 250 pounds (113 kg), Crocker, like Huntington, never gave a cent to charities or public institutions.

Hopkins was reputedly the kindest among them. Crocker ridiculed him for being too conservative in business ever to become rich. "Thin as a fence post," Hopkins was a vegetarian who refused to smoke, drink, curse, gamble or spend money. "One man works hard all his life and ends up a pauper," according to Crocker. "Another man, no smarter, makes $20,000,000. Luck has a hell of a lot to do with it." Further, having $20,000,000 ($455 million in 2023) was "against Hopkins's better judgment," and he acted "as if he wanted to apologize for his millions." [60]In partnership with Huntington, his main talent was to travel about the state buying merchandise cheap and keeping it in his warehouse until it was scarce, at which time the price would rise as high as the market would bear.

All died very wealthy men.

Crocker oversaw construction of the railroad, and in this way the Big Four came to control the company. The Crocker Construction Company charged excessively high prices for track laying, causing a dip in company profits. Fearing for their investments, many shareholders sold out at depressed prices; the Big Four took advantage of the slide by purchasing shares, thus cheating the other investors, and permitting a Big Four takeover. Methods such as these have been illegal for many years, but at the time the stock market was a dangerous jungle; if one suffered, too bad. One was personally responsible for having risked the money in the first place. In 1875 journalist Samuel Williams (1826-81) wrote of those days: "A happy turn in stocks makes a millionaire of a man who yesterday could not be trusted for a pair of boots."[61]

In 1863, when the cost and difficulty of track laying nearly caused the Big Four to throw in the towel, Governor Stanford, himself one of the Big Four, got the state to grant $1.5 million ($36,661,569 in 2023) to assist the builders. Such a conflict of interest would be illegal today, but then it was admired as sharp politicking.

The work pushed forward, but it was hardly clear sailing. Enemies of the project sent agents into the working camps with disturbing propaganda. The trans-Sierra stage lines feared the competition that the railroad threatened. They spread pernicious stories that the steel rails shipped around the Horn would be indefinitely delayed, circulated the rumor that the men would be laid off without pay, and finally turned from gossip to sabotage, wrecking some supply trains. Causing to circulate wild stories of huge gold discoveries in new and remote areas, they successfully tempted workers to desert by the hundreds. The railroad was under contract to the federal government to finish the task by a given time or suffer penalties that would bankrupt it and its owners.

These labor difficulties led to Crocker's importing Chinese workers. He had gone to San Francisco, meditating on his problem as he walked the muddy streets, until one morning he sprang into action. A sailing ship from China, with fifty Chinese coolies (outsourced unskilled labor particularly from

South China or India), was docking. Crocker rushed to the dock and herded the Chinese workers down the gangplank into waiting boxcars, and they were rushed off to the hills before they or anyone but Crocker knew where they were going. Since they spoke no English, they were immune to the propaganda of the railroad's enemies.

Crocker's construction superintendent was James Strobridge (1827-1921). He was convinced that to handle the heavy work of railroad building, a man had to stand at least six feet (1.83 m) tall and weigh at least 200 pounds (90.71 kg). Such fellows were not abundant. The men who had come to California to look for gold had come to get rich quick, and there was simply no way one could do that working for the railroad at a dollar a day ($19.05 in 2023), plus board.

Early in 1865, Strobridge advertised all over California for 5,000 husky men who wanted "constant and permanent work." This might have been a mistake as gold miners tended to be anything but "constant and permanent." Someone suggested Chinese labor to him, but Strobridge shot back, "I will not boss Chinese. I will not be responsible for the work done on the road by Chinese labor. From what I've seen of them, they're not fit laborers anyway." As white workers deserted, Crocker bellowed in return, "Hire the Chinese."

Strobridge decided to try a few, and with sinking heart looked at the first batch Crocker sent up. Their average weight was 110 pounds (50 kg) and there was not a single six-footer among them. He was sure that a week's work would kill them all. They were assigned to easy jobs around the camp. These were completed quickly and competently. Strobridge cautiously tried out a Chinese crew on a grading job.

After a week, it was obvious that the Chinese, whose ancestors had, after all, built the Great Wall, built a smoother grade than any white construction crew previously hired. Strobridge telegraphed the company headquarters: SEND UP MORE COOLIES. [62]

Crocker liked his Chinese. They did not strike, they were cheap, and they were loyal. Crocker wrote of them: "Wherever we put them, we found them good, and they worked themselves into our favor to such an extent that if we found we were in a hurry for a job of work, it was better to put Chinese on it at once." The Chinese soon became known as "Crocker's Pets," or to those who ridiculed the Chinese difficulty in pronouncing the English r, "Cholly Clockel's Pets."

On the other hand, white labor required a meat meal with their daily pay, demanded hazard pay when working with explosives and would strike to get their point across. San Francisco labor leaders denounced this use of Chinese labor, but Crocker proceeded with the imports. It would lead to fearsome consequences in less than a decade.

Day after day, week after week - in blazing sun, in sandstorms, and in the torrential rains that pounded the high Sierra - Crocker and his foreman marched up and down the line of labor urging the men on, driving the shiftless, inspiring the tired, cheering with the enthusiastic, pleading, cursing, and commanding. Crocker liked to throw his heftiness around. "Why," he reminisced, "I used to go up and down the road. . . like a mad bull, stopping along wherever there was anything amiss, and raising Old Nick with the boys that were not up to time."[63]

Slowly, inevitably, the road of steel wound up the western slopes of the Sierra. Ten thousand men labored. Fifteen tunnels were built.

One of the major obstacles was Cape Horn beyond Colfax.

This landmark was a perpendicular thousand feet (305 m). Crocker's Chinese, lowered in baskets, chiseled a passage around the rock and for many years train passengers got a tingling sensation when they realized there was nothing beneath their feet except the floorboards, railroad bed and a thousand feet of space to the American River. The bed is still narrow, but it has been widened by a few feet, depriving today's Amtrak passengers of that hair-raising experience.

Chinese railroad workers in the snow of the Sierra Nevada Mountains. Illustration by Civil War painter Joseph Becker (1841-1910). (via shmoop.com)

The greatest obstacle for track laying was Summit Tunnel, a quarter mile (402 m) of hard granite, impossible to blast or chisel. The black powder often just backfired without shattering the stone. Five hundred Chinese worked three shifts boring into the rock from both ends; then a shaft was sunk at the center so that workmen could be lowered to a point where they could drill out from the middle. The workers counted their progress by inches (1 inch=2.54 cm). The rains came, making mud and washing out the supply lines. Rains were but a prelude to heavy snows - 45 feet (13.7 m) fell in the winter of 1866-67. The workers' huts were buried under the snow, and shafts had to be drilled to provide air, tunnels hundreds of feet (1 foot=30.4 cm) long had to be dug through the snow to work sites, and of the few workers who remained, the others having been killed in weather-related perils or having departed to seek more promising work, a scant few survived the work on a meager diet of cornmeal and tea.

Heavy snows heralded another threat - avalanche. Some workers were buried clutching their picks and shovels and would not be found until spring thaw. In September 1867, however, the "impossible" Summit Tunnel was completed. Oddly, Crocker had been willing to use a new discovery, nitroglycerine, while scorning the newly invented steam drill in favor of the old-fashioned hand drill.

By December 1867 the Central Pacific had laid only 130 miles (209 km) of track out of Sacramento, but the slowest, most difficult work was done. In June 1868 the Central Pacific reached the state line.

**

"Deep and wide the wheels of progress have passed on;
the silent pioneer is gone."

-Joaquin Miller

**

The Race with the Union Pacific

Meanwhile, building west from Omaha came the Union Pacific Railroad. Its construction boss was Greenville Dodge[64] (1831-1916), a hard driver like Crocker. As a Union major general he had been asked by Lincoln to choose the eastern terminus of the railroad on the Missouri River, based on his pre-war experience with railroad building in Iowa, and chose Omaha. In 1865, while avoiding an Indian war party in the Laramie Mountains in Wyoming, he found the pass for the Union Pacific along the Platte River. In 1866 he resigned from the army and became the Union Pacific's chief engineer. Most of his laborers were Irish immigrants.

The Union Pacific had an easier time of it, laying track westward across the prairies and up along the gradual ascent of the Rockies. By December 1867 the Union Pacific had laid 500 miles (805 km) of track. Now, however, the Union Pacific was going to tackle the Rockies, and its cocky owners would find out about snow, miserable cold, and avalanches at high altitude. Suddenly Crocker and his partners woke up to the fact that there was a race going on for the greatest land grants and the most cash. The Union Pacific had had a long stretch without mountains and had achieved a head start over the Central Pacific. It appeared that the lines might join in western Nevada. The race was finally on. Crocker bought train plows to clear the tracks of snow through the mountains, but they derailed because of ice on the tracks, so he ordered snow sheds built in the High Sierra to prevent the usual thirty-foot (9.1 m) drifts' impeding a train's passing.

Down the eastern slope of the Sierra wound the ribbons of steel. Truckee was left far behind; sheer mountains of hard rock gave way to rolling foothills once more, and then on to the flat, arid, blistering plains of Nevada.

Across Nevada and toward Salt Lake construction was fairly easy. Behind were the high, rugged mountains, replaced by much smaller rises and flat desert. The cost of rails and ties skyrocketed because they had to be brought so much farther than in California. To speed things up Crocker made deals with the Shoshones and Brigham Young: with the Indians to hunt for meat for the crew and with the Mormons to grade the track beds on the approach to their capital at Salt Lake City.

Using an assembly line technique, Crocker drove his Chinese to lay ten miles (16 km) per day. The result was usually a shoddy affair, and almost immediately after completion much of this track had to be torn up and re-laid.

In one of the great "Oh, oh!" moments in history, the two companies' surveyors started to pass each other going in opposite directions: The two lines might not meet but go parallel to each other! The situation stayed relatively peaceful while only the surveyors were involved, but when the construction crews worked their way into the same Utah neighborhood, sometimes laying track only 100 feet (30.5 m) apart, Crocker's Chinese and Dodge's Irishmen got physical. Fists and pick handles evolved into dynamite as means to thwart the opposing team and win the race.

The Central Pacific was aiming north of Salt Lake while the Union Pacific was heading south to Salt Lake City. By the time the Central Pacific reached Brigham City and the Union Pacific reached Ogden, Congress realized the parallel expenses and ordered that the two lines be joined at Promontory Point, a barren spot near Ogden.

Crocker and Union Pacific vice president Thomas Durant (1820-85) posted a $10,000 bet ($208,931 in 2023) that Crocker's men could lay ten miles [16 km] of track in a day. Crocker, believing in his Chinese, boasted that his crew of 14,000 was not only the largest civilian work force in the world, but the best.

The Union Pacific had once laid just a hair over eight miles (12.9 km) of track in a day and had never stopped gloating about it, galling Crocker no end. For one thing, the Union Pacific crews had put in 20-hour workdays to achieve this feat, a circumstance Crocker deemed unfair. Accordingly,

Crocker and Strobridge assembled a crew of 848 men, 41 carts and horse teams and five trainloads of material. Crocker invited a Union Pacific delegation to watch the show. On April 28,1869 Crocker won his bet with Durant - ten miles (16 km) and 56 feet (17 m) of track were laid in less than twelve hours!

At 7:15 A.M. on that day, Crocker turned his eight Irish tracklayers loose along with hundreds of Chinese support troops. The *San Francisco Evening Bulletin's* correspondent described the scene in almost Dickensian detail:

> Each of the four men ran thirty feet (9.1 m) with one hundred and twenty-five tons (4.53 metric tons). Each of the other four men lifted and placed one hundred and twenty tons (109 metric tons) at their end of the rails. The distance traveled was over ten miles (16 km), besides extra walking... Those eight men would not consent to shift, and are proud of their work. They, like all Central Pacific men, are water-drinkers. Immediately in front of the eight are three pioneers, who, with shovel and by hand, set the ties thrown by the front teams in position; while this is doing, another party are distributing spikes and fresh bolts at each end of the rail, while some of the party are regulating the gauge. These track layers are a splendid force, and have been settled and drilled until they move like machinery...Beside the track layers come the spike-starters, who place the spikes needed in position; then comes a reverend-looking old gentleman who packs the rails and uses the line, and, by motion of his hands, directs the track-straighteners. The next men to the spike-drivers are the bolt screwers, quite a large force. Behind them come the tampers, four hundred strong, with shovels

and crowbars. They level the track by raising or lowering the ends of the ties, and shovel in enough ballast to hold them firm. When they leave it, the line is fit for trains running twenty-five miles (40.2 km) an hour. When all the iron thrown on the track has been laid, the handcarts run to the extreme front, and the locomotive and iron train come as close to the front as possible; another two miles (3.2 km) of iron is thrown off, and the process repeated. Alongside of the moving force are teams hauling tools, and water-wagons, and Chinamen, with pails strung over shoulders, moving among the men with water and tea...The scene is a most animated one. From the first pioneer to the last tamper, perhaps two miles, there is a thin line of 1000 men advancing a mile, an hour; the iron cars, with their. . . freight, running up and down; mounted men galloping backward and forward. Far

in the rear are trains of material, with four or five locomotives, and their water-tanks and cars. . . Keeping pace with the track-layers was the telegraph construction party, hauling out, and hanging, and insulating the wire, and when the train of offices and houses stood still, connection was made with the operator's office, and the business of the road transacted..."

With supreme contempt for the Union Pacific, Crocker, at 1:30 P.M., stopped work for lunch. An hour later the crews went back to work; by 7:00 P.M., they had finished more than ten miles (16 km) of track. To prove that the work in this case was well done, a locomotive chugged over the new line in forty minutes.

In the Union Pacific camp there was some delay, the cause of which was reported by the same correspondent:

The loose population that has followed up the track-layers of the Union Pacific is turbulent and rascally. Several shooting scrapes have occurred among them lately. Last night [27 April] a whiskey-seller and a gambler had a fracas, in which the 'sport' shot the whiskey dealer, and the friends of the latter shot the gambler. Nobody knows what will become of these riff-raff when the tracks meet, but they are lively enough now and carry off their share of the plunder from the working men. [65]

On May 10, 1869 - nearly a century after Portolá and Serra had planted the first colony at San Diego - California was joined to the East in a ceremony that turned into celebrations continuing through several days and nights.

It was a brilliant, sparkling day as thousands of cheering men gathered to witness the joining. After a quiet moment of prayer, a dozen men lifted the last steel rail and settled it into place on a tie made of laurel with pre-drilled holes. A golden spike, composed of 17.6 karat copper-alloyed gold prepared for the occasion and given by San Francisco builder David Hewes (1822-1915), was set in place. A sledgehammer was handed to Stanford, who swung a mighty swing and missed. But the hitting of the spike was to be the signal for a telegraph operator to flash a message to Washington, D. C. There, a magnetic ball was dropped from a pole high above the Capitol dome. In San Francisco cannons were fired, church bells and fire bells rang, and ships in the bay tooted their steam whistles. Durant, with the quick aid of those more skilled, drove the spike into its laurel track bed, and celebrations broke out at the Utah site.

The telegraphers recorded and transmitted the scene:

Early in the afternoon of May 10 at the Omaha office of Western Union a special circuit was started. As inquiries flooded into Omaha, the telegraph operator tapped out: TO EVERYBODY: KEEP QUIET. WHEN THE LAST SPIKE IS DRIVEN AT PROMONTORY POINT WE WILL SAY 'DONE.' DON'T BREAK THE CIRCUIT BUT WATCH FOR THE SIGNALS OF THE BLOWS OF THE HAMMER.

At 12:27 P.M. a message came from Promontory: ALMOST READY. HATS OFF: PRAYER BEING OFFERED.

After a short silence, Promontory again signaled: WE HAVE GOT DONE PRAYING. THE SPIKE IS ABOUT TO BE PRESENTED.

From Chicago: WE UNDERSTAND. ALL ARE READY IN THE EAST.

From Promontory: ALL READY NOW, THE SPIKE WILL SOON BE DRIVEN. THE SIGNAL WILL BE THREE DOTS FOR THE COMMENCEMENT OF THE BLOWS.

At 12:47 P.M from Promontory: DONE![66]

The golden spike that joined the lines was replaced by a regular steel one and since 1898 has been the property of Stanford University. A cross-country trip that only a decade earlier had taken two to six months, depending on the chosen route, was now accomplished in a week.

Only ten years earlier congressmen and businessmen had scoffed at Judah as crazy, impractical, a dreamer. Now, East and West were united because of the "crazy man's" dream.

Chapter Nine END NOTES

[1] Sandra Sizer Frankiel. *California's Spiritual Frontiers: Religious Alternatives in Anglo-Protestantism, 1850-1910.* (Berkeley: University of California Press, 1988), p. 16.

[2] Kevin Starr, *Americans and the California Dream, 1850-1915* (New York: Oxford University Press, 1973), pp. 16-21; John B. McGloin, SJ, San Francisco: The Story of a City (San Rafael: Presidio Press, 1979), pp. 60-61; Frankiel, California's Spiritual Frontiers, ch. 1 passim.

[3] Elizabeth M. Smith, "William Roberts: Circuit Rider of the Far West," *Methodist History* 20 (January 1982), pp. 60-74.

[4] Archdiocese of San Francisco, "History of the Archdiocese of San Francisco: An Immigrant Church," http://www.sfarchdiocese.org/home/archdiocese/archdiocesan-history.

[5] P.G.&E. California Originals: "Mother Russell – Mixer of mercy and moxie." *PG&E Progress.* 58, no. 1 (January 1981). Chris Enns, "Wild Women of the West: Sister Mary Baptist Russell," Cowgirl Magazine (September 25, 2018), https://cowgirlmagazine.com/sister-mary-baptist-russell/

[6] *California As I Saw It: First-Person Narratives of California's Early Years, 1849-1900: Rev. William C. Pond, Gospel Pioneering: reminiscences of early Congregationalism in California, 1833-1920.* Introduction by Professor John Wright Buckham. (Oberlin OH: The News, 1921), p. 63, https://catalog.loc.gov/vwebv/holdingsInfo?searchId=21277&recCount=25&recPointer=0&bibId=5914366

[7] Will Bagley, *Blood of the Prophets: Brigham Young and the Massacre at Mountain Meadows.* (Norman: University of Oklahoma Press, 2002), p. 233, passim.

[8] *California As I Saw It: First-Person Narratives of California's Early Years, 1849-1900*: Pond, p. 68.

[9] Kevin Starr, "A pioneer teacher," *San Francisco Sunday Examiner & Chronicle,* May 3, 1981, p. B-3; Mildred Hoover, *Historic Spots in California.* (Stanford University Press, 1990), p. 413. Will C. Wood, "Early Vision of Semple, Swett Realized in

Broad, Firm Educational System." The Museum of the City of San Francisco from The Bulletin Diamond Jubilee Edition (September 1925), sfmuseum.org/hist3/schools.html

[10] Heald's College closed in 2015.

[11] P.G.&E. California Originals: "John Swett: Education's pioneer activist." *PG&E Progress*, 57, no. 8 (August 1980).

[12] "Swett, John (1830-1913)." *American Eras.* (1997), http://www.encyclopedia.com/doc/1G2-2536601204.html.

[13] "USF: The Memory", *View*, Vol 2, No 4 (December 1980). *View* was the official publication of the University of San Francisco Alumni Association.

[14] "California's First Theatre,", http://www.parks.ca.gov/?page_id=959.

[15] It is currently (2024) closed due to needed structural repairs.

[16] *"Drifting About or what Jeems Pipes of Pipesville...,"* Internet Archive, https://archive.org/details/driftingaboutorw00mass.

[17] "Passed in Peace...Sam Tetlow", *Los Angeles Times*, May 21, 1898, p. 5. "The Career of Maguire," *San Francisco Call*, January 22, 1896, p. 13.

[18] Elizabeth Kerri Mahon, "Scandalous Women: Lola Montez – Uncrowned Queen of Bavaria" (16 Oct 2007), http://scandalouswoman.blogspot.com/2007/10/lola-montez-uncrowned-queen-of-bavaria.html; Mike Rapport, *1848: Year of Revolution.* (New York: Basic Books, 2008), p. 58.

[19] Hugh Chisholm, "Booth, Edwin Thomas," *Encyclopaedia Britannica*, 11th ed., 1911, p. 239.

[20] Katherine Saunders, "Booth Family Story Rivaled Fiction," *Lewiston Journal Magazine Section*, March 8, 1980, p. 15.

[21] Charles Nahl. Images, http://www.google.com/search?q=charles+nahl&hl=en&gbv=2&tbm=isch&oq=&gs_l= ; Audubon, J. W. Images, http://www.google.com/search?q=J.+w.+audubon&hl=en&gbv=2&prmd=ivns&source=lnms&tbm=isch&sa=X&ei=w91SVcqpCJC NyASGn4CoAQ&ved=0CAUQ_AU ; William Jewett. Images, http://www.google.com/search?q=william+jewett%2C+artist&hl=

en&gbv=2&tbm=isch&oq=&gs_l= .

[22] Edward Vischer. Images, http://www.google.com/search?q=edward+vischer&hl=en&gbv=2&tbm=isch&oq=&gs_l=; Millie Robbins, "A Traveling Importer Who Turned to Art", *San Francisco Chronicle*, May 31, 1974, p. 21.

[23] Peter Palmquist and Thomas Kailbourn, *Pioneer Photographers of the Far West: A Biographical Dictionary, 1840-1865*. (Stanford University Press, 2000), p. 138.

[24] Catherine Hoover and Gary Kurutz, "The Golden Wit of the Gold Rush Days: solace and delight of the Argonaut," *CHSC*, July 1979, pp. 3-5.

[25] Nathan Barker, "The California Gold Diggers: Song and Chorus." Music: Adapted and arranged by Nathan Barker. Lyrics: Jesse Hutchinson [, Jr.]. (Boston: S. W. Marsh, 1849), http://www.oocities.org/unclesamsfarm/songs/hoforcalifornia.htm.

[26] *California As I Saw It: First-Person Narratives of California's Early Years, 1849-1900: Daniel Knower, The Adventures of a Forty-Niner*. (Albany NY: Weed-Parsons: 1894), p. 150, https://catalog.loc.gov/vwebv/holdingsInfo?searchId=21474&recCount=25&recPointer=1&bibId=7721799

[27] James Melvyn Lee, *History of American Journalism*. (Boston: Houghton-Mifflin, 1923), p. 263.

[28] Lee, *History of American Journalism*, p. 240.

[29] Hank Chapot, "San Francisco Newspapers: Unfinished History" Shaping San Francisco, http://foundsf.org/index.php?title=San_Francisco_Newspapers; Muir Dawson, "Southern California Newspapers, 1851-1876: A Short History and a Census part 1" Historical Society of Southern California Quarterly 32, no 1 (March 1950), pp. 5-44.

[30] Beasely, *Negro Trail Blazers*, pp. 251-53; Susan Bragg, "Bell, Philip Alexander," http://www.blackpast.org/aaw/bell-philip-alexander-1808-1889.

[31] Jana Noel, "Jeremiah B. Sanderson: Educator and Tireless Campaigner for Educational and Civil Rights of 'Colored Citizens' in Early California". Paper presented at the 2004 Annual Conference of the American Educational Studies Association, Kansas City MO,

November 3-7, 2004.

[32] Lee, *History of American Journalism*, p. 349.

[33] There had been a hand-written one with trail gossip, *The Golden Switch*, put out by Joseph Webb at Dayton in 1854-58.

[34] Ronald James, "Joseph Goodman," Nevada Humanities-Online Nevada Encyclopedia, (2008), accessed 16 July 2015, http://www.onlinenevada.org/articles/joseph-goodman; Mayan Date Correlation, http://mayan-calendar.com/ancient_correlation.html.

[35] Pioneer Valley: Louise A. (Smith) Clappe, accessed April 21, 2015, https://pvhn2.wordpress.com/1800-2/louise-amelia-smith-clappe-aka-dame-shirley/; Lori Lee Wilson, "A Lady's Life in the Gold Rush," *History Net*, http://www.historynet.com/california-gold-rush. After the divorce her husband practiced in the Sandwich Islands and then moved to St. Louis, remarried, and served as medical doctor in the Union Army's campaign at Vicksburg. Letters to his second wife are at the State Historical Society of Missouri, http://shs.umsystem.edu/manuscripts/invent/2430.pdf.

[36] For all ten see "Bound for California." San Francisco News and Stories: 1800s. The Maritime Heritage Project, http://www.maritimeheritage.org/news/minersten.htm.

[37] Roger Olmstead, *Scenes of Wonders & Curiosity: Selected... from Hutchings' California Magazine 1856 through 1861.* (Berkeley: Howell-North, 1962), pp. 372-76, 383.

[38] Gary Scharmhorst, *Bret Harte: Opening the American Literary West.* (Norman: University of Oklahoma Press, 2000), p. 51.

[39] Kevin Starr, *Americans and the California Dream: 1850-1915*, p. 289; Bagwell, "Joaquin C.H. Miller, the poet of the Sierras," *The [Oakland] Montclarion,* June 18, 1980, pp. 6-7.

[40] Caughey, *California*, 3rd ed., pp.149, 258; Lavender, *California*, pp. 212-14; Hunt and Sánchez, *Short History of California*, p. 75.

[41] James Mooney, "Mission Indians of California," *The Catholic Encyclopedia*, (1913) vol 10, p. 374.

[42] Cf Elizabeth Godfrey, "Yosemite Indians; Yesterday and Today (1941)," http://www.yosemite.ca.us/library/yosemite_indians/history.html and "Yosemite's Chief Tenaya – What the Park Service Won't Tell You," http://yosemitenews.info/forum/read.php?1,14740.

[43] California Department of Parks and Recreation. Fort Humboldt State Park, "Brief History of Fort Humboldt, 1853-1866" typescript, n.d. Also, Captain U.S. Grant was company commander at Fort Humboldt from January to July 1854, and felt so miserable, because of a dispute with his commander and because of the boredom and loneliness, that he resigned his commission. Edward Bonekemper III, *Ulysses S. Grant: A Victor, Not a Butcher.* (Washington DC: Regnery, 2010), pp 10-11. Also see "The Mendocino Indian War," *Oakland Tribune Magazine*, July 29, 1923, p. 10.

[44] Weldon Fairbanks Heald, "The [William Penn] Abrams Diary," Notes and Correspondence, *Sierra Club Bulletin* 32, no. 5 (May 1947), pp. 126-27.

[45] Annie R. Mitchell, "Major James D. Savage and the Tulareños," *California Historical Society Quarterly* 28, n. 4 (1949), pp. 324-325.

[46] Lafayette Houghton Bunnell, *Discovery of the Yosemite, and the Indian War of 1851.* (1880; repr. Grand Rapids MI: Revell, 1892), p. 54.

[47] Bunnell, *Discovery of Yosemite and the Indian War of 1851*, p. 61.

[48] Bunnell, *Discovery of Yosemite and the Indian War of 1851*, p. 84.

[49] John Muir, *The Yosemite.* (New York: Century, 1912), p. 233.

[50] *Reports from Lt. Treadwell Moore to the Pacific Division of the Mariposa Indian War of 1852,* http://www.yosemite.ca.us/library/reports_from_lt_tredwell_moore/.

[51] Hine, Robert V. and Mack Faragher, John, *The American West: A New Interpretative History,* (Yale University Press: 2000), p. 249.

[52] Albert Hurtado, *Indian Survival on the California Frontier.* (New Haven: Yale University Press, 1990), pp. 144-47.

[53] Vee Bee, review of *A California Portfolio: The Golden State in Words and Pictures,* by Davis Dutton, *San Bernardino Sun,* July 26, 1970, p. 46, https://www.newspapers.com/image/61299753/.

[54] "His Poetry Soured Wells Fargo When Black Bart Heisted Cargo," *Fresno Bee,* July 27, 1975, p. D-1.

[55] "Charlie Parkhurst: The stagecoach driver with a secret," *PG&E Progress* 56, no. 12 (December 1979).

[56] "A Brief History of Wells Fargo," (San Francisco: Wells Fargo Bank, 1971), "The Heroes' Rewards;" Kathy Weiser, "James Wales Miller," Trailblazers, Cowboys, & Stagecoach Kings, p. 3, , http://www.legendsofamerica.com/we-trailblazerlist3.html#James%20Wales%20Miller; John Boessenecker, *Badge and Buckshot: Lawlessness in Old California.* (Norman: University of Oklahoma Press, 1993), pp. 37-58.

[57] "The S.S. Brother Jonathan," Del Norte County Historical Society, https://delnortehistory.org/the-ss-brother-jonathan/#:~:text=With%20the%20loss%20of%20over,1990's%2C%20the%20wreck%20was%20salvaged; Cf. Jonathan Franks, "Treasure Hunt," *Boys' Life,* (June 1996), p. 41, https://books.google.com/books?id=L_8DAAAAMBAJ&pg=PA38#v=onepage&q&f=false

[58] Richard White, Railroaded: The Transcontinentals and the Making of Modern America. (New York: Norton, 2011), p. 216; E. Kimbark McColl, *The Shaping of a City: Business and Politics in Portland, Oregon, 1885 to 1915.* (Portland: Georgian Press, 1976), p. 40; Joseph Gaston, *Centennial History of Oregon, 1811-1911.* (Chicago: S. J. Clarke, 1912), p. 526.

[59] From photographs and drawings, we can make a general observation that corpulence was more unusual in the 19th century than in today's world.

[60] Irving Stone, *Men to Match My Mountains*, p. 145.

[61] Samuel Williams, "The City of the Golden Gate," *Scribner's Monthly Magazine* 10, no. 3 (July 1875), p. 271.

[62] American Experience – Transcontinental Railroad,

http://www.pbs.org/wgbh/americanexperience/films/tcrr/ - General Article: Workers of the Central Pacific Railroad, Workers of the Union Pacific Railroad

[63] Russell Marshall Utley and Francis A. Ketterson, *Golden Spike*. (Washington: Government Printing Office, 1969), p. 14.

[64] Sometimes spelled Grenville.

[65] Utley and Ketterson, *Golden Spike*, pp. 40-42.

[66] Joan and Gene Olson, *California Times and Trails*. (Grants Pass, OR: Windyridge, 1977), pp. 151-84.

Chapter Nine FURTHER READING

1. American Experience – Transcontinental Railroad. http://www.pbs.org/wgbh/americanexperience/films/tcrr/.

2. General Article: Impact of the Transcontinental Railroad, People and Events:Thomas Clark Durant, Charles Crocker, Edwin Bryant Crocker, Collis Huntington, Grenville Dodge, Leland Stanford, Mark Hopkins, Oakes Ames, Theodore Judah.

3. Bowers, Q. David. *The Treasure Ship S.S. Brother Jonhathan: Her Life and Loss, 1850-1865.* Wolfeboro NH: Bowers and Merena Galleries, Inc, 1999.

4. Crampton, C. G. *The Mariposa Indian War.* Salt Lake City: University of Utah Press, 1975.

5. Derby, George. *Phoenixiana.* New York: Appleton, 1903.

6. Fender, Stephen. *Plotting the Golden West.* New York: Cambridge University Press, 1981.

7. Foley, Doris. *The Divine Eccentric.* New York: Ballantine, 1973.

8. Harte, Bret. *Tales of the Gold Rush.* New York: Heritage, nd.*

9. Holdredge, Helen. *Mammy Pleasant.* New York: Ballantine, 1972.

10. Hoopes, Chad. *Domesticate or Exterminate.* Redwood Coast Press: 1975.

11. Howard, Robert. *Hoofbeats of Destiny.* New York: Ballantine, 1974.

12. Khoury, Michelle. "Wicked California: Leisure and Morality during the Gold Rush, 1848-1860s." Historical Perspectives: Santa Clara University Undergraduate Journal of History, Series II. Vol. 17, Article 9 (2012).

https://scholarcommons.scu.edu/cgi/viewcontent.cgi?article=1050 &context=historical-perspectives

13. Moak, Sim. *The Last of the Mill Creeks*. Chico: 1923.

14. "More Glimpses of Manifest Destiny," *Daily Alta California*, February 3, 1869, p. 2.

15. Museum of the City of San Francisco. "Transcontinental Railroad - Driving the Last Spike." Accessed July 8, 1998. www.sfmuseum.org/hist1/rail.html.

16. Native American History. The Worst Slaughter of Indian Peoples in United States History – the Indians of California. www.facebook.com/nativeamericanhistory2015/videos/770341126 425953/?fref=nf.

17. *New York Times*, "William Randolph Hearst, Journalist, Dies at 85". May 15, 1993.

18. Twain, Mark. *Roughing It* .1872. Reprint, New York: Signet, 1962.

19. Wheat, Carl. *The Shirley Letters*. New York: Ballantine, 1971.

20. Williams, Greg. "Early San Francisco Theater". https://www.foundsf.org/index.php?title=Early_San_Francisco_Th eater

INDEX

411, 473
Baker, Edward, 400, 422
Balboa, Vasco Núñez de, 82
Baldwin, E. J. "Lucky", 515
Bale, Edward Turner, 284, 292
Bancroft Library, 107, 167, 465
Bancroft, Hubert, 140, 462
Bandini, Arcadia, 288
Bandini, Juan, 246, 288, 328
Bandits, 403, 463
Bank of America, 9
Bank of California, 447, 453, 455
banking
    banking, 432, 511, 512
banking, see also specific institutions
    post-Gold Rush, 446
Banning, Phineas, 438, 509
Baranov, Alexander, 262
Barreneche, Juan Antonio, 189
Barry, Felipe, 158
Bartleson, John, 295, 329
Battle of Domínguez Rancho (Battle of the Old Woman's Gun), 318
Bay of Smokes, *see also* Los Angeles (city), 102
Beale, Edward, 507
Bear Flag Revolt, 312, 314, 315
Becknell, William, 276
Beckwourth, Jim, 280, 327
Beecher, Henry Ward, 516
Belden, Josiah, 305
Bell, Alexander (filibusterer), 406
Bell, James Madison, 420
Bell, John C., 417
Bell, Philip, 420, 487
Bella Union Hotel, 433
Ben Wright's Massacre, 495
Benton, Thomas Hart, 310, 364
Bering, Vitus, 135
Bernal de Pynadero, Bernardo, 121

Bidwell, John, 295, 329
Bierce, Ambrose, 491, 492
Big Bear Lake, 22, 298
Bigler, Henry, 339, 384
Billings, Frederick, 460
Black Bart, 510, 511, 537
blacks, 175, 419, 420
Bodega, Juan Francisco de la, 169
Bolaños, Francisco de, 101
Boling, John, 503
Bolton, Herbert Eugene, 107, 172
Bonaparte, Joseph, 235
Booth, John Wilkes, 354, 482
Booth, Junius, 482
Booth, Junius Brutus Jr., 482
Boston Men, 261
Botta, Paul Emile, 331
Bouchard, Hippolyte de, 240
Bourbon administrative reforms, 142
Bovee, William, 443
Branciforte, 208, 209, 305, 380
Brannan, Sam, 337, 383, 395, 409, 475, 515
Brass Plate (Drake), 106, 107
Breen, Patrick, 301
Bridger, Jim, 280, 282
Briggs, Martin, 422
British, 107, 136, 142, 190, 202, 212, 216, 218, 226, 236, 263, 269, 272, 284, 286, 287, 290, 293, 303, 305, 306, 307, 315, 327, 331, 357, 395, 406, 410, 411, 421, 426, 453, 474, 479
Broderick, David, 412
Brown, Grafton T., 483
Brown, John Henry, 360
Browne, J. Ross, 491, 511
Bucareli, Antonio María de, 163
Buchanan, James, 308, 415
Buck, Franklin, 354, 385, 425, 466
Buena Vista, 24, 56, 167, 321, 380, 381
buffer colonies, 168
Bulette, Julia, 450, 469

542

545

infrastructure, 515
Inquisition, 94, 138
intendente, 137
Irish, 11, 299, 306, 331, 451, 481, 527, 529
irrigation, 18, 25, 26, 162, 193
Isabel I, 77
Isabell, Olive Mann, 476
Isabella II, 239
Italians, 299, 347, 348
Iturbe, Juan de, 120, 131
Iturbide, Agustín de (Agustín I), 238
Iturrigaray, José de, 235
Jackson, Andrew, 240, 302, 303
Jackson, David Edward, 277
Jackson, Helen Hunt, 191, 258
Jamaica, 79
Janin, Henry, 454
Japan, 15, 30, 78, 104, 109, 206, 264, 444
Japanese
  citizenship, 444
Jenkins, John, 396
Jesuits, 117, 122, 124, 125, 127, 128, 129, 132, 138, 139, 166,
  295, 473, 477, 479
Jewett, William, 483, 534
Jews, 348, 433, 434, 435, 436
John B. Weller, 413
John Bigler, 414
John C. Calhoun, 374
John C. Frémont, 281, 308
John McDougal, 378, 499
Johns Hopkins University, 477
Johnson, John Neely, 400, 414
Jones, Thomas ap Catesby, 305
Jones, William Carey, 459
Jones, Wilson W., 433
Jordan, David Starr, 520
José Castro, 251, 252, 308, 317
José Figueroa, 247
José María Flores, 317

Rezanov, Nikolai, 212
rice Christians, 123
Richard Mason, 337, 364
Riley, Bennett, 369
ritual ceremonies, 62
Riverside County, 53, 180
Roberts, Sam, 394
Roberts, William, 472, 533
Robideaux, Antoine, 294
Robinson, Alfred, 271, 288, 305, 336
Robles, Juan José, 147
Rockwell, Porter, 338
Roman, Anton, 491
Romualdo Pacheco, 244, 287, 463
Roop, 381
Roosevelt, Theodore, 132
Rotchev, Alexander, 265
Rousseau, Jean Jacques, 128
Rowland, John, 298
Royal Presidio Chapel, 199
Ruiz, Francisco, 219
Ruiz, María Amparo, 320
Russell, Mary Baptist, 473, 533
Russian American Company, 262, 263, 286
Russian Pacific fleet, 426
Russians (see also European immigrants), 129, 135, 136, 137,
    165, 168, 190, 212, 214, 216, 222, 239, 240, 261, 262, 263,
    265, 266, 267, 268, 273, 293, 326, 365
Ryan, Belle, 398
Ryan, William, 360
Sacramento (city), 14, 19, 23, 24, 25, 36, 39, 40, 49, 53, 167,
    220, 221, 223, 267, 272, 274, 282, 283, 293, 296, 301, 338,
    345, 357, 358, 367, 378, 379, 380, 392, 400, 402, 419, 420,
    421, 432, 436, 437, 440, 457, 464, 470, 474, 482, 485, 486,
    487, 488, 512, 513, 514, 516,518, 519, 521, 526
Sacramento Bee, 49, 487
Sacred Expeditions, 137, 140, 141, 143
Salas, José Mariano, 243
Salinian, 53

Villalobos, Ruy López de, 104
Villard, Henry, 515
vineyards, see wineries, 8, 11, 26, 289, 296, 441, 442
Virgin of Guadalupe, 90
Virginia & Truckee Railroad, 449
Virginia City, 435, 448, 449, 450, 452, 453, 469, 488, 489
Vischer, Edward, 483, 534
visitador, 128, 129, 137, 138, 140, 286
visitas, 117
Voltaire, 128
Waddell, James, 426
Wakamatsu Colony, 444
Walker, Joseph, 280, 299, 497
Walker, William, 291, 410, 464
Wappo Indians, 249
War of the Reform, 409
Warner, J. J., 328
Wars, 46, 59, 242, 493
Wash, Robert, 470
Washo, 53
Watling Island, 78
wealth-as-status, 58
Webb, Charles Henry, 491
Weber, Charles, 340, 358
Webster, Daniel, 305, 366, 374
Wells Fargo, 2, 9, 457, 458, 509, 510, 511, 512, 514, 515, 537, 538
Wells, Butterfield & Company, 457
Wells, Henry, 457
Whaley house, 402
Whigs, 302, 375, 376, 411, 414
Whitney, Asa, 515
Wilkes, Charles, 273, 327
Wilkins, James A., 345
William Fargo, 457
William Richardson, 284, 286, 398
Wilmot Proviso, 373
Wilmot, David, 373
Wilson, Benjamin D., 298

Made in the USA
Las Vegas, NV
29 December 2024

15540044R00325